# Thomas Jefferson and the Wall of Separation between Church and State

# Thomas Jefferson
*and the*
# Wall of Separation
*between*
# Church and State

Daniel L. Dreisbach

NEW YORK UNIVERSITY PRESS
*New York and London*

NEW YORK UNIVERSITY PRESS
New York and London

Library of Congress Cataloging-in-Publication Data
Dreisbach, Daniel L.
Thomas Jefferson and the wall of separation between church and state /
Daniel L. Dreisbach.
p. cm.
Includes bibliographical references and index.
ISBN 0-8147-1935-X (acid-free paper)
1. Jefferson, Thomas, 1743–1826—Views on church and state.
2. Jefferson, Thomas, 1743–1826—Correspondence. 3. Danbury
Baptist Association. 4. Jefferson, Thomas, 1743–1826—Literary art.
5. Metaphor—Political aspects—United States—History—18th century.
6. Church and state—United States—History—18th century. 7. Religion
and politics—United States—History—18th century. I. Title. II. Series.
E332.2 .D74 2002
973.4'6'092—dc21          2002003333

New York University Press books are printed on acid-free paper,
and their binding materials are chosen for strength and durability.

Manufactured in the United States of America
10 9 8 7 6 5 4 3 2 1

*For Joyce*

A patient pursuit of facts, and cautious combination and comparison of them, is the drudgery to which man is subjected by his Maker, if he wishes to attain sure knowledge.
    —Thomas Jefferson, *Notes on the State of Virginia*

# Contents

# 1

# Introduction
## *The Creation of an American Metaphor*

Congress shall make no law respecting an establishment of
religion, or prohibiting the free exercise thereof.
    —First Amendment, U.S. Constitution (1791)

[Mr. Jefferson's reply to the Danbury Baptist Association] may be
accepted almost as an authoritative declaration of the scope and
effect of the [first] amendment thus secured.
    —Chief Justice Morrison Waite, *Reynolds v. United States* (1879)[1]

In the words of Jefferson, the [First Amendment] clause against
establishment of religion by law was intended to erect 'a wall of
separation between church and State.' . . . That wall must be kept
high and impregnable. We could not approve the slightest breach.
    —Justice Hugo L. Black, *Everson v. Board of Education* (1947)[2]

On New Year's Day, 1802, President Thomas Jefferson
penned a letter to the Danbury Baptist Association of Connecticut. In
his written address, he used the celebrated "wall of separation"
metaphor to describe the First Amendment relationship between religion and civil government. Jefferson wrote, in sweeping, memorable
phrases:

Believing with you that religion is a matter which lies solely between
Man & his God, that he owes account to none other for his faith or his
worship, that the legitimate powers of government reach actions only,
& not opinions, I contemplate with sovereign reverence that act of the
whole American people which declared that *their* legislature should

1

"make no law respecting an establishment of religion, or prohibiting the free exercise thereof," thus building a wall of separation between Church & State.[3]

The missive, he said, provided an opportunity to disseminate his views on the constitutional relationship between church and state and, in particular, to explain his reasons for refusing to issue presidential proclamations of days for public fasting and thanksgiving.[4]

The First Amendment religion clause states: "Congress shall make no law respecting an establishment of religion, or prohibiting the free exercise thereof."[5] The "wall of separation" metaphorically represents this constitutional provision. The Amendment, however, differs in significant respects from Jefferson's felicitous phrase. The former prohibits the creation of laws "respecting an establishment of religion" (excepting, perhaps, laws to protect religious exercise), thereby limiting civil government; the latter, more broadly, separates "church" and "state," thereby restricting the actions of, and interactions between, *both* the church and the civil state. The First Amendment's laconic text imposes explicit restrictions on Congress only. A wall, by contrast, is a bilateral barrier, a structure of unambiguous demarcation that inhibits the movement of traffic from one side to the other. The separation principle, interpreted strictly, proscribes all admixtures of religion and politics, denies all governmental endorsement of and aid for institutional religion, and promotes a religion that is strictly voluntary and essentially private, personal, and nonpolitical. It inhibits religious intrusions on public life and politics as much as political intrusions on religion and the rights of conscience.[6] Whether Jefferson's metaphor merely makes explicit that which is implicit in the constitutional arrangement or whether it exceeds—and, indeed, reconceptualizes—the constitutional mandate has sustained a lively debate since the mid-twentieth century.

Occasionally, a figure of speech is thought to encapsulate so thoroughly an idea or concept that it passes into the language as the standard expression of that idea. Such is the case with the graphic phrase "wall of separation between church and state," which for more than half a century has profoundly influenced church-state law, policy, and discourse. The metaphor is simple and concrete and appears to bring clarity to constitutional language that "is at best opaque" and enigmatic.[7] Although nowhere to be found in the U.S. Constitution, the trope is accepted by many Americans as a pithy description of the constitutionally prescribed church-state arrangement. "In the broad definition of the term," according to one observer, "Jefferson's phrase about the wall between church and state has become a proof text for the First Amendment."[8] Another commentator wrote:

> [Jefferson's] words "a wall of separation between church and state" are not simply a metaphor of one private citizen's language; they reflect accurately the intent of those most responsible for the First Amendment; and they came to reflect the majority will of the American people. The words "separation of church and state" are an accurate and convenient shorthand meaning of the First Amendment itself; they represent a well-defined historical principle from the pen of one who in many official statements and actions helped to frame the authentic American tradition of political and religious liberty.[9]

Jefferson's architectural metaphor, in the course of time, has achieved virtual canonical status and become more familiar to the American people than the actual text of the First Amendment.[10]

More important, jurists have found the metaphor irresistible, adopting it not only as an organizing theme of church-state jurisprudence but also as a virtual rule of constitutional law. According to Leonard W. Levy, "history has made the wall of separation real. The wall is not just a metaphor. It has constitutional existence."[11] "The metaphor of the 'wall of separation' between church and state," another commentator observed,

> has become an enduring element of First Amendment analysis. Resurrected from Jefferson by the Supreme Court in 1879, since 1947 the vision of the wall seems to have molded almost all attempts to analyze the First Amendment's control over the Government's relationship to religion. Indeed, [Supreme] Court opinions, and scholarly analyses of those opinions, have relied on it so much that the "wall of separation" has become more than a mere symbol or a basis for analysis; it is a rule of law.[12]

In 1879, the U.S. Supreme Court first referenced Jefferson's address to the Danbury Baptist Association. The Court concluded, following a lengthy excerpt from the letter, "Coming as this does from an acknowledged leader of the advocates of the measure [i.e., the First Amendment], it [Jefferson's Danbury letter] may be accepted almost as an authoritative declaration of the scope and effect of the [first] amendment thus secured."[13]

Nearly seven decades later, the Court "rediscovered" Jefferson's figurative language, elevating it to authoritative gloss on the First Amendment religion provisions. The "wall" was the unifying theme of Justice Hugo L. Black's majority opinion in the landmark decision in *Everson v. Board of Education* (1947):

> The "establishment of religion" clause of the First Amendment means at least this: Neither a state nor the Federal Government can set up a church. Neither can pass laws which aid one religion, aid all religions, or prefer one religion over another. Neither can force nor influence a person to go to or to remain away from church against his will or force him to profess a belief or disbelief in any religion. No person can be punished for entertaining or professing religious beliefs or disbeliefs, for church attendance or non-attendance. No tax in any amount, large or small, can be levied to support any religious activities or institutions, whatever they may be called, or whatever form they may adopt to teach or practice religion. Neither a state nor the Federal Government can, openly or secretly, participate in the affairs of any religious organizations or groups and *vice versa*. In the words of Jefferson, the [First Amendment] clause against establishment of religion by law was intended to erect "a wall of separation between church and State.". . . That wall must be kept high and impregnable. We could not approve the slightest breach.[14]

Justice Black's gloss on the metaphor (and the Amendment) has come to dominate modern political and legal discourse, which is not surprising, because the metaphor's current fame dates from its reemergence in *Everson*. In *McCollum v. Board of Education* (1948), the following term, Justice Black confirmed the extent to which the Court had constitutionalized the "wall" metaphor: "The majority in the *Everson* case, and the minority as shown by quotations from the dissenting views . . . , agreed that the First Amendment's language, properly interpreted, had erected a wall of separation between Church and State."[15] In the years since *Everson* and *McCollum*, federal and state courts have referenced Jefferson's celebrated phrase almost too many times to count. Remarkably, the Jeffersonian metaphor has eclipsed and supplanted constitutional text in the minds of many jurists, scholars, and the American public.

Although the Danbury letter was published in partisan newspapers shortly after it was written, the "wall" metaphor never attained great currency in the nineteenth and early twentieth centuries. Indeed, by the early twentieth century, it apparently had slipped into obscurity in both public and private papers. And there it would likely have remained had it not been rediscovered by Justice Black in *Everson*. The *Everson* ruling marked the metaphor's entrance into public consciousness; shortly thereafter, its use proliferated in legal, political, and popular discourse.[16]

The pervasive influence of the "wall" in law, policy, and discourse raises some important questions. For example, is the "wall" metaphor an accurate and adequate representation of the First Amendment? Does the "wall," in short, illuminate or obfuscate the meaning of the First Amendment? Did Jefferson intend that his metaphor would encapsulate a universal, prudential, and/or constitutional rule of American church-state relations? How have legal, political, and popular constructions of the metaphor evolved over two centuries? Is the "wall of separation" referenced by courts and commentators and attributed to Jefferson the same "wall" constructed by Jefferson in 1802? Is it appropriate, as a matter of constitutional law, for a metaphor from a presidential missive to supplement or supplant constitutional text? These are among the questions addressed in this study.

No phrase in American letters has more profoundly influenced discourse and policy on church-state relations than Jefferson's "wall of separation."[17] The bibliography at the end of this volume confirms that enough books and articles to fill a small library have been written on the "wall" metaphor. So why another book on the subject? Because, prior to my 1997 article in the *Journal of Church and State*, very little had been written that examined in detail the text and political context of the Danbury letter, which contains Jefferson's trope.[18] Instead, most books and articles on the "wall" simply presume that the First Amendment erected a "wall of separation" and make that presumption their point of departure for discussing the Supreme Court's church-state jurisprudence. The extensive and continuing reliance of courts on the metaphor invites further scrutiny of Jefferson's imaginative phrase. Simply stated, insofar as the judiciary appropriated Jefferson's metaphor and then misconstrued that metaphor in its application, as critics allege, church-state jurisprudence may lack analytical merit and legitimacy.

This book recounts the story of Jefferson's correspondence with the Danbury Baptist Association; reflects on Jefferson's deliberations in framing his famous missive; tracks the entrance of the celebrated "wall of separation" into political and legal discourse; and investigates the metaphor's origins, uses, and interpretations. The book compiles the correspondence between Jefferson and the Connecticut Baptists, as well as other letters that informed Jefferson's famous pronouncement. This volume is a sourcebook for jurists and scholars who use Jefferson's metaphor.

The New England Baptists and their struggle for religious liberty are introduced in chapter 2. This chapter also briefly describes the political climate that surrounded the rancorous presidential campaign of 1800 and that prevailed in the early days of Jefferson's first administration. Chapter 3 compiles and reproduces for the first time complete and reliable transcripts of the Danbury Baptist Association's address to Jefferson, the preliminary and final drafts of Jefferson's response, and correspondence between Jefferson and cabinet advisers regarding the president's reply. Chapter 4 explores Jefferson's understanding of the metaphor and sets forth a "jurisdictional" (or structural) interpretation of the "wall" consistent with the text of the Danbury letter and the context in which it was written. Although Jefferson is often credited with coining the metaphor, chapter 5 discusses references to a "wall of separation" in a church-state context made prior to Jefferson's use of the phrase. Attention is focused on references to a "wall of separation" by Richard Hooker, the sixteenth-century Anglican theologian; Roger Williams, the seventeenth-century colonial champion of religious liberty; and James Burgh, an eighteenth-century British political writer widely read in revolutionary America. From the late eighteenth century to the present, numerous metaphorical barriers have been proposed to safeguard religious liberty. Chapter 6 identifies and discusses various alternatives to, and refinements of, the "wall." Chapter 7 briefly tracks the entrance of the metaphor into political and legal discourse and surveys judicial comment on the U.S. Supreme Court's reliance on the "wall" as the theme of many church-state pronouncements. The eighth and final chapter discusses the uses of metaphors in the law and reflects on the continuing utility and appeal of Jefferson's metaphor to participants in church-state debate.

This book is about a metaphor—a metaphor that has shaped American church-state law, politics, and discourse. The book is primarily descriptive, and it seeks to avoid the polemical and ideological cant that polarizes students of church and state. It does not comprehensively examine Thomas Jefferson's church-state views. Nor does it, more generally, study the concept of separation of church and state, American church-state relationships, or church-state jurisprudence, although the book touches on all these topics. Jefferson's views on church-state relations have been more closely scrutinized than those of any other American, and the leading scholarship on this subject is referenced in this volume's notes and bibliography. Separation of church and state as a political, theological, and legal concept and church-state relationships in the American experience also have been the subject of much scholarship over the course of two centuries. Anson Phelps Stokes's magisterial *Church and State in the United States*, 3 vols. (1950), is the most comprehensive work to date on these topics. A more recent work of note is Philip Hamburger's *Separation of Church and State* (2002), which traces the separation concept in the American experience from the colonial era to the mid-twentieth century.[19] The bibliography directs readers to additional literature on this subject.

Although this book is about a metaphor only, its narrow focus is of broad significance. Today, the "wall of separation" is the defining motif for the constitutional role of religion in American public life. It has become the *locus classicus* of the notion that the First Amendment separated religion and the civil state, thereby mandating a secular polity. Indeed, the "wall" has become a cherished symbol for a strict separationist policy that champions a secular order in which religious influences are systematically removed from public life. At the same time, the "wall" is viewed with suspicion by pious citizens who believe that religion is an "indispensable support" for social, political, and civic prosperity.[20] The role of religion in public life and the extent to which the Constitution separates religion and civil government have long been among the most contentious issues in America. Jefferson's vivid metaphor has been decisive in setting the tone and the agenda for an ongoing national conversation on these vital matters. For as long as Americans care deeply about religion and politics, the "wall of separation" will, no doubt, continue to provoke controversy, as its proponents and opponents debate whether it clarifies or distorts constitutional doctrines regarding the nonestablishment and the free exercise of religion. An examination of Jefferson's celebrated metaphor, crafted two centuries ago, given its continuing impact on political and legal thought, casts light not only on the past but also on the future role of religion in American public life.

# 2

## The President, a Mammoth Cheese, and the "Wall of Separation"

### *Jeffersonian Politics and the New England Baptists*

The greatest Cheese in America, for the greatest Man in America.
—Address of the inhabitants of Cheshire, Massachusetts (1802)[1]

Sir, we have attempted to prove our love to our President, not in words alone, but in deeds and in truth. . . . [W]e send you a CHEESE . . . as a pepper-corn of the esteem which we bear to our Chief Magistrate.
—Address of the inhabitants of Cheshire, Massachusetts (1802)[2]

The celebrated East Room [of the White House] was still unfinished, although Jefferson had recently used it to give shelter to the largest cheese ever made in the United States. This odoriferous miracle of American inventiveness most appropriately furnished that noble chamber until the electorate finally ate it.
—Gore Vidal, *Burr: A Novel* (1973)[3]

On the first day of 1802, President Thomas Jefferson received a gift of mythic proportions. Amid great fanfare, a "mammoth" Cheshire cheese was delivered to the President's House by the itinerant Baptist preacher and political gadfly Elder John Leland (1754–1841).[4] It measured more than four feet in diameter, thirteen feet in circumference, and seventeen inches in height; once cured, it weighed 1,235 pounds. According to eyewitnesses, its crust was painted red and emblazoned with Jefferson's favorite motto: "Rebellion to tyrants is obedience to God."[5]

The prodigious cheese was made by the predominantly Baptist and staunchly Republican citizens of Cheshire, a small farming community in the Berkshire Hills of western Massachusetts. At the turn of the century, the Federalist party dominated New England politics, and the Congregationalist church was legally established in Massachusetts. The religious dissenters created the cheese to celebrate Jefferson's recent electoral victory over his Federalist rival, John Adams, and to commemorate his long-standing devotion to religious liberty. Cheshire, according to local lore and extant electoral records, voted unanimously for Jefferson in the election of 1800. (Tradition has it that, with Leland's guidance, Cheshire's conversion to Jeffersonian Republicanism was so thorough that when the first lone Federalist ballot was cast in the village, it was summarily thrown out because the selectmen were sure it was a mistake.)[6] The cheese makers were both a religious and a political minority that had been subjected to legal discrimination in a Commonwealth dominated by a Congregationalist-Federalist establishment.[7]

The idea to make a giant cheese to celebrate Jefferson's election (and, perhaps, to market Cheshire's chief agricultural commodity)[8] was announced from the pulpit by Leland and enthusiastically endorsed by his congregation.[9] Much preparation and many materials were required for such a monumental project. Organizers had to calculate the quantity of available milk and instruct housewives on how to prepare and season the curds uniformly and to guard against contamination. No ordinary cheese press could accommodate a cheese of such gargantuan dimensions, so a modified "cyder" press with a reinforced hoop was constructed. On the morning of July 20, 1801, the devout Baptist families of Cheshire, in their finest Sunday frocks, turned out with pails and tubs of curds for a day of thanksgiving, hymn singing, and cheese pressing at the centrally located farm of Elisha Brown, Jr. The cheese was distilled from the single day's milk production of nine hundred or more "Republican" cows. (Since this was a gift for Mr. Jefferson, the new Republican president, the milk of "Federalist" cows was scrupulously excluded.[10] Many months later, when the cheese began to spoil, Leland purportedly alleged that the decay was caused by the curds of one or two Federalist cows that had found their way into and contaminated the cheese.)[11]

In September 1801, the Boston *Mercury and New-England Palladium* published an "Epico-Lyrico Ballad" that commemorated the festive and worshipful summer day on which the cheese was pressed:

> From meadows rich, with clover red,
>    A thousand heifers come;
> The tinkling bells the tidings spread
> The milk-maid muffles up her head,
>    And wakes the village hum. . . .
>
> The circling throng an opening drew
>    Upon the verdant grass,
> To let the vast procession through,
> To spread their rich repast in view,
>    And Elder J. L. pass.
>
> Then Elder J.————with lifted eyes,
>    In musing posture stood,
> Invoked a blessing from the skies,
> To save from vermin, mites and flies,
>    And keep the bounty good.
>
> Now mellow strokes, the yielding pile
>    From polished steel receives,
> And shining nymphs stand still awhile,
> Or mix the mass with salt and oil,
>    With sage and savory leaves.
>
> Then, sexton-like, the patriot troop,
>    With naked arms and crown,
> Embraced, with hardy hands, the scoop,
> And filled the vast expanded hoop,
>    While beetles smacked it down.
>
> Next girding screws, the ponderous beam,
>    With heft immense, drew down,
> The gushing whey, from every seam
> Flowed through the streets, a rapid stream,
>    *And shad came up to town.*[12]

## A Peppercorn for Mr. Jefferson

The month-long procession that bore the giant cheese to Washington attracted enormous public attention. Large crowds turned out all along the route to witness the spectacle. The cheese was transported down the eastern seaboard by sloop and sleigh, arriving in the Federal City on the evening of December 29 in a "waggon drawn by six horses."[13] (By the time it reached Baltimore, one wag reported, the ripening cheese, now nearly six months removed from the cows, was strong enough to walk the remaining distance to Washington.)[14] The "Mammoth Priest," as the press dubbed Leland, recounted that, "all the way there and on my return" to Massachusetts, he frequently paused to preach to "large congregations" of curious onlookers.[15] The trek to Washington was covered extensively by the popular press, and, as newspapers of the day often had partisan Federalist or Republican affiliations, the mammoth cheese was either ridiculed or praised respectively.[16] (Even a few Republicans regarded the cheese as a monument to folly.)[17]

In one of the most curious spectacles witnessed in the nation's capital, Jefferson personally received the cheese on New Year's morning. The Washington press corps reported that the cheese was conveyed down Pennsylvania Avenue on a dray drawn by two horses. Dressed in his customary black suit and respectable "Republican" shoes, the president stood in the White House doorway, arms outstretched, eagerly awaiting the cheese's arrival.[18] The gift was received with an exchange of cordial expressions of mutual admiration and gratitude and exuberant cheese tasting.[19] The cheese makers heralded their creation as "the greatest cheese in America, for the greatest man in America." In an address that accompanied the cheese, a committee of Cheshire citizens wrote:

> [W]e console ourselves, that the Supreme Ruler of the Universe, who raises up men to achieve great events, has raised up a JEFFERSON for this critical day, to defend Republicanism and to baffle all the arts of Aristocracy.
>
> Sir, we have attempted to prove our love to our President, not in words alone, but in deeds and in truth. With this address, we send you a CHEESE . . . as a pepper-corn of the esteem which we bear to our Chief Magistrate, and as a sacrifice to Republicanism. It is not the last stone in the Bastile [*sic*], nor is it of any great consequence as an article

of worth, but, as a free-will offering, we hope it will be favorably received.

The cheese was bestowed, said the Cheshire citizens, "as a pepper-corn of the esteem which we bear to our Chief Magistrate," as a "mite into the scale of Democracy."[20] (A peppercorn is a token or something trivial offered in return for a favor.) The colossal cheese symbolized political support among New England's religious dissenters for Jeffersonian Republicanism, the new administration, and the president's celebrated defense of religious liberty. This most unusual gift, Jefferson informed his son-in-law, Thomas Mann Randolph, Jr., is "an ebullition of the passion of republicanism in a state where it has been under heavy persecution."[21]

The president and the eccentric parson had crossed paths before. Leland was an unrefined, self-educated preacher-farmer.[22] He was an ardent individualist and a staunch democrat who throughout his adult life admired Jefferson's devotion to democratic principles and the rights of conscience.[23] Although a native New Englander, Leland spent nearly fifteen years as an itinerant preacher in central Virginia, where he emerged a leader among the Commonwealth's Baptists. He was instrumental in allying the Baptists with Jefferson and Madison in the bitter Virginia struggle to disestablish the Anglican Church and to secure freedom for religious dissenters. In 1791, Leland returned to New England, where he fought arduously and successfully for disestablishment and religious liberty in Connecticut and Massachusetts.[24] According to L. H. Butterfield, Leland "was as courageous and resourceful a champion of the rights of conscience as America has produced."[25] The Baptist parson was effusive in his praise for the new president. Upon receiving news of Jefferson's election, Leland enthused:

This exertion of the American genius, has brought forth the *Man of the People*, the defender of the rights of man and the rights of conscience, to fill the chair of state. . . . Pardon me, my hearers, if I am over-warm. I lived in Virginia fourteen years. The beneficent influence of my hero was too generally felt to leave me a stoic. What may we not expect, under the auspices of heaven, while JEFFERSON presides, with *Madison* in state by his side. Now the greatest orbit in America is occupied by the brightest orb.[26]

The model for Leland's grand gesture may have been the prodigious gifts bestowed on John Wilkes (1725–1797), the profane and profligate English radical lionized by the American "sons of liberty" for his legal assault on general warrants in England and for his spirited defense of liberty on both sides of the Atlantic.[27] In the late 1760s, admirers in the American colonies showered Wilkes with colossal offerings of tobacco, "curious hams," and other agricultural produce.[28] There were also more recent precedents for giving leaders extraordinary cheeses as expressions of political admiration and gratitude. Leland may have been familiar with, and inspired by, these curiosities. In 1786, the whalers of Nantucket, having been rescued from ruin by new concessions that the Marquis de Lafayette had secured for American oil in France, presented him with a five hundred-pound cheese manufactured from the milk of their own cows.[29] In October 1801, the *Gazette of the United States* reported that, in 1792, the village of Norleach, in Cheshire, England, had presented King George III with a 1,350-pound cheese.[30] Clearly, Leland's cheese garnered much more publicity than these earlier curiosities. Interestingly, the attention given the mammoth cheese spawned imitations. In January 1807, for example, William Woods, of Baltimore, wrote the president, asking him to accept "as a small token of respect" a "Mammoth Cheese in Miniature (made in the place whence came the Mammoth Cheese)."[31] In an episode strikingly reminiscent of, if not inspired by, the Leland spectacle, in 1835 a Jacksonian partisan from Oswego County, New York, made a fourteen-hundred-pound cheddar cheese four feet in diameter and two feet thick. A team of twenty-four gray horses drew the wagon, draped in bunting, that carried the behemoth on a triumphant three hundred-mile journey to Washington, where it was ceremoniously presented to President Andrew Jackson, Jefferson's political heir. The "Jackson cheese" cured for nearly two years in the White House vestibule. At a raucous levee on Washington's Birthday in 1837, in the twilight of Jackson's administration,[32] the president threw open the White House doors to all citizens to sample the monster cheese. A Jacksonian mob descended on the executive mansion and "demolished the mammoth cheddar within two hours and left only a few scraps to grace the presidential table."[33]

Before it was fully cured, Leland's mammoth cheese had been woven into New England folktales and legends. It was also irresistible fodder for political satirists, who memorialized it in doggerel verse and satirical scribblings.[34] The verse in particular was printed and reprinted in newspapers up and down the Atlantic seaboard. One humorist playfully suggested that the president would relish the cheese more if there were a "Mammoth Apple Pye" to accompany it.[35] A Republican bard commemorated the episode in a widely circulated "Ode":

> Most Excellent—far fam'd and far fetch'd CHEESE!
>     Superior far in smell, taste, weight and size,
>     To any ever form'd 'neath foreign skies,
> And highly honour'd—thou wert made to please,
>     The man belov'd by all—but stop a trice,
>     Before he's praised—I too must have a slice. . . .
>
> God bless the Cheese—and kindly bless the makers,
>     The givers—generous—good and sweet and fair,
>     And the receiver—great beyond compare,
> All those who shall be happy as partakers;
>     O! may no traitor to his country's cause
>     E'er have a bit of thee between his jaws.
>
> Some folks may sneer, with envy in their smiles,
>     And with low wit at ridicule endeavour,
>     Their sense and breeding's shewn by their behaviour,
> Well—let them use Aristocratic wiles,
>     Do what they can—and say just what they please,
>     RATS love to nibble at good Cheshire Cheese.[36]

The Federalists unmercifully lampooned in poetic narratives both the gift and its recipient. The cheese, to one Federalist poet, was a metaphor for Jefferson's craven character:

> In this great cheese I [Jefferson] see myself portray'd,
>     My life and fortunes in this useless mass,
> I curse the hands, by which the thing was made,
>     To them a cheese, to me a looking-glass. . . .
>
> Like to this cheese, my outside, smooth and sound,
>     Presents an aspect kind and lasting too;
> When nought but rottenness within is found,
>     And all my seeming rests on nothing true.[37]

Another wit translated the Cheshire citizens' presentation address into verse, noting, as had Leland, that the cheese had been made by freeborn

farmers and not by African slaves. Jefferson's opponents relished expos-
ing the slaveholding president's hypocrisy in advocating democracy and
egalitarianism. The verse included a litany of Jefferson's alleged failings
before turning to the subject at hand:

> Words are but air, and cannot prove
> To you, kind sir, our ardent love;
> We therefore send it (hope 'twill please)
> By Parson *Leland* in a CHEESE,
> Drawn by a lusty six-horse team,
> *The pepper-corn of our esteem.*
> Old fashion'd folks in ancient times,
> (When doing penance for their crimes)
> Offer'd up lambs' and bullocks' blood,
> A sacrifice to appease *their* God.
> But we with faith and plighted vows,
> Now offer up the milk of cows.
> Think not, dear sir that 'tis a stone
> By *"infuriate man"* from Bastile [*sic*] thrown;
> 'Twas made of milk, pray sir believe it,
> A free will offering, so receive it.
> Perhaps you may suspect this thing
> Was made by Lords, to please their King;
> 'Twas made by *our own Cheshire ladies,*
> And making Cheese their only trade is;
> By their fair hands the curd was made,
> Without one sooty slave to aid;
> *'Tis not with us as in Virginia,*
> *Where dairy maids all come from Guinea.*
> Now, from your well assorted dish,
> We ask for this nor loaf, nor fish;
> The Democratic scale is light,
> We therefore just throw in this *mite,*
> In hopes, when weigh'd 'gainst milk and cream,
> The Fed'ral scale will kick the beam,
>     Democracy triumphant reigns,
> Gives us great joy, relieves our pains;
> These burthens, which we could not weather,
> Are now as light as hum bird's feather;
> Once, men in power had our neglect,
> But now, *the homage of respect.*
>     We would have stamp'd on this great Cheese,

> Some pretty lines, your Grace to please,
> But stamps of all sorts we detest,
> And therefore tho't it would be best
> To send it from its native press,
> In homespun democratic dress.
>  May *all our gods*[38] your life preserve,
> That you may long your country serve;
> Then for your last reward you'll reap
> The blessings of eternal sleep.[39]

Presidential friends and foes alike agreed that this was no ordinary cheese. This was a cheese of which legends are made.

## *"A Wall of Separation"*

On the same New Year's Day that Jefferson welcomed Elder Leland to the President's House, he penned a missive to the Danbury Baptist Association. The president used the occasion to articulate his views on the constitutional relationship between church and state. More specifically, Jefferson had been under Federalist attack for refusing to issue executive proclamations setting aside days for national fasting and thanksgiving, and, even though the Baptists had not requested such a proclamation, he wanted to explain his policy on this delicate matter.[40] With this controversy in mind, Jefferson wrote:

> Believing with you that religion is a matter which lies solely between Man & his God, that he owes account to none other for his faith or his worship, that the legitimate powers of government reach actions only, & not opinions, I contemplate with sovereign reverence that act of the whole American people which declared that *their* legislature should "make no law respecting an establishment of religion, or prohibiting the free exercise thereof," thus building a wall of separation between Church & State.[41]

The celebrated "wall of separation" metaphor, conceived by Jefferson in 1802, would, in the course of time, be accepted by many Americans as an authoritative expression of the First Amendment and adopted by courts as a virtual rule of constitutional law.

Jefferson was inaugurated the third president of the United States on March 4, 1801, following one of the most bitterly contested presidential elections in American history. His religion, or the alleged lack thereof, emerged as a critical issue in the campaign.[42] The Federalists vilified him as an unreformed Jacobin, libertine, and atheist. The campaign rhetoric was so vitriolic that, when news of Jefferson's election swept across the country, housewives in Federalist New England were seen burying the family Bibles in their gardens or hiding them in wells because they fully expected the Holy Scriptures to be confiscated and burned by the new administration in Washington.[43]

Jefferson's Federalist foes did not invent the stinging accusation of atheism and infidelity.[44] His ardent advocacy of the rights of conscience and disestablishment in revolutionary Virginia first raised the suspicion of religious traditionalists that Jefferson was not an orthodox Christian. Thomas E. Buckley, a leading historian of church and state in Virginia, observed: "More than twenty years earlier, when Jefferson first proposed what became the Statute for Religious Freedom, writers in the Richmond press argued that he was, at best, a Deist whose ideas promised to spread 'Atheism' and 'impiety.'"[45] Suspicions that Jefferson was a dangerous, demoralizing infidel were exacerbated by the publication of his *Notes on the State of Virginia*, in the mid-1780s, in which he audaciously opined, "it does me no injury for my neighbor to say there are twenty gods, or no god. It neither picks my pocket nor breaks my leg."[46] This passage, perhaps more than any other, was quoted by detractors, who called him an infidel and an atheist,[47] and it came back to haunt him in a mocking query posed by the Federalist *Gazette of the United States* in the 1800 campaign:

THE GRAND QUESTION STATED.

At the present solemn and momentous
epoch, the only question to be asked by every
American, laying his hand on his heart,
is, "Shall I continue in allegiance to

GOD—AND A RELIGIOUS
PRESIDENT [John Adams];

or impiously declare for
JEFFERSON—AND NO GOD!!!"[48]

Jefferson's fidelity to the faith and his corresponding fitness for high office were challenged in the 1796 presidential contest;[49] in 1798, Timothy Dwight, president of Yale College and a Congregationalist minister, forewarned that the election of the Jeffersonian Republicans and their atheistic allies might usher in a Jacobin regime in which "we may see the Bible cast into a bonfire, the vessels of the sacramental supper borne by an ass in public procession, and our children . . . chanting mockeries against God . . . [to] the ruin of their religion, and the loss of their souls."[50]

These long-simmering questions about Jefferson's religion exploded in the campaign of 1800. In the most influential pamphlet of the campaign, obviously calculated to ruin Jefferson among pious constituents, the Dutch Reformed clergyman William Linn, from New York, denounced candidate Jefferson, charging him with "disbelief of the Holy Scriptures" and the "rejection of the Christian Religion and open profession of Deism."[51] "No professed deist, be his talents and acquirements what they may, ought to be promoted to this place by the suffrages of a Christian nation. . . . [T]he election of any man avowing the principles of Mr. Jefferson," Linn concluded ominously,

> would . . . destroy religion, introduce immorality, and loosen all the bonds of society. . . . Let the first magistrate be a professed infidel, and infidels will surround him. . . . It is certain that infidelity leads to licentious manners; and these again to the destruction of all social order and happiness. . . . [T]he voice of the nation in calling a deist to the first office must be construed into no less than rebellion against God. . . . Though there is nothing in the constitution to restrict our choice, yet the open and warm preference of a manifest enemy to the religion of Christ, in a Christian nation, would be an awful symptom of the degeneracy of that nation, and I repeat it, a rebellion against God.[52]

In another widely circulated pamphlet, the Presbyterian minister John Mitchell Mason declaimed that it would be "a crime never to be forgiven" for the American people to confer the office of chief magistrate "upon an open enemy to their religion, their Redeemer, and their hope, [and it] would be mischief to themselves and sin against God." Jefferson's "favorite wish," Mason continued, was

> to see a government administered without any religious principle among either rulers or ruled. Pardon me, Christian: this is the morality

of devils, which would break in an instant every link in the chain of human friendship, and transform the globe into one equal scene of desolation and horror, where fiend would prowl with fiend for plunder and blood. . . . Mr. Jefferson has comprized the radical principles of infidelity in its utmost latitude. . . . This point being settled, one would think that you could have no difficulty about the rest, and would instantly and firmly conclude, "Such a man ought not, and as far as depends on me, shall not, be President of the United States!"[53]

Republican pamphleteers answered the charges laid at Jefferson's feet and defended his candidacy for president. Jefferson was portrayed as a leader of uncommon liberality, tolerance, and benevolence—a wise and enlightened man who celebrated human reason and zealously defended constitutional government, civil and religious liberty, and separation between religion and politics.[54] Republicans vehemently denied that Jefferson was an atheist or infidel. "[M]y information is that he is a sincere professor of christianity—though not a noisy one," wrote Tunis Wortman.[55] A less diplomatic John Beckley, erstwhile clerk of the House of Representatives and a Republican zealot, bawled in a campaign pamphlet: "Read, ye fanatics, bigots, and religious hypocrites, of whatsoever clime or country ye be—and you, base calumniators, whose efforts to traduce are the involuntary tribute of envy to a character more pure and perfect than your own, read, learn, and practise the RELIGION OF JEFFERSON, as displayed in the sublime truths and inspired language of HIS ever memorable 'Act for establishing religious freedom.'"[56]

One pocket of support for Jeffersonian politics in the otherwise rabidly Federalist New England existed among the Baptists. The Danbury Baptist Association wrote to Jefferson, on October 7, 1801, congratulating him on his election to the "chief Magistracy in the United States." Civic and religious associations often wrote messages of courtesy and appreciation to newly elected presidents. The Connecticut Baptists celebrated Jefferson's zealous advocacy for religious liberty and chastised those who criticized him "as an enemy of religion Law & good order because he will not, dares not assume the prerogative of Jehovah and make Laws to govern the Kingdom of Christ." They expressed the heartfelt desire "that the sentiments of our beloved President, which have had such genial Effect already, like the radiant beams of the Sun, will shine & prevail through all these States and all the world till Hierarchy and tyranny be destroyed from the Earth."[57]

Organized in 1790, the Danbury Baptist Association was an alliance of "twenty-six churches, most of them in the Connecticut Valley, stretching from Suffield to Middletown and including several as far west as Amenia, New York." By the turn of the century, William G. McLoughlin reported, "[t]hese twenty-six churches had a total of 1484 members but this number could be multiplied by five to include all the nominal adherents of these churches."[58] The Connecticut Baptists were a religious minority in a state where Congregationalism was the established church. They were drawn to Jefferson's political cause because of his unflagging commitment to religious liberty.[59] The Danbury Baptists were thus among a minority of Republican partisans who lived in a bastion of ardent Federalist sentiment.[60] In short, like the Cheshire cheese makers, they were outsiders, a beleaguered religious and political minority in a state where a Congregationalist-Federalist axis dominated political life.

## *"An Outrage upon Religion"*

Jefferson conceived the Danbury letter as an instrument for explaining his refusal to issue religious proclamations designating days for public thanksgiving and fasting.[61] Many pious citizens lamented his abandonment of this venerable tradition and were soon to be alarmed by his use of an unambiguously separationist metaphor. James H. Hutson has speculated that Jefferson, fully anticipating that his response to the Danbury Baptists would unleash vicious Federalist accusations of political atheism, adopted a strategy to neutralize the religion issue and to reassure pious constituents of all political stripes that he was a friend of religion. Elder John Leland, that foremost opponent of a church-state union who was in the Federal City to deliver the mammoth cheese, had accepted an invitation to preach in the Hall of the House of Representatives on Sunday, January 3. The president perceived that participation in religious services in one of the nation's most public fora with one of its most famous parsons would be a public relations bonanza.[62] Moreover, the president "evidently concluded that, if Leland found nothing objectionable about officiating at worship on public property, he could not be criticized for attending a service at which his friend was preaching. Consequently, 'contrary to all former practice,' Jefferson appeared at church services in the House on Sunday, Jan. 3, two days after recommending in his reply to the Danbury Baptists 'a wall of separation between church and state.'"[63]

The Reverend Dr. Manasseh Cutler, a Congregationalist clergyman and a Federalist member of the U.S. Congress from Massachusetts, derisively reported on the service:

> Last Sunday [3 January], Leland, the cheesemonger, a poor, ignorant, illiterate, clownish preacher (who was the conductor of this monument of human weakness and folly [the mammoth cheese] to the place of its destination), was introduced as the preacher to both Houses of Congress, and a great number of gentlemen and ladies from I know not where. The President, contrary to all former practice, made one of the audience. Such a performance I never heard before, and I hope never shall again. The text was, "And behold a greater than Solomon is here [Matthew 12:42; Luke 11:31]." The design of the preacher was principally to apply the allusion, not to the person intended in the text, but to *him* who was then present. Such a farrago, bawled with stunning voice, horrid tone, frightful grimaces, and extravagant gestures, I believe, was never heard by any decent auditory before. Shame or laughter appeared in every countenance. Such an outrage upon religion, the Sabbath, and common decency, was extremely painful to every sober, thinking person present.[64]

Attending religious services in the Capitol, Hutson argued, alleviated the president's public relations problems, for he correctly anticipated that participation in public worship would be reported in newspapers throughout the land. "In presenting Jefferson to the nation as a churchgoer, this publicity offset whatever negative impressions might be created by his refusal to proclaim thanksgiving and fasts and prevented the erosion of his political base in God-fearing areas like New England . . . [and offered] symbolic support for religious faith and for its beneficent role in republican government."[65] In the remaining years of his presidency, Jefferson frequently attended similar religious services.[66]

Federalist leaders predictably and cynically ascribed political motives to Jefferson's church attendance. "Sarcastically commenting on the president's 'ardent zeal' in riding through a rainstorm in December 1802 to get to church in the House, Representative Manasseh Cutler of Massachusetts remarked: 'Although this is no kind of evidence of any regard to religion, it goes far to prove that the idea of bearing down and overturning our religious institutions, which, I believe, has been a favorite object, is now given up. The political necessity of paying some respect to the religion of the country is now felt.'"[67] Hutson has countered the Federalist critics, noting that, before January 1802, in both the Federal City and the Old Dominion, Jefferson had attended worship services on government property. "The consistency of Jefferson's convictions on this matter," Hutson concluded,

> acquits him of the Federalist charge that in attending public worship in the House he was indulging his habitual hypocrisy. That attending church in the Capitol served Jefferson's political objective of appeasing the average Federalist is indisputable, but he was not being false to himself. . . . That he supported throughout his life the principle of government hospitality to religious activity (provided always that it be voluntary and offered on an equal-opportunity basis) indicates that he used the wall of separation metaphor in a restrictive sense.[68]

Jefferson thus opposed a federal religious establishment, but, as the nation's head of state, he personally encouraged and symbolically supported religion by attending public church services in the Capitol.[69]

## Two Symbols of Religious Liberty

The communications of the Cheshire and the Danbury Baptists, two loyal Republican communities, coincidentally commanded the president's attention on the same day. The "monster" cheese, as Jefferson reportedly called it,[70] symbolized the same issues and themes addressed by the Danbury Baptists. The Cheshire cheese mongers and the Danbury Baptists alike viewed themselves as persecuted and marginalized religious and political minorities in New England states firmly controlled by a Congregationalist-Federalist establishment. Both Baptist communities celebrated Jefferson's election as the harbinger of a new dawn of religious liberty. Jefferson, in return, expressed solidarity with the persecuted New England Baptists in their aspirations for political acceptance and religious liberty.

From the summer of 1801 to the spring of 1802, the mammoth cheese received extensive coverage in the popular press. Even before it was fully cured, the cheese had been woven into New England folklore.

By late January 1802, copies of the Danbury Baptists' address and Jefferson's reply were appearing in New England Republican journals.[71] At the time, parallels were noted between the Cheshire and the Danbury Baptists' communications to the president and the concurrence of their concerns. Newspapers reported on the mammoth cheese and the "wall of separation" in the same column.[72]

Accounts vary as to what eventually happened to the legendary cheese. A pungent remnant remained in the executive mansion for at least a year, and perhaps for another two years or more, where it was prominently displayed and served at important Republican party functions. According to one graphic account, the decaying, maggot-infested remains were unceremoniously dumped into the Potomac River.[73]

The mammoth cheese was for a brief season at once the most celebrated and the most lampooned object in America, but in the course of time it faded from public memory as an emblem of the religious dissenters' aspirations for liberty of conscience.[74] Jefferson's "wall," by contrast, represented an idea quietly "sow[n] . . . among the people" that, over two centuries, to continue Jefferson's own gardening metaphor, has "germinate[d] and become rooted among their political tenets."[75] Today, the "wall" stands as a defining image of the prudential and constitutional role of religion in American public life.

# 3

# "Sowing Useful Truths and Principles"

## Thomas Jefferson and the Danbury Baptist Association

I have generally endeavored to turn [citizen addresses] to some account, by making them the occasion, by way of answer, of sowing useful truths & principles among the people, which might germinate and become rooted among their political tenets.

—Thomas Jefferson to Levi Lincoln (1802)[1]

[T]he clergy [entertain] a very favorite hope of obtaining an establishment of a particular form of Christianity through[out] the United States. . . . [T]hey believe that any portion of power confided to me, will be exerted in opposition to their schemes. And they believe rightly: for I have sworn upon the altar of God, eternal hostility against every form of tyranny over the mind of man.

—Thomas Jefferson to Dr. Benjamin Rush (1800)[2]

In October 1801, the Danbury Baptist Association sent a letter to Thomas Jefferson expressing "great satisfaction" in his "appointment to the chief Magistracy in the United States."[3] In the new president, the Connecticut Baptists found an ardent defender of religious liberty, a matter of vital concern to a minority sect in a state dominated by a Congregationalist establishment. The Baptists were eager to broadcast their support for the new administration in Washington and to repudiate Jefferson's critics in the bitter presidential campaign just ended. The president, in turn, was receptive to the Baptists' address, because it afforded him an opportunity to reassure pious constituents that, contrary to Federalist invective, he was a friend of religion.

The Danbury Baptists' letter precipitated an immediate flurry of correspondence between Jefferson and his political advisers, as the president contemplated his response. Jefferson promptly drafted a letter in reply and submitted it to the two New England Republicans in his cabinet, Postmaster General Gideon Granger, of Connecticut, and Attorney General Levi Lincoln, of Masssachusetts. In a brief note to the president, on December 31, Granger said he thought the letter was excellent as written. The following day, New Year's Day, Jefferson took time away from greeting and entertaining well-wishers to solicit Lincoln's advice. He sent the draft letter to Lincoln, with a cover note explaining his objectives in writing the Baptists. The attorney general responded the same day, and, before the day's end, Jefferson revised the missive to conform to Lincoln's recommendations, signed, and released the letter.

The complete, accurate transcriptions of six letters generated in Jefferson's exchange with the Baptists are reprinted in this chapter, including correspondence between Jefferson and the Danbury Baptist Association (both a preliminary draft and the final version of Jefferson's letter) and between Jefferson and his political advisers. These documents are preserved in the Jefferson papers at the Library of Congress.[4]

## Political Dynamite

Letters of courtesy, like the one sent by the Danbury Baptists, were not particularly welcomed by the president, but neither were they to be lightly dismissed with merely a cordial response in kind. Rather, Jefferson thought such correspondence furnished an occasion for "sowing useful truths & principles among the people, which might germinate and become rooted among their political tenets."[5]

Civic and religious associations often wrote congratulatory messages to newly elected presidents. In the early days of his first administration, for example, George Washington received some two dozen letters from religious societies and congregations. Presidential responses to constituent letters and citizen petitions were a favored and effective vehicle used by early presidents to communicate on matters of principle and policy or to shape public opinion.[6] Jefferson, in particular, made frequent use of this medium for articulating and disseminating his political views.[7]

The political context and subtext of Jefferson's famous epistle are difficult to miss. His reply was packed with political dynamite, and he was worried that it could prove damaging to his administration and to the Republican cause. If the past was a reliable guide, Jefferson knew that whatever he wrote to the Danbury Baptists would soon be widely publicized and, in all likelihood, reprinted in Baptist and partisan organs throughout the country. Thus, his response bears signs of careful deliberation.

Although the Danbury Baptists did *not* request a religious proclamation,[8] Jefferson thought their letter provided an opportunity to explain why he declined to follow the tradition established by Presidents George Washington and John Adams in designating days for public fasting and thanksgiving.[9] Critics had castigated Jefferson for departing from the practice of his presidential predecessors and virtually all state chief executives, who routinely designated days for prayer, fasting, and thanksgiving.[10] Jefferson thought it was improper, pursuant to the First Amendment, for the federal chief executive to issue religious proclamations. Insofar as it was appropriate for any human authority to direct religious exercises or issue religious proclamations, Jefferson believed this was a matter best left to the private citizens, religious societies, or state and local governments.[11]

Jefferson's reply to the Baptist Association was a vehicle for communicating his views on a delicate and divisive political issue. Constance B. Schulz described the purpose of the response broadly as Jefferson's way of conveying his true convictions on matters of faith and morality to loyal "Republicans in New England, who might be sensitive to or confused by" the Federalist press's unrelenting attacks on Jefferson's alleged immorality and irreligion.[12] Edward S. Corwin, the late dean of American constitutional scholars, speculated that Jefferson's Federalist tormentors were the intended audience. The missive, Corwin quipped, "was not improbably motivated by an impish desire to heave a brick at the Congregationalist-Federalist hierarchy of Connecticut, whose leading members had denounced him two years before as an 'infidel' and 'atheist.'"[13]

A growing enmity between Jefferson and the New England clergy was palpable and mutual.[14] Clerical attacks on Jefferson are documented in the preceding chapter; Jefferson's slings against the "irritable tribe of priests"[15] became more frequent during the course of the presidential campaign of 1800.[16] His anger was directed toward those Federalist ministers who had banded together against him for essentially political reasons. An increasingly anticlerical Jefferson wrote: "The clergy, by getting themselves established by law, & ingrafted into the machine of government, have been a very formidable engine against the civil and religious rights of man."[17] In a particularly bitter missive to Levi Lincoln, an anguished Jefferson went so far as to compare his persecution at the hands of the New England clergy with the crucifixion of Christ: "from the clergy I expect no mercy. They crucified their Saviour, who preached that their kingdom was not of this world; and all who practise on that precept must expect the extreme of their wrath. The laws of the present day withhold their hands from blood; but lies and slander still remain to them."[18] Jefferson never fully recovered from the wounds suffered in the campaign. "What an effort, my dear Sir, of bigotry in politics and religion have we gone through!" he wrote Joseph Priestley shortly after his inauguration. "The barbarians really flattered themselves they should be able to bring back the times of Vandalism, when ignorance put everything into the hands of power and priestcraft."[19] New England would be slow to embrace Republican principles, Jefferson confided to a correspondent, "on account of the dominion of the clergy, who had got a smell of union between Church and State."[20] He was convinced that the clergy's ultimate ambition was nothing less than the establishment of a national church. Years later, when Connecticut finally severed formal ties between church and state, Jefferson rejoiced that "this den of the priesthood is at length broken up, and that a Protestant Popedom is no longer to disgrace the American history and character."[21] Candidate Jefferson acknowledged to his friend Dr. Benjamin Rush, in September 1800, that his election would displease the clergy, "especially the Episcopalians and Congregationalists," who entertain "a very favorite hope of obtaining an establishment of a particular form of Christianity through[out] the United States. . . . The returning good sense of our country threatens abortion to their hopes, and they believe that any portion of power confided to me [as president], will be exerted in opposition to their schemes. And they believe rightly," Jefferson exclaimed with words now inscribed in marble on the walls of his memorial in Washington, D.C., "for I have sworn upon the altar of God, eternal hostility against every form of tyranny over the mind of man."[22] This is, indeed, one of Jefferson's most "noble and immortal pronouncements"; but, as Fred C. Luebke has remarked, "when his words are understood in the light of their context, they constitute first of all a bitter declaration of war on the clergy whose intemperate attacks had repeatedly struck at the core of his sensitive nature."[23]

Philip Hamburger has argued that the separation principle expressed in the Danbury letter was introduced by Republican partisans in the malignant campaign of 1800 "to browbeat Federalist clergy for preaching about politics"; in short, it was used "to deter Federalist clergymen from exercising their freedom of religion and speech." The "Federalist ministers inveighed against Jefferson, often from their pulpits, excoriating his infidelity and deism," and Republicans elevated separation of religion and civil government to a political principle "to separate Federalist clergymen from politics" and to discourage "preaching against Jefferson."[24] In the Danbury letter, Hamburger argued, Jefferson deftly transposed a phrase used by his Republican supporters from a political to a constitutional context. In so doing, he not only sought "to support his Baptists allies [in New England]," but also, "[m]ore broadly, he hoped to reprimand his clerical and Federalist opponents and to propagate his own, profoundly anticlerical, vision of the relationship of religion to politics."[25]

Drawing on the recently revealed text of a preliminary draft of the Danbury letter,[26] James H. Hutson, at the Library of Congress, similarly has argued that the Danbury letter served both to soothe Jefferson's allies and to frustrate his enemies. It was a political statement written to reassure Jefferson's Baptist constituents in New England of his continuing commitment to their religious rights and to strike back at the Federalist-Congregationalist establishment in Connecticut for shamelessly vilifying him as an "infidel" and an "atheist" in the rancorous presidential campaign. More specifically, Jefferson used the Danbury letter to explain his refusal to "proclaim fastings & thanksgivings"[27] and thus to diffuse a thorny political controversy that his Federalist opponents had used to bait him in their continuing campaign to smear him as an enemy of religion. Indeed, the propriety of executive thanksgiving and fast-day proclamations was a highly politicized issue in both the Adams and the Jefferson administrations, exploited by partisans on all sides to demonize their political opponents.[28] Before posting his considered response, Jefferson solicited the political advice and comment of "his chief consultants on New England," Attorney General Lincoln and Postmaster General Granger.[29] Jefferson's own notes reveal that political considerations guided his revision of the letter. He explained, for example, that a sentence in a preliminary draft was omitted from the final version "on the suggestion that it might give uneasiness to some of our republican friends."[30] Only days after it was written, the letter was reprinted in partisan Republican newspapers, where it served its maximum political purpose.[31] (This suggests that Jefferson was writing for an audience beyond the Danbury Baptists–including, perhaps, the New England Federalists.) Jefferson candidly acknowledged in his letter to Lincoln an objective to use statements, such as his reply to the Baptists, to inform the people's "political tenets."[32] For these and other reasons, Hutson concluded that the president "regarded his reply to the Danbury Baptists as a political letter, not as a dispassionate theoretical pronouncement on the relations between government and religion." In short, "it was meant to be a political manifesto, nothing more."[33]

One need not agree fully with Hutson's conclusions to recognize that Jefferson was acutely aware of the political implications of his pronouncement on a delicate church-state issue. Although the president responded to the Baptists within two days of receiving their address, his letter shows every mark of careful deliberation. He wrote and rewrote key passages and solicited the input of two cabinet advisers intimately familiar with New England politics. This manuscript record controverts the claims of critics who discount or belittle the Danbury letter as a hastily drafted "little address of courtesy," lacking deliberation or precision.[34] Despite the effort he invested in the address, Jefferson could not have foreseen the pervasive and enduring impact the letter would have on American politics and jurisprudence two centuries later.

### Danbury Baptist Association to Thomas Jefferson

The Danbury Baptist Association's letter celebrated Jefferson's election, affirmed the Baptists' devotion to religious liberty, and chastised those who had criticized the new president "as an enemy of religion Law & good order" because he refused as civil magistrate to craft "Laws to govern the Kingdom of Christ." Interestingly, the Baptists drew a parallel between the persecution they experienced under Connecticut laws and that suffered by Jefferson at the hands of establishmentarians. Although the letter was drafted nearly a year after the presidential election, the Baptists explained that their message was written at "the first opportunity which we have enjoy,d in our collective capacity, since your Inauguration." A notation in the margin of the preserved manuscript indicates that the letter, dated October 7, 1801, was received by the president on December 30, 1801. For reasons unknown, it took nearly three months for the missive to reach the president's desk. The Baptists wrote:

The address of the Danbury Baptist Association, in the State of Connecticut; assembled October 7th. AD 1801.
To *Thomas Jefferson* Esq. President of the united States of America.

Sir,

Among the many millions in America and Europe who rejoice in your Election to office; we embrace the first opportunity which we have enjoy,d in our collective capacity, since your Inauguration, to express our great satisfaction, in your appointment to the chief Magistracy in the United States: And though our mode of expression may be less courtly and pompious than what many others clothe their addresses with, we beg you, Sir to believe, that none are more sincere.

Our Sentiments are uniformly on the side of Religious Liberty—That Religion is at all times and places a Matter between God and Individuals—That no man ought to suffer in Name, person or effects on account of his religious Opinions—That the legitimate Power of civil Government extends no further than to punish the man who *works ill to his neighbour*: But Sir. our constitution of government is not specific. Our antient charter, together with the Laws made coincident therewith, were adopted as the Basis of our government, At the time of our revolution; and such had been our Laws & usages, & such still are; that Religion is consider,d as the first object of Legislation; & therefore what religious privileges we enjoy (as a minor part of the State) we enjoy as favors granted, and not as inalienable rights: and these favors we receive at the expence of such degrading acknowledgements, as are inconsistent with the rights of fre[e]men. It is not to be wondered at therefore; if those, who seek after *power & gain* under the pretence *of government & Religion* should reproach their fellow men—should reproach their chief Magistrate, as an enemy of religion Law & good order because he will not, dares not assume the prerogative of Jehovah and make Laws to govern the Kingdom of Christ.

Sir, we are sensible that the President of the united States, is not the national Legislator, & also sensible that the national government cannot destroy the Laws of each State; but our hopes are strong that the sentiments of our beloved President, which have had such genial Effect already, like the radiant beams of the Sun, will shine & prevail through all these States and all the world till Hierarchy and tyranny be destroyed from the Earth. Sir, when we reflect on your past services, and see a glow of philanthropy and good will shining forth in a course of more than thirty years we have reason to believe that America,s God has raised you up to fill the chair of State out of that good will which he bears to the Millions which you preside over. May God strengthen you for the arduous task which providence & the voice of the people have cal,d you to sustain and support you in your Administration against all the predetermin,d opposition of those who wish to rise to wealth & importance on the poverty and subjection of the people———

And may the Lord preserve you safe from every evil and bring you at last to his Heavenly Kingdom through Jesus Christ our Glorious Mediator.

Signed in behalf of the Association,

> Neh,h Dodge        )
> Ephm Robbins      )        The Committee[35]
> Stephen S. Nelson  )

The established Congregational ministry, in alliance with the Federalists, continued to dominate the institutions of politics and public policy in Connecticut at the start of the nineteenth century. The Baptists ruefully reported that, under the laws and traditions of the state, their "religious privileges" were not recognized as "inalienable rights." They bitterly resented policies that required them to petition the established powers for the modest religious privileges extended to them. Religious dissenters, especially the Baptists, had long chafed under Connecticut's "Standing Order." The Congregationalists and "the Federalists," one historian remarked, "were so closely allied that the party of the government and the party of the [ecclesiastical] Establishment were familiarly and collectively known as the 'Standing Order.'"[36] Congregationalists enjoyed many privileges, and dissenters suffered many disabilities, both social and legal, under this regime. Most important, all citizens, Congregationalists and dissenters alike, had to pay taxes for the support of the established church, civil authorities imposed penalties for failure to attend church on Sunday or to observe public fasts and thanksgivings, and positions of influence in public life were reserved for Congregationalists. Dissenters were often denied access to meetinghouses, their clergy were not authorized to perform marriages, and dissenting itinerant preachers faced numerous restrictions and harassment by public officials.

In the 1770s, as the push for independence from England gained momentum, the legislature had begun to dismantle elements of the standing order. This development signaled the expanding political clout of dissenters and a growing spirit of toleration. Dissenters were permitted to worship in congregations of their own choosing, tax exemption was extended to the estates of clergymen from all denominations, and the Toleration Act of 1784 exempted dissenters from the tax for the Congregational Church upon certification that they were active members of another religious body. These modest concessions did not fully satisfy the Baptists and other dissenters who were agitating for disestablishment and religious liberty.[37] By the turn of the century, the standing order was beginning to unravel, although the Congregational Church was not formally disestablished until 1818. When they wrote to Jefferson in 1801, the Danbury Baptists understood that, as a matter of federalism, the national government had little authority to "destroy" the odious "Laws of each State." Nonetheless, they hoped the new president's liberal sentiments on religious liberty would "shine & prevail through all these States and all the world till Hierarchy and tyranny be destroyed from the Earth."

The issue of foremost importance to the Baptists was whether "religious privileges" (and the rights of conscience) are rightly regarded as "inalienable rights" or merely as "favors granted" and subject to withdrawal by the civil state. The Baptists, of course, believed that religious liberty was an inalienable right, and they were deeply offended that the religious privileges of dissenters in Connecticut were treated as favors that could be granted or denied by the political authorities. They outlined the basic principles that undergirded their claim to religious liberty. The Baptists described religion as an essentially private matter between an individual and his God. No citizen, they reasoned, ought to suffer civil disability on account of his religious opinions. The legitimate powers of civil government reach actions, but not opinions. These were principles Jefferson embraced, and he reaffirmed them in his reply to the Baptists.


## Preliminary Draft of Thomas Jefferson's Response to the Danbury Baptist Association

Jefferson drafted a response to the Danbury Baptists, which he circulated for comment from the attorney general and the postmaster general. This draft contains revisions presumably made by Jefferson subsequent to Lincoln's and Granger's comments. The manuscript confirms that Jefferson worked on the letter with meticulous care and planned effect. Significantly, this draft of the letter, with scribbled amendments and a margin note that explains one major change, was retained in Jefferson's papers, along with a copy of the final version. The president, apparently, wanted to preserve a record of his preliminary draft and the explanation for the revisions made to it. Indeed, the fact that he kept the rough draft, as if it pained him to relinquish its excised portions, suggests that great deliberation was invested in the letter.[38] Jefferson lined through key words and passages in the draft response, which are italicized in the transcription that follows.


To messrs. Nehemiah Dodge, Ephraim Robbins, & Stephen S. Nelson a committee of the Danbury Baptist association in the state of Connecticut.

Gentlemen

The affectionate sentiments of esteem & approbation which you are so good as to express towards me, on behalf of the Danbury Baptist association, give me the highest satisfaction. my duties dictate a faithful & zealous pursuit of the interests of my constituents, and, in proportion as they are persuaded of my fidelity to those duties, the discharge of them becomes more & more pleasing.

Believing with you that religion is a matter which lies solely between man & his god, that he owes account to none other for his faith or his worship, that the legitimate powers of government reach actions only and not opinions, I contemplate with sovereign reverence that act of the whole American people which declared that <u>their</u> legislature should make no law respecting an establishment of religion, or prohibiting the free exercise thereof;

thus building a wall of *eternal* separation between church and state. [Congress thus inhibited from acts respecting religion, and the Executive authorised only to execute their acts, I have refrained from prescribing even *those* occa-
prescribed indeed legally where an
sional performances of devotion, *practised indeed by the* Executive *of another*
a national
*nation as/is* the legal head of *it's* [*sic*] church, but subject here, as religious exercises only to the voluntary regulations and discipline of each respective sect.] *confin-*
adhering to this expression of the supreme will of the nation in behalf of the rights of conscience,
*ing myself therefore to the duties of my station, which are merely temporal,*
*adhering to/concurring with this great act of national legislation in behalf of the rights of*
*be assured that your religious rights shall never be infringed by any act*
*conscience*            sincere satisfaction
*of mine, and that* I shall see with *friendly dispositions* the progress of those sentiments which tend to restore to man all his natural rights, convinced he has no natural right in opposition to his social duties.

     I reciprocate your kind prayers for the protection and blessing of the common father and creator of man, and tender you for yourselves and
your religious
*the Danbury Baptist* association, assurances of my high respect & esteem.

Th: Jefferson<br>Jan. 1. 1802

Note: In the manuscript, a line is drawn around the sentence bracketed in this transcription, and the following comment in the same hand is written in the left margin: "this paragraph was omitted on the suggestion that it might give uneasiness to some of our republican friends in the eastern states where the proclamation of thanksgivings etc by their Executive is an antient habit, & is respected."[39]

The italicized text in this transcription is lined through, inked out, or otherwise marked for deletion in the original, handwritten manuscript. Five lines were marked for deletion. Another three complete lines and portions of several others were inked out. Much of the text that was marked through is illegible. (The excised portions constitute approximately one-third of the original text—seven of twenty-five lines.) When, precisely, and in what order Jefferson made the various revisions and deletions to the text is not clear. Based on the responses of his cabinet advisers who received this document, one can deduce that sections were deleted after the political consultants returned their comments.

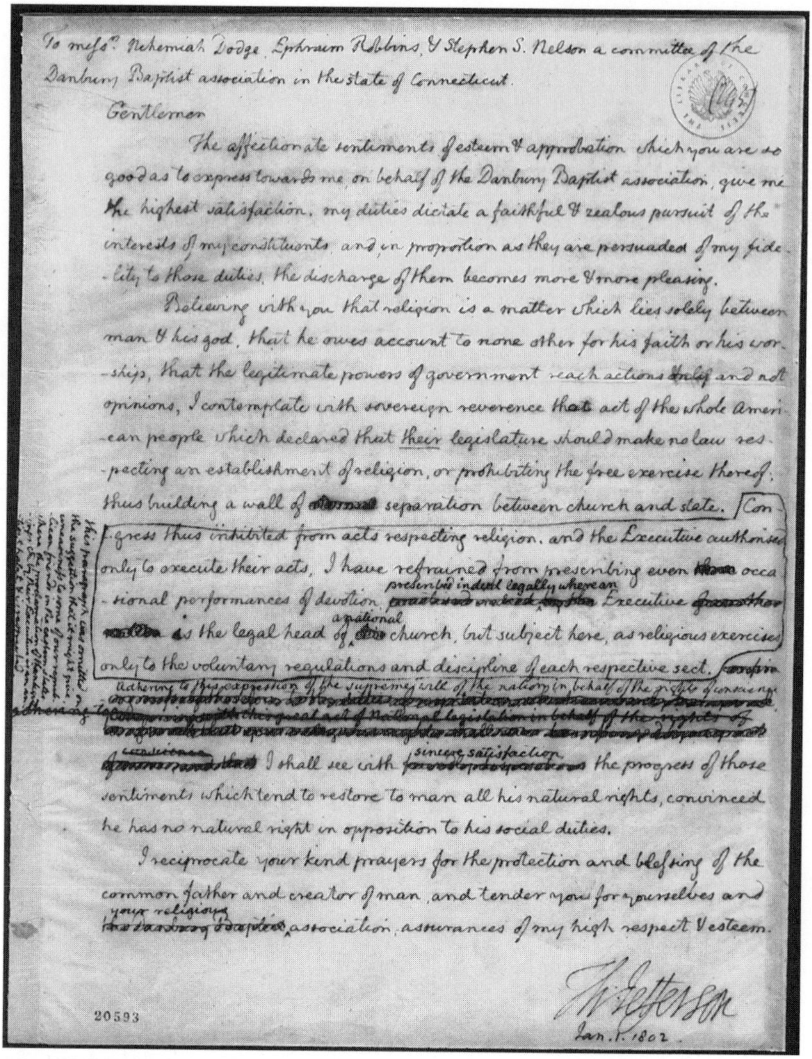

Fig. 3.1. Jefferson's draft letter to the Danbury Baptist Association, Jan. 1, 1802, as edited by Jefferson. Courtesy, Library of Congress, Washington, D.C.

The one margin note clearly indicates that at least some of the revisions and notations were made after Jefferson had received this feedback.

In 1998, this draft of Jefferson's handwritten letter was scientifically analyzed by the Federal Bureau of Investigation in its state-of-the-art laboratory. The FBI used digital photography and computer analysis to clarify inked-out words and phrases.[40] The transcription here relies on

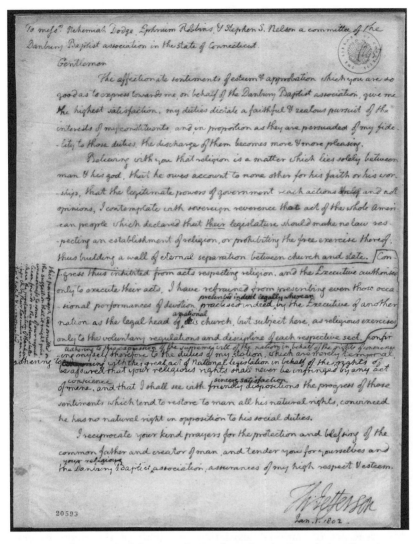

*Fig. 3.2.* Jefferson's draft letter to the Danbury Baptist Association, Jan. 1, 1802, as restored by the FBI Laboratory. Courtesy, Library of Congress, Washington, D.C.

the FBI's analysis of the document. "When [the FBI photography expert] enlarged the image greatly," the *New York Times* reported, "the difference between the ink Jefferson used when he wrote the letter and the ink he used in striking out the offending material became clear. . . ."[41] This indicates that Jefferson made revisions to the text at a time subsequent to the preparation of the initial draft.[42]

The most substantial revision to the preliminary draft was the deletion of the following sentence: "Congress thus inhibited from acts respecting religion, and the Executive authorised only to execute their acts, I have refrained from prescribing even occasional performances of devotion, prescribed indeed legally where an Executive is the legal head of a national church, but subject here, as religious exercises only to the voluntary regulations and discipline of each respective sect." Jefferson inked out what appears to be the word "those" between the words "even" and "occasional." Also, the clause that reads, "prescribed indeed legally where an Executive is the legal head of a national church" initially read "practised indeed by the Executive of another nation as the legal head of it's [*sic*] church." A line is drawn around this entire sentence, and the following comment in the same hand is written in the left margin: "this paragraph was omitted on the suggestion that it might give uneasiness to some of our republican friends in the eastern states where the proclamation of thanksgivings etc by their Executive is an antient habit, & is respected."

The draft letter reveals that Jefferson wrote and rewrote the last sentence of the second paragraph. He first wrote:

> confining myself therefore to the duties of my station, which are merely temporal, be assured that your religious rights shall never be infringed by any act of mine, and that I shall see with friendly dispositions the progress of those sentiments which tend to restore to man all his natural rights, convinced he has no natural right in opposition to his social duties.

He then apparently amended this sentence to read: "concurring with this great act of national legislation in behalf of the rights of conscience" (Jefferson apparently intended this sentence to continue with "I shall see with friendly dispositions the progress of those sentiments . . ." from the initial draft). The opening words "concurring with" were replaced with "adhering to." Both of these versions were inked out before Jefferson wrote the final version, which reads:

> adhering to this expression of the supreme will of the nation in behalf of the rights of conscience, I shall see with sincere satisfaction the progress of those sentiments which tend to restore to man all his natural rights, convinced he has no natural right in opposition to his social duties.

At some point, Jefferson replaced "friendly dispositions" in the initial draft with "sincere satisfaction." In the final sentence, Jefferson initially wrote "the Danbury Baptist association" and later replaced it with "your religious association."

As previously noted, Jefferson suffered in silence throughout the bitter 1800 presidential campaign, declining to answer publicly the relentless and vicious accusations that he was an atheist. But, in his reply to the Danbury Baptists, he struck back. James H. Hutson has alleged that, in the circled sentence and inked-out lines, the Republican president launched a subtle, yet inflammatory, political smear against John Adams and the Federalist proponents of religious proclamations by the executive:

> Jefferson took the gloves off when he asserted that the proclamations of thanksgivings and fasts were "practiced indeed by the Executive of another nation as the legal head of its church," i.e., by George III, King of England. By identifying the proclamation of thanksgivings and fasts as "British," Jefferson damned them, for in the Republican lexicon British was a dirty word, a synonym for "Anglomane," "Monocrat," "Tory," terms with which the Republicans had demonized the Federalists for a decade for their alleged plans to reverse the Revolution by reimposing a British-style monarchy on the United States. One of the most obnoxious features of the Federalists' American monarchy, as the Republicans depicted their putative project, was a church established by law, and Jefferson doubtless expected those who read his message to understand that, by supporting "British" fasts and thanksgivings, the Federalists were scheming, as always, to open a door to the introduction of an ecclesiastical tyranny.
>
> In indicting the Federalists for their "Tory" taste for thanksgivings and fasts, Jefferson was playing rough. Thanksgivings and fasts had regularly been celebrated in parts of the country since the first settlements: to sully them with Anglophobic mudslinging, generated by the partisan warfare of his own time, as Jefferson did, was a low blow.[43]

Jefferson, Hutson continued, "had at least three objectives in playing the British card":

> One was to give the Federalist mudslingers a taste of their own medicine by letting them smart under the epithet of monarchism as he had

under the insult of infidelity. Jefferson also wanted to make it clear that he regarded religious proclamations as yet more British weeds that needed to be pulled from the American political system. It followed that Jefferson expected the American public to conclude that he refused to proclaim thanksgivings and fasts, not because he was irreligious, but because he was an American patriot who would not genuflect at the altar of British monarchy as Federalist leaders had done.[44]

Jefferson's preoccupation with the British continued into the next sentence. By repudiating executive thanksgiving and fast-day proclamations, Jefferson said he was confining himself "to the duties of my station, which are merely temporal." The term "temporal," "a strong word meaning secular, was a British appellation for the lay members of the House of Lords, the Lords Temporal, as opposed to the ecclesiastical members, the Lords Spiritual."[45] His use of the term, Hutson maintained,

> shows the degree to which Jefferson was preoccupied with British monarchical practices, for the king of England, as head of the established national church, combined spiritual and temporal functions just as the House of Lords combined spiritual and temporal peers. In contrast to Federalist leaders whom Republicans suspected of seeking a similar blending in the American presidency, Jefferson wanted it known that a truly republican chief magistrate, which he intended to be, would act in a manner "merely temporal," or in a strictly secular way.[46]

Jefferson must have rethought inserting these provocative passages, characterized by Hutson as political mudslinging with their subtle reference to British monarchical practices. Upon reflection, and after consultation with his political advisers, he excised these portions from the final version of his letter.

Some revisions, also arguably dictated by political considerations, may have been designed to soften the strict separationist tenor of the missive. For example, in drawing attention to the "merely temporal" nature of his office, Jefferson drew distinct lines between the jurisdictions of the sacred and of the secular. President Jefferson explained that, because he confined himself "to the duties of my station, which are merely temporal," he was unable to take executive action on religious matters, such as appointing days for public thanksgiving and fasting. In short, the secular (or "temporal"), as well as the federal, character of his office denied him the authority to issue religious proclamations.[47] Significantly, Jefferson deleted "merely temporal" as a description of his presidential duties—a phrase that emphasized the exclusively secular nature of his office and the separation between sacred and secular duties.

Jefferson deleted another word that emphasized an emphatic and enduring separation between the church and the civil state. In the draft letter, Jefferson initially wrote "wall of eternal separation." He struck out "eternal" as a modifier of "separation," thereby diluting the strict separationist tenor of his "wall of separation." One can only speculate whether Jefferson softened the force of his metaphor to reflect a moderation in his own views or to placate an audience that might be offended by such rigid adherence to a strict separationist perspective.[48] Hutson opined that Jefferson removed "merely temporal" and "eternal" because they "sounded so uncompromisingly secular."[49]

Among the excised passages was a separation argument of a very different variety. In the preliminary draft, Jefferson succinctly made a separation-of-powers argument for why he, as president, could not exercise authority in religious matters: "Congress thus inhibited from acts respecting religion, and the Executive authorised only to execute their acts, I have refrained from prescribing even occasional performances of devotion."[50] (The First Amendment explicitly restricts the powers of Congress only: "Congress shall make no law. . . .") Because the powers of the executive are derivative of the creative powers of the legislature, Jefferson concluded that he, as president, could not assume power over matters (such as religion) denied Congress. The text suggests, and Jefferson's actions as president confirm, that he concluded that the *federal* chief executive was as powerless to issue religious proclamations (that is, to prescribe "performances of devotion") or to take other actions on matters pertaining to religion as he believed the U.S. Congress to be pursuant to the First Amendment.

Why did Jefferson delete these politically acerbic and separationist words and phrases? Did he make these revisions for reasons of politics or of principle, that is, to appeal to political constituents or to reflect his own convictions? According to Hutson, he "apparently made these changes because he thought the original phrases would sound too antireligious to pious New England ears."[51] Political advisers impressed upon him that such rhetoric not only would needle his Federalist foes but also could alienate potential Republican converts in New England. Hutson further posited that Jefferson came to realize that these words, "which sounded so uncompromisingly secular . . . did not accurately reflect the conviction he had reached by the beginning of 1802 on the role of government in religion." Although Jefferson would never compromise his view that civil government could not "legally establish one creed as official truth and support it with its full financial and coercive powers," Hutson suggested that Jefferson had come around to accept that the civil state, "kept within its well-appointed limits, . . . could provide 'friendly aids' to the churches."[52]

The Danbury letter cannot be fully understood apart from the extraordinary political milieu in which Jefferson wrote it. The missive was deliberately crafted both to reassure pious constituents that Jefferson was a friend of religion and the rights of conscience and "to respond to a malignant and persistent Federalist campaign of political defamation."[53] The volatile political forces that shaped Jefferson's letter did not strip the document of all principle, nor did Jefferson abandon for political reasons long-standing views on church-state relationships. Core Jeffersonian principles remained in the edited letter. His substantive revisions may have softened the letter's political and rhetorical force. These emendations, however, did not deprive the epistle of its potency, as is confirmed by its expansive and enduring influence on American political and judicial discourse.

### Thomas Jefferson to Attorney General Levi Lincoln

Jefferson was keenly aware of the political implications of his epistolary pronouncement on the delicate subject of church and state. Before posting his considered response, he solicited the political (and perhaps legal)[54] advice and comment of "his chief consultants on New England," Attorney General Lincoln and Postmaster General Granger.[55] Jefferson first turned to Granger, of Connecticut, and then, perhaps desiring a more discerning view, solicited a second opinion, this one from Lincoln, of Massachusetts. In a brief note to Lincoln, Jefferson identified his objectives and political concerns in framing a temperate response to the Danbury Baptists:

Th: J. to mr. Lincoln

Averse to recieve [*sic*] addresses, yet unable to prevent
them, I have generally endeavored to turn them to some
account, by making them the occasion, by way of answer, of
sowing useful truths & principles among the people, which
might germinate and become rooted among their political
tenets. the Baptist address now inclosed admits of a
condemnation of the alliance between church and state, under
the authority of the Constitution. it furnishes an occasion
too, which I have long wished to find, of saying why I do not
proclaim fastings & thanksgivings, as my predecessors did.
the address to be sure does not point at this, and it's [*sic*]
introduction is awkward. but I foresee no opportunity of
doing it more pertinently. I know it will give great offence
to the New England clergy: but the advocate for religious
freedom is to expect neither peace nor forgiveness from them.
will you be so good as to examine the answer and suggest any
alterations which might prevent an ill effect, or promote a
good one among *the people*? you understand the temper of those
in the North, and can weaken it therefore to their stomachs:
it is at present seasoned to the Southern taste only. I would
ask the favor of you to return it with the address in the
course of the day or evening. health & affection.

Jan. 1. 1802.[56]

Jefferson outlined two objectives of his address to the Baptists: he
wished, first, to broadcast "a condemnation of the alliance between
church and state, under the authority of the Constitution" and, second,
to explain why he declined to follow his presidential predecessors in issuing proclamations for public fastings and thanksgivings. The letter
thus addressed matters of both constitutional principle and politics. Jefferson understood the political delicacy in crafting such a letter, and he
urgently solicited the advice of Lincoln, an experienced hand in New
England politics. Jefferson knew well the mood of his fellow southern-
ers, but he needed help communicating to his northern constituents. Although conceding that he could "expect neither peace nor forgiveness"
from "the New England clergy,"[57] he wished to avoid offending their

followers. After all, he was eager to expand the Republican base in New England. He looked to Lincoln for suggestions "which might prevent ill effect, or promote a good one among <u>the people</u>." (Jefferson underlined "the people," emphasizing his interest in the honest citizens of New England, as opposed to the detested clergy.) Perhaps most revealing is the president's request that Lincoln "weaken" the language in order to make the letter more palatable to New England tastes. This seems to confirm that provocative passages were excised to moderate (or "weaken") Jefferson's rhetoric and that political considerations guided Jefferson's revision of the draft response.

Jefferson confided in Lincoln his hope that the letter would contain "useful truths & principles" that "might germinate and become rooted among [the people's] political tenets." A plausible reading of this passage is that, although Jefferson believed that his separationist construction of the First Amendment revealed "useful truths & principles," he implicitly conceded that these ideas were not yet political tenets accepted by the people. The admission that "his position did not reflect then-prevailing public attitudes," observed one scholar, makes it difficult to maintain that the general separationist themes of the Danbury letter (or, at least, their most radical, sweeping implications) were widely and popularly accepted in the founding era as the proper construction of the constitutional principles that govern church-state relations.[58]

## Attorney General Levi Lincoln to Thomas Jefferson

In compliance with the president's request, Levi Lincoln perused the draft letter and returned his comments within hours, leaving time for Jefferson to make final revisions to the document before the day's end. The attorney general registered grave concern that the letter, as originally written, could give needless political offense to Republicans and potential allies in New England. Lincoln wrote:

The President   )                      Jany 1s. 1802—
of the U. States )

      Sir I have carefully considered the subject you did me
the honor of submiting to my attention. The people of the
five N England Governments (unless Rhode Island is an

exception) have always been in the habit of observing fasts
and thanksgivings in performance of proclamations from their
respective Executives. This custom is venerable being handed
down from our ancestors. The Republicans of those States
generally have a respect for it. They regreted very much the
late conduct of the legislature of Rhode Island on this
subject. I think the religious sentiment expressed in your
proposed answer of importance to be communicated, but that it
would be best to have it so guarded, as to be incapable of
having it construed into an implied censure of the usages of
any of the States. Perhaps the following alteration after the
words "but subject here" would be sufficient, vis [?], only
to the voluntary regulations & discipline of each respective
sect, as mere religious exercises, and to the particular
situations, usages & recommendations of the several States,
in point of time & local circumstances. With the highest
esteem & respect.

yours, Levi Lincoln[59]

The attorney general counseled caution and tact in the manner of Jefferson's expression. Not only the Federalists-Congregationalists but also the Republicans in New England, he warned, might be offended by Jefferson's departure from the ancient and solemn tradition of executive appointment of days for public thanksgiving and religious observance. To disparage this venerable custom "with an 'implied Censure,' by representing it, as Jefferson had done, as a tainted, tory ceremony" might play well south of the Hudson River, but Lincoln feared it could prove politically disastrous in northern districts.[60]

Jefferson may have needed some convincing, because Republicans nationally had successfully opposed President John Adams's religious proclamations.[61] Lincoln offered as proof of his assertion a recent controversy in Rhode Island. During its October 1801 session, the Rhode Island legislature rejected a resolution calling for the observance of "a day of public and solemn prayer, praise and thanksgiving, to Almighty God" and requesting "his excellency the Governor . . . to issue his proclamation accordingly,"[62] as had been the custom in preceding years.[63] By a vote of forty-one to twenty-four, the House rejected a motion that recommended a day of thanksgiving, the prevailing sentiment apparently being that it was inappropriate for the General Assembly to intervene in matters of religion. One representative declared that he viewed such an observance "as an arbitrary act, which might be proper under the government of a Pope; but was contrary to the republican principles of our Government—that the General Assembly had no right to meddle in religious concerns."[64] This legislative departure from a "custom of our forefathers, which had long been adhered to in this state," generated controversy and consternation among traditionalists.[65] The following year, the legislature returned to the practice of appointing days for "public thanksgiving, prayer and praise, to Almighty God."[66] Significantly, Lincoln informed the president that Republicans, not just Federalists, regretted the Rhode Island legislature's departure from the solemn and venerable "habit of observing fasts and thanksgivings."

Lincoln recommended that Jefferson modify the following sentence by acknowledging the propriety of state traditions in these matters:

> Congress thus inhibited from acts respecting religion, and the Executive authorised only to execute their acts, I have refrained from prescribing even occasional performances of devotion, prescribed indeed legally where an Executive is the legal head of a national church, but subject here, as religious exercises only to the voluntary regulations and discipline of each respective sect.

Jefferson heeded Lincoln's advice, but not by revising the sentence as Lincoln recommended; rather, he deleted the entire sentence, fearing, he said, "that it might give uneasiness to some of our republican friends in the eastern states where the proclamation of thanksgivings etc by their Executive is an antient habit, & is respected." (The excised language included the only oblique reference to executive proclamations of religious devotion, which Jefferson told Lincoln was an issue he wanted to address in the letter.)

## Postmaster General Gideon Granger to Thomas Jefferson

The dated correspondence indicates that Jefferson solicited the advice of Gideon Granger before turning to Levi Lincoln. Granger, a Connecticut Republican whom Jefferson "entrusted with important party responsibilities in Connecticut," was well placed to remark on the political ramifications of the president's letter.[67] The Jefferson papers do not include a record of the president's solicitation of the postmaster general's comments on the draft address. Granger's written response indicates that he received either the same request Jefferson subsequently sent to Lincoln or a similarly worded one.[68] The postmaster general replied:

> G. Granger presents his compliments to The Presidt. and assures him he has carefully & attentively perused the inclosed Address & Answer— The answer will undoubtedly give great Offence to the established Clergy of New England while it will delight the Dissenters as they are called. It is but a declaration of Truths which are in fact felt by a great Majority of New England, & publicly acknowledged by near half of the People of Connecticut; It may however occasion a temporary Spasm among the Established Religionists yet his mind approves of it, because it will "germinate among the People,, and in time fix "their political Tenets,,—He cannot therefore wish a Sentence changed, or a Sentiment expressed equivocally—A more fortunate time can never be expected.————[69]

Granger registered less political concern than Lincoln with Jefferson's response to the Connecticut Baptists. Indeed, he opined that the president had expressed truths embraced by the "great Majority" of New Englanders, including nearly half the citizens of Connecticut. Therefore, he recommended that nothing be changed, even though Jefferson's response might "occasion a temporary Spasm among the Established Religionists." Interestingly, this advice contrasted sharply with Lincoln's assessment that New Englanders across the political spectrum respected the ancient practice of designating days for public fasting and thanksgiving and might be offended by Jefferson's departure from this tradition.

## Final Version of Thomas Jefferson's Response to the Danbury Baptist Association

Granger and Lincoln responded within hours to the president's request for comments on his draft reply to the Danbury Baptists, and their advice informed Jefferson's final edition of the address. Lincoln's political advice, in particular, is reflected in the last iteration. Significantly, the final text makes no mention of "performances of devotion" (noted in the initial draft), even though Jefferson had told Lincoln he wanted to use the letter to explain why he declined to "proclaim fastings & thanksgivings." Jefferson wrote:

To messrs. Nehemiah Dodge, Ephraim Robbins, & Stephen S. Nelson, a committee of the Danbury Baptist association in the state of Connecticut.

Gentlemen

The affectionate sentiments of esteem and approbation which you are so good as to express towards me, on behalf of the Danbury Baptist association, give me the highest satisfaction. my duties dictate a faithful & zealous pursuit of the interests of my constituents, & in proportion as they are persuaded of my fidelity to those duties, the discharge of them becomes more and more pleasing.

Believing with you that religion is a matter which lies solely between Man & his God,[70] that he owes account to none other for his faith or his worship, that the legitimate[71] powers of government reach actions only, & not opinions, I contemplate with sovereign reverence that act of the whole American people which declared that their legislature should "make no law respecting an establishment of religion, or prohibiting the free exercise thereof,"[72] thus building a wall of separation between Church & State. adhering to this expression of the supreme will of the nation in behalf of the rights of conscience, I shall see with sincere satisfaction the progress of those sentiments which tend to restore to man all his natural rights, convinced he has no natural right in opposition to his social duties.

I reciprocate your kind prayers for the protection & blessing of the common father and creator of man, and tender you for yourselves & your religious association, assurances of my high respect & esteem.

Th: Jefferson<br>Jan. 1. 1802.[73]

Memorable phrases and key principles in the second paragraph of Jefferson's reply correspond to language in the second paragraph of the Baptists' address. Both letters, for example, asserted, in similar language, that religion is an essentially private matter. The Baptists wrote "[t]hat Religion is at all times and places a Matter between God and Individuals." Religion, Jefferson agreed, is a "matter which lies solely between Man & his God."[74] Both maintained, in Jefferson's words, that "the legitimate powers of government reach actions only, & not opinions."[75] The Baptists opined "[t]hat the legitimate Power of civil Government extends no further than to punish the man who *works ill to his neighbour*." The theme of federalism sounded by the Baptists was echoed in Jefferson's reply. The Baptists drew on sentiments Jefferson had championed in the celebrated Statute of Virginia for Establishing Religious Freedom and in other public pronouncements on the rights of conscience.

*Fig. 3.3.* Comparison of Four Texts

| Jefferson's "Bill for Establishing Religious Freedom" (1779) | Jefferson's *Notes on the State of Virgina*, Query XVII (1780s) | Danbury Baptist Association's letter to Jefferson (Oct. 1801) | Jefferson's letter to Danbury Baptist Association (Jan. 1802) |
|---|---|---|---|
| | But our rulers can have authority over such natural rights only as we have submitted to them. The rights of conscience we never submitted, we could not submit. We are answerable for them to our God. | Religion is at all times and places a Matter between God and Individuals | religion is a matter which lies solely between Man & his God |
| no man . . . shall be enforced, restrained, molested, or burthened in his body or goods, nor shall otherwise suffer, on account of his religious opinions or belief | | no man ought to suffer in Name, person or effects on account of his religious Opinions | |
| that the opinions of men are not the object of civil government, nor under its jurisdiction; that to suffer the civil magistrate to intrude his powers into the field of opinion and to restrain the profession or propagation of principles . . . is a dangerous falacy, which at once destroys all religious liberty . . . ; that it is time enough for the rightful purposes of civil government for its officers to interfere when principles break out into overt acts against peace and good order . . . | The legitimate powers of government extend to such acts only as are injurious to others. But it does me no injury for my neighbour to say there are twenty gods, or no god. It neither picks my pocket nor breaks my leg. | the legitimate Power of civil Government extends no further than to punish the man who works ill to his neighbour | the legitimate powers of government reach actions only, & not opinions  • • •  [man] has no natural right in opposition to his social duties. |

Jefferson, no doubt, was genuinely offended by discrimination against religious minorities in Connecticut, and he expressed the desire that the rights of conscience protected from infringement by the federal government be enjoyed by all citizens. Following his metaphoric construction of the First Amendment, Jefferson wrote: "adhering to this expression of the supreme will of the nation in behalf of the rights of conscience, I shall see with sincere satisfaction the progress of those sentiments which tend to restore to man all his natural rights, convinced he has no natural right in opposition to his social duties." Jefferson's remarks parallel the desire expressed by the Danbury Baptists in their address: "our hopes are strong that the sentiments of our beloved President, which have had such genial Effect already, like the radiant beams of the Sun, will shine & prevail through all these States and all the world till Hierarchy and tyranny be destroyed from the Earth." Both Jefferson and the Baptists understood that, as a matter of federalism, the nation's chief executive could not disturb church-state relationships and policies that concerned religious liberty in the respective states. In their letter, the Baptists observed: "Sir, we are sensible that the President of the united States, is not the national Legislator, & also sensible that the national government cannot destroy the Laws of each State." Jefferson's "wall," strictly speaking, was a metaphoric construction of the First Amendment, which governed relations between religion and the *national* government. His "wall," therefore, did not specifically address relations between religion and *state* authorities. It is not self-evident that Jefferson thought the metaphor, more generally, described his views on the constitutional and prudential relationship between religion and *all* civil government.

Jefferson undoubtedly anticipated a hostile reception to his letter among New England establishmentarians. Even with the most politically sensitive portions of the draft reply removed, Jefferson's separationist rhetoric carried political risks. Perhaps to blunt the criticism of, or to needle, those who read into his metaphor animosity toward religion, Jefferson used pious rhetoric at several points in the letter. For example, he said he "contemplate[d] with sovereign reverence" the First Amendment protections.[76] In the closing paragraph, the president "performed an avowedly religious act of offering prayers on behalf of his Baptist correspondents":[77] "I reciprocate your kind prayers for the protection & blessing of the common father and creator of man."

Jefferson's locution reframed the First Amendment, shifting the terms of church-state debate in subtle but significant ways that both pleased and displeased his pious correspondents. The Baptists, William G. McLoughlin observed,

> could readily sympathize with the liberal rationalists' efforts to extend liberty of conscience by weakening the established system, just as they sympathized with the attempt of the French Revolution to overthrow the Papal establishment. But as Christian pietists they shared with the . . . ministers [of the established church] a fear of increasing secularism and irreligion. Yet to choose either side in the debate would have been inconsistent. To aid the Congregational clergy was to bolster the Standing Order. To aid the rationalist would prevent creation of a Christian nation. . . . Their future lay in a middle way between liberal secularism and an establishment. But not until the Standing Order was overthrown did their alternative—evangelical voluntarism and rule by the Christian majority—emerge clearly in New England. Meanwhile the dissenters had to consider both sides.[78]

Jefferson's letter highlighted the Baptists' dilemma. On the one hand, they celebrated Jefferson's ardent advocacy for the rights of conscience and nonestablishment. On the other hand, the erection of a "wall of separation" that could inhibit the influence of Christianity on an increasingly secular public life and culture may have alarmed them. Jefferson's metaphor subtly reframed the First Amendment in terms of *separation* between church and state, rather than *nonestablishment* (or disestablishment).[79] These terms were not interchangeable in the religious dissenters' lexicon.[80] The New England Baptists had framed their agenda in terms of disestablishment, but they did not want religious influences separated from public life and policy.

The language of "church and state" may have appealed to the Baptists in at least one respect. As the historian Jon Butler has observed, Jefferson "subtly shifted the First Amendment's meaning in the most complex ways" when he described an ideal "wall of separation between Church & State." His use of "the term *church* inevitably narrowed the meaning of an amendment concerned instead with religion and government." The word "church," rather than "religion," in Jefferson's restatement of the First Amendment emphasized that the constitutional separation was between ecclesiastical *institutions* and the civil state. This choice of language, no doubt, appealed to pious, evangelical Protestant dissenters who disapproved of established churches but believed that religion played an indispensable role in public life and republican government.[81] (The actual phrase of the First Amendment is "establishment of religion," which, like "church," in the language of the day connoted an institution.)

The effect of Jefferson's rhetoric, whether by design is not clear, was to reconceptualize the First Amendment in ways that may have alarmed evangelical dissenters. Although the Baptists and their fellow dissenters undoubtedly approved of Jefferson's use of the narrow institutional term "church," rather than the more encompassing First Amendment term "religion," they may have been discomfited by the wall imagery. A wall of separation between church and state, given the bilateral nature of the barrier, imposes restraints on both the civil state and religion. Whereas the First Amendment forbids certain laws and, in this way, limits civil government, Philip Hamburger has observed, the phrase made famous by Jefferson seems to require that church and state stay apart and thus, apparently, limits not only civil government but also religious organizations.[82] Although no friend of religious establishments, many evangelical dissenters resisted efforts to inhibit religion's ability to influence public life and culture, to deprive religious leaders of the civil liberty to participate in politics armed with political opinions informed by religious values, and to restrain the freedom of churches to define and advance their own mission and ministries, whether spiritual, social, or civic.[83] Hamburger suggested that the Danbury Baptists, who "did not publish or otherwise take notice of the letter they received from Jefferson," were discomfited by, and thus reluctant to embrace, the president's reply. The "wall" metaphor elevated to constitutional principle a separation of church and state that limited both civil government and religion. The Baptists, by contrast,

> merely sought disestablishment and did not challenge the widespread assumption that republican government depended upon the people's morals and thus upon religion. Yet such was the implication of the establishment [ministers'] charge. In these circumstances, in which the Baptists' opponents could bring them into disrepute by hinting that they wanted a separation of religion and government, the Baptists may have been hesitant to publish a letter that would have seemed to confirm this allegation.[84]

In his magisterial history of New England Baptists, William G. McLoughlin similarly argued that the Baptists were uncomfortable with the premises of Jefferson's separationist position:

> Despite their great admiration of Jefferson as the spokesman for separa-
> tion of church and state, the New England Baptists dissociated them-
> selves from the deistic and anticlerical premises on which he based his
> stand. As lineal descendants of the Puritans they deplored Jefferson's the-
> ological position. No New England Baptist, for example, ever utilized Jef-
> ferson's phrase about "the wall of separation," though he had obviously
> coined this term with the Connecticut Baptists specifically in mind.[85]

One interpretation of the "wall" that links the letter's opening substantive clauses ("that religion is a matter which lies solely between
Man & his God, that he owes account to none other for his faith or his
worship, that the legitimate powers of government reach actions only,
& not opinions") with the famous metaphoric clause suggests that Jefferson located his "wall" between religious opinion (the realm of the
church) and conduct subversive of peace and public order (the realm of
the civil state). Whereas mere *religious opinion* was beyond the reach of
civil magistrates, the civil state could legitimately regulate *religious conduct* that threatened good order. Jefferson apparently thought there
would be little need for such a wall in an ideal world, because, as he explained in the next sentence, he was "convinced [that man] has no natural right in opposition to his social duties." Although this interpretation is rooted in the text, few commentators have located Jefferson's
"wall" specifically between religious opinion and practices. This may
have been the Supreme Court's view of the "wall" in *Reynolds v. United
States* (1879), a case concerned with legislation that prohibited the
Mormon practice of polygamy.[86] The *Reynolds* Court was clearly focused on whether the Constitution granted Congress authority to prohibit *conduct* motivated by religious belief but deemed subversive of
good order. One cannot be certain that either Jefferson or the *Reynolds*
Court thought this was precisely what the "wall" separated.

What were the seeds of "useful truths & principles" sown in the
Danbury letter? A universal principle of church-state separation applicable at all levels of civil government—local, state, and federal—was *not*
among the seeds deliberately sown. Jefferson explicitly stated that his

project was to address church-state relations "under the authority of the Constitution,"[87] and he clearly recognized that the First Amendment, with its metaphoric barrier, was applicable to the federal government only. So what were the seeds, or new principles, in the Danbury letter that Jefferson hoped would "germinate and become rooted" in American political soil? One seed was a broad interpretation of the First Amendment nonestablishment provision that prohibited not only the establishment of a particular church but also executive proclamations of public thanksgiving and prayer. Jefferson's construction of the nonestablishment language was much more expansive than virtually all previous interpretations and that held by his contemporaries.[88] The seed of another idea was sown, although it is not clear whether Jefferson, within the context of federalism, deliberately sowed this seed or whether it was the inevitable, but unintended, product of his rhetoric. In either case, the "wall of separation" metaphor reconceptualized the First Amendment in terms of *separation* between church and (federal) state, rather than nonestablishment and free exercise of religion. Jefferson's graphic phrase, in the course of time, constitutionalized the separationist concept. Both of these seeds informed an emerging separationist construction of the First Amendment, but, again, it must be emphasized that, as a matter of federalism, Jefferson's separationist interpretation of the First Amendment was applicable only at the federal level and did not affect church-state policies in the respective states.

How much significance did Jefferson attach to the "wall of separation" metaphor? Did he regard it as the defining motif of his church-state views? The "wall" was neither Jefferson's first nor his last word on the constitutional and prudential relationship between church and state. So far as the extant evidence indicates, he never again used the "wall" metaphor.[89] Its absence is particularly noteworthy in his second inaugural address and in his letter to the Reverend Samuel Miller, which, like the Danbury letter, purportedly addressed Jefferson's views on the propriety of the executive appointment of days for religious observance.[90] In short, there is little evidence that Jefferson thought this figure of speech expressed a universal principle, encapsulated the most salient features of his church-state views, or was his definitive word on the First Amendment.

# 4

# "What the Wall Separates"

## A *Jurisdictional Interpretation of the "Wall of Separation"*

[A]greement, in the abstract, that the First Amendment was designed to erect a "wall of separation between church and State,"
does not preclude a clash of views as to what the wall separates.
—Justice Felix Frankfurter,
*McCollum v. Board of Education* (1948)[1]

Before I built a wall I'd ask to know
What I was walling in or walling out,
And to whom I was like to give offence.
—Robert Frost, "Mending Wall" (1914)[2]

Certainly, no power to prescribe any religious exercise, or to assume authority in religious discipline, has been delegated to the
General Government. It must then rest with the States, as far as it
can be in any human authority.
—Thomas Jefferson to Samuel Miller (1808)[3]

What does the "wall" separate? On the surface, at least, the
answer seems straightforward: the "wall" separates "church" and
"state." The answer, however, is more ambiguous than it may appear at
first blush. What is meant by "church"? What is meant by "state"?
Does the "wall" require that *all* matters respecting a "church" or, more
broadly, "religion" be separated from the civil state? Does "state" include civil government in all its forms, at the local, state, and national
levels? Did Jefferson's "wall," insofar as it metaphorically represented

the First Amendment, affect only relationships between the federal government and an "establishment of religion"? These questions interested Thomas Jefferson, and they are of great consequence to us today. They raise issues fundamental to the structure of our constitutional system.

The "wall" Jefferson erected in his letter to the Danbury Baptists served primarily to separate state and nation in matters pertaining to religion, rather than to separate ecclesiastical and all governmental authorities. The principal importance of his "wall," like the First Amendment it metaphorically represents, is its clear demarcation of the legitimate jurisdictions of federal and state governments on religious matters. In short, the "wall" constructed by Jefferson separated the federal regime on one side and ecclesiastical institutions and state governments on the other. This jurisdictional (or structural) interpretation of the metaphor is rooted in the text, structure, and historic, pre-Fourteenth Amendment understanding of the Bill of Rights, in general, and of the First Amendment, in particular.[4] This view is buttressed by the text of the Danbury letter (including evidence gleaned from a preliminary draft), as well as by Jefferson's explanation of the letter and his stance on specific church-state issues apparently addressed in his correspondence with the Connecticut Baptists.[5]

## Jefferson and Thanksgiving Day Proclamations

Jefferson said that he wanted to use his reply to the Danbury Baptists to explain why he, as president, declined to issue religious proclamations. Although President Jefferson refused to designate a day for public fasting, thanksgiving, and prayer, his general views on the propriety of such proclamations by civil magistrates are not entirely free of ambiguity. His refusal to issue religious proclamations, despite some political costs, is often portrayed as an example of his principled commitment to church-state separation.[6] Jefferson's stance on religious proclamations merits further scrutiny.

In his correspondence with Levi Lincoln, Jefferson said that the Danbury letter "furnishes an occasion too, which I have long wished to find, of saying why I do not proclaim fastings & thanksgivings, as my predecessors [Presidents Washington and Adams] did."[7] Jefferson, perhaps, wanted to address this topic since religious proclamations had emerged as a sensitive political issue in the days leading to the election of 1800. When, in March 1799, President John Adams recommended a national "day of solemn humiliation, fasting, and prayer," his political adversaries depicted him as a tool of conservative religionists intent on establishing a national church.[8] "A general suspicion prevailed," Adams recounted more than a decade later, "that the Presbyterian Church [which was presumed to be behind the proclamation] was ambitious and aimed at an establishment as a national church." Although disclaiming any involvement in such a scheme, Adams ruefully reported that he "was represented as a Presbyterian [which he was not] and at the head of this political and ecclesiastical project. The secret whisper ran though all the sects, 'Let us have Jefferson, Madison, Burr, anybody, whether they be philosophers, Deists, or even atheists, rather than a Presbyterian President.'"[9] This reservoir of opposition to "national fasts and thanksgivings," according to Adams, cost him the election in 1800. Jefferson was the political beneficiary, if not the instigator, of this sentiment and, no doubt, was eager to go on the record denouncing presidential religious proclamations. This episode challenges the often-repeated claim that Jefferson steadfastly refused to issue religious proclamations despite the substantial political costs of such a stance, thereby emphasizing that his position was principled. Clearly, political benefits, as well as costs, accompanied action on either side of this controversial practice.[10]

In the Danbury letter, Jefferson concluded that the First Amendment prohibited the president of the United States from issuing religious proclamations.[11] Yet, as president, he employed rhetoric in official utterances that, in terms of religious content, was virtually indistinguishable from the traditional thanksgiving day proclamations issued by his presidential predecessors and by state chief executives.[12] Jefferson used language skillfully to play both sides of this fractious controversy. He satisfied disestablishmentarians by declining to issue official religious proclamations, yet he used religious rhetoric in public pronouncements that appealed to pious constituents who thought social tranquillity required leaders to cultivate religious morality and to acknowledge God publicly in the life of the nation. In his first inaugural address, for example, after gratefully acknowledging "an overruling Providence," Jefferson wrote: "And may that Infinite Power which rules the destinies of the universe, lead our councils to what is best, and give them a favorable issue for your peace and prosperity."[13] His first annual message to Congress brims with thanksgiving:

While we devoutly return thanks to the beneficent Being who has been pleased to breathe into them the spirit of conciliation and forgiveness, we are bound with peculiar gratitude to be thankful to him that our own peace has been preserved through so perilous a season, and ourselves permitted quietly to cultivate the earth and to practice and improve those arts which tend to increase our comforts.[14]

His second annual message opened with the following thanksgiving: "When we assemble together, fellow citizens, to consider the state of our beloved country, our just attentions are first drawn to those pleasing circumstances which mark the goodness of that Being from whose favor they flow, and the large measure of thankfulness we owe for his bounty."[15] Jefferson concluded his second inaugural address by asking Americans to join with him in prayer that the "Being in whose hands we are . . . will so enlighten the minds of your servants, guide their councils, and prosper their measures, that whatsoever they do, shall result in your good, and shall secure to you the peace, friendship, and approbation of all nations."[16] His public papers are replete with similar expressions of thanksgiving and devotion.[17] More important to the present discussion, Jefferson had a hand in crafting proclamations for religious observances when he was an elected official in his native Commonwealth. A careful scrutiny of Jefferson's public record on this issue buttresses a jurisdictional interpretation of the "wall" erected in the Danbury letter.

In marked contrast to the separationist message of the Danbury letter, Jefferson demonstrated a willingness to issue religious proclamations in colonial and state government settings. For example, as a member of the House of Burgesses, on May 24, 1774, he participated in drafting and enacting a resolution designating a "Day of Fasting, Humiliation, and Prayer."[18] Jefferson recounted in his *Autobiography*:

We were under conviction of the necessity of arousing our people from the lethargy into which they had fallen, as to passing events [the Boston port bill]; and thought that the appointment of a day of general fasting and prayer would be most likely to call up and alarm their attention. . . . [W]e cooked up a resolution . . . for appointing the 1st day of June, on which the portbill was to commence, for a day of fasting, humiliation, and prayer, to implore Heaven to avert from us the evils of civil war, to inspire us with firmness in support of our rights, and to turn the hearts of the King and Parliament to moderation and justice.[19]

Jefferson seemed pleased with this accommodation between religion and the civil state in May 1774.[20] In 1779, when Jefferson was governor of Virginia, he issued a proclamation appointing "a day of publick and solemn thanksgiving and prayer to Almighty God."[21] (This proclamation was issued after Jefferson had penned his famous "Bill for Establishing Religious Freedom.") Also, in the late 1770s, as chair of the Virginia Committee of Revisors, he was chief architect of a revised code that included a measure entitled "A Bill for Appointing Days of Public Fasting and Thanksgiving."[22] This legislation apparently was framed by Jefferson and introduced in the Virginia legislature by James Madison on October 31, 1785.[23] The bill authorized "the Governor, or Chief Magistrate [of the Commonwealth], with the advice of the Council," to designate days for thanksgiving and fasting and to notify the public by proclamation. Far from simply granting the governor power to appoint "days of public fasting and humiliation, or thanksgiving," the bill included the following punitive provision:

> Every minister of the gospel shall on each day so to be appointed, attend and perform divine service and preach a sermon, or discourse, suited to the occasion, in his church, on pain of forfeiting fifty pounds for every failure, not having a reasonable excuse.[24]

Although the measure was never enacted, it was sponsored by Madison, and a surviving manuscript copy of the bill bears a notation in the "clerk's hand" that indicates that it was "endorsed" by Jefferson.[25] The final disposition of this legislation is unimportant to the present discussion. The relevant consideration here is that Jefferson and Madison jointly sponsored a bill that authorized Virginia's chief executive to designate days in the public calendar for fasting and thanksgiving.

## Federalism and the U.S. Bills of Rights

How can one reconcile Jefferson's record on religious proclamations in Virginia with the position he took in the Danbury letter? A careful review of Jefferson's actions throughout his public career suggests that he believed, as a matter of federalism, that the national government had no jurisdiction in religious matters, whereas state governments were authorized to accommodate and even prescribe religious exercises. Therefore, Jefferson saw no inconsistency in authoring a religious proclamation as a state official and refusing to release a similar proclamation as the federal chief executive. The "wall" metaphor was not offered as a general pronouncement on the prudential relationship between religion and all civil government; rather, it was, more specifically, a statement delineating the legitimate constitutional jurisdictions of the federal and state governments on matters pertaining to religion. It arguably had less to do with the separation between church and all civil government than with the separation between the federal and state governments. Jefferson's "wall," strictly speaking, was gloss on the First Amendment. As a figurative device to illuminate the First Amendment, the "wall" cannot, as a constitutional construct, exceed the scope and function of the First Amendment. One way to interpret the metaphor is to ascertain Jefferson's understanding of the First Amendment.

The U.S. Constitution provided for a national government of limited, strictly delegated, and enumerated powers. Those matters not explicitly entrusted to the federal government were assumed to be reserved by the individual or by the states (so far as they legitimately resided in any governmental authority). "American federalism as formulated in the Constitution," Mark DeWolfe Howe noted, "made national disability the rule and national power the exception."[26] Because the new federal government had delegated powers only, and affirmative power in the religious sphere had not been so delegated, it was acknowledged that authority over religious matters was not extended to the federal regime, and the states were free to maintain their own church-state arrangements and policies. Moreover, by imposing its restrictions specifically on "Congress," the First Amendment affirmed, by implication, that the states retained authority to determine church-state policies within their respective jurisdictions.[27] Neither the Article VI, clause 3 ban on religious tests for federal officeholders nor the First Amendment religion provisions were "laid upon the individual states. . . . Broad as were the principles upon which the national government was based, the matter of church establishment or dis-establishment, of taxation compulsory or voluntary contribution, of test acts, oaths and religious qualifications for office, was left entirely to the discretion of the sovereign states."[28] Each state was free to define the content and scope of civil and religious liberties within its territory and to structure church-state arrangements pursuant to its own constitution, declaration of rights, and statutes.[29] Indeed, some states retained religious establishments well into the nineteenth century. In short, ratification of the U.S. Constitution, in 1788, and the Bill of Rights, in 1791, had no immediate legal effect on church-state arrangements in the states and altered nothing in matters regarding federal involvement with religion. These great documents merely made explicit the jurisdictional policies that were already implicit in the constitutional order.

The federal Bill of Rights, which includes the First Amendment, served a dual purpose: to assure the citizenry that the federal government would not encroach upon the civil and religious liberties of individuals and to guarantee the states that the federal government would not usurp the states' jurisdiction over civil and religious liberties.[30] The Bill of Rights embodied a principle of federalism; it was essentially a states' rights document. "Indeed, the federalism of the Bill of Rights was widely regarded in 1791 as far more important than the protection it afforded to the individual. Odd as it may seem today, the First Amendment was not only a guarantee to the individual that Congress could not establish a national religion, but also a guarantee to the states that they were free to determine the meaning of religious establishment within their jurisdictions, and to newly establish, maintain, or disestablish religion as they saw fit."[31] This accords with Edward S. Corwin's observation that "the principal importance of the [First] Amendment lay in the separation which it effected between the respective jurisdictions of State and nation regarding religion, rather than in its bearing on the question of the Separation of Church and State."[32]

This was the prevailing interpretation of the Bill of Rights and the First Amendment shared by Jefferson and his contemporaries. Chief Justice John Marshall, writing for a united Court in *Barron v. Baltimore* (1833), declared that the liberties guaranteed in the Bill of Rights "contain no expression indicating an intention to apply them to the state governments."[33] Specifically addressing religious liberty in the Constitution, the Supreme Court ruled unanimously, in *Permoli v. Municipality* (1845), that "[t]he Constitution makes no provision for protecting the citizens of the respective States in their religious liberties; this is left to the state constitutions and laws: nor is there any inhibition imposed by the Constitution of the United States in this respect on the states."[34] Justice Joseph Story concurred, in his authoritative *Commentaries on the*

*Constitution of the United States* (1833). The purpose of the First Amendment, he wrote, was "to exclude from the national government all power to act upon the subject [of religion]."[35] He further opined that "the whole power over the subject of religion is left exclusively to the state governments, to be acted upon according to their own sense of justice, and the state constitutions."[36]

## A Jurisdictional Interpretation of the "Wall"

Jefferson embraced this jurisdictional (or structural) view, which was virtually unchallenged in the founding era. Religion was a subject reserved to the jurisdictions of the individual, religious societies, and state governments; the federal government was denied all authority in matters pertaining to religion.[37] "To the united nation [national government]," Jefferson wrote in an 1801 address to the Rhode Island General Assembly, "belongs our external and mutual relations; to each State severally the care of our . . . religious freedom."[38] Jefferson thought other important First Amendment rights were similarly subject to state jurisdiction. For example, notwithstanding his commitment to a free press, he acknowledged, in an 1804 letter to Abigail Adams, that regulation of the press was a matter of state sovereignty: "While we deny that Congress have a right to control the freedom of the press, we have ever asserted the right of the States, and their exclusive right, to do so."[39] He expressed this jurisdictional (or structural) view in various contexts and at various times during his long public career. Indeed, it was a centerpiece of his political philosophy.

Although he frequently iterated this theme, it was never more succinctly stated than in his 1798 draft of "The Kentucky Resolutions," written in opposition to the Alien and Sedition Laws:

> *Resolved*, That it is true as a general principle, and is also expressly declared by one of the amendments to the Constitution, that "the powers not delegated to the United States by the Constitution, nor prohibited by it to the States, are reserved to the States respectively, or to the people" [Tenth Amendment]; and that no power over the freedom of religion, freedom of speech, or freedom of the press being delegated to the United States by the Constitution, nor prohibited by it to the States, all lawful powers respecting the same did of right remain, and were re-

served to the States or the people: that thus was manifested their determination to retain to themselves the right of judging how far the licentiousness of speech and of the press may be abridged without lessening
their useful freedom, and how far those abuses which cannot be separated from their use should be tolerated, rather than the use be destroyed. And thus also they guarded against all abridgment by the
United States of the freedom of religious opinions and exercises, and retained to themselves the right of protecting the same, as this State, by a
law passed on the general demand of its citizens, had already protected
them from all human restraint or interference. And that in addition to
this general principle and express declaration, another and more special
provision has been made by one of the amendments to the Constitution,
which expressly declares that "Congress shall make no law respecting
an establishment of religion, or prohibiting the free exercise thereof, or
abridging the freedom of speech or of the press" [First Amendment]:
thereby guarding in the same sentence, and under the same words, the
freedom of religion, of speech, and of the press: insomuch, that whatever violates either, throws down the sanctuary which covers the others,
and that libels, falsehood, and defamation, equally with heresy and
false religion, are withheld from the cognizance of federal tribunals.[40]

Jefferson returned to this theme in the waning days of his presidency.
The Reverend Samuel Miller, one of the very few prominent Presbyterian clergymen to endorse Jefferson's administration, wrote to the president, requesting him to "recommend to the nation a day of *religious observance.*"[41] Jefferson's response, in a letter dated January 23, 1808, is
of more than passing interest, because it grappled with issues identical
to those Jefferson said he wished to address in the Danbury letter. He
affirmed his abiding commitment to the rights of conscience and re-
stated his reasons, rooted in federalism, for refusing to issue executive
religious proclamations:

I have duly received your favor of the 18th, and am thankful to you for
having written it, because it is more agreeable to prevent than to refuse
what I do not think myself authorized to comply with. I consider the
government of the United States as interdicted by the Constitution from
intermeddling with religious institutions, their doctrines, discipline, or
exercises. This results not only from the provision that no law shall be
made respecting the establishment or free exercise of religion [First

Amendment], but from that also which reserves to the States the powers not delegated to the United States [Tenth Amendment]. Certainly, no power to prescribe any religious exercise, or to assume authority in religious discipline, has been delegated to the General [i.e., federal] Government. It must then rest with the States, as far as it can be in any human authority. But it is only proposed that I should *recommend*, not prescribe a day of fasting and prayer. That is, that I should *indirectly* assume to the United States an authority over religious exercises, which the Constitution has directly precluded them from. . . .

I am aware that the practice of my predecessors may be quoted. But I have ever believed, that the example of State executives led to the assumption of that authority by the General Government, without due examination, which would have discovered that what might be a right in a State government, was a violation of that right when assumed by another. Be this as it may, every one must act according to the dictates of his own reason, and mine tells me that civil powers alone have been given to the President of the United States, and no authority to direct the religious exercises of his constituents.[42]

In his letter to Samuel Miller, as in the Kentucky Resolutions, Jefferson tied together the First and Tenth Amendments to explain his reasons, rooted in the principles of federalism and strictly delegated powers, for refusing to designate a day for religious observance. He took the position that, because no authority to appoint days for religious observance was delegated to the federal government (including the nation's chief executive), one had to assume, pursuant to the Tenth Amendment and the principle of limited federal powers, that authority in this matter was "reserved to the States respectively, or to the people."[43] Jefferson, in short, acknowledged state sovereignty, rather than federal supremacy, in matters of religious liberty and establishment.[44] He did not think that the principle of federalism was inconsistent or at odds with the goals of separationism, inasmuch as both were concerned with checking the power of civil government, thereby protecting the rights of conscience.[45] The states, Jefferson believed, provided a valuable check on the abuse of these rights by the federal regime. The separation of powers and checks and balances, which were indispensable features of American federalism, provided vital protections for liberty that, in Jefferson's view, were arguably more important than a declaration of rights.[46] Although Jefferson, no doubt, desired each state through its respective constitutions and laws to protect the natural rights of citizens, it is unlikely that he thought the First Amendment, with its "wall of separation," was the appropriate device to achieve this goal. The use of a First Amendment wall to protect dissenters' religious rights in the states would have dangerously undermined that other great protector of civil and religious liberty—federalism.

Additional confirmation that the "wall of separation" was erected between religious establishments (i.e., church) and the federal regime is found in Jefferson's second inaugural address, delivered in March 1805. Historians report that this passage, like the Danbury letter, was written to explain his opposition to executive proclamations recommending religious observances:[47]

> In matters of religion, I have considered that its free exercise is placed by the constitution independent of the powers of the general [i.e., federal] government. I have therefore undertaken, on no occasion, to prescribe the religious exercises suited to it; but have left them, as the constitution found them, under the direction and discipline of State or Church authorities acknowledged by the several religious societies.[48]

The second inaugural address and the letter to Samuel Miller were, in a sense, Jefferson's own commentary on the "wall of separation" insofar as they both concerned issues identical to those raised in the Danbury letter. These documents, the record suggests, addressed the president's authority to designate days in the national calendar for public thanksgiving, fasting, and prayer. Jefferson thought it was important that religious practices remain voluntary and that jurisdiction over religious matters be retained by the individual and religious societies; however, insofar as the civil state had legitimate authority to take actions pertaining to religion, such authority, pursuant to the First and Tenth Amendments, was retained by the respective *state* governments.

Strictly speaking, Jefferson's "wall" was a metaphoric construction of the First Amendment, which governed relations between religion and the *national* government. His "wall," therefore, did not and *could not* specifically address relations between religion and *state* authorities. It is not self-evident that Jefferson thought the metaphor, more generally, usefully represented a universal, prudential doctrine of church-state relations that governed the interactions between religious institutions and *all* civil government—local, state, and federal. Jefferson's "wall" expressly described the First Amendment and, thus, is appropriately construed in the context of the federalism design for the Bill of Rights.[49]

Jefferson qualified his separationist stance with another separation of powers argument. A constitutional question addressed in the Danbury letter was whether the First Amendment restricted only the *Congress* in matters respecting an establishment of religion or whether its prohibitions extended to the coequal branches of the federal government (and, indeed, to the entire federal government), thereby denying the executive branch the prerogative to issue religious proclamations. "I contemplate with sovereign reverence," Jefferson wrote, "that act of the whole American people [i.e., the First Amendment] which declared that their legislature [i.e., the federal Congress] should 'make no law respecting an establishment of religion, or prohibiting the free exercise thereof [First Amendment religion provisions],' thus building a wall of separation between Church & State." (By using the phrase "that act of the whole American people" and by underlining the word "their," Jefferson emphasized that the prohibitions of the First Amendment were imposed on the federal Congress only.) Because the powers of the executive are derivative of the creative powers of the legislature, Jefferson concluded that he, as president, could not assume power over matters (such as religion) denied Congress. This separation of powers argument was made forcefully in a sentence Jefferson included in the preliminary draft but deleted from the final version of the Danbury letter: "Congress thus inhibited from acts respecting religion, and the Executive authorised only to execute their acts, I have refrained from prescribing even occasional performances of devotion."[50] The text suggests, and Jefferson's actions as president confirm, that he concluded that the *federal* chief executive was as powerless to issue religious proclamations (that is, to prescribe "performances of devotion") or to take other initiatives on matters pertaining to religion as he believed the U.S. Congress to be, pursuant to the First Amendment. This argument relating to the three branches of the federal government coincided with the federalism argument. The powers explicitly denied Congress were, in short, the powers denied all branches and agencies of the federal government. Therefore, the president, like Congress, must refrain from prescribing "performances of devotion."[51]

Jefferson took seriously the jurisdictional prohibition on federal involvement with religion, and in this respect he was more separationist than virtually all of his contemporaries.[52] He went further than most national public figures of his day in limiting the federal government's acknowledgment of, or interaction with, religion. (In this respect, Jefferson made a substantive contribution to an evolving view of religion's role in the federal republic.) Many of Jefferson's contemporaries, by contrast, did not believe that thanksgiving day proclamations by the national executive constituted an "establishment of religion" or a direct exercise of power over the subject of religion; thus, they did not view the practice as a violation of the nonestablishment provision or of federalism principles.[53] By taking the position that thanksgiving day proclamations by the federal chief executive offended the First Amendment, Jefferson adopted a more extreme view than the First Federal Congress and his two presidential predecessors. Indeed, his views on this matter were outside the mainstream. The strictures of the First and Tenth Amendments notwithstanding, the First Congress, which framed the First Amendment, called on President George Washington to appoint "a day of public thanksgiving and prayer"[54] and appointed legislative chaplains paid from the public treasury.[55] Both Presidents Washington and Adams designated days in the public calendar for religious observance.[56] By staking out a radical separationist position (in both the church-state and the federalism senses) *at the federal level*, Jefferson was sowing principles that, as he implicitly conceded in his letter to Levi Lincoln, were not yet political tenets widely and popularly accepted by the people.[57] Some have argued that, within the context of federalism, Jefferson used his famous metaphor to reconceptualize the First Amendment in terms of "separation," rather than "nonestablishment" and "free exercise" of religion.[58] If so, then here, too, he sowed principles that had not yet taken root in American political soil.

## A First Amendment "Wall"

The Danbury letter touched on a variety of issues worthy of analysis, one of which was the principle of church-state separation. A comprehensive examination of Jefferson's church-state views is beyond the scope of this chapter. The purpose and function of the "wall" he erected, however, are under review. The "wall of separation" was a figurative device unquestionably used to describe the First Amendment, which explicitly prohibited Congress from making laws "respecting an establishment of religion, or prohibiting the free exercise thereof." Prior to incorporation by way of the Fourteenth Amendment,[59] the First Amendment imposed its restrictions only on Congress and, by extension, Jefferson concluded, the entire federal regime.[60] In short, the "wall" Jefferson erected in the Danbury letter was between the federal government on one side and church authorities and state governments on the other. (This, in essence, is the same as arguing that Jefferson believed the First Amendment erected two distinct walls of separation: one between the federal goverment and religious institutions, thereby preventing the establishment of a national church, and the other between the federal and the state governments on matters pertaining to religion, thereby preventing the federal regime from interfering with religious establishments and practices endorsed by state governments.) The "wall" reassured New England Baptists and others that the First Amendment inhibited the federal government from interfering with their religious exercise. Pursuant to the First and Tenth Amendments and the purely executive nature of his office, President Jefferson concluded that, while state governments had the authority to act on matters pertaining to religion, such power was denied the entire federal government, including the national chief executive. Accordingly, Jefferson saw no contradiction in authoring a religious proclamation as a *state* official and refusing to issue a similar proclamation as the *federal* chief executive.

Jefferson clearly disapproved of discrimination against the Baptists in Connecticut. He looked forward to the "progress of those sentiments which tend to restore to man all his natural rights." It is unlikely, however, that Jefferson thought that the First Amendment "wall," which he described in the Danbury letter, was the device to achieve the "progress of those sentiments" at the state level.[61] More important, the use of a "wall" erected by the First Amendment as an instrument for church-state separation in the respective sovereign states would have been contrary to the fundamental principle of federalism; the unchallenged jurisdictional (or structural) understanding of the federal Bill of Rights; and Jefferson's commitment to a limited federal government, the sovereignty of the states, and a separation of powers between the state and national governments that served to protect the liberties of the people.[62] It is plausible, even likely, that Jefferson desired each state, through its respective constitutions and laws, to erect its own wall of separation between ecclesiastical and state authorities,[63] but these state walls would not be the same First Amendment "wall" described in the Danbury letter. There is every reason to believe that he would have wanted the

Figure 4.1. A Jurisdictional or Structural View of
Jefferson's "Wall of Separation"

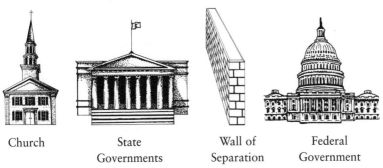

| Church | State Governments | Wall of Separation | Federal Government |

states to follow the model implemented in Virginia with passage in 1786 of his celebrated "Statute for Establishing Religious Freedom."[64] In his 1808 letter to the Reverend Miller, Jefferson once again ardently defended the rights of conscience with arguments applicable, it would seem, to both state and federal magistrates;[65] but while he specifically denied that the federal government had the "power to prescribe any religious exercise," he acknowledged that such power "rest[s] with the States, as far as it can be in any human authority." Notwithstanding the useful purposes Jefferson thought were served by the First Amendment "wall," he understood that its strictures were not imposed on state governments or on the voluntary religious societies.

Jefferson's "wall," like the First Amendment, affirmed the policy of federalism. This policy emphasized that all governmental authority over religious matters was allocated to the states. The metaphor's principal function was to delineate the legitimate jurisdictions of state and nation on religious issues. Insofar as Jefferson's "wall," like the First Amendment, was primarily jurisdictional (or structural) in nature, it offered little in the way of a substantive right or universal principle of religious liberty.[66] This controverts the conventional notion that Jefferson's metaphor encapsulated a general constitutional, prudential, and libertarian doctrine of church-state relationships and religious liberty. Indeed, a jurisdictional understanding of the "wall" raises serious questions regarding the way the metaphor is typically used by courts and commentators and recommends an honest reappraisal of the propriety of its conventional use in church-state discourse. There is no evidence that Jefferson considered the metaphor the quintessential symbolic expression of his church-state views. There is little evidence to indicate that Jefferson thought the metaphor encapsulated a *universal* principle of religious liberty or of the prudential relationships between religion and *all* civil government (local, state, and federal). There is much evidence, as set forth in this chapter, that the "wall" has been used in ways—rhetorically and substantively—that its architect almost certainly would not have recognized and, perhaps, would have repudiated.

# 5

# Early References to a "Wall of Separation"

## *Prefiguring the Jeffersonian Metaphor*

[There are those who hold] that *Bishops* may not meddle with the affairs of the commonwealth because they are governors of another corporation, which is the *Church*, nor *Kings*, with making laws for the *Church* because they have government not of this corporation, but of another divided from it, the *Commonwealth*, and the walls of separation between these two must forever be upheld.
—Richard Hooker (circa 1590s)[1]

[T]he faithful labors of many witnesses of Jesus Christ, extant to the world, abundantly proving that . . . when they have opened a gap in the hedge or wall of separation between the garden of the church and the wilderness of the world, God hath ever broke down the wall itself, removed the candlestick, and made His garden a wilderness, as at this day.
—Roger Williams (1644)[2]

Build an impenetrable wall of *separation* between things *sacred* and *civil*.
—James Burgh (1767)[3]

Although Thomas Jefferson is often credited with coining the "wall of separation" metaphor, he was not the first to use it in a church-state context. The image of a wall or similar barrier separating the realms of the church and the civil government can be found in Western political and theological literature centuries before Jefferson penned the

Danbury Baptist letter.[4] A separation between ecclesiastical and civil authorities was, for example, a familiar theme in both the Renaissance and the Reformation eras.[5]

Separationist rhetoric was used by numerous writers to advance diverse arguments and to serve a variety of theological and political purposes. This rhetoric made occasional reference to a wall of separation, a structure of unambiguous demarcation that would differentiate between the sacred and the temporal, between ecclesiastical and civil institutions and/or jurisdictions. A wall, for some theorists, was a symbol of protection and freedom; for others, it was a restrictive structure that imposed undue restraints on the proper roles of both church and state in civil society. Some thought a wall of separation shielded individual conscience from the rough and corrupting hands of civil or clerical authorities. Religious dissenters, in particular, hoped that placement of a wall between church and state would ensure a measure of autonomy from religious establishments in the exercise of religion. There were those who believed that a wall safeguarded the purity of religious truth and Christ's church from a fallen world; still others thought that it protected the civil state from ecclesiastical interference or domination.

Separationist themes emerged from the Renaissance and, later, from the Reformation. The language of separation is found in the writings of theological reformers. John Witte, Jr., observed that "[Martin] Luther, John Calvin, Thomas Cranmer, Menno Simons, and other sixteenth-century reformers all began their movements with a call for freedom from this ecclesiastical regime—freedom of the individual conscience from intrusive canon laws and clerical controls, freedom of political officials from ecclesiastical power and privileges, freedom of the local clergy from central papal rule and oppressive princely controls."[6] Early in his reformation ministry, Martin Luther (1483–1546) wrote of a "paper wall" between the "spiritual estate" and the "temporal estate."[7] In his *Institutes of the Christian Religion*, John Calvin (1509–1564) asserted that the "spiritual kingdom" and the "political kingdom" "must always be considered separately" because there is a great "difference and unlikeness . . . between ecclesiastical and civil power," and it would be unwise to "mingle these two, which have a completely different nature."[8] The Anabaptists, who believed they were in the world but not of the world, emphatically rejected the close identification of state and church that had been prevalent in Western Christendom since the reign of Constantine. They believed that the secular kingdom should be separated from the church of Christ. No true Christian, they maintained, should exercise the sword of temporal authority, and no civil magistrate should exercise jurisdiction in spiritual matters, because this is under the authority of God alone.[9] Although the civil state was instituted and ordained by God and is "necessary in the 'world,' that is, among those who do not heed or obey Christ's teachings, it is not necessary among the true disciples of Christ."[10] Menno Simons (1496–1561), a leader of the nonviolent wing of the Dutch Anabaptists, spoke of a "Scheidings-maurer"—a "separating wall" or "wall of separation" between the realms of the true church and a fallen world. In a December 1548 epistle, Menno Simons wrote: "You see, our people have always insisted that the church (*Gemeente*) must be entirely outside (*buiten*) the world. We must have a *Scheidingsmaurer* between us."[11]

Jefferson, clearly, was not the first to use the "wall of separation" metaphor in discourse on the relationship between religion and civil government. Although one cannot be sure he was familiar with earlier references to the figure of speech (indeed, in some cases he could not have known of the metaphor's use), there is little doubt that he knew of at least two works that made use of the masonic metaphor long before he wrote to the Connecticut Baptists. This chapter profiles three references to a wall of separation that predate the Danbury Baptist letter. Attention is focused on references to a "wall of separation" by Richard Hooker, the sixteenth-century Anglican apologist; Roger Williams, the seventeenth-century colonial champion of religious liberty and the founder of Rhode Island; and James Burgh, an eighteenth-century British political writer popular in revolutionary America. Each of these writers lived in different ages, and each used the metaphor for purposes different from those of the others, and from Jefferson's.

## Richard Hooker: "The Walls of Separation between . . . the Church and the Commonwealth"

The Anglican divine and theologian Richard Hooker (1554–1600) described "walles of separation between . . . the *Church* and the *Commonwealth*" in his magnum opus *Of the Laws of Ecclesiastical Polity*.[12] His treatise was an apology for the English ecclesiastical establishment (i.e., the Elizabethan settlement promulgated in the 1559 Acts of Supremacy and Uniformity) "against the attacks of the Puritan

Presbyterians on the one hand and against the Roman Catholics on the other."[13] The eighth and final book of *Ecclesiastical Polity,* published posthumously in the mid-seventeenth century from Hooker's notes, addressed "the distinction of the church and the commonwealth in a Christian kingdom."[14] Both revelation and reason, he argued, supported the organic identity of church and state as coextensive aspects of a unified Christian society. He believed, further, that "the episcopal form of government was best for the Church of England, and that Church and state were two aspects of the same commonwealth, a commonwealth in which both were rightly under the monarch."[15] "[W]ith us one society is both the *Church* and *Commonwealth* . . . whole and entire . . . under one chief Governor," he wrote.[16] Hooker contended that the crown was invested with powers both temporal and spiritual. This was the English model in which "power in causes *Ecclesiastical* is by the laws of this Realm annexed unto the *Crown.*"[17] He renounced those who would gather all authority ecclesiastical and spiritual unto the Church and deny Christian princes the supreme power to defend truth and to protect and provide for the Christian religion and spiritual matters. Indeed, he feared that the Puritans denied royal supremacy in order to elevate the clergy, thereby destroying the essential identity of church and state. Hooker, in short, eschewed walls of separation between church and state.

Hooker specifically criticized the Puritan reformers for advocating "a necessary separation perpetual and personal between the *Church* and *Commonwealth.*" He described and attributed to the Puritans a "wall of separation" that arguably caricatured and, indeed, marginalized and denigrated the church-state views of the Puritan separatists. He granted that a "*Church* and a *Commonwealth* . . . are things in nature the one distinguished from the other." The distinction, however, is formal and definitional, not substantial. He rejected the argument that

> the *Church* and the *Commonwealth* are corporations not distinguished only in nature and definition, but in subsistence perpetually severed, so that they that are of the one can neither appoint, nor execute in whole nor in part the duties which belong unto them, which are of the other, without open breach of the law of *God,* which hath divided them, and doth require that being so divided they should distinctly and severally work as depending both upon *God* and not hanging one upon the other's approbation for that which either hath to do.[18]

There are not any members of the Church of England, Hooker observed, who are not also citizens of the commonwealth. Therefore, in a frequently cited passage, he argued by geometrical analogy that, just as the same line of a triangle can be either a base or a side, depending on its position, so the same community of Christians may properly be described as either members of the church or the commonwealth, "depending on whether it is considered generally as a politic society or specifically as a politic society embracing the true religion, Christianity."[19] Hooker explained:

> So albeit properties and actions of one kind do cause the name of a Commonwealth, qualities and functions of another sort the name of a *Church* to be given unto a multitude, yet one and the selfsame multitude may in such sort be both and is so with us, that no person appertaining to the one can be denied to be also of the other.[20]

The mature politic society cares for more than mere temporal and economic concerns; rather, it seeks "to care for that which tendeth properly unto the soul's estate" and things spiritual.[21] Accordingly, one scholar wrote, Hooker "is able to acknowledge both that the religious is different from the secular (in the sense that different offices and activities will be specifically concerned with each) and that they are unavoidably related (in the sense that the same body of individuals has both secular and religious ends)."[22]

Hooker proceeded directly from his geometrical metaphor to outline the error he attributed to the Puritan reformers. The Puritans viewed church and commonwealth as two distinct and perpetually separated corporations, different in nature and ends. They thought that preservation of true religion—Christianity—required the church's independence; accordingly, they sought to vest authority for church governance in small presbyteries or local congregations (not in an episcopacy, which Hooker supported), removed from the crown's control. Hooker, however, ardently defended royal supremacy over the church:

> Contrariwise (unless they against us should hold that the *Church* and the *Commonwealth* are two both distinct and separate societies, of which two the one comprehendeth always persons not belonging to the other) that which they do, they could not conclude out of the difference between the *Church* and the *Commonwealth*; namely, that *Bishops* may

not meddle with the affairs of the commonwealth because they are governors of another corporation, which is the *Church*, nor *Kings*, with making laws for the *Church* because they have government not of this corporation, but of another divided from it, the *Commonwealth*, and the walls of separation between these two must forever be upheld. They hold the necessity of personal separation which clean excludeth the power of one man's dealing in both, we of natural which doth not hinder, but that one and the same person may in both bear a principal sway.[23]

Thus, Hooker viewed the "walls of separation" as an unfortunate impediment that prevents the Christian prince from protecting and providing for the spiritual estate.[24] More generally, Hooker lamented a separation between church and commonwealth, which he feared would lead to a diluted religious experience and an irreligious political culture. In contrast to the Puritan dissenters, Hooker favored both "the Christianizing of the public domain and the publicizing of Christianity."[25]

Jefferson was familiar with *Ecclesiastical Polity* and knew of Hooker's eminence as an Anglican apologist and political theorist. One cannot be certain, however, that he had read this particular passage or that this was the source of his "wall" metaphor.[26] Jefferson had a copy of *Ecclesiastical Polity* in his personal library; indeed, it was among the volumes he sold to the Library of Congress.[27]

## Roger Williams: "The Hedge or Wall of Separation"

A century and a half before Jefferson penned the Danbury letter, the colonial champion of religious liberty, Roger Williams (1603?–1683), erected a "wall of separation" to serve a purpose arguably different from that of Jefferson's "wall." Williams's earlier, lesser-known, and essentially theological expression was used in stark contrast to Jefferson's later and primarily political version.[28] Williams's construction of the "wall" is found in a 1644 tract entitled "Mr. Cotton's Letter Lately Printed, Examined and Answered." The radical Separatist Williams, who agitated for a complete separation of the civil state from the true church as a necessary precondition for liberty of conscience, had clashed with the preeminent Massachusetts clergyman John Cotton.[29] A conservative Puritan divine, Cotton promoted the idea that there was one objective, revealed truth of God articulated to a Christian society by the visible, organized church and defended by a civil state (ordained by God) and by godly civil magistrates.[30] Williams, unlike Cotton, denied the civil magistrate jurisdiction in spiritual affairs, including all authority to invade the sacred recesses of the soul and to coerce conformity to religious beliefs and conduct.

In a response to Cotton, Williams set forth the necessity for a "hedge or wall of separation":

> [T]he faithful labors of many witnesses of Jesus Christ, extant to the world, abundantly proving that the church of the Jews under the Old Testament in the type and the church of the Christians under the New Testament in the antitype were both separate from the world; and that when they have opened a gap in the hedge or wall of separation between the garden of the church and the wilderness of the world, God hath ever broke down the wall itself, removed the candlestick, and made His garden a wilderness, as at this day. And that therefore if He will ever please to restore His garden and paradise again, it must of necessity be walled in peculiarly unto Himself from the world; and that all that shall be saved out of the world are to be transplanted out of the wilderness of the world, and added unto His church or garden.[31]

Williams held that a "wall of separation" was peculiarly appropriate to safeguard the "most sweet and fragrant *Garden* of the *Church*"[32] (and religious truth) from the rough and corrupting hand of the world.[33] "When the imagination of Roger Williams built the wall of separation," according to the legal historian Mark DeWolfe Howe, "it was not because he was fearful that without such a barrier the arm of the church would extend its reach. It was, rather, the dread of the worldly corruptions which might consume the churches if sturdy fences against the wilderness were not maintained."[34] Any breach in the "wall" would transform "His garden" into a "wilderness." In contrast, the Enlightenment perspective attributed to Jefferson viewed a "wall of separation" as a device to safeguard the secular polity "against ecclesiastical depredations and excursions" or to protect civil society from sectarian strife.[35] Howe concluded that "if the First Amendment codified a figure of speech[,] it embraced the believing affirmations of Roger Williams and his heirs no less firmly than it did the questioning doubts of Thomas Jefferson and the Enlightenment."[36] Howe lamented that, in the modern mind, the Enlightenment construction of the "wall" had eclipsed Williams's religious motives.[37]

Critics have charged that Howe's interpretation of Williams's "wall" is simplistic, if not erroneous. For example, both David Little and William Lee Miller contended that Williams believed that both the civil state and the church have their proper, divinely ordained functions and that, contrary to Howe's suggestion, Williams was as critical of the pretensions of ecclesiastical authority to encroach upon the legitimate activities of the civil state as he was of the tendency of civil authorities to regulate the church.[38] Similarly disputing Howe's characterization of Williams's "wall," Timothy L. Hall observed that "Williams viewed it as a sign of disrespect for the secular city when the church usurped the authority God had granted to the civil magistrate. He thus complained that the clergy, relying on state support, had made civil magistrates 'but steps and stirrups to ascend and mount up into their rich and honorable seats and saddles.'"[39]

Several commentators have speculated that, in his message to the Danbury Baptists, Jefferson deliberately borrowed a figure of speech used by Roger Williams, who was briefly a Baptist and was revered in Baptist circles. Howe opined that Jefferson's figurative language "could easily, perhaps even properly, be read as an ingratiating effort to echo a Baptist orthodoxy."[40] Although Jefferson almost certainly knew of Roger Williams, there is little, if any, direct or even circumstantial evidence that Jefferson was familiar with Williams's use of the "wall" metaphor. In his religious biography of Jefferson, Edwin S. Gaustad reported that "[n]o evidence survives of Jefferson's or Madison's having read Roger Williams."[41] Williams's works, which for the most part were published in England and not widely circulated in the colonies, were largely forgotten until the Massachusetts Baptist apologist and historian Isaac Backus rediscovered them in 1773.[42] His writings did not became generally accessible to an American audience until they were republished in the nineteenth century.[43] Other commentators have argued more broadly that Williams's views had a negligible impact on the development of religious liberty in the founding era. "As for any direct influence of his thought on the ultimate achievement of religious liberty in America," Perry Miller bluntly concluded, "he had none."[44] Nonetheless, Mark DeWolfe Howe's twentieth-century commentary provoked a lively and continuing debate on whether the constitutional church-state arrangement accords with the evangelical vision attributed to Williams or the secular vision ascribed to Jefferson.

## James Burgh: "An Impenetrable Wall of Separation"

A plausible source for Jefferson's "wall" metaphor is the work of the dissenting Scottish schoolmaster James Burgh (1714–1775). Although largely unknown to modern audiences, this radical Whig Commonwealthman was "one of Britain's foremost spokesmen for political reform," whose writings influenced political thought in revolutionary America.[45] Jefferson read and admired the Scotsman's work and almost certainly encountered Burgh's use of the "wall of separation" metaphor in his extensive readings.

The Real Whigs or Commonwealthmen, with whom Burgh is often associated,

> espoused the right of resistance, separation of powers, freedom of thought, religious toleration, the secularization of education, and the extension of the rights of Englishmen to all mankind, including the less privileged sections of British society. . . . [T]hey advocated reforms including the extension of the franchise, reapportionment of legislative representation, annual parliaments, rotation in office, and the exclusion of placemen and pensioners from the House of Commons.[46]

Burgh and his fellow reformers shared a faith in "science, education, and the application of the principles of correct reason to the problems of the day. Earnestly dedicated to doing right, they believed in the power of moderate common sense and knowledge to improve the lot of their fellow men."[47] In the words of Isaac Kramnick, these "English reformers of the American revolutionary era were, in fact, committed partisans of modernity, of liberal individualism, and of market society."[48]

Burgh was prominent in a circle of reform-minded intellectuals of the 1760s that included Richard Price and Joseph Priestley.[49] Other influential reform advocates of the era, such as "Cato" (John Trenchard and Thomas Gordon) and Henry St. John, Viscount Bolingbroke, also shared ideological links with this group. In keeping with the Commonwealthman tradition, Burgh promoted reforms in various areas of

mid-eighteenth-century English life, including parliamentary government, the standing army, public education, rhetoric and grammar,
public morals and manners, poor relief, and religious toleration. He
not only promoted his own reforms but also drew on and popularized
the ideas of others. His three-volume magnum opus, *Political Disquisitions* (1774–1775), was a veritable sourcebook of reform ideas.[50] Forrest McDonald described it as a "popularized version of the *Cato cum
Bolingbroke* gospel."[51]

Burgh was a man of faith, as well as a man of reason. Indeed, he was
preoccupied with religion, which was the wellspring of his politics and
his moral code.[52] In this respect, he was not alone among the Commonwealthmen, who were "dominated and controlled" by religion. As
Colin Bonwick observed, "Religious belief . . . suffused their entire understanding of political morality and behavior and nourished their con-
ceptualization of social and governmental processes."[53]

Burgh brought to his writings a dissenter's zeal for religious toleration and a distrust of established churches. Indeed, his antipathy to ecclesiastical establishments was a logical extension of his staunch defense
of religious toleration.[54] Burgh thought religion was a matter between
God and one's conscience; he contended that two citizens with different
religious views are "both equally fit for being employed, in the service
of our country."[55] He alerted readers to the potential corrupting influences of established churches. Danger existed, he warned, in "a church's
getting too much power into her hands, and turning religion into a mere
state-engine."[56] Therefore, in his work *Crito* (1766, 1767), Burgh proposed building "an impenetrable wall of *separation* between things *sacred* and *civil*."[57] He dismissed the conventional argument that the public administration of the church was necessary to preserve religion's
salutary influence in society.

> I will fairly tell you what will be the consequences of your setting up
> such a mixed-mungrel-spiritual-temporal-secular-ecclesiastical establish-
> ment. You will make the dispensers of religion *despicable* and *odious* to
> all men of sense, and will destroy the *spirituality*, in which consists the
> whole *value*, of religion. . . .
>
> Shew yourselves superior to all these follies and knaveries. Put into
> the hands of the *people* the clerical emoluments; and let them give them
> to whom they will; *choosing* their public teachers, and maintaining

them decently, but *moderately*, as becomes their *spiritual* character. We have in our times a proof, from the conduct of some among us, in respect of the appointment of their public administrators of religion, that such a scheme will answer all the necessary purposes, and prevent infinite corruption; —*ecclesiastical* corruption; the most odious of all corruption.

Build an impenetrable wall of *separation* between things *sacred* and *civil*. Do not send a *graceless* officer, reeking from the arms of his *trull*, to the performance of a *holy* rite of *religion*, as a test for his holding the command of a regiment. To *profane*, in such a manner, a religion, which you pretend to *reverence*; is an impiety sufficient to bring down upon your heads, the roof of the sacred building you thus defile.[58]

Burgh concluded that entanglements between religion and the civil state led to the very corruption that establishmentarians argued was countered by an ecclesiastical establishment.

Jefferson admired and recommended Burgh's writings. In 1790, he advised Thomas Mann Randolph, his future son-in-law, that a young man preparing for a legal career should read, among other works, Smith's *Wealth of Nations*, Montesquieu's *Spirit of Laws* (with reservations), Locke's "little book on Government," the *Federalist*, Burgh's *Political Disquisitions*, and Hume's *Political Essays*.[59] In 1803, while president, he even "urged" one of Burgh's books on Congress.[60] Given his enthusiasm for Burgh's work, it is plausible that Jefferson's construction of the First Amendment was influenced by Burgh's recommendation for "an impenetrable wall of separation."

Jefferson was not the only American in the founding era who admired Burgh's writings. John Adams wrote that he had "contributed somewhat to make the [Political] Disquisitions more known and attended to in several parts of America" and reported that the work was "held in as high estimation by all my friends as they are by me."[61] The Philadelphia publisher of *Political Disquisitions* (who "published [the treatise in America] on a subscription basis within sixteen months of the English" edition)[62] listed more than one hundred prominent American "encouragers" or subscribers, including George Washington, Thomas Jefferson, Samuel Chase, John Dickinson, John Hancock, Robert Morris, Benjamin Rush, Roger Sherman, and James Wilson.[63] Oscar and Mary Handlin, the first twentieth-century authors to "rediscover"

Burgh, opined that the Scotsman "was as close to American thought as any European of his time."[64]

For various reasons, Burgh's considerable influence on the founding generation has been relegated to a historical footnote.[65] If, in fact, Jefferson appropriated Burgh's figure of speech in the Danbury letter, then the Scotsman's most enduring impact on American political thought may well be the "wall" metaphor.[66] Interestingly, Burgh dedicated the second volume of *Crito* "To The Good People of BRITAIN OF THE TWENTIETH CENTURY," because he expected "twentieth-century gentlemen and ladies to be of a more composed way of thinking than my contemporaries."[67] The "wall" metaphor did not emerge as a popular symbol of church-state relations in the United States until the second half of the twentieth century, since *Everson v. Board of Education* (1947). Burgh was perhaps correct to believe that only a "twentieth-century" audience would be receptive to his ideas. In the Danbury letter, Jefferson, like Burgh, seems to have looked forward to a day when there would be wide acceptance of his understanding of the rights of conscience.[68]

## Conclusion

Although the "wall of separation" metaphor is usually attributed to the sage of Monticello, it featured in church-state discourse and literature long before Jefferson wrote to the Danbury Baptist Association. There is no conclusive proof that Jefferson was familiar with any of these early references to the wall of separation. Indeed, he was probably unaware of Roger Williams's use of the metaphor, even though today Williams is celebrated as a colonial champion of religious liberty who influenced the distinctive American approach to church-state relations. Jefferson was possibly, even probably, acquainted with passages from the writings of Richard Hooker and James Burgh in which the metaphor appears. Burgh's trope, and the manner in which it was used, most closely resembles the phrase made famous by Jefferson. In any case, this chapter is a reminder that the "wall of separation" metaphor has a long history in Western theological and political discourse. For nearly half a millennium, at least, it has been used by individuals from diverse backgrounds and perspectives to serve a variety of functions in the always delicate and often vexing relations between church and state.

# 6

# Creating "Effectual Barriers"
## *Alternative Metaphors in Defense of Religious Liberty*

[I]f I could now conceive that the general Government might ever be so administered as to render the liberty of conscience insecure, I beg you will be persuaded that no one would be more zealous than myself to establish effectual barriers against the horrors of spiritual tyranny, and every species of religious persecution.

—George Washington to the United Baptist Churches
of Virginia (1789)[1]

I must admit, moreover, that it may not be easy, in every possible case, to trace the line of separation, between the rights of Religion & the Civil authority, with such distinctness, as to avoid collisions & doubts on unessential points.

—James Madison to Jasper Adams (1833)[2]

Jefferson was not alone among his American contemporaries in championing metaphoric barriers for protecting civil and religious liberties. Indeed, late-eighteenth- and nineteenth-century literature is replete with various figurative barriers erected to safeguard civil liberty in general and religious liberty in particular. Some of these barriers were constructed before the Danbury letter, and some after. Most, if not all, pre-twentieth-century alternatives to the "wall" were made without reference to, or even knowledge of, Jefferson's now famous construction. In more recent times, various commentators have proposed alternatives to, or refinements of, Jefferson's figurative language. This chapter surveys some of the notable barriers built in defense of civil and religious liberties.

## *"Effectual Barriers"*

In the days following his inauguration, President George Washington received a flood of congratulatory addresses from diverse sources, including some two dozen religious societies and congregations. These messages, in the words of a Virginia Baptist association, were "shouts of congratulations" and praise for Washington's services in war and peace and for his elevation to the chief magistracy of the United States.[3] In May 1789, Washington replied to one such address from the United Baptist Churches in Virginia. In his letter, written only months before Congress drafted the First Amendment, the president praised the Baptists throughout America for being "uniformly, and almost unanimously, the firm friends to civil liberty, and the persevering Promoters of our glorious revolution." He reaffirmed the "sentiment, that every man, conducting himself as a good citizen, . . . ought to be protected in worshipping the Deity according to the dictates of his own conscience."[4]

Addressing Baptists' fears that religious liberty was inadequately safeguarded under the new federal Constitution, he also wrote that, if the Constitution "might possibly endanger the religious rights of any ecclesiastical Society" or if the federal "Government might ever be so administered as to render the liberty of conscience insecure," then he would labor zealously "to establish effectual barriers against the horrors of spiritual tyranny, and every species of religious persecution."[5] Commentators have observed that this graphic imagery prefigured Jefferson's First Amendment "wall of separation between church and state." Conrad Henry Moehlman, for example, remarked that

> Washington's phrase "effectual barriers against the horrors of spiritual tyranny" was the forerunner of Jefferson's "wall of separation between church and state." Both loved figures of speech: Washington, the military man, thought of "barriers"; Jefferson, the man of home life, thought of a substantial, separating, secure wall around his estate. A barrier is the equivalent of a wall, especially when it is "effectual."[6]

Noting that both Washington and Jefferson crafted barrier metaphors in their responses to Baptist associations, one Washington scholar remarked that Baptists "look upon [Washington's trope] as the forerunner of Jefferson's 'wall of separation between church and state.'"[7]

Although Washington's imagery at least superficially resembles Jefferson's better known metaphor, Washington's conceit differs from Jefferson's in one vital respect. Washington was writing to the minority Baptist community in Virginia, which had grave reservations about the 1787 Constitution crafted in Philadelphia because they feared that it provided insufficient security for liberty of conscience and religious freedom. Washington did not suggest that "effectual barriers" are normally desirable, nor did he argue that a barrier between religion (or religious rights) and the civil state is a necessary precondition for religious liberty. Rather, he used the subjunctive mood to express a condition that he did not believe had existed. "If I could have entertained the slightest apprehension that the Constitution framed in the Convention . . . might possibly endanger the religious rights of any ecclesiastical Society," the president wrote, then

> certainly I would never have placed my signature to it; and if I could now conceive that the general [i.e., federal] Government might ever be so administered as to render the liberty of conscience insecure, I beg you will be persuaded that no one would be more zealous than myself to establish effectual barriers against the horrors of spiritual tyranny, and every species of religious persecution—For you, doubtless, remember that I have often expressed my sentiment, that every man, conducting himself as a good citizen, and being accountable to God alone for his religious opinions, ought to be protected in worshipping the Deity according to the dictates of his own conscience.[8]

Again, Washington did not make the normative case for a wall of separation. He did not advocate the erection of a constitutional barrier between church and state. Rather, he expressed a willingness to "establish effectual barriers" to separate people of faith from "religious persecution" and "spiritual tyranny" if warranted by circumstances.

## *"Great Barriers"*

In the summer of 1785, James Madison drafted an eloquent and passionate statement on religious liberty and church-state relations. His "Memorial and Remonstrance against Religious Assessments," which was printed and distributed throughout Virginia for popular endorsement, was a forceful, reasoned response to a pending proposal in the Virginia legislature to levy a tax, or general assessment, to support "teachers of the Christian religion." Madison's petition was so effective in galvanizing anti-assessment sentiment that it precipitated the demise of the general assessment legislation and facilitated the passage of Jefferson's celebrated Statute of Virginia for Establishing Religious Freedom (1786).[9] In the second paragraph of the "Memorial and Remonstrance," Madison argued that "[t]he preservation of a free Government requires not merely, that the metes and bounds which separate each department of power be invariably maintained; but more especially that neither of them be suffered to overleap the great Barrier which defends the rights of the people."[10] The "great barrier" circumscribes the power of the civil state; it "stands against the sovereignty of the state," John T. Noonan, Jr., observed.[11] This metaphor emphatically affirms that the peoples' religious rights, as Madison asserted, are "unalienable," "*natural and absolute.*"[12] This was a departure, indeed, from the old-world regime of religious *toleration*, in which religious exercise was a mere privilege that the civil state could grant or revoke at its pleasure. Madison believed that religious exercise was a fundamental and irrevocable right, possessed equally by all citizens, that must be placed beyond the reach of civil magistrates. At least one scholar has linked Madison's metaphor with Jefferson's: "That barrier, the limitation of legislative jurisdiction, is the political palisade before the 'wall of separation,' in Jefferson's famous metaphor for the First Amendment, which is to be erected between church and state."[13]

Madison was apparently fond of this metaphor. On other occasions, he celebrated Jefferson's Statute for Establishing Religious Freedom, which Madison had shepherded through the Virginia legislature in the dramatic and rancorous church-state battles of the mid-1780s, as a great and permanent "barrier" that circumscribes governmental infringements on religious liberty and the rights of conscience. In his "Detached Memoranda," Madison described the Virginia Statute as "a true standard of Religious liberty: its principle the great barrier ag[ain]st usurpations on the rights of conscience."[14] "The great barrier, here uncapitalized," Noonan observed, "is what the Memorial and Remonstrance had insisted upon. Natural rights are excepted from political authority."[15] Writing to George Mason's grandson in 1826, he wrote: "the celebrated bill 'establishing religious freedom' enacted into [?] a permanent barrier against future attempts on the rights of conscience, as declared in the great charter prefixed to the Constitution of the State."[16]

Other examples of this metaphor are found in the literature of the era. Tench Coxe, the Philadelphia political economist and prolific Federalist pamphleteer, wrote to Madison in June 1789:

> I observe you have brought forward the amendments you proposed to the federal Constitution. I have given them a very careful perusal, and have attended particularly to their reception by the public. The most decided friends of the constitution admit (generally) that they will meliorate the government by removing some points of litigation and jealousy, and by heightening and strengthening the barriers between necessary power and indispensable liberty.[17]

On the same subject, Senator Richard Henry Lee, a Virginia anti-Federalist, wrote to his cousin, Charles Lee:

> The enclosed paper will shew you the amendments passed the H[ouse] of R[epresentatives] to the Constitution. . . . I was surprised to find in the Senate that it was proposed we should postpone the consideration of Amendments until Experience had shewn the necessity of any—As if experience was more necessary to prove the propriety of those great principles of Civil liberty which the wisdom of Ages has found to be necessary barriers against the encroachments of power in the hands of frail Men![18]

## *"Certain Fences"*

Jefferson himself used another barrier metaphor—fences—for the protection of the people's rights. In a letter to Noah Webster, Jr., dated December 4, 1790, Jefferson noted that there are certain rights, such as "freedom of religion," that the people need not "surrender . . . to our ordinary governors . . ., and which experience has nevertheless proved they will be constantly incroaching on, if submitted to them." He then observed "[t]hat there are also certain fences which experience has proved peculiarly efficacious against wrong, and rarely obstructive of right, which yet the governing powers have ever shewn a disposition to weaken and remove."[19] A fence, although clearly a barrier and a structure of demarcation, suggests a construct less impermeable than a high, solid wall or a great and permanent barrier.[20]

## *"Line of Separation"*

Of all the alternatives to, or refinements of, Jefferson's figurative language, perhaps the most significant was coined by Jefferson's friend and colleague, James Madison. In an 1833 letter to the Reverend Jasper Adams, a South Carolina educator and moral philosopher who had solicited the elder statesman's opinion on the relation of Christianity to civil government in the United States, Madison crafted a metaphor more subtle than Jefferson's "wall." Madison wrote of a "line of separation" that acknowledged the shifting intersection of religious rights and the civil state: "I must admit, moreover, that it may not be easy, in every possible case, to trace the line of separation, between the rights of Religion & the Civil authority, with such distinctness, as to avoid collisions & doubts on unessential points."[21]

Proponents of Madison's "line of separation" metaphor argue that it describes more precisely than Jefferson's "wall" the actual relationship between religious rights and civil authority in the United States.[22] The word "wall" conjures up the image of "two distinct and settled institutions in the society once and for all time separated by a clearly defined and impregnable barrier."[23] A wall also tends to set "the two sides at odds with one another, as antagonists."[24] A line, in contrast with a wall, is fluid and adaptable to changing relationships and can be overstepped.[25] Richard P. McBrien remarked: "Madison's 'line,' unlike Jefferson's 'wall,' does not suggest something solid and unchanging, cemented in place once and for all by the nation's founders. A line has length, but not breadth. It can move constantly, even zigzag."[26] Therefore, as Madison noted, it is not easy to "trace the line of separation . . . with such distinctness, as to avoid collisions & doubts on unessential points."[27]

The "line" metaphor has not been without its critics, including justices of the U.S. Supreme Court. In an influential opinion in *McCollum v. Board of Education* (1948), Justice Felix Frankfurter opined: "Separation means separation, not something less. Jefferson's metaphor in describing the relation between Church and State speaks of a 'wall of sep-

aration,' not of a fine line easily overstepped."[28] Frankfurter's strict separationist dictum has been cited frequently in subsequent case law.
Other critics have argued that a line does not capture the impenetrable,
unyielding barrier envisioned by the framers of the First Amendment
nonestablishment provision and by Thomas Jefferson. Edwin S. Gaustad remarked that, according to Jefferson, the First Amendment "did
not draw pale lines in invisible ink between the civil and ecclesiastical
estates: it built a *wall.*"[29] Commentators, such as Richard P. McBrien,
have noted that "theoretical appeals to the 'wall of separation' notwithstanding, the Court has adopted, *in practice*, the Madisonian rather
than the Jeffersonian metaphor."[30] Indeed, the Court has made frequent
use of the line metaphor in church-state opinions.

Justice William Brennan, concurring in the famous 1963 school
prayer case, wrote: "The fact is that the line which separates the secular from the sectarian in American life is elusive." Nevertheless, he
continued, there is a "line we must draw between the permissible
and the impermissible."[31] In *Board of Education v. Allen* (1968), Justice Byron White observed that "*Everson* and later cases have shown
that the line between state neutrality to religion and state support of
religion is not easy to locate."[32] Chief Justice Warren Burger, in *Walz
v. Tax Commissioner of New York City* (1970), acknowledged that
the "course of constitutional neutrality in this area cannot be an absolutely straight line; rigidity could well defeat the basic purpose of
these [First Amendment] provisions. . . . No perfect or absolute separation is really possible."[33] He returned to the metaphor in *Lemon
v. Kurtzman* (1971), conceding candidly that the Court "can only
dimly perceive the lines of demarcation in this extraordinarily sensitive area of constitutional law. . . . In the absence of precisely stated
constitutional prohibitions, we must draw lines." The Chief Justice
then compared the "line" with Jefferson's more famous metaphor:
"Judicial caveats against entanglement must recognize that the line of
separation, far from being a 'wall,' is a blurred, indistinct, and variable barrier depending on all the circumstances of a particular relationship."[34] This provocative passage has been quoted and paraphrased by scores of federal and state courts. Other jurists have similarly observed that the line of separation between church and state
is neither straight nor easily determined.[35] Numerous lower federal
and state courts have used the line metaphor in church-state rulings.[36]

## More Walls and Other Metaphors

Since the Supreme Court rediscovered the "wall" in *Everson v. Board of Education* (1947),[37] church-state literature has been replete with alternatives to, refinements of, and recharacterizations of Jefferson's famous metaphor. These twentieth-century alternatives, unlike earlier metaphoric barriers suggested by Washington and Madison, were crafted with knowledge of, and in response to, Jefferson's construct, as interpreted by the modern Court. Presented here are a few samples of the countless modern redesigns of the wall, some thoughtful, some pedestrian.

Critics have argued that the Court itself, with its inventive use of adjectives, recharacterized the "wall" that Jefferson built. Justice Hugo L. Black, writing for the Court in *Everson*, asserted that the First Amendment "wall must be kept high and impregnable."[38] Justice Wiley B. Rutledge used equally sweeping rhetoric in his *Everson* opinion, arguing that the First Amendment's purpose "was to create a complete and permanent separation of the spheres of religious activity and civil authority by comprehensively forbidding every form of public aid or support for religion."[39] One can only speculate whether Jefferson would have described his wall as "high and impregnable" or "complete and permanent."[40]

The religious commentator Martin E. Marty recommended that the area "where church and state are to be separated" be referred to as a "zone." "Distinctions here," he opined, "are not and cannot ever become neat."[41] Harold D. Hammett similarly acknowledged a zone of interaction between church and state. He rejected the "wall" erected by the modern Supreme Court as a "homogenized" wall "composed of useless, isolated particles which merely dangle; they do not keep anything out of anything." In its place he would construct "two parallel walls" with the institutions of church and state on the most opposite exterior sides and acknowledge a zone between the two walls where both church and state have legitimate functions.[42]

Mark Weldon Whitten proposed the metaphor of a "barbed-wire fence." Such fences, he wrote,

> are erected for a purpose, a part of which is to warn against, and to impede, passage and trespass between certain areas.

Barbed wire fences are far from impregnable or impassable barriers, for one may with some care go over, under, or through them, and one may do so for good reasons. The specific location of a barbed wire fence may not be an infallible indication of where the line of separation between properties actually exists, and the particular location of the fence may be more pragmatically than legally based. A fence might require repositioning if challenged as to its pragmatic value or legal standing.

Nevertheless, one ought to proceed with caution before, during, and after deciding to traverse a barbed wire fence. There are, or at least were, good reasons for that fence's being placed where it is. It is a good assumption that one should not pass through such barriers without appropriate justification. One should also recognize that any such decision to circumvent a barbed wire fence may carry very real risks and costs. So it is with church-state separation.[43]

A number of courts and commentators have espoused a "permeable" wall. Mary C. Segers, a self-described "moderate accommodationist," advocated "a very permeable wall of separation between religion and politics."[44] Chief Justice Malcolm M. Lucas, of the California Supreme Court, opined that "the religion clauses represent not a 'wall of separation' but a permeable membrane."[45] Proponents of a high wall frequently lament that the wall is crumbling, has gaping holes, has a "major crack," or has come to resemble "Swiss cheese."[46] One federal judge remarked that "this wall," in the context of present litigation, "more resembles a moveable partition";[47] another federal court characterized the First Amendment wall as a "parchment barrier."[48]

James H. Hutson signaled approval for the wall metaphor "if it is understood as a wall of the kind that existed during the cold war, impenetrable through most of its length but punctuated by checkpoints. Jefferson," Hutson continued, "would have had no objection if, at these checkpoints, government invited religion to pass through and make itself at home in the use of its spaces, structures, and facilities, provided that it treated equally everyone who wanted to come along."[49] Stephen L. Carter opined "that in order to make the Founders' vision compatible with the structure and needs of modern society, the wall has to have a few doors in it."[50] Along the same lines, another commentator noted that a wall "need not be without a gate (which is not the same as a mere 'gap'): a gate would allow for some passage from one side to the other, but would keep the passage limited and orderly."[51] "An occasional window in the wall of separation" is another popular architectural innovation proposed by commentators.[52]

Hutson is not alone in blending Jefferson's figurative language with cold war imagery. A brief filed by amici curiae in *Everson* invoked the image of an "iron curtain" only a few months after Winston Churchill's celebrated speech at Westminster College on March 5, 1946, in which he popularized the phrase. The brief writers worried that the "legitimate 'wall'" would be "transformed . . . into an illegitimate 'iron curtain' separating areas between which there should be free passage."[53] The *"erection of a false 'wall' (or a wall in the wrong place)*," the amici warned prophetically and ominously, could restrict the rights of religious citizens to full participation in civil society and to full access to public benefits.[54] In the early 1950s, the Court of Appeals of New York invoked the "iron curtain" in a landmark case that challenged the constitutionality of New York City's "released time" program, which allowed parents to withdraw their children from public schools one hour a week to receive religious instruction. "It is thus clear beyond cavil," the New York court instructed,

> that the Constitution does not demand that every friendly gesture between church and State shall be discountenanced. The so-called "wall of separation" may be built so high and so broad as to impair both State and church, as we have come to know them. Indeed, we should convert this "wall", which in our "religious nation", Church of Holy Trinity v. United States, 143 U.S. 457, 470, is designed as a reasonable line of demarcation between friends, into an "iron curtain" as between foes, were we to strike down this sincere and most scrupulous effort of our State legislators, the elected representatives of the People, to find an accommodation between constitutional prohibitions and the right of parental control over children.[55]

Critics of the "high and impregnable" wall of separation erected in *Everson* and championed by the American Civil Liberties Union and other advocates of strict separation frequently reference the "iron curtain" in their literature. Unlike Hutson's constructive allusion to the cold war wall, these characterizations are decidedly pejorative and, one suspects, calculated not only to emphasize the impenetrability of the modern Supreme Court's "wall" but also to associate the Court's "wall" with atheistic communist regimes (many of which espoused absolute church-state separation in law and policy) and the strictly secular culture promulgated by a "high and impregnable" barrier. Not a few writers have described the "wall" erected by the modern judiciary as a "Berlin Wall."[56] One commentator has said that the Court's "metaphorical 'wall' invokes a mental image" not only of the "iron curtain" but also of the much more ancient, yet similarly forbidding, "Great Wall of China."[57]

Stephen L. Carter has denounced the modern judiciary's construction of a "single-sided wall" that confines, indeed imprisons, the community of faith but imposes few corresponding restraints on the civil state's ability to interfere with religion and religious institutions. The state, acting through its judges, "decides when religion has crossed the wall of separation. . . . Unsurprisingly, then, religion is often found to have breached the wall, whereas the state almost never is."[58] "The separation of church and state, in its contemporary rendition," Carter lamented, "represents little more than an effort to subdue the power of religion, to twist it to the ends preferred by the state."[59] This is a perversion of the historical and constitutional origins of the separation principle, Carter complained. The single-sided wall erected in the First Amendment was designed to protect religion from interference by the civil state but not to protect the civil state from religious influences. "Simply put, the metaphorical separation of church and state originated in an effort to protect religion from the state, but not the state from religion."[60] Carter concluded that, for the religious community, the modern judicial construction of the "wall" is a "prison wall." "So the wall of separation turns out to be not a garden wall but prison wall, surrounding the church to keep the people of the garden [referencing Roger Williams's metaphor for the true church] inside, with barbed-wire escarpments, angled inward, lest the religious try to clamber over."[61]

The most ironic characterization of the "wall" erected by the modern Supreme Court was suggested by one of the Court's own justices. Frustrated by hopelessly confusing church-state jurisprudence, Justice Robert H. Jackson quipped that, absent sure "legal guidance" in church-state matters, the justices "are likely to make the legal 'wall of separation between church and state' as winding as the famous serpentine wall designed by Mr. Jefferson for the University he founded."[62] Justice Lewis F. Powell, Jr., clearly not amused, curtly dismissed Jackson's sardonic musing that Jefferson's figurative "wall," as interpreted by the Court, had become as winding as the serpentine walls.[63]

The "wall" metaphor, like all metaphors, is imperfect in capturing the complexities and nuances of the constitutional concept it figuratively represents. Nonetheless, there is an obvious appeal to Jefferson's "wall" that invites courts and commentators to make creative use of this metaphor or something like it. The expansive influence and controversial application of the "wall" since the mid-twentieth century have prompted jurists, scholars, and polemicists to propose various alternatives to, or refinements of, the metaphor. These new metaphors have sought to rebut and supplant a misleading trope, correct perceived inadequacies of the "wall," or simply facilitate fresh insights about, and understandings of, prudential and constitutional relationships between church and state. The alternatives range from modifying the old barrier concept, such as a wall with gates, to creating wholly new metaphors, such as the public square.[64] Given the power of metaphor to shape reality, redesigning old metaphors or fashioning new ones has the potential to alter long-standing perceptions and to reconstruct legal, political, and popular rules that govern church-state relationships. For as long as the "wall" continues to inform church-state law, policy, and discourse, courts and commentators will be tempted to reimagine and redesign the wall to better represent the First Amendment and its goals.

# 7

## "Useful Truths and Principles . . . Germinate and Become Rooted" in the American Mind

*Jefferson's Metaphor Enters Political and Juridical Discourse*

I have generally endeavored to turn [citizen addresses] to some account, by making them the occasion, by way of answer, of sowing useful truths & principles among the people, which might germinate and become rooted among their political tenets.
—Thomas Jefferson to Levi Lincoln (1802)[1]

Metaphors in law are to be narrowly watched, for starting as devices to liberate thought, they end often by enslaving it.
—Judge Benjamin N. Cardozo, *Berkey v. Third Ave. Ry. Co.* (1926)[2]

Thomas Jefferson's message to the Danbury Baptist Association was published almost immediately. This must have pleased the president, who hoped that the "useful truths & principles" sown in the letter "might germinate and become rooted among [the people's] political tenets."[3] The celebrated "wall" metaphor, in the course of time, took root in American political and legal soil and profoundly influenced, if not defined, public debate on the constitutionally prescribed relationship between church and state in the United States.

By late January 1802, printed copies of the Danbury Baptists' address and Jefferson's reply began appearing in New England Republican newspapers.[4] The documents were often accompanied by an editorial comment. The (Boston) *Independent Chronicle*, for example, republished this commentary from the *Salem Register*:

> The *Danbury Baptist Association* has addressed the President of the United States, and have confirmed from his lips, their favorite truth— that *"religion is a matter which lies solely between a man and his God."* This christian sect, by attaching itself strongly to the present administration, has gained great success in every part of the Union. The accessions to it are unprecedented in any denomination which has spread itself in America.[5]

Following its initial publication in early 1802, the letter was not reprinted in a forum accessible to a wide audience for another half century. The missive was not included in the first collection of Jefferson's papers, published in 1829, not long after the great Virginian's death.[6] Another quarter century passed before it was published in a new collection of Jefferson's writings. In 1853, Henry A. Washington was commissioned by the U.S. government to compile a comprehensive edition of Jefferson's works.[7] Washington's nine-volume collection included both Jefferson's letter to Levi Lincoln and the final response to the Danbury Baptists.[8] The Washington edition of the Jefferson papers was reprinted in 1868 and again in 1871. Virtually all twentieth-century anthologies of Jefferson's works reproduced Washington's flawed transcription of the Danbury letter. Two major editions of Jefferson's writings were published around the turn of the century, one edited by Paul Leicester Ford and the other by Andrew A. Lipscomb and Albert Ellery Bergh. Only the latter, the Thomas Jefferson Memorial Association edition of *The Writings of Jefferson*, included Jefferson's reply to the Danbury Baptists.[9] The missive reached an even larger audience when it was reprinted in several popular one-volume compilations of Jefferson's writings published in the mid-twentieth century.[10]

## The "Wall" Enters Political and Scholarly Discourse

The entrance of the "wall" metaphor into popular and scholarly discourse is difficult to track. Occasional references to the metaphor and to the Danbury letter can be found in nineteenth-century church-state commentaries. For example, the respected nineteenth-century jurist and U.S. attorney general Jeremiah S. Black spoke of a "wall" in an 1856 lecture on religious liberty in the United States:

> The manifest object of the men who framed the institutions of this country, was to have a *State without religion*, and a *Church without politics*—that is to say, they meant that one should never be used as an engine for any purpose of the other, and that no man's rights in one should be tested by his opinions about the other. As the Church takes no note of men's political differences, so the State looks with equal eye on all the modes of religious faith. The Church may give her preferment to a Tory, and the State may be served by a heretic. Our fathers seem to have been perfectly sincere in their belief that the members of the Church would be more patriotic, and the citizens of the State more religious, by keeping their respective functions entirely separate. For that reason they built up a wall of complete and perfect partition between the two.[11]

In his acclaimed 1857 biography of the third president, Henry S. Randall drew attention to Jefferson's correspondence with the Danbury Baptists. He referenced, but did not quote, Jefferson's response to the Baptists and reproduced in full the president's letter to Levi Lincoln.[12] The church historian Philip Schaff excerpted the Danbury letter in his influential paper, *Church and State in the United States* (1888).[13] Schaff's monograph, written for the American Historical Society on the centenary of the U.S. Constitution, was the authoritative work on American church-state relations for the next half century. Significantly, the literature generated by the Liberal League, the leading late-nineteenth-century strict separationist advocacy organization, conspicuously failed to take note of the Danbury letter and the "wall" metaphor.[14] Another half century or more would pass before Jefferson's architectural phrase would become a familiar feature of legal and political rhetoric.

## The "Wall" Enters the American Legal Lexicon

The phrase "wall of separation" entered the lexicon of American constitutional law in 1879. In *Reynolds v. United States*, the U.S. Supreme

Court opined that the Danbury letter "may be accepted almost as an authoritative declaration of the scope and effect of the [first] amendment thus secured."[15] The Court reprinted the heart of Jefferson's address—the second paragraph—in its entirety, citing Henry A. Washington's collection of Jefferson's papers. Despite the significance the Court attached to the letter, Jefferson's figurative language is generally characterized as obiter dictum. Robert M. Hutchins, among other scholars, expressed the conventional view that the "wall" metaphor "played no role" in the Supreme Court's decision.[16] Chief Justice Morrison R. Waite, who authored the opinion, "wanted to use another phrase in Jefferson's letter to support his decision: he could not edit the letter to leave out the wall. The remark of Jefferson on which the Chief Justice relied was that the powers of government could reach only the actions of men, not their opinions."[17] The *Reynolds* Court, which was focused on the *legislative powers* of Congress to criminalize the Mormon practice of polygamy,[18] was apparently drawn to this passage because of Henry Washington's mistranscription of "legitimate powers" as "legislative powers."[19] Given this focus, the Court might have had little or no interest in the Danbury letter and the "wall" metaphor might not have entered the American legal lexicon *but for* this erroneous transcription.

The *Reynolds* Court seasoned its written opinion with a historical narrative of the dramatic church-state battles in revolutionary Virginia, which, the Court suggested, informed the content and meaning of the subsequently enacted First Amendment religion provisions. Later courts would similarly delve into this history in their church-state analyses.[20] How and why was the U.S. Supreme Court directed to Virginia church-state history and the Danbury letter when drafting its opinion in *Reynolds*? Neither the Danbury letter in general nor the "wall" metaphor in particular appeared in the formal record before the Court, including lower court rulings and the parties' legal briefs. The Court's reliance on Jefferson's 1802 epistle as "an authoritative declaration of the scope and effect of the [first] amendment thus secured,"[21] and, indeed, the letter's elevation to virtual constitutional status are surprising, because, as the American Minister to France from 1785 to 1789, Jefferson participated in neither the Constitutional Convention nor the First Federal Congress. The First Congress debated the content of a provision, which came to be known as the First Amendment, in the summer of 1789 and approved the final text in September; Jefferson returned to

American shores in November 1789. Thus, his influence on the actual text of the First Amendment was at most indirect.[22]

George Reynolds's free exercise of religion claim received only casual treatment until the case reached the nation's high court. The reasons for Chief Justice Waite's sudden interest in the First Amendment claims will be left for others to explore.[23] The immediate question is how Waite was introduced to the Danbury letter. One scholar has argued plausibly that George Bancroft, the most eminent historian of the age and a towering intellectual presence in the nation's capital, sparked the Chief Justice's "interest in the religious issue" and brought Jefferson's writings to the jurist's attention.[24] During his first years on the Court, Waite lived next door to the historian on H Street, where the two apparently formed a fast friendship and became frequent correspondents. "When Waite began preparing the *Reynolds* opinion," his biographer reported, "he turned to Bancroft for information about the original intent behind the religion clause of the first amendment."[25] Addressing Reynolds's religious liberty defense, Waite noted that the word "religion" is not defined in the First Amendment. "Unable to define the indefinable, he in effect shifted his inquiry to an examination of 'religious freedom' whose meaning he sought in 'the history of the times in the midst of which the provision was adopted.'"[26] He briefly noted ecclesiastical establishments in the late colonial era and their gradual demise in the revolutionary and early national periods. Waite was particularly drawn to Virginia's dramatic and bitter disestablishment battles, quoting James Madison's eloquent "Memorial and Remonstrance against Religious Assessments." He was especially moved by Jefferson's celebrated Statute of Virginia for Establishing Religious Freedom, one of the documents Bancroft furnished to the Chief Justice.[27] Historians and jurists, not surprisingly, have been drawn to the saga of church and state in revolutionary Virginia, Leonard W. Levy noted, "because the sources are uniquely ample, the struggle was important and dramatic, and the opinions of Madison, the principal framer of the First Amendment, and of Jefferson were fully elicited."[28] After noting the demands of Jefferson and others that freedom of religion be guaranteed in the federal constitution, Waite introduced contributions by Jefferson, indicating "the true distinction between what properly belongs to the church and what to the State."[29] He quoted first the Virginia Statute and then the Danbury letter.

Although Bancroft specifically referenced the Virginia Statute in his correspondence with the jurist, it is unclear "how Waite came across the letter to the Danbury Baptists." The Chief Justice's biographer has speculated that "Bancroft may have referred him to it in a conversation, or Waite, who worked very systematically, may have decided to track down Jefferson's later statements on the first amendment once he had looked at the Virginia Statute on Religious Freedom."[30] In any case,

> [the] Chief Justice warmly acknowledged his neighbor's aid. Writing to him on January 4, 1879, he "again" expressed "my thanks for the information given as to the history of the free religion clause in the constitution." "With your assistance," he continued, "I have been able to set forth, somewhat clearly I hope, the scope and effect of that provision."[31]

A fortnight later, Waite sent the famous historian "a copy of the [*Reynolds*] opinion" so that, he wrote Bancroft, "you may see what use has been made of your facts."[32]

Nearly seven decades later, in the landmark case of *Everson v. Board of Education* (1947), the Supreme Court returned to the metaphor: "In the words of Jefferson, the [First Amendment] clause against establishment of religion by law was intended to erect 'a wall of separation between church and State.' . . . That wall," the justices concluded in a sweeping separationist declaration, "must be kept high and impregnable. We could not approve the slightest breach."[33] Jefferson's words were woven neatly into the *Everson* ruling, which, like *Reynolds*, was replete with references and allusions to history, especially the roles played by Jefferson and Madison in the Virginia disestablishment struggles.[34]

Citing no source or authority other than *Reynolds*,[35] Justice Hugo L. Black, writing for a majority of five justices, invoked the Danbury letter's "wall of separation" passage. Black and his judicial brethren had likely encountered the metaphor more recently in briefs filed in *Everson*. Two briefs, filed by amici curiae in support of opposing parties, referenced the metaphor approvingly. One was the submission of the American Civil Liberties Union (ACLU). In an extended discussion of American history that emphasized Virginia's disestablishment controversies and supported the proposition that "separation of church and state is a fundamental American principle," the ACLU attorneys quoted the single clause in the Danbury letter that contains the "wall of separation" image.[36] Raising further the wall's profile, the ACLU returned to the trope twice more in the brief. It warned of the "extremities to which school boards may go in the direction of breaching the historic wall of separation between church and state."[37] The challenged state statute, the ACLU ominously concluded, "constitutes a definite crack in the wall of separation between church and state. Such cracks have a tendency to widen beyond repair unless promptly sealed up."[38] The other brief was filed jointly by the National Council of Catholic Men and the National Council of Catholic Women in support of the challenged state law, which authorized the use of state resources to transport children to and from parochial schools. This brief anticipated the controversy that would accompany the rediscovery of Jefferson's "wall." On the one hand, the National Councils argued that "[t]he Jeffersonian metaphor of a 'wall of separation' between Church and State has validity" and that the "wall" "is not undermined, breached or cracked by this transportation law."[39] While not disavowing the validity and use of the metaphor, the National Councils argued, on the other hand, that the "wall," "[l]ike any metaphor[,] . . . must be closely analyzed in order that its true content may be revealed."[40] They charged that the appellant's argument distorted "the principle of separation of Church and State by the erection of a false 'wall' not between Church and State but between the State and a large area of the State's own interests."[41] The appellant, they suggested, had been "misled by the metaphor" and had "transformed the legitimate 'wall' into an illegitimate 'iron curtain' separating areas between which there should be free passage."[42] The lamentable result, they concluded, was that "the exercise of parental choice in the matter of education [i.e., the choice of a parochial school education] necessarily 'wall[ed] off' some citizens from participation in ordinary educational benefits" to which they are entitled.[43]

*Everson* launched the metaphor into public consciousness. Although the Danbury letter had been reprinted in popular anthologies of Jefferson's writings in the years immediately preceding *Everson*,[44] the metaphor's current fame and pervasive influence in popular, political, and legal discourse date from its rediscovery by the *Everson* Court. Shortly after the ruling was handed down, the metaphor began to proliferate in books and articles.[45] Protestants and Other Americans United for the Separation of Church and State, a leading strict separationist advocacy organization, wrote the figurative phrase into its 1948 founding manifesto. Among the "immediate objectives" of the new organization was "[t]o resist every attempt by law or the administration of law further to widen the breach in the wall of separation of church and state."[46] In a 1949 best-selling anti-Catholic polemic, *American Freedom and Catholic Power*, Paul Blanshard advocated an uncompromising political and legal platform that favored "a wall of separation between church and state."[47]

The Danbury letter was cited frequently and favorably in the cases that followed *Everson*. The next term, in *McCollum v. Board of Education* (1948), Justice Black revisited the "wall," essentially constitutionalizing the Jeffersonian phrase he had relied on in *Everson*: "The majority in the *Everson* case, and the minority as shown by quotations from the dissenting views . . . ," Black asserted confidently, "agreed that the First Amendment's language, properly interpreted, had erected a wall of separation between Church and State."[48] This passage illustrates Black's blithe substitution of Jefferson's figurative language for the literal text of the First Amendment. "[N]ow no longer enclosed in quotation marks," Joseph H. Brady observed, the metaphor had "come of age!"[49] Perhaps to needle Black, whose *Everson* ruling he thought disastrously compromised separationist principles,[50] Justice Felix Frankfurter reasserted his doctrinaire separationist stance: "Separation means separation, not something less. Jefferson's metaphor in describing the relation between Church and State speaks of a 'wall of separation,' not of a fine line easily overstepped."[51] Justice Stanley F. Reed reproduced the Danbury letter's critical second paragraph in a footnote to his dissenting *McCollum* opinion.[52] (The justices made more than a dozen references to the metaphor in *McCollum* alone.)

The Danbury letter figured prominently in *Braunfeld v. Brown* (1961), a case that upheld a statute that disallowed Sunday commerce. Chief Justice Earl Warren, who announced the judgment of the Court, reprinted the letter's second paragraph in its entirety in the service of the proposition, previously stated in *Reynolds*, that "legislative power over mere opinion is forbidden but it may reach people's actions when they are found to be in violation of important social duties or subversive of good order, even when the actions are demanded by one's religion."[53] The Court's use of italics and accompanying commentary suggest that, as in the *Reynolds* case, the erroneous transcription of "legitimate powers of government" as "legislative powers of government" attracted the Court's attention to the letter.

In *Engel v. Vitale* (1962), the first of the major school prayer decisions, the Court left no doubt as to the constitutional status and continuing relevance of the "wall." "[P]etitioners argue," wrote Justice Black for the Court, that "the State's use of the [New York State Board of] Regents' prayer in its public school system breaches the constitutional wall of separation between Church and State. We agree with that contention."[54] This set the stage for subsequent cases the following term that held that state-sponsored prayer and Bible reading in public schools are unconstitutional.[55]

The "wall" continued to figure prominently in the rhetoric of church-state jurisprudence in the Burger and Rehnquist courts. In *Larkin v. Grendel's Den* (1982), Chief Justice Warren E. Burger, who had earlier expressed misgivings about Jefferson's imagery,[56] praised the metaphor: "Jefferson's idea of a 'wall' . . . was a useful figurative illustration to emphasize the concept of separateness. . . . [T]he concept of a 'wall' of separation is a useful signpost."[57] "The concept of a 'wall' of separation is a useful figure of speech probably deriving from [the] views of Thomas Jefferson," Burger opined in *Lynch v. Donnelly* (1984). "The metaphor has served as a reminder that the Establishment Clause forbids an established church or anything approaching it. But the metaphor itself," the Chief Justice cautioned, "is not a wholly accurate description of the practical aspects of the relationship that in fact exists between church and state."[58] Concurring in *McDaniel v. Paty* (1978), Justice William Brennan remarked: "Our decisions interpreting the Establishment Clause have aimed at maintaining erect the wall between church and state."[59]

A common refrain heard from jurists and commentators in recent decades is that the Supreme Court, having enthusiastically embraced the "wall" metaphor in *Everson* and its immediate progeny, quietly abandoned it toward the end of the twentieth century.[60] The Court still invoked Jefferson's trope, at least rhetorically, but, in practice, the justices implemented a less restrictive line of demarcation between church and state. Occasional murmurs that the metaphor lacked clarity or mischaracterized First Amendment doctrine were heard from the bench in the decades that followed *Everson*. In 1985, then Justice William H. Rehnquist famously renounced the "wall," lecturing his colleagues that the "'wall of separation between church and State' is a metaphor based on bad history, a metaphor which has proved useless as a guide to judging. It should be frankly and explicitly abandoned."[61] Justice John Paul Stevens led a rearguard action, plaintively urging his fellow justices to "resurrect the 'high and impregnable' wall between church and state constructed by the Framers of the First Amendment."[62]

## Judicial Criticisms of the Metaphor

Judicial uses of the "wall" have not been without criticism and controversy. A year after *Everson*, Justice Stanley F. Reed denounced the Court's reliance on the metaphor. "A rule of law," he protested, "should not be drawn from a figure of speech."[63] More than a decade later, in the first school prayer case, *Engel v. Vitale*, Justice Potter Stewart similarly cautioned his judicial brethren. The Court's task in resolving complex constitutional controversies, he opined, "is not responsibly aided by the uncritical invocation of metaphors like the 'wall of separation,' a phrase nowhere to be found in the Constitution."[64] The following term, in the 1963 school prayer case, Justice Stewart left no doubt that he believed that the nuance and complexity of the "First Amendment cannot accurately be reflected in a sterile metaphor which by its very nature may distort rather than illumine" the issues before the Court.[65] Justice Robert H. Jackson quipped in *McCollum* that, absent sure "legal guidance" in this matter, the justices "are likely to make the legal 'wall of separation between church and state' as winding as the famous serpentine wall designed by Mr. Jefferson for the University he founded."[66] In *Gillette v. United States* (1971), Justice Thurgood Marshall warned that "[t]he metaphor of a 'wall' or impassable barrier between Church and State, taken too literally, may mislead constitutional analysis."[67] A few months later, Chief Justice Warren E. Burger seemingly disavowed the metaphor:

> Candor compels acknowledgment, moreover, that we can only dimly perceive the lines of demarcation in this extraordinarily sensitive area of constitutional law. . . . Judicial caveats against entanglement must recognize that the line of separation, far from being a "wall," is a blurred, indistinct, and variable barrier depending on all the circumstances of a particular relationship.[68]

Chief Justice Rehnquist, perhaps the most vociferous critic of the "wall," concluded:

It is impossible to build sound constitutional doctrine upon a mistaken understanding of constitutional history, but unfortunately the Establishment Clause has been expressly freighted with Jefferson's misleading metaphor for nearly 40 years. Thomas Jefferson was of course in France at the time the constitutional Amendments known as the Bill of Rights were passed by Congress and ratified by the States. His letter to the Danbury Baptist Association was a short note of courtesy, written 14 years after the Amendments were passed by Congress. He would seem to any detached observer as a less than ideal source of contemporary history as to the meaning of the Religion Clauses of the First Amendment.

. . . There is simply no historical foundation for the proposition that the Framers [of the First Amendment] intended to build the "wall of separation" that was constitutionalized in *Everson*.

Notwithstanding the absence of a historical basis for this theory of rigid separation, the wall idea might well have served as a useful albeit misguided analytical concept, had it led this Court to unified and principled results in Establishment Clause cases. The opposite, unfortunately, has been true; in the 38 years since *Everson* our Establishment Clause cases have been neither principled nor unified. Our recent opinions, many of them hopelessly divided pluralities, have with embarrassing candor conceded that the "wall of separation" is merely a "blurred, indistinct, and variable barrier," which "is not wholly accurate" and can only be "dimly perceived." *Lemon v. Kurtzman*, 403 U.S. 602, 614 (1971); *Tilton v. Richardson*, 403 U.S. 672, 677-678 (1971); *Wolman v. Walter*, 433 U.S. 229, 236 (1977); *Lynch v. Donnelly*, 465 U.S. 668, 673 (1984).

Whether due to its lack of historical support or its practical unworkability, the *Everson* "wall" has proved all but useless as a guide to sound constitutional adjudication. . . .

But the greatest injury of the "wall" notion is its mischievous diversion of judges from the actual intentions of the drafters of the Bill of Rights. The "crucible of litigation," . . . is well adapted to adjudicating factual disputes on the basis of testimony presented in court, but no amount of repetition of historical errors in judicial opinions can make the errors true. The "wall of separation between church and State" is a metaphor based on bad history, a metaphor which has proved useless as a guide to judging. It should be frankly and explicitly abandoned.[69]

The judiciary's extraordinary reliance on the "wall" metaphor raises questions of great importance. For example, is the "wall" metaphor an accurate and adequate representation of the First Amendment? Does the "wall," in other words, illuminate or obfuscate the meaning of the First Amendment? Did Jefferson intend that his metaphor would encapsulate a universal, prudential, and/or constitutional rule of American church-state relations? Is the "wall of separation" referenced by courts and commentators and attributed to Jefferson the same "wall" as that constructed by Jefferson in 1802? Is it appropriate, as a matter of constitutional interpretation and law, for a metaphor from a presidential message to supplement or supplant constitutional text? Additional questions concerning the interpretive relevance of Jefferson's letter are raised by the extant documentary records, which include a preliminary draft of Jefferson's missive to the Danbury Baptists. What insights into the writer's intentions does an edited manuscript yield? Is this particular letter—with or without revisions—of any value to the judicial or policy decision maker seeking to interpret and implement constitutional principles governing church-state relations? If so, should any weight be given to passages and principles expressed in the draft letter but left out of the final version? Should greater weight be given to passages Jefferson deleted but left decipherable than to lines he completely obliterated? Those who defend the use of Jefferson's letter in contemporary legal and policy decision making must confront these questions.

"It is one of the misfortunes of the law," Justice Oliver Wendell Holmes observed, "that ideas become encysted in phrases and thereafter for a long time cease to provoke further analysis."[70] Justice Frankfurter similarly warned that the "uncritical use of words bedevils the law. A phrase begins life as a literary expression; its felicity leads to its lazy repetition; and repetition soon establishes it as a legal formula, undiscriminatingly used to express different and sometimes contradictory ideas."[71] Figures of speech designed to simplify and liberate thought end often by trivializing or enslaving it. Therefore, as Judge Benjamin N. Cardozo counseled, "[m]etaphors in law are to be narrowly watched."[72] Critics of judicial reliance on Jefferson's "wall" metaphor say this is advice that courts would do well to heed.

# 8

# Conclusion
## The Re-Creation of Church-State Law, Policy, and Discourse

WALL, *n.* [L. *vallum*; Sax. *weal*; D. *wal*; Ir. Gaelic, *balla* and *fal*; Russ. *val*; W. *gwal*.] A work or structure of stone, brick or other materials, raised to some highth, and intended for a defense or security. *Walls* of stone, with or without cement, are much used in America for fences on farms; *walls* are laid as the foundations of houses and the security of cellars. *Walls* of stone or brick form the exterior of buildings, and they are often raised round cities and forts as a defense against enemies.
> —Noah Webster, *An American Dictionary* (1828)[1]

[A]ll thinking . . . is metaphorical.
> —Robert Frost (1930)[2]

But the greatest thing by far is to be a master of metaphor.
> —Aristotle, *Poetics* (4th century B.C.)[3]

The wall metaphor is ubiquitous in Western literature. Throughout the ages, writers have been drawn to the motif.[4] A wall conjures up the image of an unambiguous, concrete barrier. It is a simple, yet dramatic and versatile figure of speech, as rich as "foundation," "fortress," "tower," "pillar," "bridge," or any other architectural metaphor.

Walls serve a variety of functions. In its most primitive form, a wall marks a boundary that separates one area from another. A wall, of course, can be the supporting structure of a building. It is "one of the sides of a room or building connecting floor and ceiling or foundation and roof."[5] Walls are often built for protection from undesirable elements, such as buffeting winds or rain or, in the case of a seawall, threatening waves or a rising tide. Retaining walls are designed to maintain the status quo, to keep soil and structures intact, safe from wind, water, or erosion. Walls can shield the senses from unwelcome sights or sounds. They can also provide sanctuary from human elements. The Great Wall of China and Hadrian's Wall, for two examples, were constructed to keep out marauding hordes; other walls, such as the Berlin Wall and prison walls, have been erected to keep people in. Walls, wrote the poet Robert Frost, are built for "walling in or walling out."[6]

All of these uses of walls have figured in the diverse applications and interpretations of the "wall of separation between church and state." Some walls have been constructed to shelter the garden of the church from the corrupting wilderness of the world; others have been erected to protect the secular polity from domination by the church or clergy; still other walls have been built simply to delineate between the sacred and the secular—between that which is God's and that which is Caesar's.

Robert Frost noted the paradox of walls in his much-anthologized poem, "Mending Wall."[7] One yearns for the boundaries and security that walls provide; yet one often chafes at the restraints on liberty imposed by barriers. "Good fences make good neighbours,"[8] said the poem's antagonist. At the same time, "Something there is that doesn't love a wall, / That wants it down."[9] (Frost clearly identified with the poem's narrator, who questioned the need for a wall.)[10] The rustic stone walls that crisscross the rocky landscape of Frost's native New England capture the contradiction. They are typically low and easily over-stepped, marking where one's property ends and a neighbor's begins. Low walls invite neighbors to meet at the wall to engage in cordial intercourse or even to pass objects between them. Walls, however, are not always welcome. They inhibit freedom of movement, to be sure. As Frost observed, even the frozen earth beneath swells in rebellion against stone walls, causing boulders to tumble and creating gaps in the barrier. Furthermore, to one involuntarily walled in or walled out, said Frost, the barrier is "like to give offence."[11]

What is the nature of the wall between church and state? Does it make for "good neighbours," or does it "give offence"? "If nowhere else, in the relation between Church and State," wrote Justice Felix Frankfurter, invoking Frost's immortal line, "'good fences make good neighbors.'"[12] "True enough!" J. M. O'Neill retorted. "But only fences that allow for cooperation, friendly intercourse. Fences so 'high and impregnable' as not to permit the slightest breach *never* make good neighbors. They are called 'spite fences' and are *never* built by good neighbors. They are only the instruments of extreme unneighborliness."[13]

Jefferson, the architect, was attentive to walls in his designs. Even today, he is remembered for the elegant "serpentine" walls he designed for his "academical village." In the pavilion gardens at the University of Virginia, in Charlottesville, Jefferson constructed graceful winding walls. He was drawn to this masonic design, which he likely first encountered during his mission to Europe, because it was at once aesthetically pleasing, structurally stable, and economical to build. The serpentine line is, indeed, visually appealing and an exotic departure from the linear, geometric patterns favored by European garden designers of the age. The meandering walls cast intriguing shadows across the terrain, evoking a sense of life and movement in the gardens. Although sensitive to aesthetics, Jefferson was eminently practical. The serpentine walls were economical because they could be safely raised, with a thickness of one brick, to a greater height with greater stability in high winds than a conventional, straight wall. Moreover, the walls not only serve as windbreakers but also present a large surface to capture radiant heat and concentrate the sun's rays on the plants that grow within the recesses of the curved walls.[14]

More than a century after their construction, Justice Robert H. Jackson whimsically referenced the serpentine walls in his critique of church-state jurisprudence. Absent sure "legal guidance" in church-state matters, Jackson quipped, the justices "are likely to make the legal 'wall of separation between church and state' as winding as the famous serpentine wall designed by Mr. Jefferson for the University he founded."[15] Some years later, Justice Lewis F. Powell, Jr., tartly dismissed the suggestion that the Court's rulings, like Jefferson's winding walls, were on a rambling or confusing course.[16] Nonetheless, a rare point of consensus among constitutional scholars is that church-state jurisprudence of the past half century has meandered across the legal landscape without clear direction or coherent principle.[17]

This final chapter considers the role of metaphor in the law. The functions and limitations of metaphor in thought and discourse are discussed first. Arguments for and against the use of the "wall of separation" metaphor in constitutional jurisprudence are then outlined and briefly examined. The chapter concludes with a few final reflections on the continuing appeal of Jefferson's famous phrase.

## Promises and Perils of Metaphors in the Law

"Metaphor," wrote Aristotle in *Poetics*, "consists in giving the thing a name that belongs to something else. . . . [A] good metaphor implies an intuitive perception of the similarity in dissimilars."[18] Metaphor pervades language and discourse. This literary device unquestionably enriches rhetoric, but metaphor is much more than merely a semantic ornament or decorative trope. Some linguists and philosophers suggest that metaphor is fundamental to thought and reasoning.[19] Indeed, some scholars argue that metaphor is indispensable to human cognition and imagination, shaping thought processes and even actions.[20] Although a metaphorical phrase may appear to be only a decorative figure of speech, it "is often a kind of 'invisible hand'" that molds arguments, enhances the weight and influence of subject concepts, and, in short, "guides events from afar without detection."[21] "In all aspects of life," wrote George Lakoff and Mark Johnson, "we define our reality in terms of metaphors and then proceed to act on the basis of the metaphors."[22] Therefore, the prevailing metaphors of a culture and those who successfully impose their metaphors on the culture, in many respects, define society's perceptions, beliefs, and even behaviors.

Metaphor is ubiquitous and necessary in legal reasoning because it is fundamental to human rationality; it is a primary mode of expression and comprehension.[23] A growing body of scholarship notes that metaphors are commonplace in law and that they shape legal thought, discourse, and doctrine.[24] This literature examines the promises and perils of metaphor in the law.[25]

Surveying the legal scholarship, Chad Oldfather identified five functions of metaphor in legal analysis and discourse. First, metaphor serves a decorative function, which is more important than the phrase implies. "Judicial opinions and legal scholarship must be persuasive in order to be successful." An opinion that is colorful, dramatic, and enjoyable to read is likely to be more influential and, perhaps, more persuasive "than one that possesses equal logical force yet is not as well-written" insofar as it captivates the reader's attention and is more likely to be referenced in subsequent opinions and scholarship. "Metaphors, regardless of whether they relate to the central analytical thrust of an opinion or article, may improve it stylistically, making it more persuasive by making it more pleasant, thus leading the reader to return to its discussion in thinking about an issue, or to quote its language in her own writing."[26] The decorative function should not be minimized.

Second, metaphor "translates the abstract concept into concrete and often vivid terms, shaping the concept with connotations and giving it a weight and carrying power independent of its true worth."[27] Metaphor can be an indispensable aid for grasping and comprehending exceedingly complex and/or abstract concepts, and, indeed, jurists laboring with such ideas are most likely to resort to metaphor. "Nonliteral language is often needed to explain the abstraction . . . that cannot be conveyed as effectively and persuasively through literal language. Through incorporation of tropes into legal opinions, what is abstruse and obscure becomes concrete and comprehensible," observed a student of metaphors in the law.[28] Metaphor is particularly appealing when "[o]ur literally expressed words fail"[29]—when the descriptive power of literal language is inadequate to convey a particularly complex or abstract concept. A metaphor not only "may render the underlying idea more concise or concrete" but also "may make it more striking or memorable by the drama of the substitution or merely by the use of the metaphor as a stylistic contrast to literal description. By connotation, the metaphor may arouse emotions associated with the metaphor and let them rub off on the subject."[30] Even concepts capable of conventional explanation can be enriched through the use of metaphor. One scholar has observed:

> By being more vivid and concrete, a metaphor also makes the accompanying doctrine more memorable to lawyers or judges in future cases. Precedent, after all, cannot do its work either as authority or by force of persuasion unless it is recollected. As the new metaphor is applied in successive cases, it is likely to acquire new shades of meaning, and the metaphor itself begins to be understood as a summary of prior applications.[31]

Herein lies much of the appeal of Jefferson's remarkably simple, yet concrete, metaphor.

Along the same lines, Oldfather argued that a third function of metaphor is "economy of expression." Again, when dealing with complex and/or abstract concepts, which may be difficult to explain in conventional, literal terms, judges find value in a metaphor's "ability to express in a few words what in literal language might take several pages."[32] Jefferson's celebrated metaphor unquestionably "condensed a wealth of concepts into a few words."[33]

Fourth, metaphor in the law functions "as a concealed form of analogical reasoning. While there may be some distinction between metaphors and analogies as they are strictly defined, they share the characteristic of comparing one concept with another for the purpose of pointing out similarities between the two that are thought to be helpful in answering an open question." The analogy, it is thought, yields new insights. A judge who invokes the "wall of separation," for example, "says that the constitutionally-prescribed relationship between religion and government is analogous to a boundary, and also says something about the nature of that boundary (i.e., that it is rigid, well-defined, etc.). The analogy here is somewhat concealed—as the analogies in metaphors often are—but it exists nevertheless."[34] "As condensed analogy," Michael Boudin observed, "metaphor has a natural appeal to lawyers versed in common law reasoning. In the common law tradition, it is an accepted method of justification for lawyers to argue, and judges to conclude, that the instant case is sufficiently 'like' the prior case that the two cases should be decided in the same way."[35]

A fifth function is metaphor's "almost magical capacity to unleash creative thought."[36] Metaphor is an invitation to consider fresh and different possibilities. At best, it opens up avenues of inquiry or perspectives not previously considered. Some may prove fruitful, others barren.[37] Metaphors link two previously unrelated things, experiences, or concepts. Once the connection is made, "one often is led to a radically different view of the underlying subject," raising new, creative possibilities for thought and analysis.[38]

While metaphor holds the promise of making language poetic and colorful, rendering abstract concepts concrete, condensing complex concepts into a few words, and provoking creative and analogical insights, metaphor also can be a source of much mischief. Metaphor is a valuable but imperfect literary device, and its uncritical use can lead to confusion and distortion.[39] As the great—perhaps the greatest—English jurist Lord Mansfield admonished, "nothing in law is so apt to mislead as a metaphor."[40] The potential perils of metaphor are inherent in its nature. As previously noted, "[m]etaphors explicitly or implicitly identify one phenomenon with another phenomenon from which the first is literally distinct."[41] A metaphor has "an understood literal meaning but [is] used nonliterally to refer to something else." It implies "some resemblance or similarity between two different things" and offers them for tacit comparison.[42] At its best, the metaphoric association of an unfamiliar and/or abstract phenomenon with something familiar and/or concrete provides comprehension, insight, and/or vital nuance. "At the heart of metaphor," however, "is a permanent paradox: metaphor enlightens by revealing common properties and by showing new connections; but because it equates two things that are not identical, the opportunity for distortion is always present."[43] By inviting us to "compare things that are not in fact identical, metaphors emphasize some traits of their subject and exclude others." The comparison, in short, is selective.[44] Indeed, "metaphor hides certain aspects of the very domains it helps us to understand," one writer candidly conceded.[45] "Half the wrong conclusions at which mankind arrive," the British Prime Minister Palmerston observed, "are reached by the abuse of metaphors, and by mistaking general resemblance or imaginary similarity for real identity."[46] The challenge of metaphor is to recognize and reject false comparisons and to discern where similarity ends and dissimilarity begins.

Metaphor pervades legal language and thought and, indeed, "consciously and unconsciously structures the way we conceive of the legal world."[47] Given the ubiquity of metaphor and its power to build, demolish, and reconstruct legal realities, metaphor in the law cannot be relied on uncritically. Jurists must be cognizant of the power and limitations of metaphor and vigilant against its misuse.

The most obvious danger of metaphor is the false, misleading, or inadequate comparison. Metaphor is essentially the comparison between two distinct phenomenon; therefore, there cannot be a complete identity between metaphor and subject. No metaphor, in short, can capture the complete essence of its subject. The emphasis on some aspects of the comparison and inattentiveness to others breeds distortion. The "wall of separation," for example, cannot possibly capture all the content and nuance of the constitutional principles governing church-state relationships. Although it may felicitously express some aspects of First Amendment law, it may seriously misrepresent or obscure others. Critics say that Jefferson's metaphor is a source of much mischief because a wall emphasizes separation to the virtual exclusion of First Amendment values such as freedom of religious exercise and association. Separation becomes the ultimate First Amendment value, crowding out all other values. Metaphors can suggest resemblances or shared attributes that are false, overstated, or deceptive. This is a core criticism of the "wall of separation." Does an immovable, bilateral wall suggest a degree of separation between church and state, or between religion and the civil government, unintended by the framers and ratifiers of the First Amendment? critics ask. Does the metaphor erroneously conflate separation and nonestablishment, thereby destroying the distinction between these two concepts? Insofar as a metaphor invites false, sloppy, or misleading comparisons, it inevitably affects the quality of analysis and understanding of the underlying concepts. If the premise of a metaphor is false, "the success of the metaphor serves only to perpetuate the falsehood." Unmasking a false or misleading—but appealing—premise is no easy task.[48] "The basic problem," Oldfather argued,

> is that a metaphor highlights certain aspects of its subject while obscuring others. Thus, for all the good that a metaphor can accomplish, the reality that we envision when we view a subject through metaphor differs from the reality of that subject as we knew it "pre-metaphor." It is not just that the meaning conveyed by a metaphor would be difficult to convey literally, or that it would take a large number of words to do so. Instead, the meaning of a subject once thought of in metaphoric terms will in a sense be polluted by the metaphor. The reader will now associate with the subject things that she would not have associated with it before, and because of the strength of these new associations might not as easily come to certain realizations about the subject.[49]

A metaphor can function like a lens, argued Thomas Ross in his influential essay, "Metaphor and Paradox." The metaphor as a lens, he suggested, "highlights and suppresses particular features of the subject idea." The lens necessarily alters or colors the examined subject. Viewing the constitutional arrangement for church-state relationships through the lens of the "wall of separation" unavoidably transforms one's view of the proper constitutional arrangement. "Even the most committed 'separationist,'" Ross remarked,

> could see the issue somewhat differently through the wall metaphor. Although the metaphor's meaning includes the separatist's doctrinal rule of separation, it also adds some things to that abstract doctrinal rule.

Seen through the lens of the "wall of separation," "church" and "state" each become monolithic entities, capable of physical separation. The metaphor suppresses the alternative sense of church and state: mere labels for the complex and bewildering array of actors, institutions, decisions, and forces which constitute "church" and "state" in our society. Instead, the metaphor highlights the sense of the reductive categories. Seen through the lens of the "wall," it seems possible in fact to achieve real and complete separation, or at least a metaphorical approximation.[50]

Insofar as metaphor informs—some say controls—legal concepts and doctrines, any distortion born of metaphor is of great consequence. A reliance on metaphor unavoidably alters the understanding of the underlying subject the metaphor describes. Metaphors inevitably graft onto their subject an emotional intensity or cultural associations that transform the understanding of the subject. If attributes of the metaphor are inaccurately, inadequately, or misleadingly assigned to the subject idea, the metaphor may reconceptualize or otherwise alter underlying legal principles or concepts. New and possibly erroneous understandings can be conveyed by metaphorical formulations. The more appealing and powerful a metaphor, the more it tends to supplant or overshadow the original concept and the more one is unable to contemplate a subject idea apart from it metaphoric formulation. "[M]etaphors have a tendency to take on a life of their own," Oldfather noted.[51] Lakoff and Johnson argued:

> New metaphors have the power to create a new reality. This can begin to happen when we start to comprehend our experience in terms of a metaphor, and it becomes a deeper reality when we begin to act in terms of it. If a new metaphor enters the conceptual system that we base our actions on, it will alter that conceptual system and the perceptions and actions that the system gives rise to.[52]

Some critics of legal metaphor have argued that judges, recognizing the power of metaphor to transform or recreate legal realities, deliberately misuse metaphors. The "unscrupulous judge," Oldfather warned, "might intentionally use it [metaphor] to obscure his reasoning or to avoid explicit consideration of a decision's consequences."[53] Courts also misuse metaphors in "an attempt to mask what the Court seems unwilling to admit: that the Court lacks a paradigm."[54] A court's invocation of a metaphor—such as the "wall of separation," which through repetition has assumed precedential and even constitutional status—can "mask the random nature of its decisions as it projects an appearance of scientific objectivity upon the Supreme Court's decisions" and creates "the impression that the Court's decision is principled."[55] Judges are also attracted to the figurative language of metaphor because they believe it can liberate them from the literal language of a constitution, statute, or some other written expression of the law. J. M. O'Neill complained that Justice Black was drawn to "an imaginary wall of separation instead of" the actual First Amendment text because the Justice "clearly preferred the freedom of the figurative language of the rhetoric of courtesy to the restrictions of the literal language of the United States Constitution."[56] Insofar as a metaphor is used to liberate or divorce a judge from a literal text, the judge runs the risk of becoming the source of the law, instead of the text the jurist is charged with interpreting. With the "wall of separation," among other metaphors, in mind, Stephen J. Safranek warned:

> The Court's abuse of metaphor will ultimately prove disastrous. The American legal system is dependent upon the use of language. The words of the Supreme Court provide guidance to lower courts and practitioners. When the Court, as the supreme interpreter of constitutional language, purposefully and intentionally hides its decisions behind deceptive metaphors, it allows other members of the profession to hide behind this confusion and encourages them to focus on outcomes, rather than reasoning. Thus, although metaphors may be powerful tools, the Supreme Court's use of metaphors frequently undermines the communication and reasoning that forms the basis of our legal system.[57]

Although metaphor has the potential to aid comprehension and provoke insight, it can also distort, mislead, and mask a hidden agenda or a lack of paradigm or principles. Controlling the influence of metaphor or rebutting an ill-conceived metaphor is not always easy. An awareness of the power of metaphor and its potential for abuse are essential to controlling it. "[U]nconscious usage means uncritical usage" of metaphor, observed one commentator.[58] The metaphor and its application must be examined critically. Hence, Benjamin Cardozo wisely admonished, "[m]etaphors in law are to be narrowly watched."[59]

## Mending Wall or Spite Fence?

The Supreme Court is keenly aware that its reliance on the "wall of separation" has been polarizing. Acknowledging the bitter controversy generated by its separationist *McCollum* opinion, Justice Black observed:

> Our insistence on "a wall between Church and State which must be kept high and impregnable" has seemed to some a correct exposition of the philosophy and a true interpretation of the language of the First Amendment to which we should strictly adhere. With equal conviction and sincerity, others have thought the *McCollum* decision fundamentally wrong and have pledged continuous warfare against it.[60]

The "wall" has become the central icon of a strict separationist dogma that champions a secular polity in which religious influences are systematically stripped from public life. Therefore, strict separationists have ardently defended a conventional separationist construction of Jefferson's "wall." With equal vigor, many religious traditionalists who favor a public role for religion and who reject the secularization of law and policy have protested the uncritical use of a metaphor not found in the Constitution, written by a man who was a member of neither the Constitutional Convention nor the First Federal Congress, to inform a secular, separationist construction of American law and policy. They contend that the "wall" misconceptualizes the original purposes of the First Amendment religion guarantees. This section summarizes the competing claims of proponents and opponents of a "wall of separation" as a defining motif of American church-state law, policy, and discourse.

## 1. *"Good Fences Make Good Neighbours": The Case for a Wall*

The "wall," proponents contend, has profitably illuminated our understanding of the constitutional arrangement for church-state relations. Defenders believe that the "wall" ably serves the previously noted functions of metaphor: making language dramatic and colorful, rendering abstract concepts concrete, and unleashing creative and analogical insights. It concretely and concisely communicates a complex constitutional principle. Moreover, the metaphor is simple and straightforward, which accounts for its remarkable appeal and utility. In *Larkin v. Grendel's Den* (1982), Chief Justice Warren E. Burger cautiously praised "Jefferson's idea of a 'wall' . . . [as] a useful figurative illustration to emphasize the concept of separateness. . . . [T]he concept of a 'wall' of separation is a useful signpost."[61] "Despite its detractors and despite its leaks, cracks, and its archways," the constitutional historian Leonard W. Levy enthused, "the wall ranks as one of the mightiest monuments of constitutional government in this nation."[62]

Insofar as the First Amendment unequivocally prohibits not only the formal recognition of, and legal preference for, one particular church (or denomination) but also all other forms of government assistance or encouragement for religious objectives,[63] then the "wall" graphically conveys the essence of the First Amendment religion provision. Given that a wall is concrete and immovable, the metaphor promises clarity and certainty to the division between civil and ecclesiastical authorities. Harold E. Fey, former editor of *The Christian Century*, championed the trope because "[t]he term 'wall' as Jefferson used it means a distinction, a limitation, a definition of fields of competence and authority. . . . It clarifies rather than confuses thought, and it encourages rather than discourages dialogue between citizens."[64] Unlike a "line of separation," which cannot always be easily discernible and can be ignored or overstepped, a wall unambiguously disrupts intercourse between church and state. Herein, thought the doctrinaire separationist Justice Felix Frankfurter, lay the virtue of a "wall": "Separation means separation, not something less. Jefferson's metaphor in describing the relation between Church and State speaks of a 'wall of separation,' not of a fine line easily overstepped."[65]

Perhaps most important, defenders of the "wall" believe that it promotes a sound prudential policy of strict separation that is good for both the civil state and religion. Absolute separation is a policy worthy of aspiration, even if one concedes that it is impossible to implement strictly. As Justice Wiley B. Rutledge remarked in *Everson*: "we have staked the very existence of our country on the faith that complete separation between the state and religion is best for the state and best for religion."[66] The Court reiterated this theme the following term and explicitly connected it to the "wall":

> For the First Amendment rests upon the premise that both religion and government can best work to achieve their lofty aims if each is left free

from the other within its respective sphere. Or, as we said in the *Everson* case, the First Amendment has erected a wall between Church and State which must be kept high and impregnable.[67]

The "wall" is often described as a vital—indeed, essential—instrument for religious liberty. "The central wisdom sustaining the concept of the wall," Marvin E. Frankel wrote,

> is that freedom of conscience is threatened when organized religion (or, indeed, organized irreligion, as in the former USSR) is brigaded with government power. It makes no essential difference whether clerics or secular ministries seek to evade the principle of separation. Either way, the resulting alliance is neither holy nor salutary. Instead, it is deadening or ominous at best; and at worst it is nasty, banal, hypocritical, degrading, and dangerous to freedom.[68]

Dissenting in *Board of Education v. Allen* (1968), a defiant Hugo L. Black opined: "And I still believe that the only way to protect minority religious groups from majority groups in this country is to keep the wall of separation between church and state high and impregnable as the First and Fourteenth Amendments provide."[69] Black left no doubt that he believed that anything less than a strict separationist policy "generates discord, disharmony, hatred, and strife among our people."[70]

A commitment to church-state separation, proponents insist, does not necessarily signal indifference, much less hostility, toward religion. Indeed, defenders of strict separation often argue that true religion flourishes when left to the voluntary support of adherents without assistance from, or entanglements with, civil government.[71] Religious liberty cannot survive as long as civil government enforces belief in religious dogma or is entangled with ecclesiastical institutions. Therefore, a "wall of separation" is a useful construct for promoting the voluntary, private support of religion and an environment in which freedom of religion can flourish. Even if one concedes that the "wall" is an imperfect conceit, it is, nonetheless, an instructive figure of speech, a fingerpost pointing toward a prudent policy of strict church-state separation.

Leading proponents are quick to defend the "wall" on historical grounds. "[I]n the writings of Jefferson and others," Justice Wiley B. Rutledge argued, "is to be found irrefutable confirmation of the [First] Amendment's sweeping content."[72] Justice Hugo L. Black, whose *Everson* opinion revived judicial interest in Jefferson's "wall," celebrated the leading roles played by Madison and Jefferson in promoting a regime of religious liberty and "in the drafting and adoption of" the First Amendment.[73] The implication is clear: great deference must be given to the considered views of Jefferson, including those expressed in the Danbury letter. The *Reynolds* Court, decades earlier, described the missive "almost as an authoritative declaration of the scope and effect of the [first] amendment thus secured," because it had been penned by "an acknowledged leader of the advocates of the measure [the First Amendment]."[74]

The "wall," in summary, promotes private, voluntary religion and freedom of conscience in a secular polity by preserving the independence of both religious institutions and the civil state from interference or domination by the other, by preventing religious establishments or even dangerous entanglements between governmental and ecclesiastical authorities, and by avoiding destructive sectarian conflict among denominations competing for governmental favor and aid. An unyielding and well-maintained "wall" serves the interests of those on both sides. Defenders of the "wall," such as Justice Frankfurter, are fond of quoting the ancient proverb made famous by Robert Frost: "'Good fences make good neighbours.'"[75]

## 2. *"Something There Is That Doesn't Love a Wall": The Case against a Wall*

Critics of the "wall" argue that the graphic metaphor has been a source of much mischief because it reconceptualizes—indeed, misconceptualizes—the First Amendment. In short, the metaphor, if taken too literally, mischaracterizes and distorts the constitutional principles that govern the relationship between religion and the civil state.[76] The First Amendment explicitly denies Congress the authority to make laws respecting an establishment of religion and granting legal preferences to one religious denomination over all others, whereas a "wall of separation" limits the activities of both the civil state and religion. Jefferson's trope uses the language of "separation between church and state," unlike the First Amendment, which speaks in terms of nonestablishment and free exercise of religion. The metaphor fails to distinguish between the concepts of "separation" and "nonestablishment."[77] Critics fear that a wall separates religion from public life and thereby promotes a religion that is strictly private and a state that is strictly secular.[78] A "high and impregnable" wall inhibits religion's ability to inform the public ethic and policy, deprives religious citizens of the civil liberty to participate in politics armed with political opinions shaped by religious principles, and infringes the freedom of churches and religious institutions to define and extend their own mission and ministries, whether spiritual, social, or civic. A high wall also makes it difficult for civil government to provide services or to grant legal exemptions to accommodate the religious exercises of citizens and communities of faith.

Detractors say that the metaphor's proponents have confused a trope for a legal principle.[79] And, indeed, few dispute that the modern judiciary has elevated the "wall of separation" to a constitutional principle. To those who say the "wall" is a reason or a principle, Robert Hutchins retorted emphatically, "[i]t is not a reason; it is a figure of speech."[80]

A wall is often a structure of enmity that tends to set "the two sides at odds with one another, as antagonists."[81] The *Everson* Court's construction of a "high and impregnable" barrier, unlike New England's low stone walls, some critics argue, unavoidably evinces a hostility toward the church and religion.[82] This "wall," they say, has been used to silence the religious voice in the marketplace of ideas and, in a form of religious apartheid,[83] to segregate faith communities behind a restrictive barrier.[84] In any case, the "wall" "privatizes religion" by restricting religion to the private sphere, "'walling off' religion from public life."[85]

The simplistic "wall" metaphor emphasizes *separation* over the free exercise of religion (to the exclusion of free exercise of religion, some fear), thus, critics say, "driving a wedge between the [First Amendment] free exercise and establishment provisions and creating the appearance of tension between them."[86] An inflexible adherence to a "high and impregnable" wall can threaten not only free exercise rights but also other First Amendment rights, such as free speech and association, of religious citizens in the public square.

A "high and impregnable" barrier between church and state, critics contend, exceeds constitutional requirements. "The First Amendment . . . does not say that in every and all respects there shall be a separation of Church and State," Justice William O. Douglas famously opined in *Zorach v. Clauson* (1952).[87] Moreover, as the Supreme Court has acknowledged, a "perfect or absolute separation" is impossible to sustain, even if it were the constitutional standard.[88]

Critics also argue that a "wall of separation" inadequately accommodates the nuance and the complexity of church-state relationships in modern society. The First Amendment, for example, may require the civil government, in the interests of free exercise of religion, to grant religious citizens a privilege or exemption from legal requirements (for example, providing military chaplains for the armed forces or tax exemption for religious institutions).[89] A "high and impregnable" wall of separation militates against such accommodation. Public policies premised on the existence of a "wall of separation" are incapable of acknowledging the nuances of constitutional doctrine, and even minor governmental accommodations of the peculiar needs of the religious community provoke cries that the "wall" is being dismantled. "[D]espite its simplicity," a critic argued, "the wall of separation produces an inflexible 'all or nothing' type of jurisprudence, which typically leaves one side jumping for joy and the other side hopping mad."[90]

The First Amendment explicitly forbids the making of certain laws and thus is a restriction on civil government only and not a restraint on religion (or the role of religion in public life). A "wall of separation" between church and state, however, restricts both the civil government and religion. Inasmuch as a wall is a bilateral, rather than a unilateral, barrier that not only prevents civil government from invading the ecclesiastical domain, as intended by the architects of the First Amendment, but also prohibits religion and the church from influencing the conduct of civil government, then the "wall" metaphor mischaracterizes the First Amendment. The various parallel guarantees in the First Amendment were entirely a check or restraint on civil government, specifically the national legislature. The free press guarantee, for example, was not written to protect the civil state from the press; rather, it was designed to protect a free and independent press from control or interference by the federal government. (Indeed, a free press was designed, in part, to serve as a check on, or a watchdog over, governmental powers.) Similarly, the religion provisions were added to the Constitution to protect religion and religious institutions from rough or corrupting interference by the federal government and not to protect the civil state from the influence of, or overreaching by, religion. Moreover, many founders believed religion and religious values liberated by the First Amendment free exercise guarantee would be, like a free press, a check on government corruption and tyranny. In summary, the First Amendment prohibition on religious establishment was a clear restraint on the power of civil government (that is, the federal government) to give legal preference to any single sect or combination of sects or to invade the religious domain. Any construction of Jefferson's "wall" that imposes restraints on entities other than civil government, critics say, exceeds the limitations imposed by the First Amendment, from which the "wall" metaphor was explicitly derived.[91]

Some critics have argued that the wall is a simplistic, jejune literary conceit that inadequately communicates—indeed, denies—the vitality of the First Amendment. In a dissenting opinion in the 1963 school prayer case, Justice Potter Stewart repudiated the Court's reliance on a "sterile metaphor which by its very nature may distort rather than illumine the problems involved in a particular case."[92] Stewart did not elaborate on why he found the "wall" a "sterile metaphor." The eminent First Amendment scholar Alexander Meiklejohn similarly found the metaphor sterile in its judicial application, complaining that the modern Supreme Court had stripped Jefferson's metaphor of its vital, organic essence and had recast it as a mechanical barrier:

> The shift in the meaning of Jefferson's "wall of separation" is a striking illustration of the change from the organic to the mechanical interpretation of a figure of speech. As one reads the words of the Rector of the University of Virginia, it is clear that the beliefs and attitudes of religion are, for him, "separated" from the other factors in education in much the same way as is the bloodstream of a living body from its other structures and functions. That bloodstream must be kept separate by the walls of the circulatory system. A break in them is disastrous. And yet the blood performs its living function only as it nourishes the whole body, giving health and vigor to all its activities. It is some such organic meaning as this which seeks expression in Jefferson's "wall of separation." But men who claim to follow him have transformed his figure into one of mechanical divisions and exclusions. They speak of his wall as if it were made of brick or stone or steel. By so doing they cut off our spiritual education from its proper field of influence. They make "private" a matter of supreme "public" importance. And the effect of that operation corresponds closely to what would happen if we should substitute for the living tissues which enclose the cortex, or the nerves, or the blood, casings of impenetrable steel.[93]

Another criticism often heard is that the "wall of separation" lacks historical legitimacy. Constitutional text, it is argued, should not be supplanted by a phrase from a private letter written by a man who was a member of neither the Constitutional Convention nor the First Federal Congress, which framed the First Amendment, and whose influence on the framing of the First Amendment was at most indirect. "There is simply no historical foundation for the proposition that the Framers [of the First Amendment] intended to build the 'wall of separation' that was constitutionalized in *Everson*," Justice William Rehnquist concluded after canvassing the pertinent history.[94] Furthermore, reliance on Jefferson's "wall" diverts attention from the more immediate and relevant legislative history of the First Amendment provisions debated in, and adopted by, the First Federal Congress in 1789. "[T]he greatest injury of the 'wall' notion," Rehnquist insisted, "is its mischievous diversion of judges from the actual intentions of the drafters of the Bill of Rights."[95] (Significantly, Hugo Black's biographer reported that the justice did not peruse the proceedings of the First Congress, which debated the provision now known as the First Amendment, until "[a]fter *Everson* was decided.")[96]

Critics complain that the "wall" provides little practical guidance for the application of First Amendment principles to real world church-state controversies, short of recommending a policy of absolute separation.[97] The problem, however, is that few Courts or even separationist partisans contend that a total and perfect separation is practical or mandated by the Constitution. In short, the "wall" is incapable of providing specific, practical guidelines that can be implemented in difficult disputes that require a delicate balancing of competing constitutional values, such as freedom of speech, association, religious exercise, and the nonestablishment of religion.

The "wall" is politically divisive. Because it is so concrete and unyielding, its very invocation forecloses meaningful dialogue regarding the prudential and constitutional role of religion, faith communities, and religious citizens in public life. The "wall" has unnecessarily infused the church-state debate in modern America with inflexibility and fostered distortions and confusion. The uncritical use of the metaphor has polarized students of church-state relations, inhibiting the search for common ground and compromise on delicate and vexing issues. It has not promoted unity or brought consensus; indeed, critics complain, it has sown discord and, in application, has frequently excluded religious citizens from public life and discourse. Jefferson's figurative language, detractors continue, has not produced the practical solutions that its apparent clarity and directness lead the wall builders to expect. Indeed, the "wall" has done what walls frequently do—it has obstructed the view. It has obfuscated our understanding of constitutional principles.[98] There is little advantage in metaphor if it is unable to bring clarity to an ambiguous or confusing text or if it fails to aid in the interpretive process. Therefore, the critics, too, evoke the poet Robert Frost, who observed in his eloquent poem, "Mending Wall": "Something there is that doesn't love a wall / That wants it down."[99]

## 3. The Wall That Black Built

Just as Thomas Jefferson's "wall" differs from the walls erected long before by Richard Hooker and Roger Williams, so, too, it could be argued, the "high and impregnable" barrier erected in 1947 by Justice Hugo L. Black and his judicial brethren in *Everson v. Board of Education* is easily distinguished from Jefferson's "wall." Although Justice Black credited the third president with building the "wall of separation," the barrier raised in *Everson* differs from Jefferson's in function and location. Much recent controversy surrounding the "wall" is less about Jefferson's metaphorical landmark and its place in history than it is about the legitimacy of the wall that Black built.

Black, unlike Jefferson, pointedly characterized his wall as "high and impregnable."[100] Even among proponents of the metaphor, this has generated much debate concerning the proper dimensions of the wall. Whereas Jefferson's "wall" explicitly separated the institutions of church and state, Black's wall, more expansively, separates religion and all civil government. Moreover, Jefferson's "wall" separated church and the federal government only. By incorporating the First Amendment nonestablishment provision into the due process clause of the Fourteenth Amendment, Black's wall separates religion and civil government at all levels—federal, state, and local. Thus, a barrier originally designed, as a matter of federalism, to separate the national and state governments, and thereby to preserve state jurisdiction in matters pertaining to religion, was transformed into an instrument of the federal judiciary to invalidate policies and programs of state and local authorities. By extending its prohibitions to state and local jurisdictions, Black

*Figure 8.1.* Two Views of the "Wall of Separation"

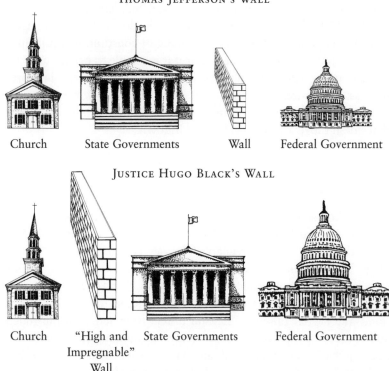

THOMAS JEFFERSON'S WALL

| Church | State Governments | Wall | Federal Government |

JUSTICE HUGO BLACK'S WALL

| Church | "High and Impregnable" Wall | State Governments | Federal Government |

turned the First Amendment, as ratified in 1791, on its head. Incorporation, in short, destroyed a vital purpose for which the First Amendment (and Jefferson's "wall") had been written.[101] Black established the "wall of separation" principle as the primary value of the First Amendment religion provisions, overshadowing the concepts of nonestablishment and free exercise of religion. The wall that Black built is the defining structure of a putatively secular polity. It represents a prudential and normative constitutional rule applicable to all relationships between religion and the civil state. The differences between the two walls is suggested by Jefferson's record as a public official in both Virginia and the nation, which shows that he initiated practices and implemented policies inconsistent with Justice Black's "high and impregnable" wall of separation.[102]

## *"Thomas Jefferson Still Survives"*

Jefferson's "wall" and its appropriation by the modern judiciary have been sources of bitter controversy since the metaphor was "rediscovered" in 1947. A civil conversation about the figurative phrase promises to enrich popular understandings, as well as judicial and political interpretations, of the prudential and constitutional role of religion in public life. Therefore, there is much to be gained by revisiting the origins, interpretations, and applications of the metaphor. Significantly, the Supreme Court, by its extensive and continuing reliance on the "wall" and, indeed, by its elevation of the metaphor to a virtual rule of constitutional law, invites this study. Insofar as the Court appropriated Jefferson's metaphor and then misconstrued that metaphor in its application, and insofar as the "wall" misconceptualizes First Amendment principles, as critics allege, the Court's jurisprudence may lack analytical merit and legitimacy.

This book focuses primarily on the history of the metaphor. Much of the modern controversy that surrounds Jefferson's "wall," by contrast, is less about the historical record than about the legal, political, and ideological uses of the metaphor in these times. Current debate centers more on defending or opposing the "wall" Justice Hugo L. Black built in *Everson* than on understanding the metaphor Jefferson used in the Danbury letter. Sadly neglected in the discussion is the historical construction of the "wall." The attention and influence appropriately accorded to the metaphor in constitutional interpretation and political discourse merit consideration, given judicial reliance on this figurative phrase. Simply put, what is the relevance of Jefferson's early-nineteenth-century trope in interpreting the Constitution and shaping public policy for the twenty-first century? This question must be asked of those who endorse the metaphor's use in contemporary law and politics.

Would American church-state law, policy, and debate be significantly different today had the "wall" not been introduced into public discourse? The contours of the church-state debate might have been similar absent the "wall," because separationist principles had been articulated in Western intellectual thought before Jefferson wrote to the Danbury Baptists, and an influential separationist perspective almost certainly would have emerged in judicial, political, and popular discourse. Absent Jefferson's metaphor, however, the debate might well have been more candid and transparent insofar as, first, separationism would have been clearly understood as only one among several plausible constructions of the First Amendment and, second, separationist partisans would have been compelled to articulate precisely the presuppositions and assumptions of their perspective, rather than gloss over them with the "wall of separation" slogan. The danger, say critics, is that, once established in church-state jurisprudence and discourse, the "wall of separation" ceased to provoke critical analysis and reevaluation. Justice Felix Frankfurter similarly warned that the repetitious, uncritical use of felicitous phrases bedevils the law: "A phrase begins life as a literary expression; its felicity leads to its lazy repetition; and repetition soon establishes it as a legal formula, undiscriminatingly used to express different and sometimes contradictory ideas."[103]

When Justice Black uttered his famous pronouncement in 1947 that the First Amendment, "[i]n the words of Jefferson, . . . erect[ed] 'a wall of separation between church and State'. . . [that] must be kept high and impregnable," he forever changed discourse on church and state in America. The "wall" metaphor entered the vocabulary of law and politics. In the course of time, it came to represent the prudential and constitutional relationship between religion and civil government, supplanting in some respects the actual text of the First Amendment. Since its introduction to public discourse, the "wall" has been a source of querulous debate. Scholars and advocates warmly debate whether the "wall" informs or distorts constitutional doctrines regarding the nonestablishment and the free exercise of religion and whether Jefferson's metaphor survives in substance or in rhetoric only. Some argue that the "wall" has been dismantled in whole or in part; others contend that the "wall" made famous by the man from Monticello was redesigned by Justice Black and his judicial brethren. There is no doubt that the "wall" remains influential in church-state rhetoric. Lost in the controversy is the historical context in which Jefferson erected his "wall." Unfortunately, the historical facts are often relegated to mere props in political and legal struggles to legitimize or delegitimize the metaphor in modern church-state policy and jurisprudence. Through it all, the "wall of separation" remains one of Jefferson's most vivid and enduring contributions to the American political and jurisprudential lexicon. Given the extensive and continuing influence of Jefferson's felicitous phrase in church-state law, policy, and discourse, it can be said, in the words of John Adams's memorable deathbed declaration, that "Thomas Jefferson still survives."[104]

# Appendices

*Documents from the Papers of
Thomas Jefferson*

APPENDIX 1

# Proclamation Appointing a Day of Fasting, Humiliation, and Prayer, May 1774

Tuesday, the 24th of May, 14 Geo. III. 1774.

This House, being deeply impressed with apprehension of the great dangers, to be derived to british *America*, from the hostile Invasion of the City of *Boston*, in our Sister Colony of *Massachusetts* bay, whose commerce and harbour are, on the first Day of *June* next, to be stopped by an Armed force, deem it highly necessary that the said first day of *June* be set apart, by the Members of this House, as a day of Fasting, Humiliation, and Prayer, devoutly to implore the divine interposition, for averting the heavy Calamity which threatens destruction to our Civil Rights, and the Evils of civil War; to give us one heart and one Mind firmly to oppose, by all just and proper means, every injury to American Rights; and that the Minds of his Majesty and his Parliament, may be inspired from above with Wisdom, Moderation, and Justice, to remove from the loyal People of America all cause of danger, from a continued pursuit of Measures, pregnant with their ruin.

*Ordered*, therefore, that the Members of this House do attend in their Places, at the hour of Ten in the forenoon, on the said first day of *June* next, in Order to proceed with the Speaker, and the Mace, to the Church in this City, for the purposes aforesaid; and that the Reverend Mr. *Price* be appointed to read Prayers, and the Reverend Mr. *Gwatkin*, to preach a Sermon, suitable to the Occasion.

*Ordered*, that this Order be forthwith printed and published.

Source: *Journals of the House of Burgesses of Virginia, 1773–1776*, ed. John Pendleton Kennedy (Richmond, Va., 1905), 124.

# Address to the Inhabitants of the Parish of St. Anne, 1774

### NOTICE OF FAST

[June, 1774]

To the Inhabitants of the parish of Saint Anne.

The members of the late house of Burgesses having taken into their consideration the dangers impending over British America from the hostile invasion of a sister colony, thought proper that it should be recommended to the several parishes in this colony that they set apart some convenient day for fasting, humiliation and prayer devoutly to implore the divine interposition in behalf of an injured and oppressed people; and that the minds of his majesty, his ministers, and parliament, might be inspired with wisdom from above, to avert from us the dangers which threaten our civil rights, and all the evils of civil war. We do therefore recommend to the inhabitants of the parish of Saint Anne that Saturday the 23d instant be by them set apart for the purpose aforesaid, on which day will be prayers and a sermon suited to the occasion by the reverend Mr. Clay at the new church on Hardware river, which place is thought the most centrical to the parishioners in General.

JOHN WALKER[1]
THOMAS JEFFERSON

*Source: The Works of Thomas Jefferson,* ed. Paul Leicester Ford, 12 vols., Federal Edition (New York: G. P. Putnam's Sons, 1904), 2:41–42.

# Bills Reported by the Committee of Revisors Appointed by the General Assembly of Virginia in 1776, 18 June 1779

*Bill Number 82: A Bill for Establishing Religious Freedom*

WELL *aware that the opinions and belief of men depend not on their own will, but follow involuntarily the evidence proposed to their minds; that*[2] Almighty God hath created the mind free, *and manifested his supreme will that free it shall remain by making it altogether insusceptible of restraint*; that all attempts to influence it by temporal punishments, or burthens, or by civil incapacitations, tend only to beget habits of hypocrisy and meanness, and are a departure from the plan of the holy author of our religion, who being lord both of body and mind, yet chose not to propagate it by coercions on either, as was in his Almighty power to do, *but to extend it by its influence on reason alone*; that the impious presumption of legislators and rulers, civil as well as ecclesiastical, who, being themselves but fallible and uninspired men, have assumed dominion over the faith of others, setting up their own opinions and modes of thinking as the only true and infallible, and as such endeavoring to impose them on others, hath established and maintained false religions over the greatest part of the world and through all time: That to compel a man to furnish contributions of money for the propagation of opinions which he disbelieves *and abhors*, is sinful and tyrannical; that even the forcing him to support this or that teacher of his own religious persuasion, is depriving him of the comfortable liberty of giving his contributions to the particular pastor whose morals he would make his pattern, and whose powers he feels most persuasive to righteousness; and is withdrawing from the ministry those temporary [temporal] rewards, which proceeding from an approbation of their personal conduct, are an additional incitement to earnest and unremitting labours for the instruction of mankind; that our civil rights have no dependance on our religious opinions, any more than [on] our opinions in physics or geometry; that therefore the proscribing any citizen as unworthy the public confidence by laying upon him an incapacity of being called to offices of trust and emolument, unless he profess or renounce this or that religious opinion, is depriving him injuriously of those privileges and advantages to which, in common with his fellow citizens, he has a natural right; that it tends also[3] to corrupt the principles of that *very* religion it is meant to encourage, by bribing, with a monopoly of worldly honours and emoluments, those who will externally profess and conform to it; that though indeed these are criminal who do not withstand such temptation, yet neither are those innocent who lay the bait in their way; *that the opinions of men are not the object of civil government, nor under its jurisdiction*; that to suffer the civil magistrate to intrude his powers into the field of opinion and to restrain the profession or propagation of principles on supposition of their ill tendency is a dangerous falacy, which at once destroys all religious liberty, because he being of course judge of that tendency will make his opinions the rule of judgment, and approve or condemn the sentiments of others only as they shall square with or differ from his own; that it is time enough for the rightful purposes of civil government for its officers to interfere when principles break out into overt acts against peace and good order; and finally, that truth is great and will prevail if left to herself; that she is the proper and sufficient antagonist to error, and has nothing to fear from the conflict unless by human interposition disarmed of her natural weapons, free argument and debate; errors ceasing to be dangerous when it is permitted freely to contradict them.

WE *the General Assembly of Virginia do enact*[4] that no man shall be compelled to frequent or support any religious worship, place, or ministry whatsoever, nor shall be enforced, restrained, molested, or burthened in his body or goods, nor shall otherwise suffer, on account of his religious opinions or belief; but that all men shall be free to profess, and by argument to maintain, their opinion*s* in matters of religion, and that the same shall in no wise diminish, enlarge, or affect their civil capacities.

AND though we well know that this Assembly, elected by the people for the ordinary purposes of legislation only, have no power to restrain the acts of succeeding Assemblies, constituted with powers equal to our own, and that therefore to declare this act [to be] irrevocable would be of no effect in law; yet we are free to declare, and do declare, that the rights hereby asserted are of the natural rights of mankind, and that if any act shall be hereafter passed to repeal the present or to narrow its operation, such act will be an infringement of natural right.

## Bill Number 84: A Bill for Punishing Disturbers of Religious Worship and Sabbath Breakers

BE it enacted by the General Assembly, that no officer, for any civil cause, shall arrest any minister of the gospel,[5] licensed according to the rules of his sect, and who shall have taken the oath[6] of fidelity to the commonwealth, while such minister shall be publicly preaching or performing religious worship in any church, chapel, or meeting-house,[7] on pain of imprisonment and amercement, at the discretion of a jury, and of making satisfaction to the party so arrested.

AND if any person shall of [on] purpose, maliciously, or contemptuously, disquiet or disturb any congregation assembled in any church, chapel, or meeting-house,[8] or misuse any such minister being there, he may be put under restraint during religious worship, by any Justice present, which Justice, if present, or if none be present, then any Justice before whom proof of the offence shall be made, may cause the offender to find two sureties[9] to be bound by recognizance in a sufficient penalty for his good behavior, and in default thereof shall commit him to prison, there to remain till the next court to be held for the same county; and upon conviction of the said offence before the said court, he shall be further punished by imprisonment and amercement at the discretion of a jury.

IF any person on Sunday[10] shall himself be found labouring at his own or any other trade or calling, or shall employ his apprentices, servants or slaves in labour, or other business, except it be in the ordinary hous[e]hold offices of daily necessity, or other work of necessity or charity, he shall forfeit the sum of ten shillings for every such offence, deeming every apprentice, servant, or slave so employed, and every day he shall be so employed as constituting a distinct offence.

## *Bill Number 85: A Bill for Appointing Days of Public Fasting and Thanksgiving*

BE it enacted by the General Assembly, that the power of appointing days of public fasting and humiliation, or thanksgiving, throughout this commonwealth, may in the recess of the General Assembly, be exercised by the Governor, or Chief Magistrate, with the advice of the Council; and such appointment shall be notified to the public, by a proclamation, in which the occasion of the fasting or thanksgiving shall be particularly set forth. Every minister of the gospel shall on each day so to be appointed, attend and perform divine service and preach a sermon, or discourse, suited to the occasion, in his church, on pain of forfeiting fifty pounds for every failure, not having a reasonable excuse.

*Source: Report of the Committee of Revisors Appointed by the General Assembly of Virginia in MDCCLXXVI* (Richmond, Va.: printed by Dixon and Holt, 1784), 58–60; William Waller Hening, ed., *The Statutes at Large; Being a Collection of all the Laws of Virginia* (Richmond, Va.: J. and G. Cochran, 1823), 12:84–86, 336–337.

APPENDIX 4

# Proclamation Appointing a Day of Publick and Solemn Thanksgiving and Prayer, November 1779

By his Excellency THOMAS JEFFERSON, Es*q*.; Governour or
Chief Magistrate of the commonwealth of *Virginia*.
PROCLAMATION.

WHEREAS the Honourable the General Congress, impressed with a grateful sense of the goodness of Almighty God, in blessing the greater part of this extensive continent with plentiful harvests, crowning our arms with repeated successes, conducting us hitherto safely through the perils with which we have been encompassed and manifesting in multiplied instances his divine care of these infant states, hath thought proper by their act of the 20th day of October last, to recommend to the several states that Thursday the 9th of December next be appointed a day of publick and solemn thanksgiving and prayer, which act is in these words, to wit.

"Whereas it becomes us humbly to approach the throne of Almighty God, with gratitude and praise, for the wonders which his goodness has wrought in conducting our forefathers to this western world; for his protection to them and to their posterity, amidst difficulties and dangers; for raising us their children from deep distress, to be numbered among the nations of the earth; and for arming the hands of just and mighty Princes in our deliverance; and especially for that he hath been pleased to grant us the enjoyment of health and so to order the revolving seasons, that the earth hath produced her increase in abundance, blessing the labours of the husbandman, and spreading plenty through the land; that he hath prospered our arms and those of our ally, been a shield to our troops in the hour of danger, pointed their swords to victory, and led them in triumph over the bulwarks of the foe; that he hath gone with those who went out into the wilderness against the savage tribes; that he hath stayed the hand of the spoiler, and turned back his meditated destruction; that he hath prospered our commerce, and given success to those who sought the enemy on the face of the deep; and above all, that he hath diffused the glorious light of the gospel, whereby, through the merits of our gracious Redeemer, we may become the heirs of his eternal glory. Therefore,

Resolved, that it be recommended to the several states to appoint THURSDAY the 9th of December next, to be a day of publick and solemn THANKSGIVING to Almighty God, for his mercies, and of PRAYER, for the continuance of his favour and protection to these United States; to beseech him that he would be graciously pleased to influence our publick Councils, and bless them with wisdom from on high, with unanimity, firmness and success; that he would go forth with our hosts and crown our arms with victory; that he would grant to his church, the plentiful effusions of divine grace, and pour out his holy spirit on all Ministers of the gospel; that he would bless and prosper the means of education, and spread the light of christian knowledge through the remotest corners of the earth; that he would smile upon the labours of his people, and cause the earth to bring forth her fruits in abundance, that we may with gratitude and gladness enjoy them; that he would take into his holy protection, our illustrious ally, give him victory over his enemies, and render him finally great, as the father of his people, and the protector of the rights of mankind; that he would graciously be pleased to turn the hearts of our enemies, and to dispence the blessings of peace to contending nations.

That he would in mercy look down upon us, pardon all our sins, and receive us into his favour; and finally, that he would establish the independence of these United States upon the basis of religion and virtue, and support and protect them in the enjoyment of peace, liberty and safety."

I do therefore by authority from the General Assembly issue this my proclamation, hereby appointing Thursday the 9th day of December next, a day of publick and solemn thanksgiving and prayer to Almighty God, earnestly recommending to all the good people of this commonwealth, to set apart the said day for those purposes, and to the several

Ministers of religion to meet their respective societies thereon, to assist them in their prayers, edify them with their discourses, and generally to perform the sacred duties of their function, proper for the occasion.

Given under my hand and the seal of the commonwealth, at *Williamsburg*, this 11th day of *November*, in the year of our Lord, 1779, and in the fourth of the commonwealth.

THOMAS JEFFERSON

*Source: The Virginia Gazette* (Dixon and Nicolson), 20 November 1779, 1; reprinted in *The Papers of Thomas Jefferson*, ed. Julian P. Boyd, 28 vols. to date (Princeton, N.J.: Princeton University Press, 1950– ), 3:177–179.

# Draft of "The Kentucky Resolutions of 1798," November 1798 (excerpt)

*Resolved*, That it is true as a general principle, and is also expressly declared by one of the amendments to the Constitution, that "the powers not delegated to the United States by the Constitution, nor prohibited by it to the States, are reserved to the States respectively, or to the people"; and that no power over the freedom of religion, freedom of speech, or freedom of the press being delegated to the United States by the Constitution, nor prohibited by it to the States, all lawful powers respecting the same did of right remain, and were reserved to the States or the people: that thus was manifested their determination to retain to themselves the right of judging how far the licentiousness of speech and of the press may be abridged without lessening their useful freedom, and how far those abuses which cannot be separated from their use should be tolerated, rather than the use be destroyed. And thus also they guarded against all abridgment by the United States of the freedom of religious opinions and exercises, and retained to themselves the right of protecting the same, as this State, by a law passed on the general demand of its citizens, had already protected them from all human restraint or interference. And that in addition to this general principle and express declaration, another and more special provision has been made by one of the amendments to the Constitution, which expressly declares that "Congress shall make no law respecting an establishment of religion, or prohibiting the free exercise thereof, or abridging the freedom of speech or of the press": thereby guarding in the same sentence, and under the same words, the freedom of religion, of speech, and of the press: insomuch, that whatever violates either, throws down the sanctuary which covers the others, and that libels, falsehood, and defamation, equally with heresy and false religion, are withheld from the cognizance of federal tribunals. That, therefore, the act of Congress of the United States, passed on the 14<sup>th</sup> day of July, 1798, intituled "An Act in addition to the act intituled An Act for the punishment of certain crimes against the United States," which does abridge the freedom of the press, is not law, but is altogether void, and of no force.

*Source: The Works of Thomas Jefferson*, ed. Paul Leicester Ford, 12 vols., Federal Edition (New York: G. P. Putnam's Sons, 1904–1905), 8:463–465.

# Correspondence with the Danbury Baptist Association, 1801–1802

*Address of the Danbury Baptist Association to Jefferson, October 1801*

The address of the Danbury Baptist Association, in the State of Connecticut; assembled October 7th. AD 1801.

To *Thomas Jefferson* Esq. President of the united States of America.

Sir,

Among the many millions in America and Europe who rejoice in your Election to office; we embrace the first opportunity which we have enjoy,d in our collective capacity, since your Inauguration, to express our great satisfaction, in your appointment to the chief Magistracy in the United States: And though our mode of expression may be less courtly and pompious than what many others clothe their addresses with, we beg you, Sir to believe, that none are more sincere.

Our Sentiments are uniformly on the side of Religious Liberty—That Religion is at all times and places a Matter between God and Individuals—That no man ought to suffer in Name, person or effects on account of his religious Opinions—That the legitimate Power of civil Government extends no further than to punish the man who *works ill to his neighbour*: But Sir. our constitution of government is not specific. Our antient charter, together with the Laws made coincident therewith, were adopted as the Basis of our government, At the time of our revolution; and such had been our Laws & usages, & such still are; that Religion is consider,d as the first object of Legislation; & therefore what religious privileges we enjoy (as a minor part of the State) we enjoy as favors granted, and not as inalienable rights: and these favors we receive at the expence of such degrading acknowledgements, as are inconsistent with the rights of fre[e]men. It is not to be wondered at therefore; if those, who seek after *power* & *gain* under the pretence *of government* & *Religion* should reproach their fellow men—should reproach their chief Magistrate, as an enemy of religion Law & good order because he will not, dares not assume the prerogative of Jehovah and make Laws to govern the Kingdom of Christ.

Sir, we are sensible that the President of the united States, is not the national Legislator, & also sensible that the national government cannot destroy the Laws of each State; but our hopes are strong that the sentiments of our beloved President, which have had such genial Effect already, like the radiant beams of the Sun, will shine & prevail through all these States and all the world till Hierarchy and tyranny be destroyed from the Earth. Sir, when we reflect on your past services, and see a glow of philanthropy and good will shining forth in a course of more than thirty years we have reason to believe that America,s God has raised you up to fill the chair of State out of that good will which he bears to the Millions which you preside over. May God strengthen you for the arduous task which providence & the voice of the people have cal,d you to sustain and support you in your Administration against all the predetermin,d opposition of those who wish to rise to wealth & importance on the poverty and subjection of the people———

And may the Lord preserve you safe from every evil and bring you at last to his Heavenly Kingdom through Jesus Christ our Glorious Mediator.

Signed in behalf of the Association,

Neh,h Dodge     )
Ephm Robbins    )    The Committee
Stephen S. Nelson  )

## *Jefferson to Danbury Baptist Association (preliminary draft)*

To messrs. Nehemiah Dodge, Ephraim Robbins, & Stephen S. Nelson a committee of the Danbury Baptist association in the state of Connecticut.

Gentlemen

The affectionate sentiments of esteem & approbation which you are so good as to express towards me, on behalf of the Danbury Baptist association, give me the highest satisfaction. my duties dictate a faithful & zealous pursuit of the interests of my constituents, and, in proportion as they are persuaded of my fidelity to those duties, the discharge of them becomes more & more pleasing.

Believing with you that religion is a matter which lies solely between man & his god, that he owes account to none other for his faith or his worship, that the legitimate powers of government reach actions only and not opinions, I contemplate with sovereign reverence that act of the whole American people which declared that <u>their</u> legislature should make no law respecting an establishment of religion, or prohibiting the free exercise thereof; thus building a wall of *eternal* separation between church and state. [Congress thus inhibited from acts respecting religion, and the Executive authorised only to execute their acts, I have refrained from prescribing even *those* occa-
                                  prescribed indeed legally where an
sional performances of devotion, *practised indeed by the* Executive *of another*
                                a national
*nation as/*is the legal head of *it's* [sic] church, but subject here, as religious exercises only to the voluntary regulations and discipline of each respective sect.] *confin-*
adhering to this expression of the supreme will of the nation in behalf of the rights of conscience,
   *ing myself therefore to the duties of my station, which are merely temporal,*
adhering to, *concurring with this great act of national legislation in behalf of the rights of*
  *be assured that your religious rights shall never be infringed by any act*
*conscience*                            sincere satisfaction
*of mine, and that* I shall see with *friendly dispositions* the progress of those sentiments which tend to restore to man all his natural rights, convinced he has no natural right in opposition to his social duties.

I reciprocate your kind prayers for the protection and blessing of the
common father and creator of man, and tender you for yourselves and your religious
*the Danbury Baptist* association, assurances of my high respect & esteem.

Th: Jefferson<br>Jan. 1. 1802

Note: In the manuscript of this draft letter, the italicized text is inked out. In addition, a line is drawn around the sentence bracketed in this transcription, and the following comment in the same hand is written in the left margin:

> this paragraph was omitted on the suggestion that it might give uneasiness to some of our republican friends in the eastern states where the proclamation of thanksgivings etc by their Executive is an antient habit, & is respected.

The manuscript of this draft letter reveals that Jefferson wrote and rewrote the last sentence of the second paragraph. He first wrote:

> confining myself therefore to the duties of my station, which are merely temporal, be assured that your religious rights shall never be infringed by any act of mine, and that I shall see with friendly dispositions the progress of those sentiments which tend to restore to man all his natural rights, convinced he has no natural right in opposition to his social duties.

He then apparently amended this sentence to read: "concurring with this great act of national legislation in behalf of the rights of conscience" (Jefferson apparently intended this sentence to continue with "I shall see with friendly dispositions the progress of those sentiments . . ." from the initial draft). The opening words "concurring with" were replaced with "adhering to." Both of these versions were inked out before Jefferson wrote the final version, which reads:

> adhering to this expression of the supreme will of the nation in behalf of the rights of conscience, I shall see with sincere satisfaction the progress of those sentiments which tend to restore to man all his natural rights, convinced he has no natural right in opposition to his social duties.

At some point, Jefferson replaced "friendly dispositions" in the initial version with "sincere satisfaction."

## *Jefferson to Attorney General Levi Lincoln*

### Th: J. to mr. Lincoln

Averse to recieve [*sic*] addresses, yet unable to prevent them, I have generally endeavored to turn them to some account, by making them the occasion, by way of answer, of sowing useful truths & principles among the people, which might germinate and become rooted among their political tenets. the Baptist address now inclosed admits of a condemnation of the alliance between church and state, under the authority of the Constitution. it furnishes an occasion too, which I have long wished to find, of saying why I do not proclaim fastings & thanksgivings, as my predecessors did. the address to be sure does not point at this, and it's [*sic*] introduction is awkward. but I foresee no opportunity of doing it more pertinently. I know it will give great offence to the New England clergy: but the advocate for religious freedom is to expect neither peace nor forgiveness from them. will you be so good as to examine the answer and suggest any alterations which might prevent an ill effect, or promote a good one among *the people*? you understand the temper of those in the North, and can weaken it therefore to their stomachs: it is at present seasoned to the Southern taste only. I would ask the favor of you to return it with the address in the course of the day or evening. health & affection.

Jan. 1. 1802.

## *Attorney General Levi Lincoln to Jefferson*

The President    )                                      Jany 1s. 1802—
of the U. States )

Sir I have carefully considered the subject you did me the honor of submitting to my attention. The people of the five N England Governments (unless Rhode Island is an exception) have always been in the habit of observing fasts and thanksgivings in performance of proclamations from their respective Executives. This custom is venerable being handed down from our ancestors. The Republicans of those States generally have a respect for it. They regreted very much the late conduct of the legislature of Rhode Island on this subject. I think the religious sentiment expressed in your proposed answer of importance to be communicated, but that it would be best to have it so guarded, as to be incapable of having it construed into an implied censure of the usages of any of the States. Perhaps the following alteration after the words "but subject here" would be sufficient, vis [?], only to the voluntary regulations & discipline of each respective sect, as mere religious exercises, and to the particular situations, usages & recommendations of the several States, in point of time & local circumstances. With the highest esteem & respect.

yours,          Levi Lincoln

## *Postmaster General Gideon Granger to Jefferson*

G. Granger presents his compliments to The Presidt. and assures him he has carefully & attentively perused the inclosed Address & Answer—The answer will undoubtedly give great Offence to the established Clergy of New England while it will delight the Dissenters as they are called. It is but a declaration of Truths which are in fact felt by a great Majority of New England, & publicly acknowledged by near half of the People of Connecticut; It may however occasion a temporary Spasm among the Established Religionists yet his mind approves of it, because it will "germinate among the People,, and in time fix "their political Tenets,,—He cannot therefore wish a Sentence changed, or a Sentiment expressed equivocally—A more fortunate time can never be expected.———

## *Jefferson to Danbury Baptist Association (final version)*

To messrs. Nehemiah Dodge, Ephraim Robbins, & Stephen S. Nelson, a committee of the Danbury Baptist association in the state of Connecticut.

Gentlemen

The affectionate sentiments of esteem and approbation which you are so good as to express towards me, on behalf of the Danbury Baptist association, give me the highest satisfaction. my duties dictate a faithful & zealous pursuit of the interests of my constituents, & in proportion as they are persuaded of my fidelity to those duties, the discharge of them becomes more and more pleasing.

Believing with you that religion is a matter which lies solely between Man & his God, that he owes account to none other for his faith or his worship, that the legitimate[11] powers of government reach actions only, & not opinions, I contemplate with sovereign reverence that act of the whole American people which declared that *their* legislature should "make no law respecting an establishment of religion, or prohibiting the free exercise thereof,"[12] thus building a wall of separation between Church & State. adhering to this expression of the supreme will of the nation in behalf of the rights of conscience, I shall see with sincere satisfaction the progress of those sentiments which tend to restore to man all his natural rights, convinced he has no natural right in opposition to his social duties.

I reciprocate your kind prayers for the protection & blessing of the common father and creator of man, and tender you for yourselves & your religious association, assurances of my high respect & esteem.

Th: Jefferson
Jan. 1. 1802.

APPENDIX 7

# Correspondence with the Citizens of Cheshire, Massachusetts, January 1802

*Address of Cheshire Citizens to Jefferson*

To Thomas Jefferson, President of the United States of America.

SIR,

Notwithstanding we live remote from the seat of our national government, and in an extreme part of our own State, yet we humbly claim the right of judging for ourselves.

Our attachment to the National Constitution is strong and indissoluble. We consider it a description of those *Powers* which the people have submitted to their Magistrates, to be exercised for *definite* purposes; and not as a charter of favours granted by a sovereign to his subjects. Among its beautiful features, the right of free suffrage, to correct all abuses. The prohibition of religious tests, to prevent all hierarchy. The means of amendment, which it contains within itself to remove defects as fast as they are discovered, appear the most prominent. But for several years past, our apprehension has been, that the genius of the government was not attended to in sundry cases; and that the administration bordered upon monarchy: Our joy, of course, must have been great on your election to the first office in the nation. Having had good evidence, from your announced sentiments and uniform conduct that it would be your strife and glory to turn back the government to its virgin purity. The trust is great! The task is arduous! But we console ourselves, that the Supreme Ruler of the Universe, who raises up men to achieve great events, has raised up a JEFFERSON for this critical day, to defend Republicanism and to baffle all arts of Aristocracy.

Sir, we have attempted to prove our love to our President, not in words alone, but in deeds and in truth. With this address, we send you a CHEESE, by the hands of Messrs. John Leland and Darius Brown as a pepper-corn of the esteem which we bear to our Chief Magistrate, and as a sacrifice to Republicanism. It is not the last stone in the Bastile [*sic*], nor is it of any great consequence as an article of worth; but, as a free-will offering, we hope it will be favorably received. The Cheese was not made by his Lordship, for his sacred Majesty; nor with a view to gain dignified titles or lucrative offices; but by the personal labour of free-born farmers (without a single slave to assist) for an elective President of a free people; with the only view of casting a mite into the scale of Democracy.

The late triumphant return of republicanism has more animated the inhabitants of Cheshire, to bear the burden of government, and treat the characters and persons of those in authority with all due respect, than the long list of alien–sedition–naval and provisional army laws, ever did.

Sir, we had some thought of impressing some significant inscription on the Cheese; but we have found such inconveniency in *stamps* on paper, that we chose to send it in a plain Republican form.

May God long preserve your life and health for a blessing to the United States, and the world at large.

*Signed by order of all Cheshire.*
P.S. *The Cheese was made July 20, 1801, and weighed 1235 lbs.*

## Jefferson to the Cheshire Citizens

To Messrs. Daniel Brown, Hezekiah Mason, Jonathan Richardson, John Waterman and John Wells junr. a Committee of the town of Cheshire, in Massachusetts.

Gentlemen,

I concur with you in the sentiments expressed in your kind address on behalf of the inhabitants of the town of Cheshire, that the Constitution of the United States is a charter of authorities and duties, not a charter of rights to its officers; and among its most precious provisions are the right of suffrage, the prohibition of religious tests, and its means of peaceable amendment. Nothing ensures the duration of this fair fabric of government so effectually as the due sense entertained by the body of our citizens, of the value of these principles and their care to preserve them.

I received with particular pleasure the testimony of good will with which your citizens have been pleased to charge you for me; it presents an extraordinary proof of the skill, with which those domestic arts, which contribute so much to our daily comfort, are practised by them, and particularly by the portion of them most interesting to the affections, the care, and the happiness of man.

To myself this mark of esteem from freeborn farmers, employed personally in the useful labours of life, is peculiarly grateful, having no wish but to preserve to them the fruits of their labour: their sense of this truth will be my highest reward.

I pray you, gentlemen, to make my thanks for their favour acceptable to them, and to be assured yourselves of my high respect and esteem.

TH: JEFFERSON

*Source: The Sun* (Pittsfield, Mass.), 8 February 1802, 1, as reprinted in John C. Harriman, ed., "'Most Excellent—far fam'd and far fetch'd Cheese': An Anthology of Jeffersonian Era Poetry," *American Magazine and Historical Chronicle* 2, no. 2 (Autumn/Winter 1986–87): 3–4. These transcripts also draw on the slightly different versions of the same documents in C. A. Browne, "Elder John Leland and the Mammoth Cheshire Cheese," *Agricultural History* 18 (1944): 149–150; L. H. Butterfield, "Elder John Leland, Jeffersonian Itinerant," *Proceedings of the American Antiquarian Society* 62 (1952): 224–225.

# Second Inaugural Address, 4 March 1805 (excerpts)

In matters of religion, I have considered that its free exercise is placed by the constitution independent of the powers of the general [i.e., federal] government. I have therefore undertaken, on no occasion, to prescribe the religious exercises suited to it; but have left them, as the constitution found them, under the direction and discipline of State or Church authorities acknowledged by the several religious societies. . . .

I shall now enter on the duties to which my fellow citizens have again called me, and shall proceed in the spirit of those principles which they have approved. I fear not that any motives of interest may lead me astray; I am sensible of no passion which could seduce me knowingly from the path of justice; but the weakness of human nature, and the limits of my own understanding, will produce errors of judgment sometimes injurious to your interests. I shall need, therefore, all the indulgence I have heretofore experienced—the want of it will certainly not lessen with increasing years. I shall need, too, the favor of that Being in whose hands we are, who led our forefathers, as Israel of old, from their native land, and planted them in a country flowing with all the necessaries and comforts of life; who has covered our infancy with his providence, and our riper years with his wisdom and power; and to whose goodness I ask you to join with me in supplications, that he will so enlighten the minds of your servants, guide their councils, and prosper their measures, that whatsoever they do, shall result in your good, and shall secure to you the peace, friendship, and approbation of all nations.

Source: The Writings of Thomas Jefferson, ed. Andrew A. Lipscomb and Albert Ellery Bergh, 20 vols. (Washington, D.C.: Thomas Jefferson Memorial Association, 1905), 3:375–383 [hereinafter Writings of Jefferson].

APPENDIX 9

# Letter from Jefferson to the Reverend Samuel Miller, 23 January 1808

WASHINGTON, January 23, 1808.

SIR,—I have duly received your favor of the 18th, and am thankful to you for having written it, because it is more agreeable to prevent than to refuse what I do not think myself authorized to comply with. I consider the government of the United States as interdicted by the Constitution from intermeddling with religious institutions, their doctrines, discipline, or exercises. This results not only from the provision that no law shall be made respecting the establishment or free exercise of religion [First Amendment], but from that also which reserves to the States the powers not delegated to the United States [Tenth Amendment]. Certainly, no power to prescribe any religious exercise, or to assume authority in religious discipline, has been delegated to the General [i.e., federal] Government. It must then rest with the States, as far as it can be in any human authority. But it is only proposed that I should *recommend*, not prescribe a day of fasting and prayer. That is, that I should *indirectly* assume to the United States an authority over religious exercises, which the Constitution has directly precluded them from. It must be meant, too, that this recommendation is to carry some authority, and to be sanctioned by some penalty on those who disregard it; not indeed of fine and imprisonment, but of some degree of proscription, perhaps in public opinion. And does the change in the nature of the penalty make the recommendation less a *law* of conduct for those to whom it is directed? I do not believe it is for the interest of religion to invite the civil magistrate to direct its exercises, its discipline, or its doctrines; nor of the religious societies, that the General Government should be invested with the power of effecting any uniformity of time or matter among them. Fasting and prayer are religious exercises; the enjoining them an act of discipline. Every religious society has a right to determine for itself the times for these exercises, and the objects proper for them, according to their own particular tenets; and this right can never be safer than in their own hands, where the Constitution has deposited it.

I am aware that the practice of my predecessors may be quoted. But I have ever believed, that the example of State executives led to the assumption of that authority by the General Government, without due examination, which would have discovered that what might be a right in a State government, was a violation of that right when assumed by another. Be this as it may, every one must act according to the dictates of his own reason, and mine tells me that civil powers alone have been given to the President of the United States, and no authority to direct the religious exercises of his constituents.

I again express my satisfaction that you have been so good as to give me an opportunity of explaining myself in a private letter, in which I could give my reasons more in detail than might have been done in a public answer; and I pray you to accept the assurances of my high esteem and respect.

*Source: Writings of Jefferson*, 11:428–430 (emphasis in the original).

# Notes

NOTES TO CHAPTER 1

1. *Reynolds v. United States*, 98 U.S. 145, 164 (1879).

2. *Everson v. Board of Education*, 330 U.S. 1, 16, 18 (1947).

3. Letter from Thomas Jefferson to Messrs. Nehemiah Dodge, Ephraim Robbins, and Stephen S. Nelson, a committee of the Danbury Baptist association in the state of Connecticut, 1 January 1802, The Papers of Thomas Jefferson (Manuscript Division, Library of Congress), Series 1, Box 89, December 2, 1801–January 1, 1802; Presidential Papers Microfilm, Thomas Jefferson Papers (Manuscript Division, Library of Congress), Series 1, Reel 25, November 15, 1801–March 31, 1802.

4. Letter from Thomas Jefferson to Levi Lincoln, 1 January 1802, The Papers of Thomas Jefferson (Manuscript Division, Library of Congress), Series 1, Box 89, December 2, 1801–January 1, 1802; Presidential Papers Microfilm, Thomas Jefferson Papers (Manuscript Division, Library of Congress), Series 1, Reel 25, November 15, 1801–March 31, 1802.

5. U.S. Constitution, amendment 1.

6. See *Amos v. Corporation of the Presiding Bishop of the Church of Jesus Christ of Latter-Day Saints*, 594 F. Supp. 791, 811 (1984), quoting Senator Samuel Ervin ("[T]he first amendment was a design to raise a wall of separation between church and state and was designed to keep the state's hands off the church and the church's hands off the state."). This passage is a slight paraphrase of Justice Robert H. Jackson's dictum in *Everson*, 330 U.S. at 26–27 (Jackson, J., dissenting) (Religious freedom "was set forth [in the Constitution] in absolute terms, and its strength is its rigidity. It was intended not only to keep the states' hands out of religion, but to keep religion's hands off the state."). See also id. at 16 ("Neither a state nor the Federal Government can, openly or secretly, participate in the affairs of any religious organizations or groups and *vice versa*.").

7. *Lemon v. Kurtzman*, 403 U.S. 602, 612 (1971).

8. Robert S. Alley, *So Help Me God: Religion and the Presidency, Wilson to Nixon* (Richmond, Va.: John Knox Press, 1972), 145.

9. R. Freeman Butts, *The American Tradition in Religion and Education* (Boston: Beacon Press, 1950), 93.

10. See Edwin S. Gaustad, "Religion," in *Thomas Jefferson: A Reference Biography*, ed. Merrill D. Peterson (New York: Charles Scribner's Sons, 1986), 282 (remarking that "[t]his powerful metaphor, once employed, became even more familiar to the American public than did the constitutional language itself"); Philip Hamburger, *Separation of Church and State* (Cambridge, Mass.: Harvard University Press, 2002), 1 ("Two centuries later, Jefferson's phrase, 'separation between church and state,' provides the label with which vast numbers of Americans refer to their religious freedom. In the minds of many, his words have even displaced those of the U.S. Constitution, which, by contrast, seem neither so apt nor so clear."); Barbara A. Perry, "Justice Hugo Black and the 'Wall of Separation between Church and State,'" *Journal of Church and State* 31 (1989): 55 ("The phrase, coined by Thomas Jefferson as an interpretive metaphor for the Establishment Clause of the First Amendment, undoubtedly is more familiar to the general public than the Amendment's actual language."); Note, "Sharpening the Prongs of the Establishment Clause: Applying Stricter Scrutiny to Majority Religions," *Georgia Law Review* 23 (1989): 1093 ("Thomas Jefferson is often identified with a metaphor probably more widely known than the text of the first amendment itself: the 'wall of separation' between church and state.").

11. Leonard W. Levy, *The Establishment Clause: Religion and the First Amendment*, 2d ed. (Chapel Hill: University of North Carolina Press, 1994), 250.

12. Harold D. Hammett, "The Homogenized Wall," *American Bar Association Journal* 53 (October 1967): 929; Hammett, "Separation of Church and State: By One Wall or Two?" *Journal of Church and State* 7 (1965): 190. See also Conrad Henry Moehlman, *The Wall of Separation between Church and State: An Historical Study of Recent Criticism of the Religious Clause of the First Amendment* (Boston: Beacon Press, 1951), 57 ("Today Jefferson's significant figure of speech is the popularly and judicially accepted summary of the religious clause of the First Amendment."); Derek H. Davis, "What Jefferson's Metaphor Really Means," *Liberty*, January/February 1997, 12 ("his letter has become a pillar of American public policy regarding the relationship between church and state").

13. *Reynolds v. United States*, 98 U.S. 145, 164 (1879).

14. *Everson*, 330 U.S. at 15–16, 18.

15. *McCollum v. Board of Education*, 333 U.S. 203, 211 (1948). See Arlin M. Adams and Charles J. Emmerich, *A Nation Dedicated to Religious Liberty: The Constitutional Heritage of the Religion Clauses* (Philadelphia: University of Pennsylvania Press, 1990), 23 ("In *Everson v. Board of Education* (1947), a seminal establishment clause case, [the Court] raised the figure of speech to con-

stitutional status."); Timothy L. Hall, *Separating Church and State: Roger Williams and Religious Liberty* (Urbana: University of Illinois Press, 1998), 4 (The Supreme Court's interpretive approach has "burdened the establishment clause with a crude form of law by metaphor, according to which the Supreme Court purported to find answers to complex issues chiefly through appeal to Jefferson's image of the 'wall of separation' between church and state. In *Everson v. Board of Education*, the Court enthroned Jefferson's metaphor."); *Separation of Church and State Committee v. City of Eugene*, 93 F.3d 617, 622 (9th Cir. 1996) (O'Scannlain, C. J., concurring) ("In *Everson v. Board of Education*, Justice Black, writing for a five-member majority, adopted Jefferson's 'wall of separation' metaphor as the theoretical centerpiece driving the religion clauses of the First Amendment. That metaphor became the focus for subsequent Establishment Clause analysis and set a philosophical tone that resonated through all post–World War II decisions regarding church and state. Operating under the assumption that the 'wall of separation' represented the Establishment Clause's correct meaning, the Court gradually developed a series of tests designed to determine if a particular governmental practice or statute impermissibly breached that wall.").

16. Following *Everson*, the "wall" metaphor began to figure prominently in the titles of books and articles on church-state topics. See, for example, Edward F. Waite, "Jefferson's 'Wall of Separation': What and Where?" *Minnesota Law Review* 33 (1949): 494–516; Moehlman, *The Wall of Separation between Church and State* (1951); Moehlman, "The Wall of Separation: The Law and the Facts," *American Bar Association Journal* 38 (April 1952): 281–284, 343–348; Loren P. Beth, "The Wall of Separation and the Supreme Court," *Minnesota Law Review* 38 (1954): 215–227.

17. See Haig Bosmajian, *Metaphor and Reason in Judicial Opinions* (Carbondale: Southern Illinois University Press, 1992), 73 ("no other metaphor has been discussed by Supreme Court justices as extensively as this 'wall.' While numerous other tropes . . . have played an important role in judicial decision making, their figurative nature has not been highlighted as much as that of the wall of separation. Further, no other judicial metaphor has been so directly defended and challenged by the justices, who have been conscious that they are relying on a metaphor that has had a great impact on court decisions related to church-state issues, especially the establishment clause of the First Amendment."); Gordon Butler, "Cometh the Revolution: The Case for Overruling McCollum v. Board of Education," *Dickinson Law Review* 99 (1995): 870 n. 111 ("The Jeffersonian 'wall of separation' has dominated Establishment Clause jurisprudence."); Joseph F. Costanzo, "Thomas Jefferson, Religious Education and Public Law," *Journal of Public Law* 8, no. 1 (1959): 97 ("the most often quoted metaphor in American legal debate"); Timothy L. Fort, "The Free Exercise Rights of Native Americans and the Prospects for a Conservative Jurisprudence

Protecting the Rights of Minorities," *New Mexico Law Review* 23 (1993): 205 n. 88 ("the use of Jefferson's comment about a 'Wall of Separation' between church and state has been elevated into a talismanic absolute with little judicial explanation of why it should be."); Philip B. Kurland, "The Religion Clauses and the Burger Court," *Catholic University Law Review* 34 (1984): 7 ("for a while [Jefferson's 'wall'] was the talisman for the Court's actions in this area" of constitutional law); Stephen J. Safranek, "Can Science Guide Legal Argumentation?: The Role of Metaphor in Constitutional Cases," *Loyola University Chicago Law Journal* 25 (1994): 371 ("the most well-known metaphor of constitutional law"), 372 (the "wall" is "the foremost paradigm of church-state relationships under the Constitution"); Note, "Alcoholics Anonymous: Anonymous Theists? *Griffin v. Coughlin* and the 'Wall of Separation between Church and State' in the New York State Prison System," *Cardozo Law Review* 19 (1998): 1469 ("Incorporated by Justice Black into his majority opinion in *Everson*, Thomas Jefferson's felicitous expression 'a wall of separation between church and state' was elevated by the Supreme Court into a definitive interpretation of the Establishment Clause."); Note, "A Page of History or a Volume of Logic?: Reassessing the Supreme Court's Establishment Clause Jurisprudence," *Denver University Law Review* 73 (1996): 512 ("Undoubtedly, Thomas Jefferson's metaphor that the Establishment Clause erects a wall of separation between church and state is the most quoted statement in the annals of Establishment Clause jurisprudence."); Note, "*Rosenberger v. Rector and Visitors of University of Virginia*: The Supreme Court Revisits the Framers' Intent behind the Religion Clauses," *Journal of Contemporary Law* 22 (1996): 492 ("The [Danbury] letter contains the most famous and oft-cited description of church-state relations. . . . Indeed, Jefferson's statement is the cornerstone of Establishment Clause jurisprudence."); Note, "Abolishing 'Separate but (Un)Equal' Status for Religious Universities," *Virginia Law Review* 77 (1991): 1234 ("the Jeffersonian metaphor of a 'wall of separation' between church and state was injected into establishment clause jurisprudence, where it remained the central motif of the Court's decisions in the following decades.").

James H. Hutson has argued that, for much of American history, another metaphor, one that expresses "a view at polar opposites to Thomas Jefferson's" metaphor, "dominated the church-state dialogue in the Anglo-American world." A Calvinist interpretation of Isaiah 49:23 instructed kings and civil magistrates to "form a nurturing bond with religious institutions within [their] jurisdiction . . . [and,] in fact, become the 'nursing father[s]' of the church." The "nursing father" metaphor, according to Hutson, was transmitted to the American colonies, where it continued to inform church-state discourse until the mid-nineteenth century. Although American constructions of the phrase evolved over time, at a minimum it stood for the proposition that civil government in general and civil magistrates in particular were obligated to model and extol lives of

Christian rectitude, protect and even encourage religion (and religious institutions), and promote laws and policies that facilitate and protect religious practices and resist laws that do not. In short, civil rulers must nurture religion as a good father cares for his children. James H. Hutson, "'Nursing Fathers': The Model for Church-State Relations in America from James I to Jefferson" (unpublished paper, 2000).

18. Daniel L. Dreisbach, "'Sowing Useful Truths and Principles': The Danbury Baptists, Thomas Jefferson, and the 'Wall of Separation,'" *Journal of Church and State* 39 (1997): 455–501.

19. Anson Phelps Stokes, *Church and State in the United States*, 3 vols. (New York: Harper and Brothers, 1950); Philip Hamburger, *Separation of Church and State* (Cambridge, Mass.: Harvard University Press, 2002).

20. The phrase "indispensable support" was used by George Washington in his "Farewell Address," 19 September 1796, *The Writings of George Washington*, ed. John C. Fitzpatrick, 37 vols. (Washington, D.C.: GPO, 1931–1940), 35:229.

Notes to Chapter 2

1. Address of the inhabitants of the town of Cheshire, Berkshire County, Massachusetts, to Thomas Jefferson, 1 January 1802. The address, with slight variations, was published contemporaneously in newspapers throughout New England. See note 20.

2. Address of the inhabitants of the town of Cheshire, Berkshire County, Massachusetts, to Jefferson, 1 January 1802.

3. Gore Vidal, *Burr: A Novel* (New York: Random House, 1973), 252.

4. Almost from the beginning, the President's mansion was known familiarly as the "White House" because of its distinctive white sandstone construction, but the appellation did not begin to appear in print until the end of the first decade of the nineteenth century. See Robert V. Remini, "Becoming a National Symbol: The White House in the Early Nineteenth Century," in *The White House: The First Two Hundred Years*, ed. Frank Freidel and William Pencak (Boston: Northeastern University Press, 1994), 18, 23–24.

5. The custom in Cheshire was to paint and stain the cheese. There is some dispute as to whether a motto was inscribed on the cheese. One published version of the Cheshire citizens' presentation address to Jefferson states that the cheese was sent without adornment. See John C. Harriman, ed., "'Most Excellent—far fam'd and far fetch'd Cheese': An Anthology of Jeffersonian Era Poetry," *American Magazine and Historical Chronicle* 2, no. 2 (Autumn/Winter 1986–87): 12. Since references to the motto appear in early accounts from late summer and early autumn of 1801 and there is no mention of it in later eyewitness reports, it is likely that the motto was not permanently impressed on the

cheese. For a discussion of Jefferson's affinity for this motto, see *The Papers of Thomas Jefferson*, ed. Julian P. Boyd, 28 vols. to date (Princeton, N.J.: Princeton University Press, 1950– ), 1:494–497, 677–679 [hereinafter *Papers of Jefferson*]; Dumas Malone, *Jefferson and His Time*, vol. 1, *Jefferson the Virginian* (Boston: Little, Brown, 1948), 242–243. For a colorful contemporaneous description of the cheese upon its arrival in Washington, see the letter written from Mount Vernon by Eleanor "Nelly" Parke Custis Lewis (George Washington's stepgranddaughter) to her friend Mrs. Charles Cotesworth Pinckney, 3 January 1802, quoted in Charles Moore, *The Family Life of George Washington* (Boston: Houghton Mifflin, 1926), 167.

6. L. H. Butterfield, "Elder John Leland, Jeffersonian Itinerant," *Proceedings of the American Antiquarian Society* 62 (1952): 214–216. One historian observed: "Under the ministrations of a political Baptist preacher [Leland], Cheshire became a Jeffersonian oasis in the desert of New England Federalism; and to this day rejoices over the fact." Moore, *The Family Life of George Washington*, 167 n. 1.

7. It was not until 1833 that Massachusetts became the last state, following Connecticut in 1818 and New Hampshire in 1819, to sever formal legal ties with an established church. See Peter S. Field, *The Crisis of the Standing Order: Clerical Intellectuals and Cultural Authority in Massachusetts, 1780–1833* (Amherst: University of Massachusetts Press, 1998); William G. McLoughlin, *New England Dissent, 1630–1883: The Baptists and the Separation of Church and State*, 2 vols. (Cambridge, Mass.: Harvard University Press, 1971); Jacob C. Meyer, *Church and State in Massachusetts: From 1740 to 1833* (Cleveland, Ohio: Western Reserve University Press, 1930); John D. Cushing, "Notes on Disestablishment in Massachusetts, 1780–1833," *William and Mary Quarterly*, 3d ser., 26 (1969): 169–190; John Witte, Jr., "'A Most Mild and Equitable Establishment of Religion': John Adams and the Massachusetts Experiment," in *Religion and the New Republic: Faith in the Founding of America*, ed. James H. Hutson (Lanham, Md.: Rowman and Littlefield, 2000), 1–40.

8. See *The Sun* (Pittsfield, Mass.), 18 January 1802, 3 ("The Cheese-makers of Cheshire begin to experience beneficial effects from the Federal abuse bestowed upon them for their *Mammoth Cheese*, as it has been generally called. It has effectually advertised the staple produce of that industrious, flourishing country town, and been the means of improving their Cheese and promoting the market of it."). See generally Evan Jones, *The World of Cheese* (New York: Alfred A. Knopf, 1989), 16–19 (discussing Leland's cheese and the history of making Cheshire and cheddar cheese in New England).

9. Leland reportedly found biblical precedent for his presentation of the cheese in the example of David recorded in I Samuel 17:18 and II Samuel 17:29. *Connecticut Journal* (New Haven), 11 February 1802, 3.

10. As a strictly voluntary enterprise, the milk of Federal cows was not requested or requisitioned.

11. Long before the giant cheese left Cheshire, another wag pondered "whether they [Cheshire citizens] expect to carry their Cheese by land or by water, or whether they expect there will be *animal* life in it sufficient to move itself." "A Mammoth Pye," *The Salem Gazette*, 25 September 1801, 2. For the fullest account of the making of the cheese, see C. A. Browne, "Elder John Leland and the Mammoth Cheshire Cheese," *Agricultural History* 18 (1944): 145–153. See also Butterfield, "Elder John Leland, Jeffersonian Itinerant," 214–229; Harriman, ed., "'Most Excellent—far fam'd and far fetch'd Cheese': An Anthology of Jeffersonian Era Poetry," 1–26; Paul W. Kieser, "President Jefferson's Mammoth Cheese," *Tradition* 5, no. 8 (August 1962): 34–42. For contemporaneous accounts, see *Impartial Observer* (Providence, R.I.), 8 August 1801, as quoted in Butterfield, "Elder John Leland, Jeffersonian Itinerant," 219–220; *Constitutional Telegraphe* (Boston), 12 August 1801, 3; *Courier of New Hampshire* (Concord), 27 August 1801, 3; *Washington Federalist*, 31 August 1801, 1.

12. "THE MAMMOTH CHEESE: An Epico-Lyrico Ballad," *The Mercury and New-England Palladium* (Boston), 8 September 1801, 1.

13. *National Intelligencer, and Washington Advertiser*, 30 December 1801, 3; *Washington Federalist*, 31 August 1801, 2 (arriving "in a waggon drawn by 5 horses").

14. Browne, "Elder John Leland and the Mammoth Cheshire Cheese," 149.

15. "Events in the Life of John Leland: Written by Himself," in *The Writings of the Late Elder John Leland*, ed. L. F. Greene (New York: printed by G. W. Wood, 1845), 32.

16. The word "mammoth," by some accounts, was first used in America as an adjective to describe the Cheshire cheese. Borrowed from the Russian name for an extinct Siberian elephant, the word was gaining currency contemporaneously in connection with Charles Willson Peale's excavation of a North American mastodon fossil in the Hudson Valley. Butterfield, "Elder John Leland, Jeffersonian Itinerant," 220–222; Charles Coleman Sellers, *Charles Willson Peale* (Philadelphia: American Philosophical Society, 1947), 2:142–144. See also Harriman, ed., "'Most Excellent—far fam'd and far fetch'd Cheese': An Anthology of Jeffersonian Era Poetry," 2 (noting that "[u]se of 'mammoth' as an adjective had derisive connotations" and was used by Republican foes, especially to suggest that Republicans possessed "exaggerated, impractical ideas").

Jefferson was familiar with the word "mammoth," having written extensively in his *Notes on the State of Virginia* (Query VI) about the prehistoric mammal that once roamed the American landscape. He argued, wrote Joseph J. Ellis, "that huge, hairy prehistoric beasts called mammoths still lived on in the unexplored American West, one of those pre-Darwinian ideas Jefferson found attractive because it supported his anti-Buffon contention that the American environment produced large animals. Federalist wits ridiculed his 'mammoth theory' over and over again, and the motif became a centerpiece of opposition sarcasm toward Jefferson's pretensions as a scientist. In the same quasi-playful mode, Jefferson's defenders countered the mammoth onslaught by presenting him with a 'mammoth cheese' weighing 1,235 pounds, reputedly from the milk of nine hundred cows, 'not one of them a federalist.'" Joseph J. Ellis, *American Sphinx: The Character of Thomas Jefferson* (New York: Alfred A. Knopf, 1997), 215 (endnotes omitted). Jefferson was eager to refute the Comte de Buffon's theory that animal life in the new world was smaller and degenerate in comparison with equivalent European species.

17. See, for example, Peter Dobbins, *The Political Farrago, or a Miscellaneous Review of Politics in the United States* (Brattleboro, Vt.: William Fessenden, 1807), 24–27.

18. *New-York Evening Post*, 7 January 1802, 3.

19. See *Washington Federalist*, 2 January 1802, 3; *Washington Federalist*, 5 January 1802, 2; *National Intelligencer, and Washington Advertiser*, 20 January 1802, 1; *Baltimore Federalist Gazette*, 6 January 1802, 2; *Boston Gazette*, 18 January 1802, 2; *Columbian Centinel, Massachusetts Federalist*, 30 January 1802, 1; *Commercial Advertiser* (New York), 9 January 1802, 3; *Connecticut Courant*, 18 January 1802, 4; *New-York Evening Post*, 7 January 1802, 3.

20. Address of the inhabitants of the town of Cheshire, Berkshire County, Massachusetts, to Jefferson, reprinted in *American Citizen and General Advertiser* (New York), 18 January 1802, 2; *American Mercury* (Hartford, Conn.), 28 January 1802, 3; *Centinel of Freedom* (Newark, N.J.), 19 January 1802, 3; *Columbian Centinel, Massachusetts Federalist*, 30 January 1802, 1; *Commercial Advertiser* (New York), 15 January 1802, 3; *Constitutional Telegraphe* (Boston), 23 January 1802, 2; *Gazette of the United States* (Philadelphia), 20 January 1802, 2–3; *Mercantile Advertiser* (New York), 16 January 1802, 3; *National Intelligencer, and Washington Advertiser*, 20 January 1802, 2; *New Hampshire Gazette* (Portsmouth), 2 February 1802, 2; *New-York Evening Post*, 16 January 1802, 2–3; *Providence Gazette*, 23 January 1802, 2–3; *The Republican; or, Anti-Democrat* (Baltimore), 13 January 1802, 3 (Baptists' address only); *Rhode Island Republican* (Newport), 23 January 1802, 3; *Salem Gazette*, 26 February 1802, 1; *Salem Register*, 25 January 1802, 2–3; *The Spectator* (New York), 16 January 1802, 2; *The Sun* (Pittsfield, Mass.), 8 February 1802, 1; *The Times, and District of Columbia Daily Advertiser* (Alexandria, Va.), 28 January 1802, 2; Harriman, ed., "'Most Excellent—far fam'd and far fetch'd Cheese': An Anthology of Jeffersonian Era Poetry," 3–4; Browne, "Elder John Leland and the Mammoth Cheshire Cheese," 149–150; Butterfield, "Elder John Leland,

Jeffersonian Itinerant," 224–225. Jefferson's response to the Cheshire citizens is reprinted in most of these journals.

21. Letter from Jefferson to Thomas Mann Randolph, 1 January 1802, as quoted in Dumas Malone, *Jefferson and His Time*, vol. 4, *Jefferson the President: First Term, 1801–1805* (Boston: Little, Brown, 1970), 108.

22. Bernard Mayo, "A Peppercorn for Mr. Jefferson," *Virginia Quarterly Review* 19 (1943): 222.

23. Herbert M. Morais, "Life and Works of Elder John Leland" (M.A. thesis, Columbia University, 1928), 44–50 (discussion of Leland's adherence to Jeffersonian political principles).

24. See generally *The Writings of the Late Elder John Leland*, ed. L. F. Greene (New York: printed by G. W. Wood, 1845); Butterfield, "Elder John Leland, Jeffersonian Itinerant," 155–242; McLoughlin, *New England Dissent*, 2:928–935; J. T. Smith, "Life and Times of the Rev. John Leland," *Baptist Quarterly* 5 (1871): 230–256; Andrew M. Manis, "Regionalism and a Baptist Perspective on Separation of Church and State," *American Baptist Quarterly* 2 (1983): 213–227 (noting both evangelical and Jeffersonian influences that shaped Leland's views on church-state separation).

25. Butterfield, "Elder John Leland, Jeffersonian Itinerant," 157.

26. John Leland, "A Blow at the Root: Being a Fashionable Fast-Day Sermon (Cheshire, 9 April 1801)," in *The Writings of the Late Elder John Leland*, 255.

27. See Pauline Maier, "John Wilkes and American Disillusionment with Britain," *William and Mary Quarterly*, 3d ser., 20 (1963): 373–395.

28. Pauline Maier, *From Resistance to Revolution: Colonial Radicals and the Development of American Opposition to Britain, 1765–1776* (New York: Random House, 1972), 161–208. Wilkes's European admirers led the way in presenting the imprisoned controversialist with extraordinary culinary provisions: "Zealous partisans vied with each other from the first in showering gifts upon the great man. 'His table,' said an eminent historian, 'was daily furnished with the most rare and costly delicacies, presented to him by admirers.' The articles of food which arrived at the gaol soon became a serious embarrassment. A piece of brawn, a firkin of rock oysters, a Cheshire cheese, a loaf of sugar, a brace of fat bucks, with turkeys, geese, and fowls, all sorts of fish and every kind of fruit, in season and out–these and similar commodities were delivered by the carrier in careless profusion several times a week. On his forty-third birthday the Chevalier d'Eon sent him a dozen smoked Russian tongues, regretting that they had not 'the eloquence of Cicero' to 'rejoice properly.'" Horace Bleackley, *Life of John Wilkes* (London: John Lane, 1917), 235–236.

29. Louis Gottschalk, *Lafayette between the American and the French Revolution* (Chicago: University of Chicago Press, 1950), 254, cited in Harriman,

ed., "'Most Excellent—far fam'd and far fetch'd Cheese': An Anthology of Jeffersonian Era Poetry," 5.

30. *Gazette of the United States*, 30 October 1801, 2, cited in Harriman, ed., "'Most Excellent—far fam'd and far fetch'd Cheese': An Anthology of Jeffersonian Era Poetry," 5.

31. Letter from [William] Woods to Jefferson, 14 January 1807, The Papers of Thomas Jefferson (Manuscript Division, Library of Congress). Mr. Woods's inscription reads in full: "Mr. Woods Grocer of Baltimore[,] Presents his best respects to Thomas Jefferson President of of [*sic*] the United States of America and begs he will please accept of a Mammoth Cheese in Miniature (made in the place whence came the Mammoth Cheese) as a small token of respect due to him for his Great Services done the United States and himself as an Individual."

32. Jackson, it has been observed, ended his presidential tenure with a party as boisterous as the legendary inaugural bash that commenced his administration. See Rufus Rockwell Wilson, *Washington: The Capital City and Its Part in the History of the Nation* (Philadelphia: J. P. Lippincott, 1902), 327 ("The close of Jackson's second term was marked by scenes hardly less exciting than those which attended his first induction into office.").

33. Robert V. Remini, *Andrew Jackson*, vol. 3, *The Course of American Democracy, 1833–1845* (Baltimore: Johns Hopkins University Press, 1984), 393–394. See also Claude G. Bowers, *The Party Battles of the Jackson Period* (Boston: Houghton Mifflin, 1922), 473; Wilson, *Washington: The Capital City*, 327–328. Commentators have drawn the inevitable comparisons between the mammoth cheeses presented to Jefferson and to Jackson. See James Parton, *The Presidency of Andrew Jackson*, ed. Robert V. Remini (New York: Harper and Row, 1967), 458 (Jackson's cheese was "twice as large, said the *Globe*, as the great cheese given to Mr. Jefferson on a similar occasion"); Benjamin Perley Poore, *Perley's Reminiscences of Sixty Years in the National Metropolis* (Philadelphia, 1886; reprint New York: AMS Press, 1971), 1:196 ("Jackson's admirers thought that every honor which Jefferson had ever received should be paid him, so some of them, residing in a rural district of New York, got up, under the superintendence of a Mr. Meacham, a mammoth cheese for 'Old Hickory.'"); John Clagett Proctor, *Proctor's Washington and Environs* (1949), 63 (same).

34. For an anthology of doggerel verse and satire published in the popular press between August 1801 and August 1802, see Harriman, ed., "'Most Excellent—far fam'd and far fetch'd Cheese': An Anthology of Jeffersonian Era Poetry," 6–26.

35. "A Mammoth Pye," *Salem Gazette*, 25 September 1801, 2. The correspondent wrote that, since the "Cheese is said to weigh *twelve hundred pounds*—the Apple Pye ought therefore to weigh at least *forty-eight hundred*, as

Mr. Jefferson, unless he has a Mammoth appetite for Cheese, will want four pounds of Pye to one of Cheese."

36. "Ode to the Mammoth Cheese Presented to Thomas Jefferson, President of the United States, By the Inhabitants of Cheshire, Massachusetts, January 1, 1802," a broadside attributed to Thomas Kennedy, reprinted in Butterfield, "Elder John Leland, Jeffersonian Itinerant," 154; Harriman, ed., "'Most Excellent—far fam'd and far fetch'd Cheese': An Anthology of Jeffersonian Era Poetry," 19–21.

37. "Reflections of Mr. Jefferson, Over the Mammoth Cheese," *Washington Federalist*, 2 April 1802, 3; *The Republican; or, Anti-Democrat* (Baltimore), 3 April 1802, 2.

38. This is a reference to Jefferson's famous statement that "it does me no injury for my neighbor to say there are twenty gods, or no god. It neither picks my pocket nor breaks my leg." Jefferson, *Notes on the State of Virginia*, Query XVII.

39. "The Greatest Cheese American! For Jefferson the Greatest Man!" *Salem Gazette*, 2 March 1802, 4.

40. Letter from Jefferson to Levi Lincoln, 1 January 1802, The Papers of Thomas Jefferson (Manuscript Division, Library of Congress), Series 1, Box 89, December 2, 1801–January 1, 1802; Presidential Papers Microfilm, Thomas Jefferson Papers (Manuscript Division, Library of Congress), Series 1, Reel 25, November 15, 1801–March 31, 1802.

41. Letter from Jefferson to Messrs. Nehemiah Dodge, Ephraim Robbins, and Stephen S. Nelson, a committee of the Danbury Baptist association in the state of Connecticut, 1 January 1802, The Papers of Thomas Jefferson (Manuscript Division, Library of Congress), Series 1, Box 89, December 2, 1801–January 1, 1802; Presidential Papers Microfilm, Thomas Jefferson Papers (Manuscript Division, Library of Congress), Series 1, Reel 25, November 15, 1801–March 31, 1802.

42. See Edwin S. Gaustad, *Sworn on the Altar of God: A Religious Biography of Thomas Jefferson* (Grand Rapids, Mich.: William B. Eerdmans, 1996), 90; James Parton, *Life of Thomas Jefferson: Third President of the United States* (Boston: James R. Osgood, 1874), 570 ("Religion . . . was an important element in the political strife of 1800. There was not a pin to choose between the heterodoxy of the two candidates."); Thomas Fleming, *The Man from Monticello: An Intimate Life of Thomas Jefferson* (New York: William Morrow, 1969), 253 ("The campaign of 1800 was the dirtiest in the history of the nation. Everything that had ever been said against Jefferson by Hamilton and others was repeated, embellished and multiplied. But it was against his religion, his supposed fondness for the atheistic worship of reason, that the Federalists chose to hurl their strongest thunderbolts."); Mark A. Noll, *One Nation under God?: Christian Faith and Political Action in America* (San Francisco: Harper and

Row, 1988), 75 ("The presidential election of 1800 was a major religious event. Not until 1928, when the Roman Catholicism of candidate Al Smith became a major issue, and then again in very recent years, was religion so obviously important in a presidential contest."); Charles F. O'Brien, "The Religious Issue in the Presidential Campaign of 1800," *Essex Institute Historical Collections* 107, no. 1 (1971): 82 ("The traditionally sensitive relation between religion and politics in the United States has rarely been more evident than in the presidential campaign of 1800."). See generally Nobel E. Cunningham, Jr., "Election of 1800," in *History of American Presidential Elections: 1789–1968*, ed. Arthur M. Schlesinger, Jr. (New York: Chelsea House, 1985 [1971]), 1:101–156; Norman De Jong, with Jack Van Der Slik, "The Presidential Election of 1800: Thomas Jefferson's Second Revolution?" in *Separation of Church and State: The Myth Revisited* (Jordan Station, Ontario, Canada: Paideia Press, 1985), 147–168; Philip Hamburger, *Separation of Church and State* (Cambridge, Mass.: Harvard University Press, 2002), chaps. 5–7; Frank Lambert, "'God— and a Religious President . . . [or] Jefferson and No God': Campaigning for a Voter-Imposed Religious Test in 1800," *Journal of Church and State* 39 (1997): 769–789; Charles O. Lerche, Jr., "Jefferson and the Election of 1800: A Case Study in the Political Smear," *William and Mary Quarterly*, 3d ser., 5 (1948): 467–491; Fred C. Luebke, "The Origins of Thomas Jefferson's Anti-Clericalism," *Church History* 32 (1963): 344–356; Constance B. Schulz, "'Of Bigotry in Politics and Religion': Jefferson's Religion, the Federalist Press, and the Syllabus," *Virginia Magazine of History and Biography* 91 (1983): 73–91 (examining the attack on Jefferson's religious views after the election of 1800).

43. Dumas Malone, *Jefferson and His Time*, vol. 3, *Jefferson and the Ordeal of Liberty* (Boston: Little, Brown, 1962), 481; David Saville Muzzey, *Thomas Jefferson* (New York: Charles Scribner's Sons, 1918), 207–208; Albert Jay Nock, *Jefferson* (New York: Harcourt, Brace, 1926), 238; James Parton, *Life of Thomas Jefferson* (Boston: James R. Osgood, 1874), 574; Henry S. Randall, *The Life of Thomas Jefferson*, 3 vols. (New York, 1857), 1:495, 2:567–568; Max J. Herzberg, "Thomas Jefferson as a Man of Letters," *South Atlantic Quarterly* 13 (October 1914): 323. Timothy Dwight warned in 1798 that under a Jeffersonian Republican regime "we may see the Bible cast into a bonfire." Timothy Dwight, *The Duty of Americans, at the Present Crisis* (New-Haven: printed by Thomas and Samuel Green, 1798), reprinted in Ellis Sandoz, ed., *Political Sermons of the American Founding Era, 1730–1805* (Indianapolis, Ind.: Liberty Press, 1991), 1382.

44. For a discussion of the meaning of "infidelity" at the start of the nineteenth century, see Sidney E. Mead, "The 'Nation with the Soul of a Church,'" in *American Civil Religion*, ed. Russell E. Richey and Donald G. Jones (New York: Harper and Row, 1974), 64–65; Martin E. Marty, *The Infidel: Freethought and American Religion* (Cleveland, Ohio: Meridian Books, 1961).

45. Thomas E. Buckley, "Reflections on a Wall," *William and Mary Quarterly*, 3d ser., 56 (1999): 795. Among the sources Buckley cited are *Virginia Gazette*, 11 September 1779 (see also 18 September 1779); [John Swanwick], *Considerations on an Act of the Legislature of Virginia, Entitled, an Act for the Establishment of Religious Freedom* (Philadelphia: printed by Robert Aitken, 1786), 1 (Jefferson's Act "seems calculated to destroy all religion, and to open the gates of scepticism and immorality to the people of that state.").

46. Jefferson, *Notes on the State of Virginia*, Query XVII. Critics saw evidence of Jefferson's infidelity and atheism in a host of other statements in the *Notes on Virginia*, including his expressed doubts about the biblical account of a universal deluge (Query VI), reflections on biological differences between the races, thereby allegedly denying the common origin of mankind in Adam (Query XIV), claim that "[t]hose who labor in the earth are the chosen people of God, if ever He had a chosen people" (Query XIX), and reservations about placing the Bible in the hands of immature school children (Query XIV). Jefferson was also widely criticized for fraternizing with the atheist leaders of the French Revolution. See Clement Clarke Moore, *Observations upon certain passages in Mr. Jefferson's Notes on Virginia: which appear to have a tendency to subvert religion, and establish a false philosophy* (New York, 1804). See generally G. Adolf Koch, *Republican Religion: The American Revolution and the Cult of Reason* (Gloucester, Mass.: Peter Smith, 1964), 265–274; Hamburger, *Separation of Church and State*, chap. 5; Eugene R. Sheridan, "Liberty and Virtue: Religion and Republicanism in Jeffersonian Thought," in *Thomas Jefferson and the Education of a Citizen*, ed. James Gilreath (Washington, D.C.: Library of Congress, 1999), 256–257.

47. See, for example, [William Loughton Smith], *The Pretensions of Thomas Jefferson to the Presidency Examined; and the Charges against John Adams Refuted* ([Philadelphia], October 1796), 36–37; [William Linn], *Serious Considerations on the Election of a President: Addressed to the Citizens of the United States* (New York, printed by John Furman, 1800), 17–19; [John Mitchell Mason], *The Voice of Warning to Christians, on the Ensuing Election of a President of the United States* (New-York: printed by G. F. Hopkins, 1800), reprinted in Sandoz, *Political Sermons*, 1461–1462. Republican partisans were apparently unperturbed by Jefferson's statement. Even the devoutly religious Elder John Leland borrowed Jefferson's rhetoric: "Government has no more to do with the religious opinions of men, than it has with the principles of mathematics. Let every man speak freely without fear, maintain the principles that he believes, worship according to his own faith, either one God, three Gods, no God, or twenty Gods; and let government protect him in so doing, i.e., see that he meets with no personal abuse, or loss of property, for his religious opinions." John Leland, *The Rights of Conscience Inalienable* (New-London, Conn., 1791), in *The Writings of the Late Elder John Leland*, 184.

48. *Gazette of the United States*, 11 September 1800, 2. This question was posed repeatedly by the *Gazette* in the course of the election season. See *Gazette of the United States*, 12 September 1800, 3; 15 September 1800, 2; 16 September 1800, 3; 17 September 1800, 2; 8 October 1800, 3; 9 October 1800, 3; 10 October 1800, 2; 11 October 1800, 2; 13 October 1800, 2. See also an article signed by "No Infidel," "GOD AND A RELIGIOUS PRESIDENT, JEFFERSON AND NO GOD," *Gazette of the United States*, 7 October 1800, 3. See generally Lambert, "'God—and a Religious President . . . [or] Jefferson and No God': Campaigning for a Voter-Imposed Religious Test in 1800," 769–789.

49. In a pamphlet written in the campaign of 1800 to answer ruinous accusations against Jefferson, DeWitt Clinton alleged that William Loughton Smith, in 1796, was the "gentleman who first raised the hue and cry about Mr. Jefferson's religion." Clinton bitterly denounced "[t]he party in opposition to [Jefferson, which] have, with their usual rancour, revived an obsolete and exploded slander, originally invented by [Smith], and with their usual industry have disseminated over the community, that Mr. Jefferson is a *deist*, if not an *atheist*." Grotius [DeWitt Clinton], *A Vindication of Thomas Jefferson; Against the Charges Contained in a Pamphlet Entitled, "Serious Considerations," &c.* (New-York: printed by David Denniston, 1800), 3, 3–4n, referencing [Smith], *The Pretensions of Thomas Jefferson to the Presidency Examined; and the Charges against John Adams Refuted.* An even earlier pamphlet charged that Jefferson possessed "no Conscience, no Religion, no Charity." *The Politics and Views of a Certain Party Examined* (Philadelphia, 1792), quoted in Lerche, "Jefferson and the Election of 1800," 470 n. 4.

50. Timothy Dwight, *The Duty of Americans, at the Present Crisis*, in Sandoz, *Political Sermons,* 1382. In the 1800 election season, Federalist editors, echoing Dwight's oration, ominously predicted: "Should the infidel Jefferson be elected to the Presidency, *the seal of death* is that moment set on our holy religion, our churches will be prostrated, and some infamous prostitute, under the title of the Goddess of Reason, will preside in the Sanctuaries now devoted to the worship of the Most High." Hudson *Bee*, 7 September 1800, reprinted from the *New-England Palladium*, quoted in Nathan Schachner, *Thomas Jefferson: A Biography* (New York: Thomas Yoseloff, 1951), 641.

51. [Linn], *Serious Considerations on the Election of a President*, 4.

52. [Linn], *Serious Considerations on the Election of a President*, 20, 24, 25–26, 28.

53. [Mason], *The Voice of Warning to Christians*, in Sandoz, *Political Sermons,* 1452, 1462, 1465. See also the warning of "a Christian Federalist": "Can serious and reflecting men look about them and doubt, that if Jefferson is elected, and the Jacobins get into authority, that those morals which protect our lives from the knife of the assassin—which guard the chastity of our wives and daughters from seduction and violence—defend our property from plunder and

devastation, and shield our religion from contempt and profanation, will not be trampled upon and exploded." *A Short Address to the Voters of Delaware* (September 1800), 3.

54. See Noble E. Cunningham, Jr., *In Pursuit of Reason: The Life of Thomas Jefferson* (Baton Rouge: Louisiana State University Press, 1987), 225–226.

55. [Tunis Wortman], *A Solemn Address, to Christians and Patriots, Upon the Approaching Election of a President of the United States: In Answer to a Pamphlet, Entitled, "Serious Considerations, &c."* (New-York, printed by David Denniston, 1800), reprinted in Sandoz, *Political Sermons,* 1499.

56. [John James Beckley], *Address to the People of the United States: With an Epitome and Vindication of the Public Life and Character of Thomas Jefferson* (Philadelphia: printed by James Carey, 1800), 7.

57. Letter from a committee of the Danbury Baptist association to Jefferson, 7 October 1801, The Papers of Thomas Jefferson (Manuscript Division, Library of Congress), Series 1, Box 87, August 30, 1801–October 15, 1801; Presidential Papers Microfilm, Thomas Jefferson Papers (Manuscript Division, Library of Congress), Series 1, Reel 24, June 26, 1801–November 14, 1801.

58. McLoughlin, *New England Dissent,* 2:920, 986.

59. See M. Louise Greene, *The Development of Religious Liberty in Connecticut* (Boston: Houghton Mifflin, 1905), 394, 407 ("[F]rom 1793 the dissenters began to lean towards affiliation with the [Jeffersonian] Democratic-Republican party, the successors to the Anti-Federal; yet it was not until toward the close of the War of 1812 that the Republican party made large gains in Connecticut and the dissenters began to feel sure that the dawn of religious liberty was at hand. . . . [T]he Republican [party] gains were greater among the Methodists and Baptists. This was partly because not a few among these dissenters associated Jefferson's party with his efforts towards disestablishment in Virginia in 1785."); Forrest McDonald, *The Presidency of Thomas Jefferson* (Lawrence: University Press of Kansas, 1976), 17 ("[R]eligious dissenters supported Jefferson because of his well-known championship of the cause of religious liberty. New England Baptists, for instance, having fought long and vainly for disestablishment, virtually idolized Jefferson.").

60. See McLoughlin, *New England Dissent,* 2:1004–1005 (commenting on the Connecticut Baptists' affiliation with the Republicans at the turn of the century); Merrill D. Peterson, *Thomas Jefferson and the New Nation: A Biography* (New York: Oxford University Press, 1970), 671 (Republicans in Connecticut "were few, outcasts of society, and systematically excluded from the state government."). For a discussion of Republican party gains in Connecticut in the early nineteenth century, especially among religious dissenters, see Greene, *The Development of Religious Liberty in Connecticut,* 393–444; McLoughlin, *New England Dissent,* 2:1006–1024; Richard J. Purcell, *Connecticut in Transition,*

*1775–1818* (Washington, D.C.: American Historical Association, 1918); Joseph Francis Thorning, *Religious Liberty in Transition: A Study of the Removal of Constitutional Limitations on Religious Liberty as Part of the Social Progress in the Transition Period* (Washington, D.C.: Catholic University of America, 1931), 93–137.

61. See chapter 3 for a discussion of, and evidence for, Jefferson's motives in writing the Danbury Baptist letter.

62. James H. Hutson, "Thomas Jefferson's Letter to the Danbury Baptists: A Controversy Rejoined," *William and Mary Quarterly*, 3d ser., 56 (1999): 785.

63. James Hutson, "'A Wall of Separation': FBI Helps Restore Jefferson's Obliterated Draft," *Library of Congress Information Bulletin* 57, no. 6 (1998): 163.

64. Letter from Manasseh Cutler to Dr. Joseph Torrey, 4 January 1802, in William Parker Cutler and Julia Perkins Cutler, *Life, Journals and Correspondence of Rev. Manasseh Cutler, LL.D.* (Cincinnati: Robert Clarke, 1888), 2:66–67; see also ibid., 2:58–59 (diary entry for 3 January 1802); Anson Phelps Stokes, *Church and State in the United States*, 3 vols. (New York: Harper and Brothers, 1950), 1:499; Butterfield, "Elder John Leland, Jeffersonian Itinerant," 226–227.

65. Hutson, "'A Wall of Separation,'" 163. See also Hutson, "Thomas Jefferson's Letter to the Danbury Baptists," 785–788; James H. Hutson, *Religion and the Founding of the American Republic* (Washington, D.C.: Library of Congress, 1998), 84–94.

66. See Ellis Sandoz, "Religious Liberty and Religion in the American Founding Revisited," in *Religious Liberty in Western Thought*, ed. Noel B. Reynolds and W. Cole Durham, Jr. (Atlanta: Scholars Press, 1996), 245 n. 1.

67. Hutson, "Thomas Jefferson's Letter to the Danbury Baptists," 786, quoting a letter from Manasseh Cutler to Dr. Joseph Torrey, 3 January 1803, in *Life, Journals and Correspondence of Rev. Manasseh Cutler*, 2:119. See also Malone, *Jefferson the President*, 199.

68. Hutson, "Thomas Jefferson's Letter to the Danbury Baptists," 789.

69. Barry Shain, "A Nation with the Soul of a Church," *Harvard Divinity Bulletin*, 28 no. 2/3 (1999): 17.

70. Jefferson, as quoted in Browne, "Elder John Leland and the Mammoth Cheshire Cheese," 150.

71. See, for example, *American Citizen and General Advertiser* (New York), 18 January 1802, 2; *American Mercury* (Hartford, Conn.), 28 January 1802, 3; *The Centinel of Freedom* (Newark, N.J.), 16 February 1802, 2–3 (Baptists' address), 23 February 1802, 3 (Jefferson's reply); *Constitutional Telegraphe* (Boston), 27 January 1802, 2; *Independent Chronicle* (Boston), 25 January 1802, 2–3; *New Hampshire Gazette* (Portsmouth), 9

February 1802, 2; *Rhode-Island Republican* (Newport), 30 January 1802, 2; *Salem Register*, 28 January 1802, 1; *The Sun* (Pittsfield, Mass.), 15 February 1802, 4.

72. See, for example, *American Citizen and General Advertiser* (New York), 18 January 1802, 2; *American Mercury* (Hartford, Conn.), 28 January 1802, 3; *Independent Chronicle* (Boston), 25 January 1802, 2–3. Modern scholars have commented on the coincidence of Leland's delivery of the cheese on the very day Jefferson wrote to the Danbury Baptists. Cushing Strout, for example, observed that Leland "blended Jeffersonianism with his own unorthodox Baptist faith and sent the Virginian, on behalf of Berkshire Republicans, a mammoth cheese, the product of nine hundred cows, on the day in 1802 that Jefferson paid tribute to the Danbury Baptists in a letter that has become the *locus classicus* of the idea that Jefferson and Baptists had joined to endorse the First Amendment for 'building a wall of separation between Church and State.' Thereafter, Connecticut Republicans asked Baptists to join them in Fourth of July celebrations." Strout, "Jeffersonian Religious Liberty and American Pluralism," in *The Virginia Statute for Religious Freedom: Its Evolution and Consequences in American History*, ed. Merrill D. Peterson and Robert C. Vaughan (New York: Cambridge University Press, 1988), 209. See also Hamburger, *Separation of Church and State*, 156–157.

73. See *Washington Federalist*, 7 July 1802, 3; Harriet Taylor Upton, *Our Early Presidents, Their Wives and Children* (Boston: D. Lothrop, 1890), 166 ("In 1805 a portion of the 'mammoth cheese' was still in existence, and was served at a Levee, along with cake and a great urn of hot punch."); Proctor, *Proctor's Washington and Environs*, 62 ("Four years hence it was served with cake and punch at the New Year reception."); Butterfield, "Elder John Leland, Jeffersonian Itinerant," 228–229.

74. When the cider press was eventually dismantled, the great wooden screw was cut into sections and distributed as relics. One of the last reminders of this episode is a concrete replica of the press, erected in Cheshire in 1940. Dedicated by the Sons of the American Revolution, the monument, with an accompanying plaque bearing Leland's likeness, is located at the corner of Church Street and School Street, a few blocks from the village center. Butterfield, "Elder John Leland, Jeffersonian Itinerant," 221 n. 147, 229; Kieser, "President Jefferson's Mammoth Cheese," 42.

75. Letter from Jefferson to Levi Lincoln, 1 January 1802.

NOTES TO CHAPTER 3

1. Letter from Thomas Jefferson to Levi Lincoln, 1 January 1802, The Papers of Thomas Jefferson (Manuscript Division, Library of Congress), Series 1, Box 89, December 2, 1801–January 1, 1802; Presidential Papers Microfilm,

Thomas Jefferson Papers (Manuscript Division, Library of Congress), Series 1, Reel 25, November 15, 1801–March 31, 1802.

2. Letter from Jefferson to Dr. Benjamin Rush, 23 September 1800, *The Writings of Thomas Jefferson*, ed. Andrew A. Lipscomb and Albert Ellery Bergh, 20 vols. (Washington, D.C.: Thomas Jefferson Memorial Association, 1905), 10:175 [hereinafter *Writings of Jefferson*].

3. Letter from a committee of the Danbury Baptist association to Jefferson, 7 October 1801, The Papers of Thomas Jefferson (Manuscript Division, Library of Congress), Series 1, Box 87, August 30, 1801–October 15, 1801; Presidential Papers Microfilm, Thomas Jefferson Papers (Manuscript Division, Library of Congress), Series 1, Reel 24, June 26, 1801–November 14, 1801.

4. The six letters reproduced in this chapter are preserved at the Manuscript Division of the Library of Congress, Washington, D.C. For a discussion concerning the provenance of Jefferson's papers in the Library of Congress archives, see "Introduction," *Thomas Jefferson Papers*, Presidential Papers Microfilm, Manuscript Division, Library of Congress, vii–xvii.

The transcription of handwritten material to printed form is often a difficult and uncertain undertaking. An effort has been made to transcribe the letters accurately, remaining as faithful to the original style as possible. The original punctuation, grammar, and capitalization, as well as anglicized, archaic, and idiosyncratic spellings and misspellings, have been retained (periods are supplied at the end of sentences whether or not they are apparent in the manuscripts). It is often unclear whether Jefferson intended to write a capital or a lower-case letter. "[H]e used capitals with extreme economy and he began each sentence with a lower-case letter." *The Papers of Thomas Jefferson*, ed. Julian P. Boyd et al., 28 vols. to date (Princeton, N.J.: Princeton University Press, 1950- ), 1:xxx [hereinafter *Papers of Jefferson*]. It is also sometimes difficult to determine whether he intended to leave a space between words or to run them together. All editorial changes are placed in brackets; doubtful readings of words in the texts are followed by a question mark in brackets.

| *Guide to Referenced Holograph Letters in the Jefferson Papers* | | | |
| --- | --- | --- | --- |
| | Original Document | In Publications | On the Web |
| Danbury Baptist Association to Jefferson, 10/7/1801 | Jefferson Papers, Library of Congress | Charles C. Haynes, *Religion in American History: What to Teach and How* (Alexandria, Va.: Assoc. for Supervision and Curriculum Development, 1990), 41–43. | http://memory.loc.gov/ammem/mtjhtml/mtjhome.html (search by keyword) |
| Jefferson to Danbury Baptist Association | Jefferson Papers, Library of | James H. Hutson, "Thomas Jefferson's Letter to the Danbury Baptists: A Controversy | http://memory.loc.gov/ammem/mtjhtml/mtjhome.html |

*Guide to Referenced Holograph Letters in the Jefferson Papers (Continued)*

| | Original Document | In Publications | On the Web |
|---|---|---|---|
| (preliminary draft) | Congress | Rejoined," *William & Mary Quarterly*, 3d Ser., 56 (Oct. 1999): 778. | (search by keyword) http://lcweb.loc.gov/ exhibits/religion/ f0605as.jpg |
| Jefferson to Danbury Baptist Association (FBI Version) | | Hutson, "Thomas Jefferson's Letter to the Danbury Baptists: A Controversy Rejoined," 779. | http://lcweb.loc.gov/ exhibits/religion/ danburys.jpg |
| Jefferson to Levi Lincoln, 1/1/1802 | Jefferson Papers, Library of Congress | | http://memory.loc. gov/ammem/mtjhtml/ mtjhome.html (search by keyword) |
| Levi Lincoln to Jefferson, 1/1/1802 | Jefferson Papers, Library of Congress | | http://memory.loc. gov/ammem/mtjhtml/ mtjhome.html (search by keyword) |
| Gideon Granger to Jefferson, 12/31/1801 | Jefferson Papers, Library of Congress | | http://memory.loc. gov/ammem/mtjhtml/ mtjhome.html (search by keyword) |
| Jefferson to Danbury Baptist Association, 1/1/1802 (final version) | Jefferson Papers, Library of Congress | Haynes, *Religion in American History: What to Teach and How*, 46–47. | http://memory.loc. gov/ammem/mtjhtml/ mtjhome.html (search by keyword) |

5. Letter from Jefferson to Levi Lincoln, 1 January 1802.

6. Daniel L. Dreisbach and Jeffry Hays Morrison, "George Washington and American Public Religion," paper presented at the annual meeting of the American Political Science Association, Washington, D.C., 3 September 2000.

7. See James H. Hutson, "Thomas Jefferson's Letter to the Danbury Baptists: A Controversy Rejoined," *William and Mary Quarterly*, 3d ser., 56 (1999): 782 ("By 1802, Americans had come to consider replies to addresses . . . as the prime instruments for the dissemination of partisan views."); Constance B. Schulz, "'Of Bigotry in Politics and Religion': Jefferson's Religion, the Federalist Press, and the Syllabus," *Virginia Magazine of History and Biography* 91 (1983): 85 (Jefferson "found ways of making his true political views known to those who could be reasonably persuaded. As president, he had used official responses to citizen petitions as a means of publicly stating important principles.").

8. A careless reading of Jefferson's letter to Levi Lincoln is the source of the frequently repeated error that the Danbury Baptists requested Jefferson to "designate a day of fasting in connection with the nation's past ordeals." Norman Cousins, ed., *"In God We Trust": The Religious Beliefs and Ideas of the American Founding Fathers* (New York: Harper and Brothers, 1958), 134. Jefferson wrote to Lincoln: "the Baptist address . . . furnishes an occasion too . . . of saying why I do not proclaim fastings & thanksgivings, as my predecessors did. *[T]he address to be sure does not point at this*" (emphasis added). Letter from Jefferson to Levi Lincoln, 1 January 1802. Although Cousins's book is, perhaps, the work most frequently cited in support of this error, others before him made the same mistake. See, for example, Nathan Schachner, *Thomas Jefferson: A Biography* (New York: Appleton-Century-Crofts, 1951), 701. For more recent examples of this error, see Isaac Kramnick and R. Laurence Moore, *The Godless Constitution: The Case against Religious Correctness* (New York: W. W. Norton, 1996), 97, 119; Robert L. Maddox, *Separation of Church and State: Guarantor of Religious Freedom* (New York: Crossroad, 1987), 25–27 (offering a dramatic, but erroneous, account of the Baptists' request).

9. For a discussion of the practices of Jefferson's two presidential predecessors in appointing days for public thanksgiving and religious observance, see Anson Phelps Stokes, *Church and State in the United States*, 3 vols. (New York: Harper and Brothers, 1950), 1:486–491.

10. For examples of Federalist complaints about Republican opposition to the designation of days for public thanksgiving, see *Newport Mercury* (Rhode Island), 24 November 1801, 2; *United States Oracle, and Advertiser* (Portsmouth, N.H.), 28 November 1801, 2; *Columbian Centinel* (Boston), 28 November 1801. See generally Hutson, "Thomas Jefferson's Letter to the Danbury Baptists: A Controversy Rejoined," 780–781.

11. Significantly, Jefferson thought it improper for civil rulers to prescribe religious exercises; yet, in his second inaugural address, he explicitly invited the American people to join him in prayer. Jefferson, Second Inaugural Address, 4 March 1805, *Writings of Jefferson*, 3:383. See generally Thomas E. Buckley, "Reflections on a Wall," *William and Mary Quarterly*, 3d ser., 56 (1999): 800.

12. Schulz, "'Of Bigotry in Politics and Religion,'" 85–86.

13. Edward S. Corwin, "The Supreme Court as National School Board," in *A Constitution of Powers in a Secular State* (Charlottesville, Va.: Michie, 1951), 106. For a brief discussion of President Jefferson's ongoing feud with Connecticut Federalists, see Schulz, "'Of Bigotry in Politics and Religion,'" 74–78. The Connecticut Federalist clergymen, in particular, had staunchly opposed Jefferson's election in 1800. See Stokes, *Church and State in the United States*, 1:408–410, 674–676.

14. See generally Edwin S. Gaustad, "Thomas Jefferson, Danbury Baptists, and 'Eternal Hostility,'" *William and Mary Quarterly*, 3d ser., 56 (1999): 802–803.

15. Letter from Jefferson to Dr. Benjamin Rush, 23 September 1800, *Writings of Jefferson*, 10:174.

16. For a discussion of the origins of Jefferson's anticlericalism in the campaign of 1800, see Fred C. Luebke, "The Origins of Thomas Jefferson's Anti-Clericalism," *Church History* 32 (1963): 344–356. See also Philip Hamburger, *Separation of Church and State* (Cambridge, Mass.: Harvard University Press, 2002), chaps. 5–7; Frank Lambert, "'God—and a Religious President . . . [or] Jefferson and No God': Campaigning for a Voter-Imposed Religious Test in 1800," *Journal of Church and State* 39 (1997): 769–789; Charles O. Lerche, Jr., "Jefferson and the Election of 1800: A Case Study in the Political Smear," *William and Mary Quarterly*, 3d ser., 5 (1948): 467–491.

17. Letter from Jefferson to Jeremiah Moor, 14 August 1800, *The Works of Thomas Jefferson*, ed. Paul Leicester Ford, 12 vols., Federal Edition (New York: G. P. Putnam's Sons, 1905), 9:143 [hereinafter *Works of Jefferson*].

18. Letter from Jefferson to Levi Lincoln, 26 August 1801, *Writings of Jefferson*, 10:275–276. See also Abraham Bishop, *Oration Delivered in Wallingford, on the 11th of March 1801, before the Republicans of the State of Connecticut, at their General Thanksgiving, for the Election of Thomas Jefferson to the Presidency, and of Aaron Burr to the Vice-Presidency, of the United States of America* (New Haven, Conn., printed by William W. Morse, 1801), 41 (the Federalist clergy "would, if they had power, and really believed themselves, actually crucify the republicans").

19. Letter from Jefferson to Dr. Joseph Priestley, 21 March 1801, *Writings of Jefferson*, 10:228.

20. Letter from Jefferson to Moses Robinson, 23 March 1801, *Writings of Jefferson*, 10:236–237.

21. Letter from Jefferson to John Adams, 5 May 1817, *Writings of Jefferson*, 15:109.

22. Letter from Jefferson to Dr. Benjamin Rush, 23 September 1800, *Writings of Jefferson*, 10:175.

23. Luebke, "The Origins of Thomas Jefferson's Anti-Clericalism," 350.

24. Hamburger, *Separation of Church and State*, 111, 112.

25. Hamburger, *Separation of Church and State*, 144. These themes are explored in great detail in ibid., chaps. 5–7.

26. See note 40.

27. Letter from Jefferson to Levi Lincoln, 1 January 1802.

28. See chapter 4 in text accompanying notes 7–10.

29. Dumas Malone, *Jefferson and His Time*, vol. 4, *Jefferson the President: First Term, 1801–1805* (Boston: Little, Brown, 1970), 109. See also Merrill D.

Peterson, *Thomas Jefferson and the New Nation: A Biography* (New York: Oxford University Press, 1970), 672 (Lincoln was "the President's chief liaison with the New England Republicans").

30. Draft letter from Jefferson to Messrs. Nehemiah Dodge, Ephraim Robbins, and Stephen S. Nelson, a committee of the Danbury Baptist association in the state of Connecticut, 1 January 1802, The Papers of Thomas Jefferson (Manuscript Division, Library of Congress), Series 1, Box 89, December 2, 1801–January 1, 1802; Presidential Papers Microfilm, Thomas Jefferson Papers (Manuscript Division, Library of Congress), Series 1, Reel 25, November 15, 1801–March 31, 1802.

31. See chapter 2, note 71.

32. Letter from Jefferson to Levi Lincoln, 1 January 1802.

33. James Hutson, "'A Wall of Separation': FBI Helps Restore Jefferson's Obliterated Draft," *Library of Congress Information Bulletin* 57, no. 6 (June 1998), 137, 163.

34. See, for example, J. M. O'Neill, *Religion and Education under the Constitution* (New York: Harper and Brothers, 1949), 83. See also ibid., 79, 81, 136 ("little letter of courtesy"), 242 ("little note of courtesy"), 199 ("figurative language of the rhetoric of courtesy"); *Wallace v. Jaffree*, 472 U.S. 38, 92 (1985) (Rehnquist, J., dissenting) ("a short note of courtesy"); Joseph H. Brady, *Confusion Twice Confounded: The First Amendment and the Supreme Court: An Historical Study* (South Orange, N.J.: Seton Hall University Press, 1954), 32 ("the short courtesy note"), 70 ("offhand little metaphor"), 174 ("casual, figurative expression"); John F. Wilson, *Public Religion in American Culture* (Philadelphia: Temple University Press, 1979), 6 ("Jefferson's casually delivered unyielding metaphor"); John Remington Graham, "A Restatement of the Intended Meaning of the Establishment Clause in Relation to Education and Religion," *Brigham Young University Law Review* 1981 (1981): 334 ("the phrase is little more than a literary flourish of innocuous significance. Yet some have seized upon this language as if it were a venerable landmark carved in legal stone."); M. G. "Pat" Robertson, "Squeezing Religion Out of the Public Square—The Supreme Court, *Lemon*, and the Myth of the Secular Society," *William and Mary Bill of Rights Journal* 4 (1995): 223 ("In an angry note he wrote to the Danbury Baptist Association in 1802, Thomas Jefferson mentioned in passing that the First Amendment Establishment Clause had built 'a wall of separation between church and State.' Inconceivable as it may be, the United States Supreme Court, starting in 1947, has built much of its present Establishment Clause jurisprudence on this off-hand phrase uttered by a man, however distinguished, who was not even present in the country when the Bill of Rights was drafted and ratified.") (footnotes omitted). But see Leonard W. Levy, *The Establishment Clause: Religion and the First Amendment*, 2d ed. (Chapel Hill: University of North Carolina Press, 1994), 247 (de-

nouncing the tendency of critics to belittle the letter); R. Freeman Butts, *The American Tradition in Religion and Education* (Boston: Beacon Press, 1950), 93–94 (Jefferson "worded *this* letter with meticulous care in order to emphasize and describe a political and constitutional *principle* which he deeply believed to be of first importance. He was not idly coining a phrase for pleasure nor hurriedly dictating a formal letter of courtesy in the midst of the pressures of more important business."); Leo Pfeffer, *Church, State, and Freedom* (Boston: Beacon Press, 1953), 118–121 (arguing that it is difficult to characterize the Danbury letter as lacking in deliberation); Robert Boston, *Why the Religious Right Is Wrong about Separation of Church and State* (Buffalo, N.Y.: Prometheus Books, 1993), 66, 221 (same); Robert S. Alley, "Public Education and the Public Good," *William and Mary Bill of Rights Journal* 4 (1995): 309–315 (same).

35. Letter from a committee of the Danbury Baptist association to Jefferson, 7 October 1801, The Papers of Thomas Jefferson (Manuscript Division, Library of Congress), Series 1, Box 87, August 30, 1801–October 15, 1801; Presidential Papers Microfilm, Thomas Jefferson Papers (Manuscript Division, Library of Congress), Series 1, Reel 24, June 26, 1801–November 14, 1801.

36. M. Louise Greene, *The Development of Religious Liberty in Connecticut* (Boston: Houghton Mifflin, 1905), 357. See generally Stokes, *Church and State in the United States*, 1:488; Christopher Grasso, *A Speaking Aristocracy: Transforming Public Discourse in Eighteenth-Century Connecticut* (Chapel Hill: Omohundro Institute of Early American History and Culture; University of North Carolina Press, 1999); Peter S. Field, *The Crisis of the Standing Order: Clerical Intellectuals and Cultural Authority in Massachusetts, 1780–1833* (Amherst: University of Massachusetts Press, 1998).

37. See Richard J. Purcell, *Connecticut in Transition, 1775–1818* (Washington, D.C.: American Historical Association, 1918), 75 ("The general Act of Toleration in 1784 in no respect met Baptist demands for a free church within a free state."); William G. McLoughlin, *New England Dissent, 1630–1883: The Baptists and the Separation of Church and State*, 2 vols. (Cambridge, Mass.: Harvard University Press, 1971), 2:985–1005.

38. See Daniel L. Dreisbach and John D. Whaley, "What the Wall Separates: A Debate on Thomas Jefferson's 'Wall of Separation' Metaphor," *Constitutional Commentary* 16 (1999): 646.

39. Draft letter from Jefferson to Messrs. Nehemiah Dodge, Ephraim Robbins, and Stephen S. Nelson, a committee of the Danbury Baptist association in the state of Connecticut, 1 January 1802, The Papers of Thomas Jefferson (Manuscript Division, Library of Congress), Series 1, Box 89, December 2, 1801–January 1, 1802; Presidential Papers Microfilm, Thomas Jefferson Papers (Manuscript Division, Library of Congress), Series 1, Reel 25, November 15, 1801–March 31, 1802.

40. See Laurie Goodstein, "Fresh Debate on 1802 Jefferson Letter," *New York Times*, 10 September 1998, A20; Diego Ribadeneira, "New Debate Flares over Jefferson's View of Church and State," *Boston Globe*, 1 August 1998, B2; Warren Fiske, "Test on Letter by Jefferson Fuels Debate on Church, State," *Virginian-Pilot* (Norfolk, Va.), 4 July 1998, A1; Carl Hartman, "Jefferson's Stance on Religion Fuels Debate," *USA Today*, 31 July 1998, 6A; Irvin Molotsky, "One of Jefferson's Enigmas, So Finally the F.B.I. Steps In," *New York Times*, 30 May 1998, A15; Larry Witham, "Very Political Jefferson Built 'Wall of Separation,'" *Washington Times*, 1 June 1998, A1; Bill Broadway, "One Nation under God," *Washington Post*, 6 June 1998, B9; Carl Hartman, "Line Uncovered in Historic Letter," *Dayton Daily News*, 6 June 1998, 7C; Martin Kettle, "Sacred Ideal Founded on Jefferson's Fudge," *Guardian* (London), 8 June 1998, 12. For an excellent analysis of the preliminary draft that draws on the FBI report, see Hutson, "'A Wall of Separation': FBI Helps Restore Jefferson's Obliterated Draft," 136–139, 163; Hutson, "Thomas Jefferson's Letter to the Danbury Baptists: A Controversy Rejoined," 775–790.

41. Molotsky, "One of Jefferson's Enigmas, So Finally the F.B.I. Steps In," A15, A18.

42. The FBI reported: "During the evaluation process, attempts to differentiate the Danbury Letter ink by filters and different lighting sources were not successful indicating that all notations and overwriting was [*sic*] prepared with the same ink. The differentiation of overwriting to text was in density of the ink and not by a separation due to a difference in chemical composition. No further destructive ink analysis was conducted due to the nature and historical value of this document." Letter from David W. Attenberger, Unit Chief, Questioned Documents Unit, Laboratory Division, Federal Bureau of Investigation, Washington, D.C. to the author, 3 December 1998. The differentiation between the text and the overwriting in the density of the ink gives some clue as to the sequence in which Jefferson made the various revisions to the letter.

43. Hutson, "'A Wall of Separation': FBI Helps Restore Jefferson's Obliterated Draft," 138.

44. Hutson, "Thomas Jefferson's Letter to the Danbury Baptists: A Controversy Rejoined," 783.

An alternative, if highly implausible, reading of this passage is that "Executive(s)" who are "the legal head of a national church" may refer to governors of states with formally established churches, and "subject here" may mean under the federal regime. Given this interpretation, Jefferson was saying that the First Amendment mandates that, under the authority of the federal government, "religious exercises" must be left "to the voluntary regulations and discipline of each respective sect," but in states (i.e., "nations") with established churches recognized by law, the "executive" may legally prescribe "performances of devotion."

45. Hutson, "'A Wall of Separation': FBI Helps Restore Jefferson's Obliterated Draft," 139.

46. Hutson, "Thomas Jefferson's Letter to the Danbury Baptists: A Controversy Rejoined," 783–784.

47. See also letter from Jefferson to the Reverend Samuel Miller, 23 January 1808, *Writings of Jefferson*, 11: 429–430 ("every one must act according to the dictates of his own reason, and mine tells me that civil powers alone have been given to the President of the United States, and no authority to direct the religious exercises of his constituents.").

48. For a brief commentary on the deletion of the word "eternal," see Robert S. Alley, "Public Education and the Public Good," *William and Mary Bill of Rights Journal* 4 (1995): 314 n. 232. This language is reminiscent of one of Jefferson's frequently quoted declarations, written in the midst of the presidential campaign of 1800: "I have sworn upon the altar of God, eternal hostility against every form of tyranny over the mind of man." Letter from Jefferson to Benjamin Rush, 23 September 1800, *Writings of Jefferson*, 10:175. Although not used in reference to the subject of church and state, Jefferson used the phrase "eternal separation" in the penultimate paragraph of early drafts of the Declaration of Independence. See Carl L. Becker, *The Declaration of Independence: A Study in the History of Political Ideas* (New York: Vintage Books, 1958 [1922]), 150, 170, 183. See also *McCollum v. Board of Education*, 333 U.S. 203, 219, 231 (1948) (Opinion of Frankfurter, J.) (twice Justice Felix Frankfurter quoted Elihu Root's declaration of "the great American principle of eternal separation between Church and State").

49. Hutson, "'A Wall of Separation': FBI Helps Restore Jefferson's Obliterated Draft," 163. These two phrases, Hutson opined, had "a clenched-teeth, defiant ring." Ibid., 139.

If political considerations guided Jefferson's revision of the letter, then Jefferson's original phrases (i.e., "wall of eternal separation" and "merely temporal") arguably reveal his true, principled strict separationist views before politics prompted him to dilute the public expression of those views. Daniel L. Dreisbach, "Thomas Jefferson and the Danbury Baptists Revisited," *William and Mary Quarterly*, 3d ser., 56 (1999): 815 n. 24.

50. Draft letter from Jefferson to Messrs. Nehemiah Dodge, Ephraim Robbins, and Stephen S. Nelson, a committee of the Danbury Baptist association in the state of Connecticut, 1 January 1802. This sentence parallels an acknowledgment made in the letter from the Baptists: "we are sensible that the President of the united States, is not the national Legislator, & also sensible that the national government cannot destroy the Laws of each State."

51. Hutson, "'A Wall of Separation': FBI Helps Restore Jefferson's Obliterated Draft," 163.

52. Hutson, "'A Wall of Separation': FBI Helps Restore Jefferson's Obliterated Draft," 163.

53. Hutson, "Thomas Jefferson's Letter to the Danbury Baptists: A Controversy Rejoined," 777.

54. See Rodney K. Smith, *Public Prayer and the Constitution: A Case Study in Constitutional Interpretation* (Wilmington, Del.: Scholarly Resources, 1987), 61 ("That Jefferson considered this reply to be significant, as a legal matter, is clear from the fact that he submitted a draft of the letter to his attorney general, Levi Lincoln, for his review.").

55. Malone, *Jefferson the President*, 109.

56. Letter from Jefferson to Levi Lincoln, 1 January 1802, The Papers of Thomas Jefferson (Manuscript Division, Library of Congress), Series 1, Box 89, December 2, 1801–January 1, 1802; Presidential Papers Microfilm, Thomas Jefferson Papers (Manuscript Division, Library of Congress), Series 1, Reel 25, November 15, 1801–March 31, 1802.

57. Letter from Jefferson to Levi Lincoln, 1 January 1802. Hutson opined that "Jefferson knew and seemed to savor the fact that his letter, as originally drafted, would give 'great offence' to the New England Federalists." Hutson, "'A Wall of Separation': FBI Helps Restore Jefferson's Obliterated Draft," 139.

58. Smith, *Public Prayer and the Constitution*, 62.

59. Letter from Levi Lincoln to Jefferson, 1 January 1802, The Papers of Thomas Jefferson (Manuscript Division, Library of Congress), Series 1, Box 89, December 2, 1801–January 1, 1802; Presidential Papers Microfilm, Thomas Jefferson Papers (Manuscript Division, Library of Congress), Series 1, Reel 25, November 15, 1801–March 31, 1802.

60. Hutson, "Thomas Jefferson's Letter to the Danbury Baptists: A Controversy Rejoined," 784; Hutson, "'A Wall of Separation': FBI Helps Restore Jefferson's Obliterated Draft," 139.

61. See chapter 4 in text accompanying notes 7–10.

62. "Resolution for a Day of Thanksgiving," *Newport Mercury*, Tuesday, 3 November 1801, 3.

63. See, for example, "Resolution Appointing a Day of Thanksgiving," Rhode Island Senate Resolution, 1 November 1800, at 34–35 (October 1800 Sess.); "Act for Thanksgiving," 1799 Rhode Island Laws at 19 (October 1799 Sess.); and "An Act Appointing a Day of Thanksgiving," 1798 Rhode Island Laws at 17–18 (October 1798 Sess.).

64. *Newport Mercury*, 3 November 1801, 3.

65. *Newport Mercury*, 3 November 1801, 3. See also *Newport Mercury*, 24 November 1801, 2.

66. "Thanksgiving Appointed," 1802 Rhode Island Laws at 22 (October 1802 Sess.).

67. *Dictionary of American Biography*, ed. Allen Johnson and Dumas Malone (New York: Charles Scribner's Sons, 1931–1932), 7:483, s.v. "Granger, Gideon."

68. Granger's letter is presented here out of chronological sequence in order to afford the reader access to Jefferson's communication to Levi Lincoln, which almost certainly was similar, if not identical, to the request sent to Granger. This is evident from the cover note Granger quoted in his reply.

69. Letter from Gideon Granger to Jefferson, December 1801, The Papers of Thomas Jefferson (Manuscript Division, Library of Congress), Series 1, Box 89, December 2, 1801–January 1, 1802; Presidential Papers Microfilm, Thomas Jefferson Papers (Manuscript Division, Library of Congress), Series 1, Reel 25, November 15, 1801–March 31, 1802. A notation on the reverse side of the manuscript reads: "Granger. Gideon. recd. Dec. 31. 1801."

70. In the preliminary draft of the letter, the first letter of "God" is not capitalized.

71. Most published collections of Jefferson's writings incorrectly transcribe this word as "legislative." See, for example, *The Writings of Thomas Jefferson*, ed. H. A. Washington, 9 vols. (Washington, D.C.: Taylor and Maury, 1853–1854), 8:113–114; *The Writings of Thomas Jefferson*, ed. Andrew A. Lipscomb and Albert Ellery Bergh, 20 vols., Library Edition (Washington, D.C.: Thomas Jefferson Memorial Association, 1905), 16:281–282; *The Life and Selected Writings of Thomas Jefferson*, ed. Adrienne Koch and William Peden (New York: Modern Library; Random House, 1944), 332; *The Complete Jefferson*, ed. Saul K. Padover (New York: Duell, Sloan and Pearce, 1943), 518–519; *The Portable Thomas Jefferson*, ed. Merrill D. Peterson (New York: Penguin Books, 1975), 303; *Writings*, notes and selections by Merrill D. Peterson (New York: Literary Classics of the United States, The Library of America, 1984), 510. This mistranscription apparently originated in Henry A. Washington's mid-nineteenth-century published collection of Jefferson's papers.

72. U.S. Constitution, amendment I.

73. Letter from Jefferson to Messrs. Nehemiah Dodge, Ephraim Robbins, and Stephen S. Nelson, a committee of the Danbury Baptist association in the state of Connecticut, 1 January 1802, The Papers of Thomas Jefferson (Manuscript Division, Library of Congress), Series 1, Box 89, December 2, 1801–January 1, 1802; Presidential Papers Microfilm, Thomas Jefferson Papers (Manuscript Division, Library of Congress), Series 1, Reel 25, November 15, 1801–March 31, 1802.

74. Richard P. McBrien remarked that the opening phrase of the second paragraph, "Believing with you that religion is a matter which lies solely between Man & his God," was written in the language of faith and clearly "express[ed] a theological judgment." Richard P. McBrien, *Caesar's Coin: Religion*

*and Politics in America* (New York: Macmillan, 1987), 64. For similar statements asserting that religion is a subject that lies solely between man and his maker, see letter from Jefferson to Mrs. M. Harrison Smith, 6 August 1816, *Writings of Jefferson*, 15:60; letter from Jefferson to Richard Rush, 31 May 1813, *Works of Jefferson*, ed. Paul Leicester Ford (New York: G. P. Putnam's Sons, 1905), 11:292; letter from Jefferson to Miles King, 26 September 1814, *Writings of Jefferson*, 14:198. McBrien further remarked about this passage that "Jefferson's ecclesiology was highly individualistic: 'I am a sect myself.' Religion pertains only to the sphere of the private." McBrien, *Caesar's Coin*, 64, quoting letter from Jefferson to Ezra Styles, Esq., 25 June 1819, *Writings of Jefferson*, 15:203.

75. Compare Jefferson's language here with that in the *Notes on the State of Virginia*: "The legitimate powers of government extend to such acts only as are injurious to others." Jefferson, "Query XVII," *Notes on the State of Virginia*, in *Life and Selected Writings of Jefferson*, 275. This comparison, along with a commentary on the Danbury letter, is noted in McBrien, *Caesar's Coin*, 64. "To needle his political opponents," Hutson suggested, Jefferson may have deliberately paraphrased this passage from the *Notes on Virginia*, "which the Federalists had shamelessly distorted in the election of 1800 in an effort to stigmatize him as an atheist." Hutson, "'A Wall of Separation': FBI Helps Restore Jefferson's Obliterated Draft," 138. See also Jefferson's language in his draft of "A Bill for Establishing Religious Freedom," which was subsequently deleted by legislative amendment: "that the opinions of men are not the object of civil government, nor under its jurisdiction." *Papers of Jefferson*, 2:546.

76. Hamburger, *Separation of Church and State*, 147.

77. John Witte, Jr., *Religion and the American Constitutional Experiment: Essential Rights and Liberties* (Boulder, Colo.: Westview Press, 2000), 50. See also Thomas G. West, "Religious Liberty: The View from the Founding," in *On Faith and Free Government*, ed. Daniel C. Palm (Lanham, Md.: Rowman and Littlefield, 1997), 5 ("Yet Jefferson closes this very same letter, written in his official capacity as president, with a prayer. . . . If today's liberals were right, Jefferson would be breaking down the wall of separation at the very moment he proclaims it."); Stephen J. Safranek, "Can Science Guide Legal Argumentation?: The Role of Metaphor in Constitutional Cases," *Loyola University Chicago Law Journal* 25 (1994): 372–373 n. 83 ("Contrary to some popular views, Jefferson was not an advocate of strict separation of church and state. . . . Ironically, Jefferson closed his letter to the Danbury Baptists with a prayer.").

78. McLoughlin, *New England Dissent*, 2:919.

79. The First Amendment prohibition is not technically a "disestablishment" measure since there was no formal ecclesiastical establishment to abolish.

80. For a discussion of the distinctions religious dissenters made among the terms "separation," "disestablishment," and "religious liberty," see Hamburger, *Separation of Church and State*, 9–14, 89–107.

81. Jon Butler, "Coercion, Miracle, Reason: Rethinking the American Religious Experience in the Revolutionary Age," in *Religion in a Revolutionary Age*, ed. Ronald Hoffman and Peter J. Albert (Charlottesville: University Press of Virginia; United States Capitol Historical Society, 1994), 29–30. See also Charles Wesley Lowry, "The Case for the Traditional American Middle Way in Church and State," *Journal of Public Law* 13 (1964): 454–455 ("Jefferson . . . shifts verbal gears" by referring to a separation of "church" and state, rather than "religion" and state, implying that he did not mean to proscribe all interaction between religion and the state.); Steven D. Smith, "Separation and the 'Secular': Reconstructing the Disestablishment Decision," *Texas Law Review* 67 (1989): 974 ("Both the devotees and the critics of the metaphor have too often parsed from Jefferson's statement only the words 'wall of separation.' In the eighteenth century understanding, the establishment clause did erect such a 'wall.' But as Jefferson said, the wall lay not between *government and religion*—that is, dividing religious values, beliefs, imagery, and rhetoric, on the one hand, and political culture, on the other—but between *church and state*.").

82. See Hamburger, *Separation of Church and State*, 11–14.

83. See Hamburger, *Separation of Church and State*, chaps. 2–4.

84. Hamburger, *Separation of Church and State*, 163, 165. William G. McLoughlin similarly noted: "Oddly the Danbury Baptist Association Minutes, although they mention writing to Jefferson, neither printed the letter to him nor mentioned his reply." McLoughlin, *New England Dissent*, 2:1005 n. 23. This may be evidence of Baptist discomfort with the letter.

85. McLoughlin, *New England Dissent*, 2:1013.

86. *Reynolds v. United States*, 98 U.S. 145 (1879).

87. Letter from Jefferson to Levi Lincoln, 1 January 1802.

88. Jefferson's definition of an *establishment* prohibited by the First Amendment was not so expansive as to include some types of governmental activities that courts in the twenty-first century would hold to be impermissible establishments of religion. During his presidency, for example, Jefferson negotiated a treaty with the Kaskaskia Indians that appropriated federal dollars for "the support of a [Catholic] priest" and "the erection of a church." "A Treaty between the United States of America and the Kaskaskia Tribe of Indians," *U.S. Statutes at Large*, 7:78–79. The treaty advanced the secular governmental goals of promoting friendship and security with these Indians and providing for the education of their children. This is one of numerous actions Jefferson took that confirms that he did not embrace an absolute separation between church and state in all circumstances. For more on this and other examples of Jefferson's use of sectarian means to advance secular governmental goals, see Robert L. Cord,

"Mr. Jefferson's 'Nonabsolute' Wall of Separation between Church and State," in *Religion and Political Culture in Jefferson's Virginia*, ed. Garrett Ward Sheldon and Daniel L. Dreisbach (Lanham, Md.: Rowman and Littlefield, 2000), 167–188; Cord, *Separation of Church and State: Historical Fact and Current Fiction* (New York: Lambeth Press, 1982).

89. Jefferson used the "wall of separation" metaphor on at least one prior occasion, albeit not in a church-state context. In a January 1798 letter to Angelica Church, Alexander Hamilton's sister-in-law, he used the figurative phrase to convey the bitter divide between Federalists and Republicans: "Party animosities here [in Philadelphia] have raised a wall of separation between those who differ in political sentiments." Letter from Jefferson to Angelica Church, 11 January 1798, *Works of Jefferson*, 7:156 (the letter in this collection is dated incorrectly "October 1792"); Dumas Malone, *Jefferson and His Time*, vol. 3, *Jefferson and the Ordeal of Liberty* (Boston: Little, Brown, 1962), 360.

90. Jefferson's Second Inaugural Address (4 March 1805) and letter to the Reverend Samuel Miller (23 January 1808) are discussed in chapter 4.

NOTES TO CHAPTER 4

1. *McCollum v. Board of Education*, 333 U.S. 203, 213 (1948) (Opinion of Frankfurter, J.). See also *Carden v. Bland*, 199 Tenn. 665, 679, 288 S.W.2d 718, 724 (1956) ("The [Supreme] Court cites Thomas Jefferson as . . . having coined the phrase that there must be 'a wall of separation between church and State.' There was no convincing argument as to just what the wall was to separate.").

2. Robert Frost, "Mending Wall," in *North of Boston* (London: David Nutt, 1914), reprinted in *Collected Poems of Robert Frost* (New York: Henry Holt, 1930), 48.

3. Letter from Thomas Jefferson to the Reverend Samuel Miller, 23 January 1808, *The Writings of Thomas Jefferson*, ed. Andrew A. Lipscomb and Albert Ellery Bergh, 20 vols. (Washington, D.C.: Thomas Jefferson Memorial Association, 1905), 11:428 [hereinafter *Writings of Jefferson*].

4. The terms "jurisdictional" and "structural" are used here synonymously to mean that the "wall" (like the First Amendment it metaphorically represents) is concerned primarily with managing (conferring and limiting) governmental powers and prerogatives between the national and the state governments on matters pertaining to religion. "Federalism" and "separation of powers" are the principal constitutional structures countenanced by these terms as used in this chapter. The primary purpose of the First Amendment nonestablishment provision, it is argued, is *not* to secure individual rights and liberties, although the structural restraints of the First Amendment (and the "wall") "can have a laudable effect on individual rights by constraining the branches of government to act only within the scope of their delegated powers." Carl H. Esbeck, "The Es-

tablishment Clause as a Structural Restraint on Governmental Power," *Iowa Law Review* 84 (1998): 3.

5. See generally Joseph F. Costanzo, "Thomas Jefferson, Religious Education and Public Law," *Journal of Public Law* 8, no. 1 (1959): 97–98 ("The meaning of a figure of speech is not self-contained; it is derivative. It loses its meaning if it is excised from its historical context and from its literal composition. Much less ought we to ignore the author's consistent conduct and thinking. The meaning of a figure of speech is wholly in its referral to related thinking on the subject.").

6. See, for example, *Marsh v. Chambers*, 463 U.S. 783, 807–808 (1983) (Brennan, J., dissenting); *Lee v. Weisman*, 505 U.S. 577, 622–624 (1992) (Souter, J., concurring).

7. Letter from Jefferson to Levi Lincoln, 1 January 1802, The Papers of Thomas Jefferson (Manuscript Division, Library of Congress), Series 1, Box 89, December 2, 1801–January 1, 1802; Presidential Papers Microfilm, Thomas Jefferson Papers (Manuscript Division, Library of Congress), Series 1, Reel 25, November 15, 1801–March 31, 1802.

8. "Proclamation for a National Fast," 6 March 1799, *The Works of John Adams, Second President of the United States*, ed. Charles Francis Adams (Boston: Little, Brown, 1854), 9:172–174.

9. Letter from John Adams to Benjamin Rush, 12 June 1812, in *The Spur of Fame: Dialogues of John Adams and Benjamin Rush, 1805–1813*, ed. John A. Schutz and Douglass Adair (San Marino, Calif.: Huntington Library, 1966), 224. See generally Edwin S. Gaustad, *Sworn on the Altar of God: A Religious Biography of Thomas Jefferson* (Grand Rapids, Mich.: William B. Eerdmans, 1996), 94–96.

10. See generally Charles Ellis Dickson, "Jeremiads in the New American Republic: The Case of National Fasts in the John Adams Administration," *New England Quarterly* 60 (1987): 187–207.

11. This was Jefferson's conclusion if, in fact, public thanksgiving and fast-day proclamations remained the principal point of his letter. Jefferson's final version of the Danbury letter did not explicitly mention the issue of "fastings & thanksgivings," and it would not be apparent from the text that this was the original object of this address were it not for his letter to Levi Lincoln. Letter from Jefferson to Levi Lincoln, 1 January 1802. The "performances of devotion" are an oblique reference to the practice of public "fastings & thanksgivings" mentioned in the preliminary draft of the Danbury letter. Draft letter from Jefferson to Messrs. Nehemiah Dodge, Ephraim Robbins, and Stephen S. Nelson, a committee of the Danbury Baptist association in the state of Connecticut, 1 January 1802, The Papers of Thomas Jefferson (Manuscript Division, Library of Congress), Series 1, Box 89, December 2, 1801–January 1, 1802; Presidential Papers Microfilm, Thomas Jefferson Papers (Manuscript Division, Library of

Congress), Series 1, Reel 25, November 15, 1801–March 31, 1802. Henry S. Randall, one of the first major biographers of Jefferson, noted, in 1857, that, although Jefferson had set out to explain why he declined "to proclaim fast and thanksgiving days, after the custom of his predecessors," the "answer to the 'Baptist Address' . . . [contained] no direct allusion to his reasons for not proclaiming fast days." Randall then raised the possibility that Jefferson may have abandoned this original purpose for the letter: "Whether Mr. Lincoln advised the suppression of the paragraph, or whether the 'awkwardness' of its introduction induced the President, on second thought, to wait for a better 'opportunity,' we are not informed." Randall, *The Life of Thomas Jefferson*, 3 vols. (New York: Derby and Jackson, 1857), 3:2.

    12. See John G. West, Jr., *The Politics of Revelation and Reason: Religion and Civic Life in the New Nation* (Lawrence: University Press of Kansas, 1996), 57. See also Thomas E. Buckley, "Reflections on a Wall," *William and Mary Quarterly*, 3d ser., 56 (1999): 797 ("Throughout his political career and particularly during his presidency, Jefferson repeatedly wove expressions of religious belief into his public statements.").

    13. Jefferson, First Inaugural Address, 4 March 1801, *Writings of Jefferson*, 3:320, 323.

    14. Jefferson, First Annual Message, 8 December 1801, *Writings of Jefferson*, 3:327.

    15. Jefferson, Second Annual Message, 15 December 1802, *Writings of Jefferson*, 3:340.

    16. Jefferson, Second Inaugural Address, 4 March 1805, *Writings of Jefferson*, 3:383.

    17. For examples, see Buckley, "Reflections on a Wall," 797–800; Thomas E. Buckley, "The Political Theology of Thomas Jefferson," in *The Virginia Statute for Religious Freedom: Its Evolution and Consequences in American History*, ed. Merrill D. Peterson and Robert C. Vaughan (New York: Cambridge University Press, 1988), 94–96.

    18. "Resolution of the House of Burgesses Designating a Day of Fasting and Prayer," 24 May 1774, *The Papers of Thomas Jefferson*, ed. Julian P. Boyd et al., 28 vols. to date (Princeton, N.J.: Princeton University Press, 1950– ), 1:105–106 [hereinafter *Papers of Jefferson*]. See also letter from Jefferson and John Walker to the Inhabitants of the Parish of St. Anne, before 23 July 1774, *Papers of Jefferson*, 1:116.

    19. Jefferson, *Autobiography*, *Writings of Jefferson*, 1:9–10.

    20. See Robert M. Healey, *Jefferson on Religion in Public Education* (New Haven, Conn.: Yale University Press, 1962), 135; Gaustad, *Sworn on the Altar of God*, 102–103 (commenting on Jefferson's role in this proclamation). Martin E. Marty observed that this resolution "is hardly a noble charter, but it does show that Jefferson did, on occasion, allow for acts that clearly contradicted the

[religious freedom] bill of 1779 and the [Virginia] statute [for religious freedom] of 1786." Marty, "The Virginia Statute Two Hundred Years Later," in *The Virginia Statute for Religious Freedom: Its Evolution and Consequences in American History*, 9.

21. "Proclamation Appointing a Day of Thanksgiving and Prayer," 11 November 1779, *Papers of Jefferson*, 3:177–179.

22. *Report of the Committee of Revisors Appointed by the General Assembly of Virginia in MDCCLXXVI* (Richmond, Va.: printed by Dixon and Holt, 1784), 59–60 [hereinafter *Report of the Revisors*]. The bill is reprinted in *Papers of Jefferson*, 2:556. This bill was part of a legislative package that included Jefferson's "Bill for Establishing Religious Freedom" and "Bill for Punishing Disturbers of Religious Worship and Sabbath Breakers." The three bills were apparently framed by Jefferson and sponsored in the Virginia legislature by James Madison. See Daniel L. Dreisbach, "A New Perspective on Jefferson's Views on Church-State Relations: The Virginia Statute for Establishing Religious Freedom in Its Legislative Context," *American Journal of Legal History* 35 (1991): 172–204; Dreisbach, "Thomas Jefferson and Bills Number 82–86 of the Revision of the Laws of Virginia, 1776–1786: New Light on the Jeffersonian Model of Church-State Relations," *North Carolina Law Review* 69 (1990): 159–211.

23. Julian P. Boyd, editor of the Jefferson papers, did not explicitly attribute authorship of this bill to Jefferson. He did not, however, reject the possibility that Jefferson drafted "A Bill for Appointing Days of Public Fasting and Thanksgiving." Boyd noted that Jefferson apparently endorsed the bill. *Papers of Jefferson*, 2:556. Other scholars have described Jefferson as the author of this bill. See, for example, Robert L. Cord, *Separation of Church and State: Historical Fact and Current Fiction* (New York: Lambeth Press, 1982), 220–221; Healey, *Jefferson on Religion in Public Education*, 135; Donald L. Drakeman, "Religion and the Republic: James Madison and the First Amendment," *Journal of Church and State* 25 (1983): 441; Comment, "Jefferson and the Church-State Wall: A Historical Examination of the Man and the Metaphor," *Brigham Young University Law Review* 1978 (1978): 657, 666.

24. *Report of the Revisors*, 60; *Papers of Jefferson*, 2:556. The punitive feature of "A Bill for Appointing Days of Public Fasting and Thanksgiving" is difficult to reconcile with that portion of Jefferson's "Bill for Establishing Religious Freedom" that declares "that no man shall be compelled to frequent or support any religious worship, place, or ministry whatsoever." *Report of the Revisors*, 58; *Papers of Jefferson*, 2:546; William Waller Hening, ed., *The Statutes at Large; Being a Collection of All the Laws of Virginia, From the First Session of the Legislature, in the Year 1619* (Richmond, Va.: J. and G. Cochran, 1823), 12:86.

25. *Papers of Jefferson*, 2:556.

26. Mark DeWolfe Howe, *The Garden and the Wilderness: Religion and Government in American Constitutional History* (Chicago: University of Chicago Press, 1965), 19–20. In *The Federalist Papers*, No. 45, James Madison observed that "[t]he powers delegated by the proposed Constitution to the federal government are few and defined. Those which are to remain in the State governments are numerous and indefinite. . . . The powers reserved to the several States will extend to all the objects which, in the ordinary course of affairs, concern the lives, liberties, and properties of the people, and the internal order, improvement, and prosperity of the State." *The Federalist Papers*, ed. Clinton Rossiter (New York: Mentor Books, 1961), 292–293.

27. See Note, "Rethinking the Incorporation of the Establishment Clause: A Federalist View," *Harvard Law Review* 105 (1992): 1706–1707 (the word "Congress" emphasizes the federalism component of the First Amendment); Esbeck, "The Establishment Clause as a Structural Restraint on Governmental Power," 15 and n. 51; Jay S. Bybee, "Taking Liberties with the First Amendment: Congress, Section 5, and the Religious Freedom Restoration Act," *Vanderbilt Law Review* 48 (1995), 1555–1566; Kurt T. Lash, "The Second Adoption of the Free Exercise Clause: Religious Exemptions under the Fourteenth Amendment," *Northwestern University Law Review* 88 (1994): 1111–1112. See also Edward S. Corwin, "The Supreme Court as National School Board," in *A Constitution of Powers in a Secular State* (Charlottesville, Va.: Michie, 1951), 109 ("the First Amendment, taken by itself, is binding only on Congress").

28. Joseph Francis Thorning, *Religious Liberty in Transition* (Washington, D.C.: Catholic University of America, 1931), 4.

29. The First Amendment, it should be emphasized, denied the national government jurisdiction over religion not because religion was thought unimportant or because governmental support for religion was generally regarded as improper but, rather, because jurisdiction in issues pertaining to "establishment" and government regulation of religion were thought appropriately reserved by the states.

30. James McClellan, *Joseph Story and the American Constitution: A Study in Political and Legal Thought* (Norman: University of Oklahoma Press, 1971), 146. Note also Jefferson's letter to James Madison in July 1788: "I hope therefore a bill of rights will be formed to guard the people against the federal government, as they are already guarded against their state governments in most instances." Letter from Jefferson to James Madison, 31 July 1788, *Papers of Jefferson*, 13:443. Samuel Adams similarly opined: "I mean, my friend, to let you know how deeply I am impressed with a sense of the Importance of Amendments; that the good People may clearly see the distinction, for there is a distinction—between the *federal* Powers vested in Congress, and the *sovereign* Authority belonging to the several States, which is the Palladium of the private, and personal rights of the Citizens." Letter from Samuel Adams to Richard

Henry Lee, 24 August 1789, in *Creating the Bill of Rights: The Documentary Record from the First Federal Congress*, ed. Helen E. Veit, Kenneth R. Bowling, and Charlene Bangs Bickford (Baltimore, Md.: Johns Hopkins University Press, 1991), 286; letter from Samuel Adams to Elbridge Gerry, 22 August 1789 in *Creating the Bill of Rights*, 284–285.

31. James McClellan, "The Making and the Unmaking of the Establishment Clause," in *A Blueprint for Judicial Reform*, ed. Patrick B. McGuigan and Randall R. Rader (Washington, D.C.: Free Congress Research and Education Foundation, 1981), 295, 314–315. See also Akhil Reed Amar, *The Bill of Rights: Creation and Reconstruction* (New Haven, Conn.: Yale University Press, 1998), 34 ("The original establishment clause, on a close reading, is not antiestablishment but pro-states' rights; it is agnostic on the substantive issue of establishment versus nonestablishment and simply calls for the issue to be decided locally.").

32. Corwin, "The Supreme Court as National School Board," 106. See also Howe, *The Garden and the Wilderness*, 29 ("the federalism of the First Amendment may be even more important than its libertarianism."); Amar, *The Bill of Rights*, 246 (establishment clause, "as originally written, stood as a pure federalism provision"). For other works that argue that the specific purpose of the First Amendment religion provisions was to preserve state sovereignty over religious matters, see Amar, *The Bill of Rights*, 32–42; Akhil Reed Amar, "The Bill of Rights as a Constitution," *Yale Law Journal* 100 (1991): 1131–1210; Chester James Antieau, Arthur T. Downey, and Edward C. Roberts, *Freedom from Federal Establishment: Formation and Early History of the First Amendment Religion Clauses* (Milwaukee: Bruce, 1964); Jonathan P. Brose, "In Birmingham They Love the Governor: Why the Fourteenth Amendment Does Not Incorporate the Establishment Clause," *Ohio Northern University Law Review* 24 (1998): 1–30; Bybee, "Taking Liberties with the First Amendment: Congress, Section 5, and the Religious Freedom Restoration Act," 1539–1633; Daniel O. Conkle, "Toward a General Theory of the Establishment Clause," *Northwestern University Law Review* 82 (1988): 1113–1194; Esbeck, "The Establishment Clause as a Structural Restraint on Governmental Power," 1–113; Wilber G. Katz, *Religion and American Constitutions* (Evanston, Ill.: Northwestern University Press, 1964), 8–10; Clifton B. Kruse, Jr., "The Historical Meaning and Judicial Construction of the Establishment of Religion Clause of the First Amendment," *Washburn Law Journal* 2 (1962): 65–141; Kurt T. Lash, "The Second Adoption of the Establishment Clause: The Rise of the Nonestablishment Principle," *Arizona State Law Journal* 27 (1995): 1085–1154 (arguing that the "original Establishment Clause expressed the principle of federalism"; however, the Establishment Clause was adopted a second time through the Fourteenth Amendment, and it then prohibited both state and federal governments from supporting or suppressing religion); James McClellan, "Hand's Writing on the Wall of Separation: The Significance of *Jaffree* in Future Cases

on Religious Establishment," in *How Does the Constitution Protect Religious Freedom?*, ed. Robert A. Goldwin and Art Kaufman (Washington, D.C.: American Enterprise Institute for Public Policy Research, 1987), 43–68; William K. Lietzau, "Rediscovering the Establishment Clause: Federalism and the Rollback of Incorporation," *DePaul Law Review* 39 (1990): 1191–1234; Note, "Rethinking the Incorporation of the Establishment Clause: A Federalist View," *Harvard Law Review* 105 (1992): 1700–1719; Stuart D. Poppel, "Federalism, Fundamental Fairness, and the Religion Clauses," *Cumberland Law Review* 25 (1995): 247–308; Joseph M. Snee, "Religious Disestablishment and the Fourteenth Amendment," *Washington University Law Quarterly* 1954 (1954): 371–407; Michael A. Paulsen, "Religion, Equality, and the Constitution: An Equal Protection Approach to Establishment Clause Adjudication," *Notre Dame Law Review* 61 (1986): 311–371; William C. Porth and Robert P. George, "Trimming the Ivy: A Bicentennial Re-Examination of the Establishment Clause," *West Virginia Law Review* 90 (1987): 109–170; Steven D. Smith, *Foreordained Failure: The Quest for a Constitutional Principle of Religious Freedom* (New York: Oxford University Press, 1995), 17–54.

33. *Barron v. Baltimore*, 32 U.S. (7 Peters) 243, 250 (1833).

34. *Permoli v. Municipality*, 44 U.S. (3 Howard) 589, 609 (1845).

35. Joseph Story, *Commentaries on the Constitution of the United States*, 3 vols. (Boston: Hilliard, Gray, 1833), 3:730, sec. 1873.

36. Story, *Commentaries on the Constitution of the United States*, 3:731, sec. 1873. See also ibid., 3:728, sec. 1871 ("The real object of the [first] amendment was . . . to exclude all rivalry among Christian sects, and to prevent any national ecclesiastical establishment, which should give to an hierarchy the exclusive patronage of the national government.").

37. This jurisdictional view was shared by Jefferson's contemporaries and was expressed in the ratification debates. See, for example, speeches of James Madison (Va.), in Jonathan Elliot, ed., *The Debates in the Several State Conventions on the Adoption of the Federal Constitution*, 2d ed., 5 vols. (Philadelphia: J. B. Lippincott, 1836) [hereinafter Elliot's *Debates*], 3:330 (12 June 1788) ("There is not a shadow of right in the general [federal] government to intermeddle with religion. Its least interference with it would be a most flagrant usurpation."), ibid., 3:93 (6 June 1788) ("The government has no jurisdiction over [religion]"); James Iredell (N.C.), in Elliot's *Debates*, 4:194–195 (30 July 1788) ("They [the Federal Congress] certainly have no authority to interfere in the establishment of any religion whatsoever; and I am astonished that any gentleman should conceive they have. . . . Each state . . . must be left to the operation of its own principles."); Richard Dobbs Spaight (N.C.), in Elliot's *Debates*, 4:208 (30 July 1788) ("As to the subject of religion . . . [n]o power is given to the general government to interfere with it at all. Any act of Congress on this subject would be a usurpation."); Edmund Randolph (Va.), in Elliot's *Debates*,

3:204 (10 June 1788) ("no power is given expressly to Congress over religion"), ibid., 3:469 (15 June 1788) ("No part of the Constitution, even if strictly construed, will justify a conclusion that the general government can take away or impair the freedom of religion."); James Wilson (Pa.), in Elliot's *Debates*, 2:455 (4 December 1787) ("we are told that there is no security for the rights of conscience. I ask the honorable gentleman, what part of this system puts it in the power of Congress to attack those rights? When there is no power to attack, it is idle to prepare the means of defence."); Tench Coxe (Pa.), "A Freeman I" (23 January 1788), in John P. Kaminski and Gaspare J. Saladino, eds., *Commentaries on the Constitution: Public and Private*, vol. 3, *18 December 1787 to 31 January 1788*, vol. XV of *The Documentary History of the Ratification of the Constitution* (Madison: State Historical Society of Wisconsin, 1984), 458 ("[Congress] cannot interfere with . . . religious . . . societies"), "A Freeman II" (30 January 1788), in ibid., 508 ("Having seen what Congress *cannot do*, let us now proceed to examine what the state governments *must or may do*. . . . 2dly. Every regulation relating to religion, or the property of religious bodies, must be made by the state governments, since no powers affecting those points are contained in the constitution."); Oliver Ellsworth (Conn.), "The Landholder, VI" (10 December 1787), in Paul Leicester Ford, ed., *Essays on the Constitution of the United States, Published during Its Discussion by the People, 1787–1788* (reprinted New York: Burt Franklin, 1970), 164 ("[There is no declaration in the proposed constitution to preserve] liberty of conscience . . . ; it is enough that congress have no power to prohibit either, and can have no temptation. This objection is answered in that the states have all the power originally, and congress have only what the states grant them."); Roger Sherman (Conn.), in *The Debates and Proceedings in the Congress of the United States*, ed. Joseph Gales (Washington: Gales and Seaton, 1834), 1st Cong., 1st sess., 1:730 (15 August 1789) ("Mr. Sherman [in the debates on the religion provision in the First Congress] thought the amendment altogether unnecessary, inasmuch as Congress had no authority whatever delegated to them by the Constitution to make religious establishments.").

38. Jefferson, Address to the General Assembly of Rhode Island and Providence Plantations, 26 May 1801, *Writings of Jefferson*, 10:263. See also letter from Jefferson to Joseph C. Cabell, 2 February 1816, *Writings of Jefferson*, 14:421 ("[T]he way to have good and safe government is not to trust it all to one, but to divide it among the many, distributing to every one exactly the functions he is competent to. Let the national government be entrusted with the defence of the nation, and its foreign and federal relations; the State governments with the civil rights, laws, police and administration of what concerns the State generally.").

39. Letter from Jefferson to Mrs. John Adams, 11 September 1804, *Writings of Jefferson*, 11:51. See Jean M. Yarbrough, *American Virtues: Thomas Jefferson*

192 | Notes to Chapter 4

on the Character of a Free People (Lawrence: University Press of Kansas, 1998), 192 ("although Jefferson opposed the Alien and Sedition Acts on the ground that the national government has no power to regulate the rights of speech and press, he has no objections to the states abridging these very liberties").

40. Jefferson, "Drafts of the Kentucky Resolutions of 1798" [November 1798], *The Works of Thomas Jefferson*, ed. Paul Leicester Ford, Federal Edition, 12 vols. (New York: G. P. Putnam's Sons, 1904–1905), 8:463–465. See generally Snee, "Religious Disestablishment and the Fourteenth Amendment," 390–392; Comment, "Jefferson and the Church-State Wall," 654–655; Kurt T. Lash, "Power and the Subject of Religion," *Ohio State Law Journal* 59 (1998): 1094–1095 (highlighting that Jefferson "read the First Amendment in conjunction with the Tenth and concluded that the restrictions of the religion clauses on the federal government were sweeping and comprehensive"); Lash, "The Second Adoption of the Free Exercise Clause: Religious Exemptions Under the Fourteenth Amendment," *Northwestern University Law Review* 88 (1994): 1111–1114 (same).

41. Samuel Miller, *The Life of Samuel Miller, D.D., LL.D.* (Philadelphia: Claxton, Remsen and Haffelfinger, 1869), 235. Miller was a self-described "warm and zealous partisan in favor of Mr. Jefferson's administration" and political principles. Long afterward, Miller wrote, he became "aware of the rottenness of his [Jefferson's] *moral* and *religious* opinions," and "my respect for him was exchanged for contempt and abhorrence. I now believe Mr. Jefferson to have been one of the meanest and basest of men. His own writings evince a hypocrisy, a selfishness, an artful, intriguing, underhand spirit, a contemptible envy of better men than himself, a blasphemous impiety, and a moral profligacy, which no fair, honest mind, to say nothing of piety, can contemplate without abhorrence." Ibid., 235, 131–132. For Miller's commentary on his correspondence with the president, see ibid., 235–237.

42. Letter from Jefferson to the Reverend Samuel Miller, 23 January 1808, *Writings of Jefferson*, 11:428–430 (emphasis in the original).

In 1832, President Andrew Jackson was asked to designate a national day for public "fasting, humiliation and prayer" in order to avert a threatening cholera epidemic. Following Jefferson's lead, he declined to issue a religious proclamation for essentially the same reasons given by his predecessor. Jackson outlined these reasons in a letter dated 12 June 1832 to the Synod of the Reformed Church of North America:

> I have the pleasure to acknowledge the receipt of your letter of the 10th instant submitting to me an extract from the minutes of the session of the general synod of the reformed church of North America relative to the general observance of a day of fasting, humiliation and prayer, which it is recommended that the President of the United States should appoint.

Whilst I concur with the synod in the efficacy of prayer, and in the hope that our country may be preserved from the attack of Pestilence and "that the judgments now abroad in the earth may be sanctified to the good of nations", I am constrained to decline the appointment of any period or mode as proper for the public manifestation of this reliance. I could not do otherwise without transcending those limits which are prescribed by the Constitution for the President and without feeling that I might in some degree disturb the security which religion now enjoys in this country in its complete seperation [*sic*] from the political concerns of the General Government.

It is the province of the pulpits and the State Governments to recommend the mode by which the people may best attest their reliance on the protecting arm of the almighty in times of great public distress. Whether the apprehension that cholera will visit our land furnishes a proper occasion for their solemn notice, I must therefore leave to their own consideration.

Letter from Andrew Jackson to the Synod of the Reformed Church, 12 June 1832, *Correspondence of Andrew Jackson*, ed. John Spencer Bassett (Washington, D.C.: Carnegie Institution of Washington, 1929), 4:447.

43. U.S. Constitution, amendment X.

44. See Amar, *The Bill of Rights*, 34 ("Jefferson . . . appears to have understood the states'-rights aspects of the original establishment clause.").

45. See letter from Jefferson to Monsieur Destutt de Tracy, 26 January 1811, *Writings of Jefferson*, 13:19 ("the true barriers of our liberty in this country are our State governments"). For similar statements affirming the vital role of states in the federal system, see Jefferson, First Inaugural Address, 4 March 1801, *Writings of Jefferson*, 3:321 ("I deem [one of] the essential principles of our government . . . the support of the state governments in all their rights, as the most competent administrations for our domestic concerns and the surest bulwarks against anti-republican tendencies"); Jefferson, Address to the General Assembly of Rhode Island and Providence Plantations, 26 May 1801, *Writings of Jefferson*, 10:263; letter from Jefferson to Joseph C. Cabell, 2 February 1816, *Writings of Jefferson*, 14:421; letter from Jefferson to Charles Hammond, 18 August 1821, *Writings of Jefferson*, 15:332; letter from Jefferson to Judge William Johnson, 12 June 1823, *Writings of Jefferson*, 15:448–451; Jefferson, The Solemn Declaration and Protest of the Commonwealth of Virginia, on the Principles of the Constitution of the United States of America, and on the Violations of them (1825), *Writings of Jefferson*, 17:442–446. See generally J. M. O'Neill, *Religion and Education under the Constitution* (New York: Harper and Brothers, 1949), 66–72 (surveying Jefferson's views on the separation of state and federal authority).

46. See *Atascadero State Hospital v. Scanlon*, 473 U.S. 234, 242 (1985), quoting *Garcia v. San Antonio Metropolitan Transit Authority*, 469 U.S. 528,

572 (1985) (Powell, J., dissenting) ("The 'constitutionally mandated balance of power' between the States and the Federal Government was adopted by the Framers to ensure the protection of 'our fundamental liberties.'").

47. Edward S. Corwin described this portion of the second inaugural address, perhaps offered in response to criticisms of Jefferson's refusal to appoint days for national religious observances, as a "more deliberate, more carefully considered evaluation by Jefferson of the religious clauses of the First Amendment" than the Danbury letter. Corwin, "The Supreme Court as National School Board," 106. See also Anson Phelps Stokes, *Church and State in the United States*, 3 vols. (New York: Harper and Brothers, 1950), 1:335 (stating that in this passage of the address Jefferson "doubtless had in mind particularly his well-known objection to presidential Thanksgiving Day proclamations"); Gaustad, *Sworn on the Altar of God*, 99–100 (indicating that this passage explicitly reaffirmed Jefferson's opposition to "presidential proclamations pertaining to religion"); *The Jeffersonian Cyclopedia*, ed. John P. Foley, 2 vols. (New York: Russell and Russell, 1900), 1:324, sec. 2902 (quoting this passage under the heading of "FAST-DAYS").

48. Jefferson, Second Inaugural Address, 4 March 1805, *Writings of Jefferson*, 3:378. The apparent source of this particular jurisdictional statement concerning church-state relations was comments offered by James Madison on a draft of Jefferson's second inaugural address. Madison recommended the following amendment to the speech, which was substantially incorporated into the final text: "as religious exercises, could therefore be neither controuled nor prescribed by us. They have accordingly been left as the Constitution found them, under the direction and discipline acknowledged within the several States." James Morton Smith, ed., *The Republic of Letters: The Correspondence between Thomas Jefferson and James Madison, 1776–1826*, 3 vols. (New York: W. W. Norton, 1995), 3:1364.

49. See Cord, *Separation of Church and State*, 115 ("By this phrase Jefferson could only have meant that the 'wall of separation' was erected 'between church and State' in regard to possible federal action. . . . Therefore, to leave the impression that Jefferson's 'separation' statement was a universal one concerning the whole of the federal and state political system is extremely misleading."); M. Stanton Evans, *The Theme Is Freedom: Religion, Politics, and the American Tradition* (Washington, D.C.: Regnery Publishing, 1994), 288 ("The wall of separation, instead, was *between the federal government and the states*, [and was] meant to make sure the central authority didn't meddle with the customs of local jurisdictions."); O'Neill, *Religion and Education under the Constitution*, 67–69, 79–83 (arguing that Jefferson's "wall" separated the federal government and one religion); Yarbrough, *American Virtues*, 189 ("Nor for all his opposition to established churches, and the special privileges they conveyed upon their members, is he [Jefferson] willing to interfere with established reli-

gions in other states. The famous 'wall of separation' that Jefferson believes the First Amendment erects between church and state is specifically intended to apply only to the federal government. . . . In the clash between religious liberty and federalism, Jefferson threw his weight behind the federal principle. If states wished to establish churches or otherwise to enforce piety and religious worship, Jefferson was prepared, however grudgingly, to countenance these actions for the sake of republican self-government, trusting that with proper instruction the people in the different states would eventually get it right without any interference from the national government."); Snee, "Religious Disestablishment and the Fourteenth Amendment," 389 (arguing that Jefferson's "wall" affirmed the principle of federalism); Comment, "Jefferson and the Church-State Wall," 645, 656–659 (arguing that Jefferson's "wall" was a study in federalism and that the "wall" described in the Danbury letter was erected only against the federal government).

50. Draft letter from Jefferson to Messrs. Nehemiah Dodge, Ephraim Robbins, and Stephen S. Nelson, a committee of the Danbury Baptist association in the state of Connecticut, 1 January 1802. This sentence parallels an acknowledgment made in the letter from the Baptists: "we are sensible that the President of the united States, is not the national Legislator, & also sensible that the national government cannot destroy the Laws of each State." Letter from a committee of the Danbury Baptist association to Jefferson, 7 October 1801, The Papers of Thomas Jefferson (Manuscript Division, Library of Congress), Series 1, Box 87, August 30, 1801–October 15, 1801; Presidential Papers Microfilm, Thomas Jefferson Papers (Manuscript Division, Library of Congress), Series 1, Reel 24, June 26, 1801–November 14, 1801. Thus, language in both the Baptists' letter and Jefferson's response confirms that it was generally understood and unchallenged, as a principle of federalism, that religion was a subject of state jurisdiction.

51. In the light of the text and structure of the First Amendment, Jefferson undoubtedly thought the First Amendment religion provisions were a restriction on civil government only and not a restraint on religion (or the role of religion in public life). Inasmuch as a wall is a bilateral, rather than unilateral, barrier that not only prevents civil government from invading the ecclesiastical domain, as intended by the architects of the First Amendment, but also prohibits religion and the church from influencing the conduct of civil government, then the "wall" metaphor mischaracterizes the First Amendment. The various parallel guarantees in the First Amendment were entirely a check or restraint on civil government, specifically the national legislature. The free press guarantee, for example, was not written to protect the civil state from the press; rather, it was designed to protect a free and independent press from control or interference by the federal government. Similarly, the religion provisions were added to the Constitution to protect religion and religious institutions from

rough or corrupting interference by the federal government, and not to protect the civil state from the influence of, or overreaching by, religion. In other words, the First Amendment prohibition on religious establishment was a clear restraint on the power of civil government (i.e., the federal government) to give legal preference to any single sect or combination of sects or to invade the religious domain. Any construction of Jefferson's "wall" that imposes restraints on entities other than civil government exceeds the limitations imposed by the First Amendment, from which the "wall" metaphor was explicitly derived. See Stephen L. Carter, *God's Name in Vain: The Wrongs and Rights of Religion in Politics* (New York: Basic Books, 2000), 67–81 (arguing that the First Amendment wall is a single-sided wall because the "religion clause of the First Amendment is designed to limit what the state can do, not what the church can do."); Stephen L. Carter, *The Culture of Disbelief: How American Law and Politics Trivialize Religious Devotion* (New York: Basic Books, 1993), 105, 115 ("the metaphorical separation of church and state originated in an effort to protect religion from the state, not the state from religion."); Richard John Neuhaus, "Contending for the Future: Overcoming the Pfefferian Inversion," *Journal of Law and Religion* 8 (1990): 119 ("The threat perceived by the framers and by sensible people since their time is the threat that government poses to religion. The establishment of a religion, the framers correctly believed, would violate the freedom of those who dissent from the established belief. . . . The religion clause [of the First Amendment], I am arguing, is entirely a check upon government, not a check upon religion. . . . The religion clause is not then, as many claim, a check upon both government and religion, nor is it a clause in which two claims are to be 'balanced' against one another. The religion clause is not to protect the state from the church but to protect the church from the state."); Richard John Neuhaus, "Establishment Is Not *the* Issue," *Religion and Society Report* 4, no. 6 (June 1987): 1, 3 (same).

52. In a preliminary draft of the Danbury letter, Jefferson raised another jurisdictional consideration. Jefferson concluded that he was unable to take executive action on religious matters since he confined himself "to the duties of my station, which are merely temporal." In short, the secular (or "temporal"), as well as the federal, character of his office denied him the authority to issue religious proclamations. Draft letter from Jefferson to Messrs. Nehemiah Dodge, Ephraim Robbins, and Stephen S. Nelson, a committee of the Danbury Baptist association in the state of Connecticut, 1 January 1802. He reiterated this point in his letter to Samuel Miller: "every one must act according to the dictates of his own reason, and mine tells me that civil powers alone have been given to the President of the United States, and no authority to direct the religious exercises of his constituents." Letter from Jefferson to the Reverend Samuel Miller, 23 January 1808.

53. See Lash, "The Second Adoption of the Establishment Clause: The Rise of the Nonestablishment Principle," 1096–1097.

54. *The Debates and Proceedings in the Congress of the United States*, ed. Joseph Gales, 42 vols. (Washington, D.C.: Gales and Seaton, 1834–1856), 1st Cong., 1st sess., 1:914 (25 September 1789); *Documentary History of the First Federal Congress of the United States of America, March 4, 1789–March 3, 1791*, ed. Linda Grant De Pauw, vol. I, *Senate Legislative Journal* (Baltimore: Johns Hopkins University Press, 1972), 1:197; *Journal of the First Session of the Senate of the United States of America* (New York: Thomas Greenleaf, 1789), 154 (26 September 1789).

55. *U.S. Statutes at Large* 1 (1789): 71 (22 September 1789).

56. For a discussion of the practices of Jefferson's two presidential predecessors in appointing days for public thanksgiving and religious observance, see Stokes, *Church and State in the United States*, 1:486–491.

57. See Rodney K. Smith, *Public Prayer and the Constitution: A Case Study in Constitutional Interpretation* (Wilmington, Del.: Scholarly Resources, 1987), 62; Daniel L. Dreisbach, "'Sowing Useful Truths and Principles': The Danbury Baptists, Thomas Jefferson, and the 'Wall of Separation,'" *Journal of Church and State* 39 (1997): 465–466.

58. See Philip Hamburger, *Separation of Church and State* (Cambridge, Mass.: Harvard University Press, 2002), chap. 7.

59. In *Cantwell v. Connecticut*, 310 U.S. 296, 303 (1940), and *Everson v. Board of Education*, 330 U.S. 1, 15 (1947), the First Amendment free exercise and nonestablishment of religion provisions, respectively, were incorporated into the "liberties" protected by the Fourteenth Amendment due process of law clause, thereby guarding these First Amendment provisions from infringement by the states. The present discussion is about Jefferson's construction of his "wall" and not about post–Fourteenth Amendment interpretations of the metaphor. It should be noted that if the jurisdictional interpretation of the First Amendment, and hence the "wall," is correct, then not only is it impossible (not to mention illogical) to "incorporate" into the "liberty" protected by the Fourteenth Amendment that which is essentially the structural assignment of authority over a specific subject matter to a particular level or branch of government (as opposed to a libertarian device that confers judicially enforceable, substantive rights upon individuals), but also the First Amendment "cannot be incorporated without eviscerating its raison d'etre." Note, "Rethinking the Incorporation of the Establishment Clause," 1709. See also Amar, *The Bill of Rights*, 34, 41–42 (as primarily a federalism provision, the establishment clause, like the Tenth Amendment, seems difficult to incorporate against the states); Donald L. Drakeman, *Church-State Constitutional Issues: Making Sense of the Establishment Clause* (Westport, Conn.: Greenwood Press, 1991), 111 (incorporation

"may have stood the eighteenth-century framers' decision on its head"); Smith, *Foreordained Failure*, 49–50; John F. Wilson, "Religion, Political Culture, and the Law," *DePaul Law Review* 41 (1992): 835–836 ("at one level of irony, the religion clauses of the First Amendment have become appropriated to specific purposes directly opposed to those that led to their adoption."); Porth and George, "Trimming the Ivy," 138-139; John E. Dunsford, "Prayer in the Well: Some Heretical Reflections on the Establishment Syndrome," *Utah Law Review* 1984 (1984): 20–21 ("It is a supreme irony of history that the establishment clause was crafted by the framers for a purpose exactly opposite from the one to which the Supreme Court has put it."); Conkle, "Toward a General Theory of the Establishment Clause," 1141; *Abington School District v. Schempp*, 374 U.S. 203, 309–310 (1963) (Stewart, J., dissenting) ("As a matter of history, the First Amendment was adopted solely as a limitation upon the newly created National Government. The events leading to its adoption strongly suggest that the Establishment Clause was primarily an attempt to insure that Congress not only would be powerless to establish a national church, but would also be unable to interfere with existing state establishments. . . . Each State was left free to go its own way and pursue its own policy with respect to religion. . . . [I]t is not without irony that a constitutional provision evidently designed to leave the States free to go their own way should now have become a restriction upon their autonomy."). Pursuant to this view, incorporating the nonestablishment provision (and Jefferson's "wall") is as nonsensical as incorporating the Tenth Amendment.

60. The Fourteenth Amendment was adopted more than six decades after Jefferson wrote to the Danbury Baptists; therefore, this study, which is concerned with Jefferson's understanding of the First Amendment and the "wall," gives only passing notice to the impact of the Fourteenth Amendment on the First Amendment and the "wall."

61. Letter from Jefferson to Messrs. Nehemiah Dodge, Ephraim Robbins, and Stephen S. Nelson, a committee of the Danbury Baptist association in the state of Connecticut, 1 January 1802, The Papers of Thomas Jefferson (Manuscript Division, Library of Congress), Series 1, Box 89, December 2, 1801–January 1, 1802; Presidential Papers Microfilm, Thomas Jefferson Papers (Manuscript Division, Library of Congress), Series 1, Reel 25, November 15, 1801–March 31, 1802. In the last sentence of the second paragraph of the Danbury letter, Jefferson wrote: "adhering to this expression of the supreme will of the nation in behalf of the rights of conscience, I shall see with sincere satisfaction the progress of those sentiments which tend to restore to man all his natural rights, convinced he has no natural right in opposition to his social duties." "[T]his expression of the supreme will of the nation" is a reference to the First Amendment, which was cited in the preceding sentence and, as previously noted, applied only to the federal government. In the second clause of the sen-

tence, it is not clear whether Jefferson was referring to a "progress of those sentiments" promoting the rights of conscience among individuals vis-à-vis the federal regime only, *pursuant to the First Amendment,* or whether he was looking forward to the "progress of those sentiments" among citizens in the states because state governments voluntarily adopted the First Amendment model. He certainly did not believe that the states were subject to the First Amendment "wall."

62. James McClellan made this same point, forcefully repudiating the Supreme Court's "incorporation" of the First Amendment and, by extension, Jefferson's "wall" in recent church-state jurisprudence: "To apply Jefferson's wall of separation theory to present cases, as the Supreme Court has done, is to lift it wholly out of context. Jefferson believed that the states were free to prescribe the nature of religious liberty within their respective jurisdictions. . . . The application of the Jeffersonian theory *against* the states, and its utilization by the federal courts in deciding how a state should behave with respect to civil liberties, is wholly contrary to the very basis of the Jeffersonian philosophy of states' rights; and it is incompatible with Jefferson's strong desire to resist the increasing powers of the Supreme Court. To say that the national courts instead of the various state courts should possess final authority in the enforcement of an absolute wall of separation between church and state is similar to arguing that the powers of the states are best preserved by transferring those powers to the federal government." McClellan, *Joseph Story and the American Constitution,* 143–144.

63. This belief may have informed Jefferson's revision of the Danbury letter. Jefferson chose not to follow Levi Lincoln's recommendation to acknowledge the propriety of state traditions of "observing fasts and thanksgivings in performance of proclamations from their respective Executives." Letter from Levi Lincoln to Jefferson, 1 January 1802, The Papers of Thomas Jefferson (Manuscript Division, Library of Congress), Series 1, Box 89, December 2, 1801–January 1, 1802; Presidential Papers Microfilm, Thomas Jefferson Papers (Manuscript Division, Library of Congress), Series 1, Reel 25, November 15, 1801–March 31, 1802. Instead, he avoided the issue by deleting the entire sentence in question. Jefferson's desire to encourage states to erect and maintain their own walls of separation may have been the reason he did not adopt Lincoln's advice.

64. See R. Freeman Butts, *The American Tradition in Religion and Education* (Boston: Beacon Press, 1950), 95 (arguing "that the federal government did not have the power under the Constitution to decide for the states what their attitudes toward religious proclamations should be, but Jefferson's whole history in Virginia showed clearly that he thought the attitude of the states should be the same as that of the federal government.").

65. Jefferson was concerned that a civil magistrate's recommendation for a day of public fasting and prayer would be, in effect, indistinguishable from a

mandatory prescription for such exercises and thereby would impose penalties on those who for reasons of conscience failed to comply. This argument applies equally to state and federal magistrates. Jefferson further argued that it is in the interests of religion to direct its own exercises, discipline, and doctrines and not to vest such matters in the hands of civil government.

66. This language is borrowed from Steven D. Smith's commentary on the First Amendment religion clauses. Smith, *Foreordained Failure*, 17. The framers and ratifiers of the religion clauses, Smith argued, deliberately declined to adopt a principle or theory of religious liberty. "They consciously chose not to answer the religion question, and they were able for the most part to avoid it . . . because of the way in which they answered the jurisdiction question—that is, by assigning the religion question to the states." Accordingly, it is futile to locate in or to extrapolate from the original meaning of the religion clauses a substantive right or principle of religious liberty. In other words, the First Amendment was calculated not to articulate a principle or theory of religious liberty but merely to specify who (or what level or branch of civil government) shall substantively address this subject matter. Ibid., 21, 25. See also Amar, *The Bill of Rights*, 34, 41–42, 246 (First Amendment was agnostic on the substantive issue of establishment versus nonestablishment and simply left matters of religion to be decided at the state level).

NOTES TO CHAPTER 5

1. Richard Hooker, *Of the Laws of Ecclesiastical Polity: Preface, Book I, Book VIII*, ed. Arthur Stephen McGrade (Cambridge: Cambridge University Press, 1989), VIII.1.2 (emphasis in the original).

2. Roger Williams, "Mr. Cotton's Letter Lately Printed, Examined and Answered," in Perry Miller, *Roger Williams: His Contribution to the American Tradition* (Indianapolis, Ind.: Bobbs-Merrill, 1953; reprinted New York: Atheneum, 1962), 98.

3. [James Burgh], *Crito, or Essays on Various Subjects*, 2 vols. (London, 1766, 1767), 2:119 (emphasis in the original).

4. This chapter focuses on constructions of a *wall* between religious and civil authorities that predate Jefferson. For an insightful, comprehensive examination of "separation of church and state" as a concept and as a constitutional standard in American history, see Philip Hamburger, *Separation of Church and State* (Cambridge, Mass.: Harvard University Press, 2002). Hamburger and others have noted that separationist themes and rhetoric have long been a feature of Western discourse. For one influential example that would have been familiar to Jefferson, see John Locke, *A Letter Concerning Toleration* (1689), in *The Works of John Locke*, 10 vols. (London, 1823), 6:9 ("I esteem it above all things necessary to distinguish exactly the business of civil government from

that of religion, and to settle the just bounds that lie between the one and the other."), 6:21 ("the church itself is a thing absolutely separate and distinct from the commonwealth. The boundaries on both sides are fixed and immovable. He jumbles heaven and earth together, the things most remote and opposite, who mixes these societies, which are, in their original, end, business, and in every thing, perfectly distinct, and infinitely different from each other.").

5. "My Kingdom is not of this world," Jesus responded to the interrogation by Pontius Pilate (John 18:36 KJV). When the Pharisees sought to trap Him by asking whether it was lawful to pay taxes to Caesar, Jesus answered: "Render unto Caesar the things which are Caesar's; and unto God the things that are God's" (Matthew 22:21 KJV; Mark 12:17; Luke 20:25; see also Romans 13:7). Christian scholars throughout the ages have elaborated on these and other sayings recorded in the Gospels that suggest a differentiation between the spiritual and the temporal kingdoms. A related theme, sounded by the Apostle Paul, called on believers to separate themselves from unbelievers (2 Corinthians 6:17; see also 2 Corinthians 6:14 KJV: "Be ye not unequally yoked together with unbelievers: for what fellowship hath righteousness with unrighteousness? And what communion hath light with darkness?"). This, too, informed the church-state arrangements adopted by some Christian sects.

6. John Witte, Jr., *Religion and the American Constitutional Experiment: Essential Rights and Liberties* (Boulder, Colo.: Westview Press, 2000), 14. See also John Witte, Jr., *Law and Protestantism: The Legal Teachings of the Lutheran Reformation* (Cambridge: Cambridge University Press, 2002), chaps. 2–4.

7. Martin Luther, *To the Christian Nobility of the German Nation* (1520), in *Three Treatises* (Philadelphia: Fortress Press, 1970), 12, 16; see also ibid., 11 ("these walls of straw and paper"). See also Dallin H. Oaks, introduction, *The Wall between Church and State*, ed. Dallin H. Oaks (Chicago: University of Chicago Press, 1963), 2 (noting Martin Luther's reference to walls).

8. John Calvin, *Institutes of the Christian Religion* (1559), ed. John T. McNeill, trans. Ford Lewis Battles, 2 vols., The Library of Christian Classics (Philadelphia: Westminster Press, 1960), bk. 3, chap. 19.15; bk. 4, chap. 11.3; bk. 4, chap. 20.1. See also John Witte, Jr., "Moderate Religious Liberty in the Theology of John Calvin," in *Religious Liberty in Western Thought*, ed. Noel B. Reynolds and W. Cole Durham, Jr. (Atlanta: Scholars Press, 1996), 112–118.

In his *Commentaries*, Calvin used a "wall of separation" metaphor on several occasions, usually to illustrate the separation of God's chosen people from the world. See, for example, John Calvin, *Commentaries on the Prophet Jeremiah and the Lamentations*, trans. John Owen (Grand Rapids, Mich.: William B. Eerdmans, 1950), 5:63 (Lecture One Hundred and Seventy-Third) (Jeremiah 49:6) ("But though God built, as it were, a wall to separate his people from aliens, it was yet his will to give some preludes of his favour, and of the calling of the Gentiles."); Calvin, *Commentaries on the Book of Genesis*, trans. John King (Grand Rapids, Mich.: William B. Eerdmans, 1948), 2:400 (Genesis 47:3) ("Now, however, their [Joseph's brethren] mean and contemptible mode of life [referencing that Egyptians abhorred shepherds, the occupation of Joseph's brethren] proves a wall of separation between them and the Egyptians. . . . [T]here is no doubt that the Lord directed their tongues, so as . . . to keep the body of the Church pure and distinct. This passage also teaches us, how much better it is to possess a remote corner in the courts of the Lord, than to dwell in the midst of palaces, beyond the precincts of the Church. Therefore, let us not think it grievous to secure a sacred union with the sons of God, by enduring the contempt and reproaches of the world."); Calvin, *Commentary upon the Acts of the Apostles*, ed. Henry Beveridge, trans. Christopher Fetherstone (Grand Rapids, Mich.: Baker Book House, 1996), 1:432–433 (Acts 10:28) ("Finally, if faith alone do purge and purify the hearts of men, unbelief doth make the same profane. But Peter compareth the Jews and the Gentiles together in this place; and because the wall of separation was pulled down, and the covenant of life is now common to them both alike, he saith that those are not to be counted aliens who are made partakers of God's adoption.").

9. Heinrich Bullinger, *Anabaptist Origins* (1561), in Walter Klaassen, ed., *Anabaptism in Outline: Selected Primary Sources* (Scottdale, Pa.: Herald Press, 1981), 300.

10. Hans J. Hillerbrand, "An Early Anabaptist Treatise on the Christian and the State," *Mennonite Quarterly Review* 32 (1958): 30–31. See also Harold S. Bender, *The Anabaptists and Religious Liberty in the Sixteenth Century* (Philadelphia: Fortress Press, 1970), 1–22; Hans J. Hillerbrand, "The Anabaptist View of the State," *Mennonite Quarterly Review* 32 (1958): 83–110; Walter Klaassen, "The Anabaptist Understanding of the Separation of the Church," *Church History* 46 (December 1977): 421–436; Klaassen, ed., *Anabaptism in Outline: Selected Primary Sources*, 244–301.

11. Letter from Menno Simons to "J.V." [perhaps Johannes Voetius, a Dutch jurist], December 1548. Menno enclosed a copy of the Schleitheim Confession (1527) in this correspondence with "J.V." This document in the Rijksarchief in the Hague, Netherlands, was brought to my attention by John Witte, Jr.

The Anabaptist principle of church-state separation, illustrated by Menno Simons's "wall of separation," was based on theological grounds different from those that informed the separationist doctrines of others in the Reformed Protestant tradition and was certainly far removed from the secular political precepts upon which the separationist principles of the Enlightenment rested. See John H. Redekop, "The State and the Free Church," in *Kingdom, Cross, and Community*, ed. John Richard Burkholder and Calvin Redekop (Scottdale, Pa.: Herald Press, 1976), 181 ("Theories about 'a wall of separation,' especially as set forth in early American history, have their root in political, constitutional, and juridical thought, not in theology or the assertions of early Anabaptist theologians.").

I am indebted to John Witte, Jr., and Philip Hamburger for bringing these Reformation references to my attention. See Witte, *Religion and the American Constitutional Experiment*, 14–17, 48–49; Hamburger, *Separation of Church and State*, chap. 1.

12. Richard Hooker, *Of the Laws of Ecclesiastical Polity: Books VI, VII, VIII*, ed. P. G. Stanwood, vol. 3 in *The Folger Library Edition of The Works of Richard Hooker*, ed. W. Speed Hill (Cambridge, Mass.: Belknap Press, Harvard University Press, 1981), 320. All other quotations in this section from *Ecclesiastical Polity*, with modernized spelling, are from Hooker, *Of the Laws of Ecclesiastical Polity: Preface, Book I, Book VIII*, ed. Arthur Stephen McGrade (Cambridge, England: Cambridge University Press, 1989).

13. Kenneth Scott Latourette, *A History of Christianity* (New York: Harper and Brothers, 1953), 812. The term "Puritan," or the equivalent term "Presbyterian," which is preferred by some scholars in this context, refers to dissenting Protestants of the Reformed theological tradition who wished to reform and purify the Church of England but declined to break fully from the Anglican establishment.

14. According to Arthur Stephen McGrade, "recently discovered working notes for the book [indicate] that Hooker had considered a more informative title [for the first chapter of Book VIII]: 'of the distinction of the church and the commonwealth in a Christian kingdom.'" McGrade, Introduction to *Of the Laws of Ecclesiastical Polity*, xxv.

15. Latourette, *A History of Christianity*, 812.

16. *Ecclesiastical Polity*, VIII.1.7.

17. *Ecclesiastical Polity*, VIII.1.2.

18. *Ecclesiastical Polity*, VIII.1.2.

19. McGrade, Introduction to *Of the Laws of Ecclesiastical Polity*, xxv, citing *Ecclesiastical Polity*, VIII.1.2.

20. *Ecclesiastical Polity*, VIII.1.2.

21. *Ecclesiastical Polity*, VIII.1.4.

22. McGrade, Introduction to *Of the Laws of Ecclesiastical Polity*, xxv.

23. *Ecclesiastical Polity*, VIII.1.2.

24. See also discussion of Hooker's use of the "wall" metaphor in Hamburger, *Separation of Church and State*, 32–38.

25. Arthur S. McGrade, "The Public and the Religious in Hooker's *Polity*," *Church History* 37 (1969): 415. For further reading on Hooker's political thought, especially as it pertains to church and state, see J. W. Allen, *A History of Political Thought in the Sixteenth Century* (London: Methuen, 1928; reprint 1960), 184–198; E. T. Davies, *The Political Ideas of Richard Hooker* (New

York: Octagon Books, 1972), 81–98; Cletus F. Dirksen, *A Critical Analysis of Richard Hooker's Theory of the Relation of Church and State* (Notre Dame, Ind.: University of Notre Dame, 1947); Robert K. Faulkner, *Richard Hooker and the Politics of a Christian England* (Berkeley: University of California Press, 1981), 151–184; Raymond Aaron Houk, Introduction to *Hooker's Ecclesiastical Polity, Book VIII* (New York: Columbia University Press, 1931); F. J. Shirley, *Richard Hooker and Contemporary Political Ideas* (London: SPCK, 1949), 106–134.

26. See Hamburger, *Separation of Church and State,* 161 (the Danbury letter "echo[ed] the words he [Jefferson] surely had read in Hooker's *Ecclesiastical Polity*").

27. E. Millicent Sowerby, comp., *Catalogue of the Library of Thomas Jefferson,* 5 vols. (Charlottesville: University Press of Virginia, 1983), 3:14.

28. See Mark DeWolfe Howe, *The Garden and the Wilderness: Religion and Government in American Constitutional History* (Chicago: University of Chicago Press, 1965), 5–31. See also Hamburger, *Separation of Church and State,* 38n. 27 (raising the possibility that Williams had seen an unpublished manuscript of the Eighth Book of Hooker's *Ecclesiastical Polity* in which the "wall" metaphor is used).

29. For a discussion of the meaning of the words "Separatist" and "Separatism" in the seventeenth century, see Timothy L. Hall, *Separating Church and State: Roger Williams and Religious Liberty* (Urbana: University of Illinois Press, 1998), 18-27.

30. See generally Irwin H. Polishook, ed., *Roger Williams, John Cotton and Religious Freedom: A Controversy in New and Old England* (Englewood Cliffs, N.J.: Prentice-Hall, 1967); Hamburger, *Separation of Church and State,* chap. 1; Sacvan Bercovitch, "Typology in Puritan New England: The Williams-Cotton Controversy Reassessed," *American Quarterly* 19 (Summer 1967): 166–191; Richard M. Gummere, "Church, State and Classics: The Cotton-Williams Debate," *Classical Journal* 54 (1958): 175–183; Elisabeth Feist Hirsch, "John Cotton and Roger Williams: Their Controversy Concerning Religious Liberty," *Church History* 10 (1941): 38–51; Henry Bamford Parkes, "John Cotton and Roger Williams Debate Toleration, 1644–1652," *New England Quarterly* 4 (1931): 735–756; Jesper Rosenmeier, "The Teacher and the Witness: John Cotton and Roger Williams," *William and Mary Quarterly,* 3d ser., 25 (1968): 408–431; George Albert Stead, "Roger Williams and the Massachusetts-Bay," *New England Quarterly* 7 (1934): 235–257.

For further discussion of Roger Williams and liberty of conscience, see Edwin S. Gaustad, *Liberty of Conscience: Roger Williams in America* (Grand Rapids, Mich.: William B. Eerdmans, 1991); Theodore P. Greene, ed., *Roger Williams and the Massachusetts Magistrates* (Boston: D. C. Heath, 1964); Timothy L. Hall, *Separating Church and State: Roger Williams and Religious Lib-*

*erty* (Urbana: University of Illinois Press, 1998); W. K. Jordan, *The Development of Religious Toleration in England* (Cambridge, Mass.: Harvard University Press, 1938), 3:472–506; Edmund S. Morgan, *Roger Williams: The Church and the State* (New York: W. W. Norton, 1967); William Lee Miller, *The First Liberty: Religion and the American Republic* (New York: Alfred A. Knopf, 1986), 153–224; Hugh Spurgin, *Roger Williams and Puritan Radicalism in the English Separatist Tradition* (Lewiston, N.Y.: Edwin Mellen Press, 1989); L. John Van Til, *Liberty of Conscience: The History of a Puritan Idea* (Phillipsburg, N.J.: Presbyterian and Reformed, 1972), 29–54.

31. Roger Williams, "Mr. Cotton's Letter Lately Printed, Examined and Answered," in *The Complete Writings of Roger Williams* (Providence, R.I.: Providence Press, 1866), 1:392. The quotation is taken from Perry Miller's modernized version in Miller, *Roger Williams: His Contribution to the American Tradition* (Indianapolis, Ind.: Bobbs-Merrill, 1953; reprinted New York: Atheneum, 1962), 98.

The motif of a protective "hedge" or "wall" was ubiquitous in the rhetoric of colonial New England. These barriers were vital structures of demarcation between the degrading "wilderness of the world" and the enclosed, fragrant "garden of the church." In a 1672 election sermon, Thomas Shepard stated: "*A wilderness is not hedged in, nor fenced about*; what is in the wilderness hath no defence, but lies open to the injury of those that will break in to Bark the Trees thereof, and root up the same; the wilderness is no Inclosure; *have I then been so to you*? have I left you without defence, without an hedge of protection? *have you not been as an inclosed garden to me, and I a wall of fire round about you*? have not I given you those walls, such Defenders, Leaders, Instruments of safety, whereby you have been hedged about, walled in, and secured?" Thomas Shepard, *Eye-Salve, or a Watch-Word From our Lord Jesus Christ unto his Churches* (Cambridge, Mass.: printed by Samuel Green, 1673), 5 (emphasis in the original). Jeremiah Shepard preached in a May 1715 election sermon: "The glorious Arm of Divine Conduct, hath fenc'd us with the hedge of Government. Oh what a favour is this! to give Government, to Establish Authority, to have a Wall of Magistracy set and kept about a People; this is a thing of unspeakable concernment; otherwise a people would be left to Anarchy and heaps of Confusion." Jeremiah Shepard, *God's Conduct of His Church through the Wilderness, with His Glorious Arm, to make Himself an Everlasting Name* (Boston: printed by John Allen, 1715), 25. Both sermons are quoted in A. W. Plumstead, ed., *The Wall and the Garden: Selected Massachusetts Election Sermons, 1670–1775* (Minneapolis: University of Minnesota Press, 1968), 2, title page. For an informative discussion of the metaphors of the "wilderness of the world" and the "garden of the church" in biblical and ecclesiastical literature, see Hamburger, *Separation of Church and State*, chap. 1. Williams was particularly fond of these metaphors. Ellis M. West observed: "Over and over Williams used the metaphor of 'garden' to refer to Christ's true church, which he thought should be protected from the 'wilderness' of earthly cultures, kingdoms, and laws." Ellis M. West, "Roger Williams on the Limits of Religious Liberty," *Annual of the Society of Christian Ethics* (1988): 141.

32. Roger Williams, *The Bloody Tenent Yet More Bloody*, ed. Samuel L. Caldwell, in *Complete Writings of Williams*, 4:333.

33. Howe, *Garden and the Wilderness*, 19. Quoting Perry Miller, Arlin M. Adams and Charles J. Emmerich similarly opined: "In contrast to Enlightenment rationalists, Roger Williams and others in the pietistic tradition built a wall of separation 'not to prevent the state from becoming an instrument of "priestcraft," but in order to keep the holy and pure religion of Jesus Christ from contamination by the slightest taint of earthly support.'" Arlin M. Adams and Charles J. Emmerich, *A Nation Dedicated to Religious Liberty: The Constitutional Heritage of the Religion Clauses* (Philadelphia: University of Pennsylvania Press, 1990), 56, quoting Perry Miller, "Roger Williams: An Essay in Interpretation," in *Complete Writings of Williams*, 7:6.

34. Howe, *Garden and the Wilderness*, 6. Justice Harry Blackmun quoted this passage in *Lee v. Weisman*, 505 U.S. 577, 608 n. 11 (1992) (Blackmun, J., concurring).

35. Howe, *Garden and the Wilderness*, 2.

36. Howe, *Garden and the Wilderness*, 9. For further comparisons of Williams's and Jefferson's uses of the "wall," see Garry Wills, *Under God: Religion and American Politics* (New York: Simon and Schuster, 1990), 350–353; Miller, *The First Liberty*, 182–183; Gaustad, *Liberty of Conscience*, 207–208; Edward J. Eberle, "Roger Williams' Gift: Religious Freedom in America," *Roger Williams University Law Review* 4 (1999): 427, 464–471; Wilber G. Katz, "Radiations from Church Tax Exemption," *Supreme Court Review* 1970 (1970): 96–97. See also Perry Miller, *Errand into the Wilderness* (Cambridge, Mass.: Belknap Press, Harvard University Press, 1956), 145–146 (comparing the church-state views of Williams and Jefferson); Hall, *Separating Church and State*, 116–145 (comparing Williams's views with those of Locke, Jefferson, and Madison). See generally Tom Gerety, "Legal Gardening: Mark DeWolfe Howe on Church and State: A Retrospective Essay," *Stanford Law Review* 38 (1986): 595–614.

37. Insofar as the First Amendment restrains the actions of civil government only and not the actions of private actors (such as religious entities), Williams's "wall of separation," as interpreted by Howe, arguably approximates the prohibitions of the First Amendment more closely than the "wall" erected in *Everson v. Board of Education*, 330 U.S. 1 (1947).

38. David Little, "Roger Williams and the Separation of Church and State," in *Religion and the State: Essays in Honor of Leo Pfeffer*, ed. James E. Wood, Jr. (Waco, Tex.: Baylor University Press, 1985), 15–16; Miller, *The First Liberty*,

182–183. See also Isaac Kramnick and R. Laurence Moore, "The Baptists, the Bureau, and the Case of the Missing Lines," *William and Mary Quarterly*, 3d ser., 56 (1999): 818 ("Williams, however, also had concerns about the way the church might intrude inappropriately into worldly matters.").

39. Hall, *Separating Church and State*, 83, quoting Roger Williams, *The Bloudy Tenet, of Persecution*, in *Complete Writings of Williams*, 3:178. Hall further noted that "Williams defined for the state a sphere of existence untroubled by religious disputes. He envisioned a notion of the secular as not antagonistic to religion but occupied with fundamentally different concerns from religion. He respected the secular city because he believed that God had instituted it and that its existence was not hostile to the existence of the church." Ibid.; Timothy L. Hall, "Roger Williams and the Foundations of Religious Liberty," *Boston University Law Review* 71 (1991): 482.

For further criticism of Howe's thesis, see Philip B. Kurland, "The Origins of the Religion Clauses of the Constitution," *William and Mary Law Review* 27 (1986): 859–860.

40. Howe, *Garden and the Wilderness*, 1–2. See also John Witte, Jr., "The Essential Rights and Liberties of Religion in the American Constitutional Experiment," *Notre Dame Law Review* 71 (1996): 400 n. 144; John Eidsmoe, *Christianity and the Constitution: The Faith of Our Founding Fathers* (Grand Rapids, Mich.: Baker Book House, 1987), 243. For a useful comparison between the perspectives of Jefferson and of various Baptists on church-state separation, see William G. McLoughlin, *Soul Liberty: The Baptists' Struggle in New England, 1630–1833* (Hanover, N.H.: Brown University Press, 1991), 249–269; Andrew M. Manis, "Regionalism and a Baptist Perspective on Separation of Church and State," *American Baptist Quarterly* 2 (1983): 213–227.

41. Edwin S. Gaustad, *Sworn on the Altar of God: A Religious Biography of Thomas Jefferson* (Grand Rapids, Mich.: William B. Eerdmans, 1996), 72. See also Wills, *Under God*, 371 ("Jefferson did not know or admire the work of Williams."); LeRoy Moore, "Roger Williams as an Enduring Symbol for Baptists," *Journal of Church and State* 7 (1965): 185 (there is little question but that Jefferson and Madison never read works by Williams); Hall, *Separating Church and State*, 117 ("influential theorists such as Locke, Madison, and Jefferson proceeded without apparent influence from Williams's ideas").

42. Thomas J. Curry, *The First Freedoms: Church and State in America to the Passage of the First Amendment* (New York: Oxford University Press, 1986), 91 (noting that "[t]he memory of Roger Williams subsided to such an extent that no library catalogue published in the American colonies listed any of his works"); Michael W. McConnell, "The Origins and Historical Understanding of Free Exercise of Religion," *Harvard Law Review* 103 (1990): 1426; Moore, "Roger Williams as an Enduring Symbol for Baptists," 186.

43. Moore, "Roger Williams as an Enduring Symbol for Baptists," 185; LeRoy Moore, "Roger Williams and the Historians," *Church History* 32 (December 1963): 432–451 (emphasizing the unavailability of Williams's writings in America before the nineteenth century). In his introduction to "Mr. Cotton's Letter Examined and Answered," Reuben Aldridge Guild noted that the "original edition of Williams's Reply to Cotton" (in which Williams mentioned the "wall of separation") is among "that class of books which" is "*excessively rare*." Guild, "Introductory Remarks," in *Complete Writings of Williams*, 1:293 (emphasis in the original). His work was not widely available in America until it was reprinted in the mid-nineteenth century. For other useful historiographical essays on Williams's contributions to American traditions, see Raymond D. Irwin, "A Man for All Eras: The Changing Historical Image of Roger Williams, 1630–1993," *Fides et Historia: Journal of the Conference on Faith and History* 26, no. 3 (1994): 6–23; Nancy E. Peace, "Roger Williams—A Historiographical Essay," *Rhode Island History* 35 (1976): 103–113.

44. Miller, "Roger Williams: An Essay in Interpretation," in *Complete Writings of Williams*, 7:10. Perry Miller also wrote that, "although Williams is celebrated as the prophet of religious freedom, he actually exerted little or no influence on institutional developments in America; only after the conception of liberty for all denominations had triumphed on wholly other grounds did Americans look back on Williams and invest him with his ill-fitting halo." Miller, *Roger Williams: His Contribution to the American Tradition*, 29. Miller further opined that Williams "exerted little or no direct influence on theorists of the Revolution and the Constitution, who drew on quite different intellectual sources." Ibid., 254. See also McLoughlin, *Soul Liberty*, 326 n. 21 (expressing agreement with Perry Miller's assessment of Williams's influence); William G. McLoughlin, *New England Dissent, 1630–1833: The Baptists and the Separation of Church and State*, 2 vols. (Cambridge, Mass.: Harvard University Press, 1971), 1:8 (remarking that "almost no one in colonial New England ever praised his [Williams's] experiment, sought his advice, quoted his books, or tried to imitate his practices"); Hall, *Separating Church and State*, 116–117 (arguing that Williams's influence on the colonial and founding eras was minimal); Ellis M. West, "Roger Williams on the Limits of Religious Liberty," 136 ("Williams's writings on religious freedom are important even though their influence on the events that led to the adoption of the First Amendment was indirect and perhaps slight."); William Lee Miller, *The First Liberty*, 217–224 (discussing Williams's influence and legacy). But see Loren P. Beth, *The American Theory of Church and State* (Gainesville: University of Florida Press, 1958), 65 ("It is probably true that Madison and Jefferson were not familiar with the writings of Roger Williams, yet it does not follow that they did not know his doctrines. They were exceedingly familiar with Baptist views on religious liberty

which had been expressed in hundreds of petitions and memorials presented to the state legislature. It is perfectly possible that some of their ideas stemmed thus indirectly from Williams."); Little, "Roger Williams and the Separation of Church and State," 7–16 (arguing that Williams indirectly influenced the American struggle for religious liberty in the founding era through John Locke and Isaac Backus); Jimmy D. Neff, "Roger Williams: Pious Puritan and Strict Separationist," *Journal of Church and State* 38 (1996): 545–546 (same); LeRoy Moore, Jr., "Religious Liberty: Roger Williams and the Revolutionary Era," *Church History* 34 (March 1965): 57–76 (arguing that Williams's influence in the revolutionary era was limited and indirect).

45. Carla H. Hay, *James Burgh, Spokesman for Reform in Hanoverian England* (Washington, D.C.: University Press of America, 1979), 30, 41–44. Hay argued that Burgh's "tome [*Political Disquisitions*] quickly secured the status in England and in America of a monumental reference work with the authority of a political classic. An impressive number of America's founding fathers and virtually all the key figures in the English reform movement were indebted to the work." Ibid., 105.

46. Hay, *James Burgh*, 3. See generally Caroline Robbins, *The Eighteenth-Century Commonwealthman: Studies in the Transmission, Development and Circumstance of English Liberal Thought from the Restoration of Charles II until the War with the Thirteen Colonies* (Cambridge, Mass.: Harvard University Press, 1959). For a more recent discussion of the Real Whigs or Commonwealthmen and their influence on American political and constitutional thought in the revolutionary era, see David N. Mayer, "The English Radical Whig Origins of American Constitutionalism," *Washington University Law Quarterly* 70 (1992): 131–208. Mayer placed Burgh squarely within this tradition. Ibid., 170.

47. Oscar Handlin and Mary Handlin, "James Burgh and American Revolutionary Theory," *Proceedings of the Massachusetts Historical Society* 73 (1961): 43. See also Hay, *James Burgh*, 28–30.

48. Isaac Kramnick, *Republicanism and Bourgeois Radicalism: Political Ideology in Late Eighteenth-Century England and America* (Ithaca, N.Y.: Cornell University Press, 1990), 205. See also Kramnick, "Republicanism Revisited: The Case of James Burgh," in *The Republican Synthesis Revisited: Essays in Honor of George Athan Billias*, ed. Milton M. Klein, Richard D. Brown, and John B. Hench (Worcester, Mass.: American Antiquarian Society, 1992), 22.

49. For a list of others included in this group, see Hay, *James Burgh*, 28–29. Benjamin Franklin also had ties with this circle, visiting them when he traveled to England. See Oscar Handlin and Mary Handlin, "James Burgh and American Revolutionary Theory," 42, 52; Verner W. Crane, "The Club of Honest Whigs: Friends of Science and Liberty," *William and Mary Quarterly*, 3d ser., 23 (1966): 210–233.

50. Caroline Robbins described the work as "perhaps the most important political treatise which appeared in England in the first half of the reign of George III." Robbins, *Eighteenth-Century Commonwealthman*, 365.

51. Forrest McDonald, "A Founding Father's Library," *Literature of Liberty* 1 (January-March 1978): 13. See also Lance Banning, *The Jeffersonian Persuasion: Evolution of a Party Ideology* (Ithaca, N.Y.: Cornell University Press, 1978), 61; Kramnick, *Republicanism and Bourgeois Radicalism*, 235–237.

52. Hay, *James Burgh*, 49. Carla H. Hay briefly traced the evolution of Burgh's religious beliefs from his early Calvinist training as the son of a Church of Scotland clergyman to a conversion "to some form of unitarianism." In his later works, he rejected Trinitarianism and other doctrines of orthodox Christianity. However, "[t]here was never any question in Burgh's mind that organized Christianity was the most valid expression of man's religious needs and duties. . . . Moreover, Burgh always believed that Protestantism was the only legitimate manifestation of the Christian faith." Hay, *James Burgh*, 49–55.

53. Colin Bonwick, *English Radicals and the American Revolution* (Chapel Hill: University of North Carolina Press, 1977), 14–15.

54. Hay, *James Burgh*, 51. The Real Whigs were early and zealous advocates of religious toleration. Mayer, "The English Radical Whig Origins of American Constitutionalism," 163. For a useful discussion of religious dissenters in England during this era, see Anthony Lincoln, *Some Political and Social Ideas of English Dissent, 1763–1800* (Cambridge: Cambridge University Press, 1938).

55. [James Burgh], *Crito, or Essays on Various Subjects*, 2 vols. (London, 1766, 1767), 2:68, as quoted in Kramnick, *Republicanism and Bourgeois Radicalism*, 232. Carla H. Hay pointed out that, "[a]lthough Burgh heartily endorsed private religious devotions, he maintained that the public expression of such sentiments was especially useful in inculcating a sense of one's obligations to God." Hay, *James Burgh*, 50.

56. *Crito*, 1:7.

57. *Crito*, 2:119 (emphasis in the original).

58. *Crito*, 2:117–119 (emphasis in the original).

59. Letter from Jefferson to Thomas Mann Randolph, 30 May 1790, *The Writings of Thomas Jefferson*, ed. Andrew A. Lipscomb and Albert Ellery Bergh, 20 vols. (Washington, D.C.: Thomas Jefferson Memorial Association, 1904), 8:31–32. Nearly a quarter of a century later, Jefferson gave the same advice to Bernard Moore; see letter from Jefferson to Bernard Moore, 30 August 1814, in Henry S. Randall, *The Life of Thomas Jefferson*, 3 vols. (New York: Derby and Jackson, 1857), 1:55.

60. H. Trevor Colbourn, "Thomas Jefferson's Use of the Past," *William and Mary Quarterly*, 3d ser., 15 (1958): 65 n. 47; Hay, *James Burgh*, 43.

61. Letter from John Adams to James Burgh, 28 December 1774, *The Works of John Adams, Second President of the United States*, ed. Charles Francis Adams (Boston: Charles C. Little and James Brown, 1851), 9:351. See also [Adams], "Novanglus," *Works of Adams*, 4:21 n. * (Burgh's *Political Disquisitions* is a "book which ought to be in the hands of every American who has learned to read."). Other scholars have noted the extent of Burgh's influence among those involved in writing the U.S. Constitution, as well as state constitutions. In his survey of European political literature that influenced late-eighteenth-century American political thought, Donald S. Lutz noted: "during the period of Constitution writing . . . a host of English Whig writers [including Burgh] becomes prominent." Lutz, "The Relative Influence of European Writers on Late Eighteenth Century American Political Thought," *American Political Science Review* 78 (1984): 193. Likewise, David Lundberg and Henry F. May's analysis of library collections of the period found that library holdings of Burgh's work "gain[ed] sharply" in the 1790s. Lundberg and May, "The Enlightened Reader in America," *American Quarterly* 28 (1976): 269.

62. Hay, *James Burgh*, 42. See generally H. Trevor Colbourn, *The Lamp of Experience: Whig History and the Intellectual Origins of the American Revolution* (Chapel Hill: University of North Carolina Press; Institute of Early American History and Culture, 1965), 19.

63. James Burgh, *Political Disquisitions: or, An Enquiry into Public Errors, Defects, and Abuses*, 3 vols. (Philadelphia, Pa., 1775), 3: "Names of the Encouragers."

64. Oscar Handlin and Mary Handlin, "James Burgh and American Revolutionary Theory," 57.

65. Oscar Handlin and Mary Handlin suggested that Burgh's influence faded because he was "an unsystematic thinker," was more of a transmitter and popularizer of ideas than a truly original theorist, and was clearly not of the same intellectual stature as Hume, Locke, or Montesquieu. Oscar Handlin and Mary Handlin, "James Burgh and American Revolutionary Theory," 38–39, 55–57. Carla H. Hay further observed that the style and format of his writings may have contributed to his passage into obscurity: "Didactic, discursive, and frequently dull, these 'grab-bags' of information [Burgh's published works] offend modern literary tastes, although they were widely read in Burgh's day. . . . Created in his limited leisure time, Burgh's compositions were little more than unpolished first drafts. Poorly organized, they were chronically repetitive and frequently rambled from one unconnected topic to another. Arguments were developed in a haphazard, almost stream-of-consciousness fashion." Hay, *James Burgh*, 4, 15.

66. Isaac Kramnick and R. Laurence Moore identified Burgh as "the original source of the metaphor, which Jefferson would use, that captures in a phrase

this entire liberal secular view of the relationship between politics and religion—the wall of separation." Kramnick and Moore, *The Godless Constitution: The Case Against Religious Correctness* (New York: W. W. Norton, 1996), 82. See also Kramnick, *Republicanism and Bourgeois Radicalism*, 232 (Burgh "could well be the source of Jefferson's" metaphor); Kramnick and Moore, "The Baptists, the Bureau, and the Case of the Missing Lines," 819 (same).

67. *Crito*, 2: dedication, 1, 3 (emphasis in the original). See also Hay, *James Burgh*, 34; Kramnick, *Republicanism and Bourgeois Radicalism*, 228.

68. See Joseph F. Costanzo, "Thomas Jefferson, Religious Education and Public Law," *Journal of Public Law* 8, no. 1 (1959): 98 ("Years before all the states cancelled their church establishments and decades before the Supreme Court would make the First Amendment meaning of religious liberty operative upon the states through the Fourteenth Amendment, Jefferson is looking forward to the day when state governments would follow the example of the federal Constitution and guarantee by law equality of religious freedom.").

Notes to Chapter 6

1. Letter from George Washington to the United Baptist Churches of Virginia, [May 1789], *The Papers of George Washington*, Presidential Series, ed. Dorothy Twohig (Charlottesville: University Press of Virginia, 1987), 2:424.

2. Letter from James Madison to the Reverend Jasper Adams, September 1833, in *Religion and Politics in the Early Republic: Jasper Adams and the Church-State Debate*, ed. Daniel L. Dreisbach (Lexington: University Press of Kentucky, 1996), 120.

3. Address of the United Baptist Churches in Virginia to George Washington, May 1789, *Papers of Washington*, 2:424 n1.

4. Letter from Washington to the United Baptist Churches of Virginia, [May 1789], *Papers of Washington*, 2:424.

5. Letter from Washington to the United Baptist Churches of Virginia, [May 1789], *Papers of Washington*, 2:424.

6. Conrad Henry Moehlman, *The Wall of Separation between Church and State: An Historical Study of Recent Criticism of the Religious Clause of the First Amendment* (Boston: Beacon Press, 1951), 86–87.

7. Paul F. Boller, Jr., *George Washington and Religion* (Dallas, Tex.: Southern Methodist University Press, 1963), 143.

8. Letter from Washington to the United Baptist Churches of Virginia, [May 1789], *Papers of Washington*, 2:424.

9. See generally Daniel L. Dreisbach, "Church-State Debate in the Virginia Legislature: From the Declaration of Rights to the Statute for Establishing Religious Freedom," in *Religion and Political Culture in Jefferson's Virginia*, ed. Garrett Ward Sheldon and Daniel L. Dreisbach (Lanham, Md.: Rowman and

Littlefield, 2000), 135–165; Dreisbach, "George Mason's Pursuit of Religious Liberty in Revolutionary Virginia," *Virginia Magazine of History and Biography* 108, no. 1 (2000): 5–44.

10. James Madison, "Memorial and Remonstrance," *The Papers of James Madison*, ed. Robert A. Rutland et al. (Chicago: University of Chicago Press, 1973), 8:299.

11. John T. Noonan, Jr., *The Lustre of Our Country: The American Experience of Religious Freedom* (Berkeley: University of California Press, 1998), 75. See also ibid., 89.

12. "Memorial and Remonstrance," *Papers of Madison*, 8:299; Douglass Adair, ed., "James Madison's Autobiography," *William and Mary Quarterly*, 3d ser., 2 (1945): 199 (emphasis in the original).

13. Eva T. H. Brann, "Madison's 'Memorial and Remonstrance': A Model of American Eloquence," in *Rhetoric and American Statesmanship*, ed. Glen E. Thurow and Jeffrey D. Wallin (Durham, N.C.: Carolina Academic Press; Claremont Institute for the Study of Statesmanship and Political Philosophy, 1984), 21. Citing this passage, Philip B. Kurland similarly linked Madison's and Jefferson's metaphors: "In this work, Madison, like Jefferson, argued that separation of church and state is necessary for the preservation of a free society." Philip B. Kurland, "The Irrelevance of the Constitution: The Religion Clauses of the First Amendment and the Supreme Court," *Villanova Law Review* 24 (1978-1979): 13 n. 71.

14. Elizabeth Fleet, ed., "Madison's 'Detached Memoranda,'" *William and Mary Quarterly*, 3d ser., 3 (1946): 554.

15. Noonan, *The Lustre of Our Country*, 84.

16. Letter from James Madison to George Mason, 14 July 1826, *Letters and Other Writings of James Madison, Fourth President of the United States*, 4 vols. (New York: R. Worthington, 1884), 3:526; *The Complete Madison: His Basic Writings*, ed. Saul K. Padover (New York: Harper and Brothers, 1953), 299n.

17. Letter from Tench Coxe to James Madison, 18 June 1789, *Papers of Madison*, 12:239.

18. Letter from Richard Henry Lee to Charles Lee, 28 August 1789, in *Creating the Bill of Rights: The Documentary Record from the First Federal Congress*, ed. Helen E. Veit, Kenneth R. Bowling, and Charlene Bangs Bickford (Baltimore: Johns Hopkins University Press, 1991), 290.

19. Letter from Thomas Jefferson to Noah Webster, Jr., 4 December 1790, *The Papers of Thomas Jefferson*, ed. Julian P. Boyd et al., 28 vols. to date (Princeton, N.J.: Princeton University Press, 1950– ), 18:132. For commentary on this passage, see Adrienne Koch, *The Philosophy of Thomas Jefferson* (New York: Columbia University Press, 1943), 141–142; David N. Mayer, *The Constitutional Thought of Thomas Jefferson* (Charlottesville: University Press of Virginia, 1994), 156-157.

20. Other references to fences in similar service can be found in the literature of the age. For example, John Jay, coauthor of the *Federalist Papers* and the first Chief Justice of the U.S. Supreme Court, spoke of the rule of law as a protective fence for a free people: "The more free the people are, the more strong and efficient ought their Governm[en]t to be; and for this plain Reason, that it is a more arduous Task to make and keep up the Fences of Law & Justice about twenty Rights than about five or six; & because it is more difficult to fence against & restrain men who are unfettered, than men who are in Yokes & Chains." John Jay, Charge to the Grand Jury of the Circuit Court for the District of Virginia, Richmond, Virginia, 22 May 1793, in Maeva Marcus et al., eds., *The Documentary History of the Supreme Court of the United States, 1789–1800,* 6 vols. to date (New York: Columbia University Press, 1985– ), 2:390.

21. Letter from James Madison to the Reverend Jasper Adams, September 1833, in *Religion and Politics in the Early Republic,* 120. In the same letter, immediately following the "line" metaphor, Madison wrote: "The tendency to a usurpation on one side, or the other, or to a corrupting coalition or alliance between them, will be best guarded against by an entire abstinence of the Government from interference, in any way whatever, beyond the necessity of preserving public order, & protecting each sect against trespasses on its legal rights by others." Ibid., 120. Therefore, it would be a mistake to construe his "line of separation" as support for something less than a separation between church and state.

22. Interestingly, during his presidency, Jefferson made occasional use of the "line of separation" metaphor, although not in a church-state context. See, for example, letter from Jefferson to Thomas Lomax, 25 February 1801, *The Writings of Thomas Jefferson,* ed. Andrew A. Lipscomb and Albert Ellery Bergh, 20 vols. (Washington, D.C.: Thomas Jefferson Memorial Association, 1905), 10:211 [hereinafter *Writings of Jefferson*]; letter from Jefferson to Mr. Pictet, 5 February 1803, *Writings of Jefferson,* 10:357; letter from Jefferson to Mrs. John Adams, 13 June 1804, *Writings of Jefferson,* 11:28; Jefferson, Sixth Annual Message, 2 December 1806, *Writings of Jefferson,* 3:423.

23. Sidney E. Mead, "Neither Church nor State: Reflections on James Madison's 'Line of Separation,'" *Journal of Church and State* 10 (1968): 350.

24. Richard P. McBrien, *Caesar's Coin: Religion and Politics in America* (New York: Macmillan, 1987), 66. See also ibid., 176–177; Christopher F. Mooney, *Public Virtue: Law and the Social Character of Religion* (Notre Dame, Ind.: University of Notre Dame Press, 1986), 30. See Terry Eastland, "In Defense of Religious America," *Commentary* 71, no. 6 (June 1981): 39 ("in today's usage the idea of a wall connotes antagonism and suspicion between the two sides thus separated."); John F. Wilson, *Public Religion in American Culture* (Philadelphia: Temple University Press, 1979), 5–6 (a comparison of Madi-

son's "subtle and rich insights" with "simplistic formulas" like Jefferson's "wall," concluding that "Madison's counsel is markedly more helpful in comprehending this grand experiment than Jefferson's casually delivered unyielding metaphor, which has perhaps finally obscured more than it has clarified this area.").

25. Cf. *McCollum v. Board of Education*, 333 U.S. 203, 231 (1948) (Opinion of Frankfurter, J.) ("Separation means separation, not something less. Jefferson's metaphor in describing the relation between Church and State speaks of a 'wall of separation,' not of a fine line easily overstepped.").

26. McBrien, *Caesar's Coin*, 66.

27. Letter from James Madison to the Reverend Jasper Adams, September 1833, in *Religion and Politics in the Early Republic*, 120.

28. *McCollum*, 333 U.S. at 231 (Opinion of Frankfurter, J.). See also *Wolman v. Walter*, 433 U.S. 229, 265 (1977) (Stevens, J., concurring in part and dissenting in part) ("The line drawn by the Establishment Clause of the First Amendment must also have a fundamental character.").

29. Edwin S. Gaustad, *Sworn on the Altar of God: A Religious Biography of Thomas Jefferson* (Grand Rapids, Mich.: William B. Eerdmans, 1996), 99 (emphasis in the original).

30. McBrien, *Caesar's Coin*, 66 (emphasis in the original). For a discussion of the Supreme Court's references to the "line" metaphor and a comparison between Madison's "line" and Jefferson's "wall," see McBrien, *Caesar's Coin*, 66–67; Mooney, *Public Virtue*, 29–32; Stephen J. Safranek, "Can Science Guide Legal Argumentation?: The Role of Metaphor in Constitutional Cases," *Loyola University Chicago Law Journal* 25 (1994): 381–389. See also Elwyn A. Smith, *Religious Liberty in the United States: The Development of Church-State Thought since the Revolutionary Era* (Philadelphia: Fortress Press, 1972), 309–325 (chapter entitled "From 'Wall' to 'Line' of Separation").

31. *Abington School District v. Schempp*, 374 U.S. 203, 231, 294 (1963) (Brennan, J., concurring).

32. *Board of Education v. Allen*, 392 U.S. 236, 242 (1968).

33. *Walz v. Tax Commissioner of New York City*, 397 U.S. 664, 669–670 (1970).

34. *Lemon v. Kurtzman*, 403 U.S. 602, 612, 614 (1971). See also id. at 614, 625 ("[T]otal separation is not possible in an absolute sense. Some relationship between government and religious organizations is inevitable. . . . [Nevertheless,] lines must be drawn.").

35. See *Friedman v. Board of County Commissioners of Bernalillo County*, 781 F.2d 777, 785 (10th Cir. 1985) (Barrett, C. J., dissenting); *Espinosa v. Rusk*, 634 F.2d 477, 483 (10th Cir. 1980) (Barrett, C. J., dissenting); *Florey v. Sioux Falls School District*, 619 F.2d 1311, 1322 (8th Cir. 1980) (McMillian, C. J., dissenting). All three of these federal circuit court opinions make this

statement in essentially identical language, citing *Committee for Public Education and Religious Liberty v. Regan*, 444 U.S. 646 (1980). This is an apparent reference to Justice Harry A. Blackmun's bitter allegation that the majority departed from precedents that "at least had fixed the line between that which is constitutionally appropriate public aid and that which is not. The line necessarily was not a straight one," Blackmun conceded. He later described the "line" as "wavering." *Committee for Public Education*, 444 U.S. at 663 (Blackmun, J., dissenting).

36. See, for example, *Doe v. Beaumont Independent School District*, 240 F.3d 462, 492 (5th Cir. 2001) (Wiener, C. J., concurring in part and dissenting in part) ("the bright line that separates the permissible from the impermissible"); *Donovan v. Tony and Susan Alamo Foundation*, 722 F.2d 397, 399 (8th Cir. 1983) ("there comes a time when secular endeavor must be recognized as such, and passes over the line separating it from the sacred functions of religious worship."); *Florey v. Sioux Falls School District*, 619 F.2d 1311, 1322 (8th Cir. 1980) (McMillian, C. J., dissenting), quoting *Abington School District v. Schempp*, 374 U.S. at 231 (Brennan, J., concurring) ("Although in my view the line of separation has become unnecessarily blurred, '[t]he fact is that the line which separates the secular from the sectarian in American life is elusive.'"); *Tanford v. Brand*, 932 F. Supp. 1139, 1142 (S.D. Ind. 1996) ("Given the complexity of the task, it is perhaps not surprising that no single criterion adequately defines the fragile line that separates religious indoctrination from a simple accommodation of religion."); *Espresso, Inc. v. District of Columbia*, 884 F. Supp. 7, 9 (D.D.C. 1995) ("the elusive line that separates"); *Verbena United Methodist Church v. Chilton County Board of Education*, 765 F. Supp. 704, 715 (M.D. Ala. 1991) (government officials must be careful that "religious uses of school property do not . . . cross the difficult-to-define line separating equal access from official sponsorship."); *Archbishop of the Roman Catholic Apostolic Archdiocese of San Juan v. Guardiola*, 628 F. Supp. 1173, 1179 (D. Puerto Rico 1985) ("The line of separation is not a wall. . . ."); *Amos v. Corporation of the Presiding Bishop of the Church of Jesus Christ of Latter-Day Saints*, 594 F. Supp. 791, 826 (D. Utah 1984) ("To determine whether a particular law crosses that line . . ."); *Bender v. Williamsport Area School District*, 563 F. Supp. 697, 710 (M.D. Pa. 1983) ("although the line separating accommodation from advancement [of religion] sometimes appears blurred, it is a line which must be drawn, and drawn with as much precision as logic and precedent will allow."); *Gaines v. Anderson*, 421 F. Supp. 337, 341, 344 (D. Mass. 1976) ("the line which separates the secular from the sectarian is an elusive one"); *Americans United for the Separation of Church and State v. Dunn*, 384 F. Supp. 714, 718 (M.D. Tenn. 1974) ("Church and State are not separated by Thomas Jefferson's 'wall,' but by a 'line.'. . ."); *Tony and Susan Alamo Foundation, Inc. v. Ragland*, 295 Ark. 12, 16, 746 S.W.2d 45, 48 (1988) ("Religious organiza-

tions entering the commercial and secular world necessarily do so with the understanding that they no longer enjoy the constitutional protection afforded religious organizations. There are no shields once they cross the line that separates church and state."); *University of Delaware v. Keegan*, 318 A.2d 135, 138 (Del. Ch. 1974) ("the thin line which separates the establishment clause from the free exercise clause"); *Seegers v. Parker*, 256 La. 1039, 1057, 241 So.2d 213, 220 (1970) ("the attempt to find and maintain the lines of separation would itself require excessive state involvement in religion"); *Clayton v. Kervick*, 56 N.J. 523, 528, 267 A.2d 503, 506 (1970) ("But the 'wall of separation' is an elusive line."); *New York State Employment Relations Board v. Christ the King Regional High School*, 90 N.Y.2d 244, 252, 682 N.E.2d 960, 966 (1997) ("If . . . a line is crossed or the wall of separation is breached . . ."); *Rhoades v. School District of Abington Township*, 424 Pa. 202, 231, 226 A.2d 53, 69 (1967) (Roberts, J., concurring) ("draw the line separating the constitutional from the unconstitutional"); *Society of Separationists v. Whitehead*, 870 P.2d 916, 942 (Utah 1993) (Stewart, J., dissenting) ("the Framers [of the Utah Constitution] sought to make clear the line that should separate church and state.").

37. *Everson v. Board of Education*, 330 U.S. 1 (1947).

38. *Everson*, 330 U.S. at 18. See also *Zorach v. Clauson*, 303 N.Y. 161, 179, 100 N.E.2d 463, 472 (1951) (Desmond, J., concurring) (noting terms "unbreachable wall" and "impassable gulf"); *Zwerling v. Reagan*, 576 F. Supp. 1373, 1375 (C.D. Cal. 1983) ("Jefferson's formidable 'wall'"); *Branch Ministries, Inc. v. Rossotti*, 40 F. Supp.2d 15, 26 (D.D.C. 1999), quoting *Christian Echoes National Ministry, Inc. v. United States*, 470 F.2d 849, 857 (10th Cir. 1972) ("the wall separating church and state [must] remain high and firm").

39. *Everson*, 330 U.S. at 31–32 (Rutledge, J., dissenting).

40. For a critique of the *Everson* Court's "high and impregnable" wall and the attribution of this wall to Jefferson, see Robert L. Cord, "Mr. Jefferson's 'Nonabsolute' Wall of Separation between Church and State," in *Religion and Political Culture in Jefferson's Virginia*, 167–188.

41. Martin E. Marty, *Church-State Separation in America: The Tradition Nobody Knows* (Washington, D.C.: People for the American Way, 1982), 7.

42. Harold D. Hammett, "The Homogenized Wall," *American Bar Association Journal* 53 (October 1967): 935; Hammett, "Separation of Church and State: By One Wall or Two?" *Journal of Church and State* 7 (Spring 1965): 202–203.

43. Mark Weldon Whitten, *The Myth of Christian America: What You Need to Know about the Separation of Church and State* (Macon, Ga.: Smyth and Helwys, 1999), 30. See also Kathlyn Gay, *Church and State: Government and Religion in the United States* (Brookfield, Conn.: Millbrook Press, 1992), 27, citing Delos B. McKown and Clifton B. Perry, "Religion, Separation, and Accommodation: A Recipe of Perfection?" *Phi Kappa Phi Journal* (Winter

1988), 2 (suggesting the metaphor of a "picket fence" for the partition between church and state).

44. Mary C. Segers and Ted G. Jelen, *A Wall of Separation?: Debating the Public Role of Religion* (Lanham, Md.: Rowman and Littlefield, 1998), 54.

45. *Sands v. Morongo Unified School District*, 53 Cal.3d 863, 892, 809 P.2d 809, 827 (1991) (Lucas, C. J., concurring). See also *American Civil Liberties Union of Illinois v. City of St. Charles*, 794 F.2d 265, 272 (7th Cir. 1986) ("'wall of separation' is not so impermeable"); Note, "*Grumet v. Board of Education of the Kiryas Joel Village School Dist.*—When Neutrality Masks Hostility—The Exclusion of Religious Communities from an Entitlement to Public Schools," *Notre Dame Law Review* 68 (1993): 788 n. 70 ("[The Court] has also concluded that the 'wall,' rather than being impenetrable, is instead a permeable barrier."); Mark C. Rahdert, "A Jurisprudence of Hope: Justice Blackmun and the Freedom of Religion," *Hamline Law Review* 22 (1998): 75 ("*Lemon* and its several companion decisions collectively represent a deliberate attempt to construct, not an impregnable wall between church and state, but a sometimes scalable wall—or, to change the metaphor, what might be regarded as a semi-permeable membrane between church and state that filters most church-state interactions out, but also lets an appreciable number and magnitude of such interactions in."); Susanna Dokupil, "A Sunny Dome with Caves of Ice: The Illusion of Charitable Choice," *Texas Review of Law and Politics* 5 (2000): 163 (posing the question, "Wall of Separation or Semi-Permeable Membrane?"); Note, "*New York State School Boards Ass'n v. Sobol*: A Commendable Attempt to Apply Confusing Establishment Clause Standards," *Villanova Law Review* 38 (1993): 774 ("Thomas Jefferson's impenetrable 'wall' of separation has been reduced to a permeable membrane that tolerates necessary interaction and contact between church and state."); Note, "The Collision of Religious Exercise and Governmental Nondiscrimination Policies," *Stanford Law Review* 41 (1989): 1209 ("the Court has recognized that the 'wall' of separation between church and state is somewhat porous"). But see Comment, "School Prayer and the Constitution: Silence Is Golden," *Maryland Law Review* 48 (1989): 1027 ("the Court has constructed an impermeable wall of separation between church and state when the government's religious activity involves public education"); Note, "Daily Moments of Silence in Public Schools: A Constitutional Analysis," *New York University Law Review* 58 (1983): 377 ("the Supreme Court has established a fairly impermeable wall of separation between church and state within elementary and secondary public schools").

46. See, for example, William Van Alstyne, "Trends in the Supreme Court: Mr. Jefferson's Crumbling Wall—A Comment on *Lynch v. Donnelly*," *Duke Law Journal* 1984 (1984): 770–787; Paul L. Hicks, "The Wall Crumbles: A Look at the Establishment Clause: *Rosenberger v. Rector & Visitors of the University of Virginia*," *West Virginia Law Review* 98 (1995): 363–395; Suzanne

H. Bauknight, "The Search for Constitutional School Choice," *Journal of Law and Education* 27 (1998): 527 ("With the Court's decision in *Everson v. Board of Education of Ewing Township* in 1947, Establishment Clause litigation built a high and impregnable wall of separation between church and state that has been deconstructed, brick by brick, in the 1980s and 1990s, leaving a not-so-high, 'holey' fence."); Note, "Separation of Church and State: *Jackson v. Benson*—The Wall Comes Tumblin' Down," *Widener Journal of Public Law* 8 (1999): 562 ("From the 1940s through 1970s, holes in the wall of separation began to appear"); *South Jersey Catholic School Teachers Organization v. St. Teresa of the Infant Jesus Church Elementary School*, 150 N.J. 575, 587, 696 A.2d 709, 715 (1997) ("major crack occurred in the 'wall of separation'"); Melissa A. Dalziel, "Religious Liberty Book Review Symposium: The Tension between a Godless Constitution and a Culture of Belief in an Age of Reason," *Brigham Young University Law Review* 1999 (1999): 862 (reporting the views of two authors that the wall currently "resembles Swiss cheese").

47. *Wilder v. Bernstein*, 848 F.2d 1338, 1350 (2nd Cir. 1988) (Cardamone, C. J., dissenting).

48. *Catholic High School Association of the Archdiocese of New York v. Culvert*, 753 F.2d 1161, 1162 (2nd Cir. 1985).

49. James H. Hutson, "Thomas Jefferson's Letter to the Danbury Baptists: A Controversy Rejoined," *William and Mary Quarterly*, 3d ser., 56 (1999): 789-790.

50. Stephen L. Carter, *The Culture of Disbelief: How American Law and Politics Trivialize Religious Devotion* (New York: Basic Books, 1993), 109. See also Note, "*Rosenberger v. Rector & Board of Visitors of the University of Virginia*: A Battle between Establishment Clause Principles and the First Amendment Clauses Further Weakens the Wall of Separation," *DePaul Law Review* 46 (1997): 577–584 (arguing that the principle of neutrality is a "door through which a state can pass through the 'wall of separation'"); Note, "When the Issue Is Funding, No News *Isn't* 'Good News': *Rosenberger v. Rector & Visitors of University of Virginia*, 115 S.Ct. 2510 (1995)," *University of Dayton Law Review* 21 (1996): 562 (the wall contains a "door that allows ideas to pass unimpeded from one side of the wall to the other.").

51. Lucas A. Swaine, "Principled Separation: Liberal Governance and Religious Free Exercise," *Journal of Church and State* 38 (1996): 597–598. See also J. M. O'Neill, *Religion and Education under the Constitution* (New York: Harper and Brothers, 1949), 83 (arguing that Jefferson would not have built a wall "completely without gates, or stiles, or friendly openings").

52. Note, "The Equal Access Act and *Mergens*: Balancing the Religion Clauses in Public Schools," *Georgia Law Review* 24 (1990): 1179. See also Nadine Strossen, "A Framework for Evaluating Equal Access Claims by Student Religious Groups: Is There a Window for Free Speech in the Wall Separating

Church and State?" *Cornell Law Review* 71 (1985): 143–183 (suggesting that free speech can be a "window" in the "wall").

53. Brief Amici Curiae of National Council of Catholic Men and National Council of Catholic Women at 35, *Everson v. Board of Education*, 330 U.S. 1 (1947).

54. Brief Amici Curiae of National Council of Catholic Men and National Council of Catholic Women at 39.

55. *Zorach v. Clauson*, 303 N.Y. 161, 172, 100 N.E.2d 463, 467–468 (1951).

56. See, for example, Gordon Butler, "Cometh the Revolution: The Case for Overruling McCollum v. Board of Education," *Dickinson Law Review* 99 (1995): 847 (the "artificial 'wall of separation' between church and state" erected in *McCollum* and its progeny, "like the Berlin Wall, must fall of its own weight."); Comment, "Take Care of Me When I Am Dead: An Examination of American Church-State Development and the Future of American Religious Liberty," *SMU Law Review* 49 (1996): 1628 (reporting a view that "likens the existing wall of separation to the Berlin Wall"), 1582 ("Indeed, Mr. Reagan's covert agenda to bring down the wall in Germany was analogous to his attempt to bring down the wall of separation between church and state."); F. LaGard Smith, *ACLU: The Devil's Advocate: The Seduction of Civil Liberties in America* (Colorado Springs, Colo.: Marcon Publishers, 1996), 27 (comparing the modern "wall" championed by the ACLU to the "Berlin Wall").

57. Safranek, "Can Science Guide Legal Argumentation?: The Role of Metaphor in Constitutional Cases," 371. See also O'Neill, *Religion and Education under the Constitution*, 82 ("Attempts have been made to use it [this wall] to achieve a division in American thought and practice as though it were as real as the Great Wall of China."); Bruce Fein, "Is This Lawsuit Necessary?" *Washington Times*, 31 July 2001, A14 (the Virginia chapter of the American Civil Liberties Union is a proselytizer for "an impermeable Chinese Wall of separation between church and state.").

58. Stephen L. Carter, *God's Name in Vain: The Wrongs and Rights of Religion in Politics* (New York: Basic Books, 2000), 79–80.

59. Carter, *God's Name in Vain*, 78.

60. Carter, *The Culture of Disbelief*, 105. See also ibid., 115 ("for most members of the Founding Generation the idea of separating church from state meant protecting the church from the state—not the state from the church."); Carter, *God's Name in Vain*, 77 ("The religion clause of the First Amendment is designed to limit what the state can do, not what the church can do.").

61. Carter, *God's Name in Vain*, 80–81.

62. *McCollum*, 333 U.S. at 238 (Jackson, J., concurring). See also Justice Jackson's admission in *Zorach*: "The wall which the Court was professing to erect between Church and State has become even more warped and twisted than

I expected." *Zorach v. Clauson*, 343 U.S. 306, 325 (1952) (Jackson, J., dissenting). Significantly, Jackson credited the Court, not Jefferson or the framers of the First Amendment, with erection of the "wall." See Joseph H. Brady, *Confusion Twice Confounded: The First Amendment and the Supreme Court: An Historical Study* (South Orange, N.J.: Seton Hall University Press, 1954), 189.

63. *Committee for Public Education and Religious Liberty v. Nyquist*, 413 U.S. 756, 761 (1973).

64. The "public square" is the space open to all citizens for public discourse that, it is thought, will inform the public ethic and policy. Greatly disputed are the precise territory included in the public square, the role of religion in this public space, and the extent to which religion may appropriately influence the public ethic and policy. See generally Richard John Neuhaus, *The Naked Public Square: Religion and Democracy in America* (Grand Rapids, Mich.: William B. Eerdmans, 1984).

NOTES TO CHAPTER 7

1. Letter from Thomas Jefferson to Levi Lincoln, 1 January 1802, The Papers of Thomas Jefferson (Manuscript Division, Library of Congress), Series 1, Box 89, December 2, 1801–January 1, 1802; Presidential Papers Microfilm, Thomas Jefferson Papers (Manuscript Division, Library of Congress), Series 1, Reel 25, November 15, 1801–March 31, 1802.

2. *Berkey v. Third Ave. Ry. Co.*, 244 N.Y. 84, 94, 155 N.E. 58, 61 (1926).

3. Letter from Jefferson to Levi Lincoln, 1 January 1802.

4. See, for example, *American Citizen and General Advertiser* (New York), 18 January 1802, 2; *American Mercury* (Hartford, Conn.), 28 January 1802, 3; *The Centinel of Freedom* (Newark, N.J.), 16 February 1802, 2–3 (Baptists' address), 23 February 1802, 3 (Jefferson's reply); *Constitutional Telegraphe* (Boston), 27 January 1802, 2; *Independent Chronicle* (Boston), 25 January 1802, 2-3; *New Hampshire Gazette* (Portsmouth), 9 February 1802, 2; *Rhode-Island Republican* (Newport), 30 January 1802, 2; *Salem Register*, 28 January 1802, 1; *The Sun* (Pittsfield, Mass.), 15 February 1802, 4.

5. (Boston) *Independent Chronicle*, 28 January 1802, 2 (emphasis in the original), reprinted from *Salem Register*, 25 January 1802, 3. This commentary was probably authored by the Reverend Dr. William Bentley, a Salem clergyman and a frequent contributor to the *Register*, who, in strikingly similar prose, recorded in his diary the same week:

> The Baptists by attaching themselves to the present administration have gained great success in the United States & greater in New England than any sect since the settlement, even beyond comparison. This seems to be a warning to the Churches of the other denominations. The late address of the Danbury Associa-

tion of Baptist Churches to President Jefferson with his answer of the present month are before the public. The president is in full consent with them upon the use of civil power in the Church. The Baptists are in their constituencies more republican than the Methodists tho' hardly much more join their profession.

The Diary of William Bentley, D.D., 2 vols. (Salem, Mass.: Essex Institute, 1907), 2:409 (diary entry for 24 January 1802).

6. Memoir, Correspondence and Miscellanies, from the Papers of Thomas Jefferson, ed. Thomas Jefferson Randolph, 4 vols. (Charlottesville, Va., 1829).

7. The Writings of Thomas Jefferson, ed. Henry A. Washington, 9 vols. (Washington, D.C.: Taylor and Maury, 1853–1854).

8. The Writings of Thomas Jefferson, ed. H. A. Washington, 8:113–114; letter from Jefferson to Mr. Lincoln, 1 January 1802, ibid., 4:427.

9. The Writings of Thomas Jefferson, ed. Andrew A. Lipscomb and Albert Ellery Bergh, 20 vols., Library Edition (Washington, D.C.: Thomas Jefferson Memorial Association, 1905), 16:281–282 [hereinafter Writings of Jefferson]. See also The Jeffersonian Cyclopedia, ed. John P. Foley, 2 vols. (New York: Russell and Russell, 1900), 1:142, sec. 1269, s.v. "Church and State."

10. See, for example, Adrienne Koch and William Peden, eds., The Life and Selected Writings of Thomas Jefferson (New York: Modern Library; Random House, 1944), 332–333 [hereinafter Life and Selected Writings of Jefferson]; Saul K. Padover, ed., The Complete Jefferson (New York: Duell, Sloan and Pearce, 1943), 518–519; John Dewey, ed., The Living Thoughts of Thomas Jefferson (New York: Longmans, Green, 1940), 102–103; Edward Boykin, ed., The Wisdom of Thomas Jefferson (New York: Doubleday, Doran, 1941), 167.

11. Jeremiah S. Black, "Religious Liberty," An Address to the Phrenakosmian Society of Pennsylvania College, Delivered at the Annual Commencement, September 17, 1856, in Essays and Speeches of Jeremiah S. Black (New York: D. Appleton, 1885), 53 (emphasis in the original). Black's remark was quoted in McCollum v. Board of Education, 333 U.S. 203, 219–220 n. 8 (1948) (Opinion of Frankfurter, J.).

12. Henry S. Randall, The Life of Thomas Jefferson, 3 vols. (New York: Derby and Jackson, 1857), 3:2.

13. Philip Schaff, Church and State in the United States; or, the American Idea of Religious Liberty and Its Practical Effects (New York: G. P. Putnam's Sons; American Historical Society, 1888), 29 n. 1. Schaff reprinted excerpts from Reynolds v. United States (1879) in which the Supreme Court for the first time cited the Danbury letter. Ibid., 121. This Court opinion, in all likelihood, introduced Schaff to the metaphor.

14. See Philip Hamburger, Separation of Church and State (Cambridge, Mass.: Harvard University Press, 2002), 302 n. 39.

15. Reynolds v. United States, 98 U.S. 145, 164 (1879).

16. It is unclear whether the *Reynolds* Court thought the "wall" was relevant to its analysis, although the conventional view is that the metaphor was not. The justices, however, firmly believed there was a "true distinction between what properly belongs to the church and what to the State." *Reynolds*, 98 U.S. at 163. They may have thought that Jefferson's "wall" separated religious opinion, which was free from government intrusion, from conduct that threatened peace and good order, which the Court held was subject to legitimate government restrictions. Of course, one cannot be certain that either Jefferson or the *Reynolds* Court thought this was precisely what the "wall" separated. Few modern commentators have located Jefferson's "wall" specifically between religious opinion and religious conduct subversive of good order. For a brief discussion of the *Reynolds* opinion suggesting that the "wall" was not superfluous language, see chapter 3 in text accompanying note 86.

17. Robert M. Hutchins, "The Future of the Wall," in *The Wall between Church and State*, ed. Dallin H. Oaks (Chicago: University of Chicago Press, 1963), 17. See also Christopher F. Mooney, *Public Virtue: Law and the Social Character of Religion* (Notre Dame, Ind.: University of Notre Dame Press, 1986), 30 ("Chief Justice Waite wanted to use another phrase in Jefferson's letter to support his decision and could not edit out 'the wall.'"); Charles C. Haynes, *Religion in American History: What to Teach and How* (Alexandria, Va.: Association for Supervision and Curriculum Development, 1990), 53 ("the first use of Jefferson's letter by the Court had less to do with the 'wall of separation' and more to do with the distinction Jefferson makes between actions and opinions in matters of religion."); Robert M. Healey, "Thomas Jefferson's 'Wall': Absolute or Serpentine?" *Journal of Church and State* 30 (1988): 443 ("Waite did not mention the 'wall' metaphor. Although it was part of the quoted paragraph, other Jeffersonian sentences supplied the standards for deciding the case."); Stephen J. Safranek, "Can Science Guide Legal Argumentation?: The Role of Metaphor in Constitutional Cases," *Loyola University Chicago Law Journal* 25 (1994): 375–376 ("[T]he wall metaphor found its way into the Court's First Amendment as an 'appearance' because the *Reynolds* Court placed no particular emphasis on the metaphor. It simply appeared in the Court's opinion as part of the Court's larger quotation from Jefferson's Danbury letter. Presumably, the Court's silence indicates that it did not view the metaphor as having any meaning independent of that of the letter itself, and the letter, in turn, only distinguished between the government's ability to legislate against an individual's actions and its absolute inability to exert any power over an individual's religious beliefs or opinions. . . . Because . . . the theme of his letter to the Danbury Baptists provided the Court with all that it believed necessary to interpret the Free Exercise Clause, the Court found no need to interpret Jefferson's 'wall' metaphor. Nevertheless, because the Court chose to cite the entire Danbury letter, the 'wall of separation' quietly found its way into constitutional law.");

Craig B. Mousin, "Confronting the Wall of Separation: A New Dialogue between Law and Religion on the Meaning of the First Amendment," *DePaul Law Review* 42 (1992): 3–5 (noting that Waite was attracted to the Danbury letter because of the distinction Jefferson made between belief and action).

18. See generally Todd M. Gillett, "The Absolution of Reynolds: The Constitutionality of Religious Polygamy," *William and Mary Bill of Rights Journal* 8 (2000): 497–534.

19. *Reynolds*, 98 U.S. at 164. This mistranscription is noted in chapter 3.

20. For more on the Court's use of history in church-state cases, see Daniel L. Dreisbach, "*Everson* and the Command of History: The Supreme Court, Lessons of History, and Church-State Debate in America," in *Everson Revisited: Religion, Education, and Law at the Crossroads*, ed. Jo Renée Formicola and Hubert Morken (Lanham, Md.: Rowman and Littlefield, 1997), 23–57; Daniel L. Dreisbach, "A Lively and Fair Experiment: Religion and the American Constitutional Tradition," *Emory Law Journal* 49 (2000): 223–253.

21. *Reynolds*, 98 U.S. at 164.

22. See also the question raised by Gerard V. Bradley: "if the wall of separation metaphor was first used in 1802 (as the Court admits it was), how could its meaning be apparent to the 1788 conventioneers who demanded nonestablishment or to the state legislators who ratified that stricture in 1790?" Bradley, *Church-State Relationships in America* (Westport, Conn.: Greenwood Press, 1987), 142–143. Joseph H. Brady further complained that, even if the metaphor means what the Court says it does, "it is obviously incorrect to substitute this private opinion for the First Amendment." Joseph H. Brady, *Confusion Twice Confounded: The First Amendment and the Supreme Court: An Historical Study* (South Orange, N.J.: Seton Hall University Press, 1954), 74.

23. See generally C. Peter Magrath, "Chief Justice Waite and the 'Twin Relic': *Reynolds v. United States*," *Vanderbilt Law Review* 18 (1965): 507–543.

24. Magrath, "Chief Justice Waite and the 'Twin Relic,'" 524.

25. Magrath, "Chief Justice Waite and the 'Twin Relic,'" 526.

26. Magrath, "Chief Justice Waite and the 'Twin Relic,'" 529, quoting *Reynolds*, 98 U.S. at 162.

27. Magrath, "Chief Justice Waite and the 'Twin Relic,'" 526.

28. Leonard W. Levy, *The Establishment Clause: Religion and the First Amendment*, 2d ed. (Chapel Hill: University of North Carolina Press, 1994), 75.

29. *Reynolds*, 98 U.S. at 163.

30. Magrath, "Chief Justice Waite and the 'Twin Relic,'" 530 n. 111.

31. Magrath, "Chief Justice Waite and the 'Twin Relic,'" 527, quoting a letter from Waite to Bancroft, 4 January 1879. The phrase "scope and effect" used in this letter was also used in the *Reynolds* opinion to introduce the Danbury letter. 98 U.S. at 164.

32. Magrath, "Chief Justice Waite and the 'Twin Relic,'" 528, quoting a letter from Waite to Bancroft, 17 January 1879.

33. *Everson v. Board of Education*, 330 U.S. 1, 16, 18 (1947). Justice Hugo L. Black wrote the majority opinion in *Everson*. For a useful discussion of Justice Black's attraction to Jefferson's metaphor as a theme of his church-state views, see Barbara A. Perry, "Justice Hugo Black and the 'Wall of Separation between Church and State,'" *Journal of Church and State* 31 (1989): 55–72. Perry remarked: "Justice Hugo L. Black, the foremost jurisprudential interpreter of the metaphor in the Supreme Court's modern era, is arguably responsible for the public's familiarity with the 'wall' doctrine." Ibid., 55.

In *Separation of Church and State*, Philip Hamburger argued that Justice Black, a former Alabama Ku Klux Klansman, was the product of a remarkable "confluence of Protestant [specifically Baptist], nativist and progressive anti-Catholic forces. . . . Black's association with the Klan has been much discussed in connection with his liberal views on race, but, in fact, his membership suggests more about [his] ideals of Americanism," especially his support for separation of church and state. "Black had long before sworn, under the light of flaming crosses, to preserve 'the sacred constitutional rights' of 'free public schools' and 'separation of church and state.'" Although he later distanced himself from the Klan, "Black's distaste for Catholicism did not diminish." Black's admixture of progressive, Baptist, Klan, and strict separationist views is best understood in terms of anti-Catholicism and, more broadly, a deep hostility to assertions of ecclesiastical authority. Separation of church and state, the Justice believed, was an American ideal of freedom from oppressive ecclesiastical authority, especially that of the Roman Catholic Church. A regime of separation enabled Americans to assert their individual autonomy and practice democracy, which Black believed was Protestantism in its secular form. In *Everson*, Black "led the Court to declare itself in favor of the 'separation of church and state.'" Hamburger, *Separation of Church and State*, 423, 434, 462, 463. See also Hugo Black, Jr., *My Father: A Remembrance* (New York: Random House, 1975), 101–105 (Black's son contended that the only thing his father had in common with the Klan was a suspicion of the Catholic Church; Black read and admired Paul Blanshard's books); Roger K. Newman, *Hugo Black: A Biography* (New York: Pantheon Books, 1994), 104, 521 (noting Black's view of Catholicism); Howard Ball, *Hugo L. Black: Cold Steel Warrior* (New York: Oxford University Press, 1996), 16 (Black opposed "the Klan's use of intimidation and violence" but "sympathized with the group's economic, nativist, and anti-Catholic beliefs"); Gerald T. Dunne, *Hugo Black and the Judicial Revolution* (New York: Simon and Schuster, 1977), 268 (Black's church-state views were informed by anti-Catholic sentiment in his native Alabama and "the anti-Catholic polemics of Paul Blanshard of the post-World War II period"). For additional examinations of anti-Catholic sentiment in twentieth-century church-state jurisprudence, see Thomas C. Berg, "Anti-Catholicism and Modern Church-State Relations," *Loyola University Chicago Law Journal* 33 (2001): 121–172 (discussing how church-state disputes in modern America have been shaped by societal attitudes toward Roman Catholicism); Edward McGlynn Gaffney, "Hostility to Religion, American Style," *DePaul Law Review* 42 (1992): 263–304 (illustrating a history of hostility to religion, especially Roman Catholicism, which is connected to confusion about church-state jurisprudence); John T. McGreevy, "Thinking on One's Own: Catholicism in the American Intellectual Imagination, 1928–1960," *Journal of American History* 84 (June 1997): 97–131 (describing the rise of anti-Catholicism among American liberal intellectuals in the mid-twentieth century and its influence on separationist judicial pronouncements in *Everson* and *McCollum*).

34. See note 20.

35. See *Wallace v. Jaffree*, 472 U.S. 38, 92 n.1 (1985) (Rehnquist, J., dissenting) (noting that "*Reynolds* is the only authority cited as direct precedent for the 'wall of separation theory.'").

36. Brief of the American Civil Liberties Union as Amicus Curiae at 8, 12, *Everson v. Board of Education*, 330 U.S. 1 (1947).

37. Brief of the American Civil Liberties Union as Amicus Curiae at 27.

38. Brief of the American Civil Liberties Union as Amicus Curiae at 34. See also the three references to the wall in Brief of the American Civil Liberties Union as Amicus Curiae on Petition for Rehearing at 2, 3, 4.

39. Brief Amici Curiae of National Council of Catholic Men and National Council of Catholic Women at 32, 33, *Everson v. Board of Education*, 330 U.S. 1 (1947).

40. Brief Amici Curiae of National Council of Catholic Men and National Council of Catholic Women at 33.

41. Brief Amici Curiae of National Council of Catholic Men and National Council of Catholic Women at 36.

42. Brief Amici Curiae of National Council of Catholic Men and National Council of Catholic Women at 35.

43. Brief Amici Curiae of National Council of Catholic Men and National Council of Catholic Women at 36.

44. See note 10.

45. See, for example, Edward F. Waite, "Jefferson's 'Wall of Separation': What and Where?" *Minnesota Law Review* 33 (1949): 494–516; Conrad Henry Moehlman, *The Wall of Separation between Church and State: An Historical Study of Recent Criticism of the Religious Clause of the First Amendment* (Boston: Beacon Press, 1951); Moehlman, "The Wall of Separation: The Law and the Facts," *American Bar Association Journal* 38 (April 1952): 281–284, 343–348; Loren P. Beth, "The Wall of Separation and the Supreme

Court," *Minnesota Law Review* 38 (1954): 215–227; Dallin H. Oaks, ed., *The Wall between Church and State* (Chicago: University of Chicago Press, 1963).

46. Joseph Martin Dawson, *Separate Church and State Now* (New York: Richard R. Smith, 1948), Appendix B, 209. See also ibid., 203 ("PROTESTANTS AND OTHER AMERICANS UNITED is determined to assert its full strength to the end that there shall be no more breaches in this wall, that the breaches already made shall be repaired, and that the complete separation of church and state in an undivided state-supported educational system shall be maintained."). See also "New Body Demands Church Separation: Protestants and Others Plan Drive, Charging Catholic Violations of Doctrine," *New York Times*, 12 January 1948, 1, 12.

47. Paul Blanshard, *American Freedom and Catholic Power* (Boston: Beacon Press, 1949), 305.

48. *McCollum v. Board of Education*, 333 U.S. 203, 211 (1948). See also Roger K. Newman, "School Prayer and the Ten Commandments in Alabama," *Cumberland Law Review* 28 (1997–1998): 4 ("the Court made Jefferson's metaphor of the 'wall of separation between church and state' into a principle of constitutional law."). Newman, Black's biographer, also offers interesting insights into Hugo Black's private views on these cases.

49. Brady, *Confusion Twice Confounded*, 130. Brady's complete sentence is as follows: "Remarkable, indeed, is the care with which he [Black] avoids the plain language of the First Amendment, with which he assiduously relies upon the Everson decision, with which he substitutes the figurative 'wall of separation' (now no longer enclosed in quotation marks—it has come of age!) for the literal language of the First Amendment, which he is supposed to be using as the measuring-rod for the Illinois law."

50. Despite its strict separationist rhetoric, the *Everson* Court upheld the New Jersey law that authorized reimbursements to parents for money expended in the transportation of their children to and from parochial schools, rejecting the minority contention that the tax-supported program constituted an "establishment of religion" in violation of the First Amendment. The dissenting justices were struck by the apparent inconsistency between the majority's separationist rhetoric and its accommodationist holding. Justice Robert H. Jackson remarked sardonically: "the undertones of the opinion, advocating complete and uncompromising separation of Church from State, seem utterly discordant with its conclusion yielding support to their commingling in educational matters." *Everson*, 330 U.S. at 19 (Jackson, J., dissenting). Justice Felix Frankfurter was particularly bitter about the majority's apparent compromise.

51. *McCollum*, 333 U.S. at 231 (Opinion of Frankfurter, J.). See also Dunne, *Hugo Black and the Judicial Revolution*, 267–268; Newman, *Hugo Black: A Biography*, 361–365; James F. Simon, *The Antagonists: Hugo Black,*

*Felix Frankfurter and Civil Liberties in Modern America* (New York: Simon and Schuster, 1989), 180–183.

52. *McCollum*, 333 U.S. at 244–245 n. 8 (Reed, J., dissenting).

53. *Braunfeld v. Brown*, 366 U.S. 599, 603–604 (1961) (Opinion of Warren, C. J.).

54. *Engel v. Vitale*, 370 U.S. 421, 425 (1962).

55. *Abington School District v. Schempp*, 374 U.S. 203 (1963).

56. See *Lemon v. Kurtzman*, 403 U.S. 602, 614 (1971).

57. *Larkin v. Grendel's Den*, 459 U.S. 116, 122–123 (1982).

58. *Lynch v. Donnelly*, 465 U.S. 668, 673 (1984).

59. *McDaniel v. Paty*, 435 U.S. 618, 637 (1978) (Brennan, J., concurring).

60. Indeed, some ardent separationists argue that the Court began its retreat from the "wall of separation" principle in *Everson* when it declined to strike down the challenged New Jersey statute.

61. *Wallace v. Jaffree*, 472 U. S. at 107 (Rehnquist, J., dissenting).

62. *Committee for Public Education and Religious Liberty v. Regan*, 444 U.S. at 671 (Stevens, J., dissenting). See also *County of Allegheny v. American Civil Liberties Union, Greater Pittsburgh Chapter*, 492 U.S. 573, 650–651 n. 7 (1989) (Stevens, J., concurring in part and dissenting in part) (same); *Capitol Square Review and Advisory Board v. Pinette*, 515 U.S. 753, 797 (1995) (Stevens, J., dissenting) ("this case illustrates the importance of rebuilding the 'wall of separation between church and State' that Jefferson envisioned.").

63. *McCollum*, 333 U.S. at 247 (Reed, J., dissenting).

64. *Engel v. Vitale*, 370 U.S. 421, 445–446 (1962) (Stewart, J., dissenting). See also William A. Stanmeyer, "Free Exercise and the Wall: The Obsolescence of a Metaphor," *George Washington Law Review* 37 (1968): 241 ("the realities of Church-State relations in our complex and changing times do not readily fit the metaphor of the 'Wall'"); Timothy L. Hall, *Separating Church and State: Roger Williams and Religious Liberty* (Urbana, Ill.: University of Illinois Press, 1998), 4 (The Supreme Court's interpretive approach has "burdened the establishment clause with a crude form of law by metaphor, according to which the Supreme Court purported to find answers to complex issues chiefly through appeal to Jefferson's image of the 'wall of separation' between church and state. In *Everson v. Board of Education*, the Court enthroned Jefferson's metaphor.").

65. *Abington School District v. Schempp*, 374 U.S. at 309 (Stewart, J., dissenting).

66. *McCollum*, 333 U.S. at 238 (Jackson, J., concurring). But see *Committee for Public Education and Religious Liberty v. Nyquist*, 413 U.S. 756, 761 (1973) (Justice Lewis F. Powell, Jr., disputing that Jefferson's metaphoric "wall" has become as winding as his famous serpentine walls). See Justice Robert H. Jackson's admission in *Zorach*: "The wall which the Court was professing to erect between Church and State has become even more warped and twisted than

I expected. Today's judgment will be more interesting to students of psychology and of the judicial processes than to students of constitutional law." *Zorach v. Clauson*, 343 U.S. 306, 325 (1952) (Jackson, J., dissenting). Significantly, Jackson credited the Court, not Jefferson or the framers of the First Amendment, with erection of the "wall." See also Brady, *Confusion Twice Confounded*, 189 ("There it is: it is not the First Amendment which erected the wall—it is the Court which has done it! At last the truth has come out.").

67. *Gillette v. United States*, 401 U.S. 437, 450 (1971).

68. *Lemon v. Kurtzman*, 403 U.S. 602, 612, 614 (1971).

69. *Wallace v. Jaffree*, 472 U.S. 38, 92, 106–107 (1985) (Rehnquist, J., dissenting). Jefferson, in fact, returned to America in November 1789, long before formal ratification of the Bill of Rights. See also *Grand Rapids School District v. Ball*, 473 U.S. 373, 400–401 (1985) (Rehnquist, J., dissenting) (chastising the Court for failing "to discuss the faulty 'wall' premise upon which those cases rest. In doing so the Court blinds itself to the first 150 years' history of the Establishment Clause."). Justice Rehnquist's reading of history in his dissenting *Jaffree* opinion was influenced by Robert L. Cord, *Separation of Church and State: Historical Fact and Current Fiction* (New York: Lambeth Press, 1982). For a scathing critique of Rehnquist's use of history, see Leo Pfeffer, "The Establishment Clause: An Absolutist's Defense," *Notre Dame Journal of Law, Ethics and Public Policy* 4 (1990): 720–729. For a brief discussion of Chief Justice Rehnquist's criticism of the "wall" metaphor, see Derek Davis, *Original Intent: Chief Justice Rehnquist and the Course of American Church/State Relations* (Buffalo, N.Y.: Prometheus Books, 1991), 94–97.

70. *Hyde v. United States*, 225 U.S. 347, 391 (1912) (Holmes, J., dissenting).

71. *Tiller v. Atlantic Coast Line Railroad Co.*, 318 U.S. 54, 68 (1943) (Frankfurter, J., concurring). See also *Lee v. Weisman*, 505 U.S. 577, 644 (1992) (Scalia, J., dissenting) ("Our Religion Clause jurisprudence has become bedeviled (so to speak) by reliance on formulaic abstractions that are not derived from, but positively conflict with, our long-accepted constitutional traditions.").

72. *Berkey v. Third Ave. Ry. Co.*, 244 N.Y. 84, 94, 155 N.E. 58, 61 (1926). Cf. *Kingston Dry Dock Co. v. Lake Champlain Transportation Co.*, 31 F.2d 265, 267 (2nd Cir. 1929) (Learned Hand remarked: "Much of the metaphor in the books merely impedes discourse, as Judge Cardozo well observes in Berkey v. Third Avenue Ry.; here, as elsewhere, it is ordinarily a symptom of confused thinking."); *United States v. Scophony Corp.*, 333 U.S. 795, 820 (1948) (Frankfurter, J., concurring) ("all instruments of thought should be narrowly watched lest they be abused."). See also Stanmeyer, "Free Exercise and the Wall: The Obsolescence of a Metaphor," 223–224 ("In recent controversies over the meaning of the American Constitution, there is probably no figure of speech more famous than the 'Wall of Separation between Church and State.' . . . Yet because

of its very popularity, this metaphor endangers public understanding of the policy it aims to express, for frequent repetition of any shorthand phrase can, if we are not careful, reduce it to the status of a slogan. And slogans are poor tools with which to fashion public policy or Constitutional doctrine. If Justice Cardozo's comment is correct, if metaphors are indeed fickle friends which 'end often by enslaving' the very thought they started out to free, then the site, contours, foundation, and usefulness of this 'Wall' must be 'narrowly watched.'"); Ronald F. Thiemann, *Religion in Public Life: A Dilemma for Democracy* (Washington, D.C.: Georgetown University Press, 1996), 42 ("Principles derived from metaphors have the advantage of capturing with vividness and felicity the essential elements of a complicated situation. They have the distinct disadvantage, however, of encouraging simplicity instead of precise analysis or fostering caricature when detailed portraiture is needed.").

NOTES TO CHAPTER 8

1. Noah Webster, *An American Dictionary of the English Language*, 2 vols. (New York: S. Converse, 1828), s.v. "Wall."

2. Robert Frost, "Education by Poetry: A Meditative Monologue," in *Collected Poems, Prose, and Plays* (New York: Library of America, Literary Classics of the United States, 1995), 720. Frost excepted from this statement "mathematical thinking."

3. Aristotle, *Poetics*, 1459a, in *The Complete Works of Aristotle*, ed. Jonathan Barnes, 2 vols. (Princeton, N.J.: Princeton University Press, 1984), 2:2334–2335.

4. Biblical literature, for example, frequently references the wall metaphor. See, for example, St. Paul's reference to a separating wall in his epistle to the Ephesians: "For Christ himself has brought us peace by making Jews and Gentiles one people. With his own body he broke down the wall that separated them and kept them enemies." Ephesians 2:14 (*Good News Bible*). For other biblical references to the wall metaphor, see Proverbs 25:28 KJV ("He that hath no rule over his own spirit is like a city that is broken down, and without walls."); I Samuel 25:16; Proverbs 18:11; Song of Solomon 8:9–10; Isaiah 5:5; Isaiah 26:1; Isaiah 62:6; Zechariah 2:5.

5. *Merriam-Webster's Collegiate Dictionary*, 10th ed. (1993), s.v. "wall."

6. Robert Frost, "Mending Wall," in *North of Boston* (London: David Nutt, 1914), reprinted in *Collected Poems of Robert Frost* (New York: Henry Holt, 1930), 48 [hereinafter "Mending Wall"].

7. Frost, "Mending Wall," 47–48. Frost also referred to the poem as "Building Wall." Jeffrey S. Cramer, *Robert Frost among His Poems: A Literary Companion to the Poet's Own Biographical Contexts and Associations* (Jefferson, N.C.: McFarland, 1996), 30.

8. For more on the ancient origins of this proverb, see George Monteiro, *Robert Frost and the New England Renaissance* (Lexington: University Press of Kentucky, 1988), 126; Cramer, *Robert Frost among His Poems*, 30–31; Addison Barker, "Notes & Queries: Good Fences Make Good Neighbors," *Journal of American Folklore* 64 (1951): 421.

9. Frost, "Mending Wall," 48.

10. See also Jeffrey Meyers, ed., *Early Frost: The First Three Books* (Hopewell, N.J.: Ecco Press, 1996), xxiii (arguing that Frost "clearly stands with the narrator who questions the very need to have a wall and repeats his belief: 'Something there is that doesn't love a wall.' That 'something,' a natural force, which breaks down the wall and indicates the poet's point of view is—of course—frost."); Mordecai Marcus, *The Poems of Robert Frost: An Explication* (Boston: G. K. Hall, 1991), 42 (noting that "Mending Wall," "often quoted out of context, is sometimes, mistakenly said to declare that 'Good fences make good neighbors,' which—as Frost sometimes had to point out—is the formula of the poem's antagonist"; noting that Frost himself suggested that he, perhaps, was both of the poem's characters; noting the pun, in the poem's opening lines, that it is frost that does not love a wall and that "makes the stones in walls" tumble). Some scholars suggest that Frost's view of walls was ambivalent. See, for example, Marion Montgomery, "Robert Frost and His Use of Barriers: Man vs. Nature toward God," in *Robert Frost: A Collection of Critical Essays*, ed. James M. Cox (Englewood Cliffs, N.J.: Prentice-Hall, 1962), 138–150 (noting Frost's ambivalent view of barriers).

11. Frost, "Mending Wall," 48. See Marcus, *The Poems of Robert Frost*, 42 (suggesting that the word "offense" was a pun on "fence"); Monteiro, *Robert Frost and the New England Renaissance*, 127 ("What finally emerges from Frost's poem is the idea that the stock reply—unexamined wisdom from the past—seals off the possibility of further thought and communication. When thought has frozen into folk expression, language itself becomes another wall, one unresponsive to that which it encircles and given over to fulfilling a new and perhaps unintended function.").

12. *McCollum v. Board of Education*, 333 U.S. 203, 232 (1948) (Opinion of Frankfurter, J.).

13. J. M. O'Neill, *Religion and Education under the Constitution* (New York: Harper and Brothers, 1949), 243 (emphasis in the original). See also *Farris v. Minit Mart Foods, Inc.*, 684 S.W.2d 845, 850 (Ky. 1984) (Wintersheimer, J., dissenting) ("The wall of separation should not become a spite fence."); Joseph H. Brady, *Confusion Twice Confounded: The First Amendment and the Supreme Court: An Historical Study* (South Orange, N.J.: Seton Hall University Press, 1954), 149 ("Deriving our specifications from the Court's own statement about a 'high and impregnable' wall we seem to arrive at what is in common parlance called a 'spite fence,' which is the public denial of good neighborliness.

The fence which makes 'good neighbors' is the low fence, allowing freedom of communication between those on either side of it, with a gate or two to allow free exchange of visits and the performance of deeds of neighborly courtesy and help. It is, in fact, this kind of a fence which has separated church and state in this country from the beginning until now, when the Supreme Court would replace it with its 'spite fence.'").

14. See Horace M. Kallen, "Jefferson's Garden Wall," *American Bookman* 1 (Winter 1944): 78–82; Silvio A. Bedini, *Thomas Jefferson: Statesman of Science* (New York: Macmillan, 1990), 475–476; Philip A. Bruce, *History of the University of Virginia*, vol. 1, *The Lengthened Shadow of One Man* (New York: Macmillan, 1920), 1:273; Desmond Guinness and Julius Trousdale Sadler, Jr., *Mr. Jefferson Architect* (New York: Viking Press, 1973), 139, 143; William Howard Adams, ed., *The Eye of Thomas Jefferson* (Washington, D.C.: National Gallery of Art, 1976), 304; "Jefferson Left Directions for Building Curved Walls," *Richmond Times-Dispatch*, 16 December 1962, H12.

15. *McCollum*, 333 U.S. at 238 (Jackson, J., concurring). Other commentators have been drawn to the modified metaphor of a serpentine wall. See, for example, A. E. Dick Howard, "The Supreme Court and the Serpentine Wall," in *The Virginia Statute for Religious Freedom: Its Evolution and Consequences in American History*, ed. Merrill D. Peterson and Robert C. Vaughan (New York: Cambridge University Press, 1988), 313–349; Robert M. Healey, "Thomas Jefferson's 'Wall': Absolute or Serpentine?" *Journal of Church and State* 30 (1988): 441–462; Note, "The Serpentine Wall of Separation between Church and State: *Rosenberger v. Rector and Visitors of the University of Virginia*," *North Carolina Law Review* 74 (1996): 1225–1258; Note, "The Serpentine Wall and the Serpent's Tongue: Rethinking the Religious Harassment Debate," *Virginia Law Review* 83 (1997): 177–206.

16. *Committee for Public Education and Religious Liberty v. Nyquist*, 413 U.S. 756, 761 (1973).

17. See John Witte, Jr., *Religion and the American Constitutional Experiment: Essential Rights and Liberties* (Boulder, Colo.: Westview Press, 2000), 2–3 ("Indeed, the Court's entire record on religious rights and liberties has become vilified for its lack of consistent and coherent principles and its uncritical use of mechanical tests and misleading metaphors."); Frederick Mark Gedicks, *The Rhetoric of Church and State: A Critical Analysis of Religion Clause Jurisprudence* (Durham, N.C.: Duke University Press, 1995), 1 (surveying scholarly consensus that church-state jurisprudence lacks coherence); Stephen L. Carter, *God's Name in Vain: The Wrongs and Rights of Religion in Politics* (New York: Basic Books, 2000), 72 (church-state jurisprudence "has become almost silly, a satire on itself, struggling to enforce an ahistorical fantasy."); Leonard W. Levy, *The Establishment Clause: Religion and the First Amendment*, 2d ed. (Chapel Hill: University of North Carolina Press, 1994), 221

("The Court has reaped the scorn of a confused and aroused public because it has been erratic and unprincipled in its decisions."); Richard John Neuhaus, "Contending for the Future: Overcoming the Pfefferian Inversion," *Journal of Law and Religion* 8 (1990): 117 ("There seems to be general agreement among constitutional scholars, 'strict separationists' and 'accommodationists' alike, that the Court's rulings on religion constitute an intellectual and judicial scandal."); Frank Guliuzza III, "The Practical Perils of an Original Intent-Based Judicial Philosophy: Originalism and the Church-State Test Case," *Drake Law Review* 42 (1993): 356–357 (surveying the scholarly consensus that church-state jurisprudence lacks coherence); Rex E. Lee, "The Religion Clauses: Problems and Prospects," *Brigham Young University Law Review* 1986 (1986): 338 ("A decent argument can be made that the net contribution of the Court's precedents toward a cohesive body of law . . . has been zero. Indeed, some would say that it has been less than zero."); William P. Marshall, "Introduction: Religion and the Law Symposium," *Connecticut Law Review* 18 (1986): 698 ("the one salient point upon which academia has reached almost universal agreement is that the policies and principles underlying religion clause jurisprudence have been inadequately explored and inconsistently applied by the judiciary."); Steven D. Smith, "Separation and the 'Secular': Reconstructing the Disestablishment Decision," *Texas Law Review* 67 (1989): 956 ("In a rare and remarkable way, the Supreme Court's establishment clause jurisprudence has unified critical opinion: people who disagree about nearly everything else in the law agree that establishment doctrine is seriously, perhaps distinctively, defective. Prevailing doctrine is widely disparaged by commentators and Supreme Court Justices alike."); Casenote, "Praise the Lord and Pass the Diplomas: Harris v. Joint School District No. 241, 41 F.3d 447 (9th Cir. 1994)," *University of Cincinnati Law Review* 64 (1996): 708 ("the Supreme Court's Establishment Clause jurisprudence may resemble the construction of the Tower of Babel more than the erection of a 'wall of separation' between church and state.").

18. Aristotle, *Poetics*, 1457b and 1459a, in *The Complete Works of Aristotle*, 2:2332, 2335. A popular dictionary defines metaphor as "a figure of speech containing an implied comparison, in which a word or phrase ordinarily and primarily used of one thing is applied to another." *Webster's New World College Dictionary*, 4th ed. (1999), s.v. "metaphor."

19. See Bernard J. Hibbitts, "Making Sense of Metaphors: Visuality, Aurality, and the Reconfiguration of American Legal Discourse," *Cardozo Law Review* 16 (1994): 235, quoting George Lakoff and Mark Johnson, *Metaphors We Live By* (Chicago: University of Chicago Press, 1980), 3 ("Today few would dismiss it [metaphor] as mere semantic decoration, ornament, or rhetorical device. Some scholars have indeed gone so far in the other direction as to suggest that metaphors are fundamental tools of thought and reasoning—so much a part of the deep structure of our mentality that 'our ordinary conceptual system . . . is

. . . metaphorical in nature.'"); Andrew Ortony, "Metaphor, Language and Thought," in *Metaphor and Thought*, ed. Andrew Ortony, 2d ed. (New York: Cambridge University Press, 1993), 2–3 (discussing a "constructivist theory" of metaphor that sees metaphor as essential to human understanding); Adam Arms, "Metaphor, Women and Law," *Hastings Women's Law Journal* 10 (1999): 257–259 (surveying the literature making this claim).

20. Hibbitts, "Making Sense of Metaphors," 236.

21. Michael Boudin, "Antitrust Doctrine and the Sway of Metaphor," *Georgetown Law Journal* 75 (1986): 396.

22. Lakoff and Johnson, *Metaphors We Live By*, 158.

23. Steven L. Winter, "Transcendental Nonsense, Metaphoric Reasoning, and the Cognitive Stakes for Law," *University of Pennsylvania Law Review* 137 (1989): 1166. See also Thomas Ross, "Metaphor and Paradox," *Georgia Law Review* 23 (1989): 1076–1077 ("Legal metaphors are indispensable pieces of the legal culture, not merely tolerated, but needed."); Arms, "Metaphor, Women and Law," 257 ("Legal discourse is pregnant with metaphor. . . . Indeed, it would be difficult to have a conversation about law without resorting to the use of metaphor.").

24. See Michael J. Yelnosky, "If You Write It, (S)he Will Come: Judicial Opinions, Metaphors, Baseball, and 'the Sex Stuff,'" *Connecticut Law Review* 28 (1996): 817–818 ("Judges may be unable to avoid the use of metaphors in their opinions because metaphors are fundamental tools of thought and language.").

25. For examples, in addition to the works already cited, see Milner S. Ball, *Lying Down Together: Law, Metaphor, and Theology* (Madison: University of Wisconsin Press, 1985), 23–27; Haig Bosmajian, *Metaphor and Reason in Judicial Opinions* (Carbondale: Southern Illinois University Press, 1992); Maureen Archer and Ronnie Cohen, "Sidelined on the (Judicial) Bench: Sports Metaphors in Judicial Opinions," *American Business Law Journal* 35 (1998): 225–248; Jan G. Deutsch, "Law as Metaphor: A Structural Analysis of Legal Process," *Georgetown Law Journal* 66 (1978) 1339–1348; Martha Grace Duncan, "In Slime and Darkness: The Metaphor of Filth in Criminal Justice," *Tulane Law Review* 68 (1994): 725–802; Burr Henly, "'Penumbra': The Roots of a Legal Metaphor," *Hastings Constitutional Law Quarterly* 15 (1987): 81–100; Adalberto Jordan, "Imagery, Humor, and the Judicial Opinion," *University of Miami Law Review* 41 (1987): 693–727; Gary Minda, "The Law and Metaphor of Boycott," *Buffalo Law Review* 41 (1993): 807–931; James R. Murray, "The Role of Analogy in Legal Reasoning," *UCLA Law Review* 29 (1982): 833–871; James E. Murray, "Understanding Law as Metaphor," *Journal of Legal Education* 34 (1984): 714–730; Lars Noah, "Interpreting Agency Enabling Acts: Misplaced Metaphors in Administrative Law," *William and Mary Law Review* 41 (2000): 1463–1530; Stephen

J. Safranek, "Can Science Guide Legal Argumentation?: The Role of Metaphor in Constitutional Cases," *Loyola University Chicago Law Journal* 25 (1994): 357–403; Elizabeth G. Thornburg, "Metaphors Matter: How Images of Battle, Sports, and Sex Shape the Adversary System," *Wisconsin Women's Law Journal* 10 (1995): 225–281; Steven L. Winter, "The Metaphor of Standing and the Problem of Self-Governance," *Stanford Law Review* 40 (1988): 1371–1516.

26. Chad M. Oldfather, "The Hidden Ball: A Substantive Critique of Baseball Metaphors in Judicial Opinions," *Connecticut Law Review* 27 (1994): 20–21. See also Boudin, "Antitrust Doctrine and the Sway of Metaphor," 403 ("As rhetoric, metaphor is able not only to shape doctrine but also to increase its weight or influence with courts.").

27. Boudin, "Antitrust Doctrine and the Sway of Metaphor," 395.

28. Bosmajian, *Metaphor and Reason in Judicial Opinions*, 47.

29. Ross, "Metaphor and Paradox," 1072.

30. Boudin, "Antitrust Doctrine and the Sway of Metaphor," 405.

31. Boudin, "Antitrust Doctrine and the Sway of Metaphor," 404.

32. Oldfather, "The Hidden Ball," 23–24.

33. Safranek, "Can Science Guide Legal Argumentation?" 372.

34. Oldfather, "The Hidden Ball," 22–23. See also Boudin, "Antitrust Doctrine and the Sway of Metaphor," 395, 406–407 ("[M]etaphor is . . . a concealed form of argument by analogy. . . . Although a metaphor may contain an argument by analogy, it is likely to be a concealed argument. . . . This concealment of arguments has distinct effects, making metaphor a sharper weapon and one more difficult to parry.").

35. Boudin, "Antitrust Doctrine and the Sway of Metaphor," 406. See also Yelnosky, "If You Write It, (S)he Will Come," 818.

36. Boudin, "Antitrust Doctrine and the Sway of Metaphor," 414.

37. Boudin, "Antitrust Doctrine and the Sway of Metaphor," 414–421.

38. Oldfather, "The Hidden Ball," 23.

39. See Thornburg, "Metaphors Matter," 226 (metaphors "have real effects and can do real harm"); Arms, "Metaphor, Women and Law," 276 ("metaphor is an imperfect tool and its uncritical use leaves important realities unilluminated").

40. Lord Mansfield, as quoted in Wesley Newcomb Hohfeld, "Fundamental Legal Conceptions as Applied in Judicial Reasoning," *Yale Law Journal* 26 (1916–1917): 711–712 n. 4.

41. Hibbitts, "Making Sense of Metaphors," 233. See also Winter, "The Metaphor of Standing," 1387 ("Metaphor can, thus, have as great a potential to mislead as to enlighten.")

42. Boudin, "Antitrust Doctrine and the Sway of Metaphor," 405. See also Arms, "Metaphor, Women and Law," 276 ("Understanding by way of

metaphor involves using one's understanding of one thing to understand something else.").

43. Boudin, "Antitrust Doctrine and the Sway of Metaphor," 421.

44. Thornburg, "Metaphors Matter," 230.

45. Arms, "Metaphor, Women and Law," 262.

46. Philip Guedella, *Palmerston, 1784–1865* (New York: G. P. Putnam's, 1927), 226.

47. Arms, "Metaphor, Women and Law," 265.

48. Boudin, "Antitrust Doctrine and the Sway of Metaphor," 420.

49. Oldfather, "The Hidden Ball," 24–25, citing Ross, "Metaphor and Paradox," 1071–1073. See also Arms, "Metaphor, Women and Law," 259–260; Archer and Cohen, "Sidelined on the (Judicial) Bench: Sports Metaphors in Judicial Opinions," 229.

50. Ross, "Metaphor and Paradox," 1064–1066. Other scholars have used the lens metaphor to explain the power and function of metaphor. See, for example, Max Black, *Models and Metaphors: Studies in Language and Philosophy* (Ithaca, N.Y.: Cornell University Press, 1962), 39–41; Winter, "The Metaphor of Standing," 1387.

51. Oldfather, "The Hidden Ball," 25.

52. Lakoff and Johnson, *Metaphors We Live By*, 145.

53. Oldfather, "The Hidden Ball," 30. See also Safranek, "Can Science Guide Legal Argumentation?" 358 ("judges often use metaphors in legal decisions to create obscurity rather than clarity").

54. Safranek, "Can Science Guide Legal Argumentation?" 360.

55. Safranek, "Can Science Guide Legal Argumentation?" 359–360.

56. O'Neill, *Religion and Education under the Constitution*, 199.

57. Safranek, "Can Science Guide Legal Argumentation?" 402–403.

58. Arms, "Metaphor, Women and Law," 262.

59. *Berkey v. Third Ave. Ry. Co.*, 244 N.Y. 84, 94, 155 N.E. 58, 61 (1926).

60. *Zorach v. Clauson*, 343 U.S. 306, 317 (1952) (Black, J., dissenting) (footnotes omitted).

61. *Larkin v. Grendel's Den, Inc.*, 459 U.S. 116, 122–123 (1982). See also *Lynch v. Donnelly*, 465 U.S. 668, 673 (1984) ("The concept of a 'wall' of separation is a useful figure of speech probably deriving from [the] views of Thomas Jefferson.").

62. Levy, *The Establishment Clause*, 250.

63. See *Everson*, 330 U.S. at 15–16 (majority opinion); id. at 31–32 (Rutledge, J., dissenting).

64. Harold E. Fey, "Problems of Church and State in the United States: A Protestant View," in *The Wall between Church and State*, ed. Dallin H. Oaks (Chicago: University of Chicago Press, 1963), 37.

65. *McCollum*, 333 U.S. at 231 (Opinion of Frankfurter, J.). See also *Wolman v. Walter*, 433 U.S. 229, 265 (1977) (Stevens, J., concurring in part and dissenting in part) ("The line drawn by the Establishment Clause of the First Amendment must also have a fundamental character.").

66. *Everson*, 330 U.S. at 59 (Rutledge, J., dissenting).

67. *McCollum*, 333 U.S. at 212. See also *Engel v. Vitale*, 370 U.S. 421, 431 (1961) (The Establishment Clause's "first and most immediate purpose rested on the belief that a union of government and religion tends to destroy government and to degrade religion.").

68. Marvin E. Frankel, "Religion in Public Life—Reasons for Minimal Access," *George Washington University Law Review* 60 (1992): 633–634.

69. *Board of Education v. Allen*, 392 U.S. 236, 254 (1968) (Black, J., dissenting).

70. *Board of Education v. Allen*, 392 U.S. at 254 (Black, J., dissenting).

71. See Levy, *The Establishment Clause*, 246.

72. *Everson*, 330 U.S. at 34 (Rutledge, J., dissenting).

73. *Everson*, 330 U.S. at 13. Jefferson was in Europe at the time the First Amendment was drafted and adopted by the First Federal Congress.

74. *Reynolds v. United States*, 98 U.S. 145, 164 (1879).

75. Robert Frost, "Mending Wall," 48. Justice Felix Frankfurter quoted Frost's poem in *McCollum*, 333 U.S. at 232 (Opinion of Frankfurter, J.) ("If nowhere else, in the relation between Church and State, 'good fences make good neighbors.'").

76. See *Gillette v. United States*, 401 U.S. 437, 450 (1971) ("The metaphor of a 'wall' or impassable barrier between Church and State, taken too literally, may mislead constitutional analysis.").

77. See generally Philip Hamburger, *Separation of Church and State* (Cambridge, Mass.: Harvard University Press, 2002), 9–14, 89–107 (noting that many Americans in the founding era, especially religious dissenters, drew sharp distinctions among the terms "separation," "disestablishment," and "religious liberty").

78. Frank Guliuzza argued that many courts and commentators promote the "wall of separation" and the equivalent notion of "separation of church and state" as an instrument for the secularization of the state and society and the privatization of religion in public life. See especially the chapter entitled "Secularization and the Wall of Separation" in Frank Guliuzza III, *Over the Wall: Protecting Religious Expression in the Public Square* (Albany: State University of New York Press, 2000), 51–69.

79. See Bosmajian, *Metaphor and Reason in Judicial Opinions*, 1 (noting that although important principles have been expressed through tropes, principles and tropes are distinctly separate).

80. Robert M. Hutchins, "The Future of the Wall," in *The Wall between Church and State*, 19. See also Paul G. Kauper, "Everson v. Board of Education: A Product of the Judicial Will," *Arizona Law Review* 15 (1973): 321 ("The use of any metaphor as a substitute for reasoning and principle is suspect, and this was early found to be the case with respect to the wall."); William A. Stanmeyer, "Free Exercise and the Wall: The Obsolescence of a Metaphor," *George Washington Law Review* 37 (1968): 224 ("Yet because of its very popularity, this metaphor [the 'wall'] endangers public understanding of the policy it aims to express, for frequent repetition of any shorthand phrase can, if we are not careful, reduce it to the status of a slogan. And slogans are poor tools with which to fashion public policy or Constitutional doctrine.").

81. Richard P. McBrien, *Caesar's Coin: Religion and Politics in America* (New York: Macmillan, 1987), 66.

82. See *County of Allegheny v. American Civil Liberties Union, Greater Pittsburgh Chapter*, 492 U.S. 573, 657 (1989) (Kennedy, J., concurring in part and dissenting in part) (warning the Court of an unjustified "latent hostility toward religion" when it acts "as jealous guardians of an absolute 'wall of separation'").

83. *Encyclopedia of Religion in American Politics*, ed. Jeffrey D. Schultz, John G. West, Jr., and Iain Maclean (Phoenix, Ariz.: Oryx Press, 1999), 210, s.v. "Religious Apartheid."

84. The late Erwin N. Griswold, former dean of the Harvard Law School and former U.S. solicitor general, remarked:

> Jefferson is often cited as the author of views leading to the absolutist approach. His "wall of separation" is the shibboleth of those who feel that all traces of religion must be barred from any part of public activity. This phrase comes from Jefferson's reply to the Danbury Baptist Association, dated January 1, 1802. It is clear that he wrote it deliberately, and with planned effect, as, before issuing it, he sent it to the Attorney General for comment. . . . What Jefferson wrote was a powerful way of summarizing the effect of the First Amendment. But it was clearly neither a complete statement nor a substitute for the words of the Amendment itself. Moreover, the absolute effect which some have sought to give to these words is belied by Jefferson's own subsequent actions and writings.

Griswold, "Absolute Is in the Dark—A Discussion of the Approach of the Supreme Court to Constitutional Questions," *Utah Law Review* 8 (1963): 174. See also "The Williamsburg Charter," in *Articles of Faith, Articles of Peace: The Religious Liberty Clauses and the American Public Philosophy*, ed. James Davison Hunter and Os Guinness (Washington, D.C.: Brookings Institution, 1990), 136 (There are those "who raise justifiable fears of an unwarranted exclusion of religion from public life. . . . [I]nterpretations of the 'wall of separation' that would exclude religious expression and argument from public life, also contradict freedom of conscience and the genius of the [First Amendment Religious Liberty] provisions."); John W. Whitehead, *The Truth about the Wall of Separation* (Charlottesville, Va.: Rutherford Institute, 1997) ("the ['wall of separation'] phrase has often been used as a bludgeon by various interest groups to suppress an entire class of citizens—religious people—from rightly exercising their basic freedoms.").

85. Kathleen M. Sullivan, "God as a Lobby," *University of Chicago Law Review* 61 (1994): 1665; Amelia J. Uelmen, "Can a Religious Person Be a Big Firm Litigator?" *Fordham Urban Law Journal* 26 (1999): 1086.

86. Mary Ann Glendon and Raul F. Yanes, "Structural Free Exercise," *Michigan Law Review* 90 (1991): 535. Paul G. Kauper argued that "the Court's adoption of Jefferson's statement about the establishment of a wall suggests that separation of church and state is the ultimate principle in the first amendment. This view is subject to the criticism so aptly made by Professor Katz that religious freedom is the ultimate value captured in the twin religion clause and that separation is a supplemental principle which is useful in so far as it serves to protect and advance religious freedom." Kauper, "Everson v. Board of Education: A Product of the Judicial Will," 321–322, citing Wilber G. Katz, "Freedom of Religion and State Neutrality," *University of Chicago Law Review* 20 (1953): 428.

87. *Zorach v. Clauson*, 343 U.S. 306, 312 (1952). See also *Lynch v. Donnelly*, 465 U.S. 668, 673 (1984) ("the Constitution [does not] require complete separation of church and state; it affirmatively mandates accommodation, not merely tolerance, of all religions, and forbids hostility toward any. Anything less would require the 'callous indifference' we have said was never intended by the Establishment Clause. Indeed, we have observed, such hostility would bring us into 'war with our national tradition as embodied in the First Amendment's guaranty of the free exercise of religion.'")(citations omitted); id. at 678 ("the Court consistently has declined to take a rigid, absolutist view of the Establishment Clause. . . . In our modern, complex society, whose traditions and constitutional underpinnings rest on and encourage diversity and pluralism in all areas, an absolutist approach in applying the Establishment Clause is simplistic and has been uniformly rejected by the Court. Rather than mechanically invalidating all governmental conduct or statutes that confer benefits or give special recognition to religion in general or to one faith—as an absolutist approach would dictate—the Court has scrutinized challenged legislation or official conduct to determine whether, in reality, it establishes a religion or religious faith, or tends to do so.").

88. *Walz v. Tax Commission of the City of New York*, 397 U.S. 664, 670 (1970) ("No perfect or absolute separation is really possible."). See also *Lemon v. Kurtzman*, 403 U.S. 602, 614 (1971) ("Our prior holdings do not call for

total separation between church and state; total separation is not possible in an absolute sense. Some relationship between government and religious organizations is inevitable."); *Committee for Public Education and Religious Liberty v. Nyquist*, 413 U.S. 756, 760 (1973) ("It has never been thought either possible or desirable to enforce a regime of total separation. . . ."); *Lynch v. Donnelly*, 465 U.S. 668, 672–673 (1984) ("as the Court has so often noted, total separation of the two is not possible. . . . [T]he [wall] metaphor itself is not a wholly accurate description of the practical aspects of the relationship that in fact exists between church and state. No significant segment of our society and no institution within it can exist in a vacuum or in total or absolute isolation from all the other parts, much less from government."); *Agostini v. Felton*, 521 U.S. 203, 233 (1997) ("Interaction between church and state is inevitable, . . . and we have always tolerated some level of involvement between the two."); *Abington School District v. Schempp*, 374 U.S. at 308–309 (Stewart, J., dissenting) ("It is, I think, a fallacious oversimplification to regard [the religion clauses] as establishing a single constitutional standard of 'separation of church and state,' which can be mechanically applied in every case to delineate the required boundaries between government and religion. We err in the first place if we do not recognize, as a matter of history and as a matter of the imperatives of our free society, that religion and government must necessarily interact in countless ways.").

89. See *Lynch v. Donnelly*, 465 U.S. at 673, 683; *Abington School District v. Schempp*, 374 U.S. at 309 (Stewart, J., dissenting).

90. Note, "The Equal Access Act and *Mergens*: Balancing the Religion Clauses in Public Schools," *Georgia Law Review* 24 (1990): 1178. See also Marci A. Hamilton, "Power, the Establishment Clause, and Vouchers," *Connecticut Law Review* 31 (1999): 824 ("Unfortunately, the metaphor can be misleading because it seems to offer an either-or proposition: there is a wall or there is not.").

91. See Neuhaus, "Contending for the Future: Overcoming the Pfefferian Inversion," 119 ("The threat perceived by the framers and by sensible people since their time is the threat that government poses to religion. The establishment of a religion, the framers correctly believed, would violate the freedom of those who dissent from the established belief. . . . The religion clause [of the First Amendment], I am arguing, is entirely a check upon government, not a check upon religion. . . . The religion clause is not then, as many claim, a check upon both government and religion, nor is it a clause in which two claims are to be 'balanced' against one another. The religion clause is not to protect the state from the church but to protect the church from the state."); Carter, *God's Name in Vain*, 67–81 (arguing that the First Amendment wall is a single-sided wall because the "religion clause of the First Amendment is designed to limit what the state can do, not what the church can do."); Stephen L. Carter, *The Culture of Disbelief: How American Law and Politics Trivialize Religious Devotion* (New

York: Basic Books, 1993), 105, 115 ("the metaphorical separation of church and state originated in an effort to protect religion from the state, not the state from religion.").

92. *Abington School District v. Schempp*, 374 U.S. at 309 (Stewart, J., dissenting).

93. Alexander Meiklejohn, "Educational Cooperation between Church and State," *Law and Contemporary Problems* 14 (1949): 61, 69.

94. *Wallace v. Jaffree*, 472 U.S. 38, 106 (1985) (Rehnquist, J., dissenting).

95. *Wallace v. Jaffree*, 472 U.S. at 107 (Rehnquist, J., dissenting).

96. Roger K. Newman, *Hugo Black: A Biography* (New York: Pantheon Books, 1994), 365.

97. See Kauper, "Everson v. Board of Education: A Product of the Judicial Will," 321 (the wall "lacks meaning and value as a guide to constitutional interpretation").

98. See Hutchins, "The Future of the Wall," 18 (the wall "has not produced those instant solutions which its apparent clarity and directness lead its devotees to expect."), 19 ("The wall has done what walls usually do: it has obscured the view. It has lent a simplistic air to the discussion of a very complicated matter. Hence it has caused confusion whenever it has been invoked. Far from helping to decide cases, it has made opinions and decisions unintelligible. The wall is offered as a reason. It is not a reason; it is a figure of speech."); *Chamberlin v. Dade County Board of Public Instruction*, 143 So.2d 21, 25 (1962) ("The [wall of separation] quotation imputed to Jefferson, written by him ten years after the adoption of the First Amendment in a letter to the Danbury Baptists of Connecticut, has done little other than cause confusion."); John F. Wilson, *Public Religion in American Culture* (Philadelphia: Temple University Press, 1979), 5 ("[W]e have been at the mercy of simplistic formulas. A good example of the latter is Thomas Jefferson's 'Wall of Separation.' Such metaphors are misleading because they misrepresent intentions underlying the resolution of social issues, as well as actual results."), 6 ("Jefferson's casually delivered unyielding metaphor . . . has perhaps finally obscured more than it has clarified this area."); Ronald F. Thiemann, *Religion in Public Life: A Dilemma for Democracy* (Washington, D.C.: Georgetown University Press, 1996), 42–43 ("Principles derived from metaphors have the advantage of capturing with vividness and felicity the essential elements of a complicated situation. They have the distinct disadvantage, however, of encouraging simplicity instead of precise analysis or fostering caricature when detailed portraiture is needed. At a time when our nation is struggling to define the proper role of religion and religiously based moral convictions within public life, the phrase 'the separation of church and state' and its attendant metaphor 'a wall of separation between church and state' serve not to clarify but to confuse. While the phrases identify one aspect of government's relation to religion, they deflect our attention from other funda-

mental features of the first amendment guarantees."); Safranek, "Can Science Guide Legal Argumentation?" 359 ("[T]he Court's misuse of the 'wall of separation' metaphor in the church and state context has resulted in considerable clouding of Establishment Clause jurisprudence and has done little to clarify important constitutional issues of church and state relations."); George W. Dent, Jr., "Religious Children, Secular Schools," *Southern California Law Review* 61 (1988): 883 ("Like many metaphors, it [Jefferson's 'wall'] is graphic and may even facilitate analysis if viewed solely as a metaphor, but if worshipped as a golden calf it can destroy clear thinking.").

99. Robert Frost, "Mending Wall," 48.

100. *Everson*, 330 U.S. at 18.

101. See Daniel L. Dreisbach and John D. Whaley, "What the Wall Separates: A Debate on Thomas Jefferson's 'Wall of Separation' Metaphor," *Constitutional Commentary* 16 (1999): 672.

102. For a discussion of Jefferson's practices and policies inconsistent with the "wall" erected by Black in *Everson*, see Robert L. Cord, "Mr. Jefferson's 'Nonabsolute' Wall of Separation between Church and State," in *Religion and Political Culture in Jefferson's Virginia*, ed. Garrett Ward Sheldon and Daniel L. Dreisbach (Lanham, Md.: Rowman and Littlefield, 2000), 167–188; Daniel L. Dreisbach, *Real Threat and Mere Shadow: Religious Liberty and the First Amendment* (Westchester, Ill.: Crossway Books, 1987), 113–134; Daniel L. Dreisbach, "Thomas Jefferson and Bills Number 82–86 of the Revision of the Laws of Virginia, 1776–1786: New Light on the Jeffersonian Model of Church-State Relations," *North Carolina Law Review* 69 (1990): 159–211; Comment, "Jefferson and the Church-State Wall: A Historical Examination of the Man and the Metaphor," *Brigham Young University Law Review* 1978 (1978): 645–674.

103. *Tiller v. Atlantic Coast Line Railroad Co.*, 318 U.S. 54, 68 (1943) (Frankfurter, J., concurring).

104. It is reported that these were the last words of John Adams, who, unaware that Jefferson had expired five hours earlier at Monticello, died on 4 July 1826, the fiftieth anniversary of the American Declaration of Independence. See Merrill D. Peterson, *The Jefferson Image in the American Mind* (New York: Oxford University Press, 1960), 3–6; Andrew Burstein, *America's Jubilee* (New York: Alfred A. Knopf, 2001), 255–286; Robert P. Hay, "The Glorious Departure of the American Patriarchs: Contemporary Reactions to the Deaths of Jefferson and Adams," *Journal of Southern History* 35 (November 1969): 543–555.

## NOTES TO THE APPENDICES

1. John Walker was Jefferson's fellow-member from Albemarle County in the Virginia House of Burgesses.

2. The italicized words in this document were deleted by amendments during the October 1785 session of the Virginia General Assembly. The Act as adopted begins: "WHEREAS, Almighty God . . ."

3. The Act replaced "also" with "only."

4. The wording here was changed to "Be it enacted by the General Assembly . . ."

5. The Act replaced "the gospel" with "religion."

6. The Act added the words "or affirmation."

7. The Act deleted the "or" preceding meeting-house and added the words "or other place of religious worship" following meeting-house.

8. The Act deleted the "or" preceding meeting-house and added the words "or other place of religious worship" following meeting-house.

9. The Act replaced "sureties" with "securities."

10. The Act replaced "Sunday" with "the sabbath day."

11. Most published collections of Jefferson's writings incorrectly transcribe this word as "legislative." The mistranscription apparently originated from *The Writings of Thomas Jefferson*, ed. H. A. Washington, 9 vols. (Washington, D.C.: Taylor and Maury, 1853–1854), 8:113–114.

12. U.S. Constitution, amendment I.

# Selected Bibliography

There is an extensive body of scholarly works on religion and politics and church–state relationships in American history. A variety of perspectives, disciplines, and emphases has enriched this literature. The following is a bibliography of selected works on the history of religion and religious liberty in America from colonial times to the mid–nineteenth century and on the social and intellectual forces that shaped political culture and church–state relations in the early Republic. Emphasis has been placed on the ample scholarship that examines the framing of the First Amendment religion provisions and the contributions of Thomas Jefferson to a distinctive American approach to church–state relations. Also included in this bibliography are works on Jefferson's religious views and literature on the "wall of separation." For a comprehensive bibliography of works on church and state in the colonial and early national periods, see John F. Wilson, ed., *Church and State in America: A Bibliographical Guide; The Colonial and Early National Periods* (Westport, Conn.: Greenwood Press, 1986).

Adams, Arlin M., and Charles J. Emmerich. *A Nation Dedicated to Religious Liberty: The Constitutional Heritage of the Religion Clauses.* Philadelphia: University of Pennsylvania Press, 1990.

———. "William Penn and the American Heritage of Religious Liberty." *Journal of Law and Religion* 8 (1990): 57–70.

Adams, Jasper. *The Relation of Christianity to Civil Government in the United States,* 2d ed. Charleston, S.C.: A. E. Miller, 1833.

Ahlstrom, Sydney E. *A Religious History of the American People.* New Haven, Conn.: Yale University Press, 1972.

Albanese, Catherine L. *Sons of the Fathers: The Civil Religion of the American Revolution.* Philadelphia: Temple University Press, 1976.

Aldrich, P. Emory. "The Christian Religion and the Common Law." *American Antiquarian Society Proceedings* 6 (April 1889–April 1890): 18–37.

Alley, Robert S., ed. *James Madison on Religious Liberty.* Buffalo, N.Y.: Prometheus Books, 1985.

Amar, Akhil Reed. *The Bill of Rights: Creation and Reconstruction.* New Haven, Conn.: Yale University Press, 1998.

Amos, Gary T. *Defending the Declaration: How the Bible and Christianity Influenced the Writing of the Declaration of Independence.* Brentwood, Tenn.: Wolgemuth and Hyatt, 1989.

Anderson, M. B. "Relations of Christianity to the Common Law." *Albany Law Journal* 20 (4 October 1879): 265–268, (11 October 1879): 285–288.

Antieau, Chester James, Phillip Mark Carroll, and Thomas Carroll Burke. *Religion under the State Constitutions.* Brooklyn, N.Y.: Central Book Co., 1965.

Antieau, Chester James, Arthur T. Downey, and Edward C. Roberts. *Freedom from Federal Establishment: Formation and Early History of the First Amendment Religion Clauses.* Milwaukee, Wis.: Bruce, 1964.

Bailyn, Bernard, ed. *Pamphlets of the American Revolution, 1750–1776.* Vol. 1, *1750–1765.* Cambridge, Mass.: Belknap Press, Harvard University Press, 1965.

Bainton, Roland H. *The Travail of Religious Liberty.* New York: Harper and Brothers, 1951.

Baird, Robert. *Religion in America; or, An Account of the Origin, Progress, Relation to the State, and Present Condition of the Evangelical Churches in the United States. With Notices of the Unevangelical Denominations.* New York: Harper and Brothers, 1844.

Baker, John S., Jr. "The Establishment Clause as Intended: No Preference among Sects and Pluralism in a Large Commercial Republic." In *The Bill of Rights: Original Meaning and Current Understanding,* edited by Eugene W. Hickok, Jr. Charlottesville: University Press of Virginia, 1991.

———."James Madison and Religious Freedom." *Benchmark* 3, nos. 1–2 (1987): 71–78.

Baldwin, Alice M. *The New England Clergy and the American Revolution.* Durham, N.C.: Duke University Press, 1928.

Banner, Stuart. "When Christianity Was Part of the Common Law." *Law and History Review* 16 (1998): 27–62.

Banning, Lance. "James Madison, the Statute for Religious Freedom, and the Crisis of Republican Convictions." In *The Virginia Statute for Religious Freedom: Its Evolution and Consequences in American History,* edited by Merrill D. Peterson and Robert C. Vaughan. New York: Cambridge University Press, 1988.

Bellah, Robert N. "Civil Religion in America." *Daedalus: Journal of the American Academy of Arts and Sciences* 96 (1967): 1–21.

———. "The Revolution and Civil Religion." In *Religion and the American Revolution,* edited by Jerald C. Brauer. Philadelphia: Fortress Press, 1976.

Bercovitch, Sacvan. *The American Jeremiad.* Madison: University of Wisconsin Press, 1978.

Berg, Thomas C. *The State and Religion in a Nutshell.* West Nutshell Series. St. Paul, Minn.: West Group, 1998.

Berman, Harold J. "Religion and Law: The First Amendment in Historical Perspective." *Emory Law Journal* 35 (1986): 777–793.

Berns, Walter. *The First Amendment and the Future of American Democracy.* New York: Basic Books, 1976.

Beth, Loren P. *The American Theory of Church and State.* Gainesville: University of Florida Press, 1958.

———. "The Wall of Separation and the Supreme Court." *Minnesota Law Review* 38 (1954): 215–227.

Billington, Ray Allen. *The Protestant Crusade, 1800–1860: A Study of the Origins of American Nativism.* New York: Macmillan, 1938; reprinted New York: Rinehart, 1952.

Blakely, William Addison, ed. *American State Papers on Freedom in Religion,* 3d ed. Washington, D.C.: Religious Liberty Association, 1943.

Blau, Joseph L. "The Wall of Separation." *Union Seminary Quarterly Review* 38 (1984): 263–288.

———. ed. *Cornerstones of Religious Freedom in America.* Boston: Beacon Press, 1949.

Bodo, John R. *The Protestant Clergy and Public Issues, 1812–1848.* Princeton, N.J.: Princeton University Press, 1954; reprinted Philadelphia: Porcupine Press, 1980.

Boles, John. *The Great Revival, 1787–1805: The Origins of the Southern Evangelical Mind.* Lexington: University Press of Kentucky, 1972.

Boller, Paul F., Jr. *George Washington and Religion.* Dallas, Tex.: Southern Methodist University Press, 1963.

———. "George Washington and Religious Liberty." *William and Mary Quarterly,* 3d ser., 17 (1960): 486–506.

Bonomi, Patricia U. *Under the Cope of Heaven: Religion, Society, and Politics in Colonial America.* New York: Oxford University Press, 1986.

Borden, Morton. *Jews, Turks, and Infidels.* Chapel Hill: University of North Carolina Press, 1984.

Bosmajian, Haig. *Metaphor and Reason in Judicial Opinions.* Carbondale: Southern Illinois University Press, 1992.

Botein, Stephen. "Religious Dimensions of the Early American State." In *Beyond Confederation: Origins of the Constitution and American National Identity,* edited by Richard Beeman, Stephen Botein, and Edward C. Carter II. Chapel Hill: University of North Carolina Press, 1987.

Bradford, M. E. *Founding Fathers: Brief Lives of the Framers of the United States Constitution,* 2d ed., rev. Lawrence: University Press of Kansas, 1994.

———. "Religion and the Framers: The Biographical Evidence." *Benchmark* 4, no. 4 (1990): 349–358.

Bradley, Gerard V. *Church–State Relationships in America.* Westport, Conn.: Greenwood Press, 1987.

Bradley, Gerard V. "Imagining the Past and Remembering the Future: The Supreme Court's History of the Establishment Clause." *Connecticut Law Review* 18 (1986): 827–843.

———. "The No Religious Test Clause and the Constitution of Religious Liberty: A Machine That Has Gone of Itself." *Case Western Reserve Law Review* 37 (1987): 674–747.

Brady, Joseph H. *Confusion Twice Confounded: The First Amendment and the Supreme Court: An Historical Study*. South Orange, N.J.: Seton Hall University Press, 1954.

Brann, Eva T. H. "Madison's 'Memorial and Remonstrance': A Model of American Eloquence." In *Rhetoric and American Statesmanship*, edited by Glen E. Thurow and Jeffrey D. Wallin. Durham, N.C.: Carolina Academic Press, 1984.

Brant, Irving. *The Bill of Rights: Its Origin and Meaning*. Indianapolis: Bobbs–Merrill, 1965.

———. "Madison: On the Separation of Church and State." *William and Mary Quarterly*, 3d ser., 8 (1951): 3–24.

Brauer, Jerald C., ed. *Religion and the American Revolution*. Philadelphia: Fortress Press, 1976.

Brewer, David J. *The United States a Christian Nation*. Philadelphia: John C. Winston, 1905.

Briceland, Alan V. "Thomas Jefferson's Epitaph: Symbol of a Lifelong Crusade against Those Who Would 'Usurp the Throne of God.'" *Journal of Church and State* 29 (1987): 285–303.

Bridenbaugh, Carl. *Mitre and Sceptre: Transatlantic Faiths, Ideas, Personalities, and Politics, 1689–1775*. New York: Oxford University Press, 1962.

Browne, C. A. "Elder John Leland and the Mammoth Cheshire Cheese." *Agricultural History* 18 (1944): 145–153.

Buckley, Thomas E. "After Disestablishment: Thomas Jefferson's Wall of Separation in Antebellum Virginia." *Journal of Southern History* 61 (1995): 445–480.

———. *Church and State in Revolutionary Virginia, 1776–1787*. Charlottesville: University Press of Virginia, 1977.

———. "The Political Theology of Thomas Jefferson." In *The Virginia Statute for Religious Freedom: Its Evolution and Consequences in American History*, edited by Merrill D. Peterson and Robert C. Vaughan. New York: Cambridge University Press, 1988.

———. "Reflections on a Wall." *William and Mary Quarterly*, 3d ser., 56 (1999): 795–800.

———. "Wall of Separation." *America* 180, no. 9 (20 March 1999): 18–19, 22–23.

Butler, Jon. *Awash in a Sea of Faith: Christianizing the American People*. Cambridge, Mass.: Harvard University Press, 1990.

Butler, Paul M., and Alfred L. Scanlan. "Wall of Separation—Judicial Gloss on the First Amendment." *Notre Dame Lawyer* 37 (1962): 288–308.

Butterfield, L. H. "Elder John Leland, Jeffersonian Itinerant." *Proceedings of the American Antiquarian Society* 62 (1952): 155–242.

Butts, R. Freeman. *The American Tradition in Religion and Education.* Boston: Beacon Press, 1950.

Calhoon, Robert M. *Evangelicals and Conservatives in the Early South, 1740–1861.* Columbia: University of South Carolina Press, 1988.

Carmody, Denise Lardner, and John Tully Carmody. *The Republic of Many Mansions: Foundations of American Religious Thought.* New York: Paragon House, 1990.

Carroll, Peter N., ed. *Religion and the Coming of the American Revolution.* Waltham, Mass.: Ginn–Blaisdell, 1970.

Carter, Stephen L. *The Culture of Disbelief: How American Law and Politics Trivialize Religious Devotion.* New York: Basic Books, 1993.

———. *God's Name in Vain: The Wrongs and Rights of Religion in Politics.* New York: Basic Books, 2000.

Carwardine, Richard J. *Evangelicals and Politics in Antebellum America.* New Haven, Conn.: Yale University Press, 1993.

Cherry, Conrad, ed. *God's New Israel: Religious Interpretations of American Destiny.* Englewood Cliffs, N.J.: Prentice–Hall, 1971.

Clebsch, William A. *From Sacred to Profane America: The Role of Religion in American History.* New York: Harper and Row, 1968.

Cobb, Sanford. *The Rise of Religious Liberty in America: A History.* New York: Macmillan, 1902.

Cogan, Neil H., ed. *The Complete Bill of Rights: The Drafts, Debates, Sources, and Origins.* New York: Oxford University Press, 1997.

Cole, Franklin P., ed. *They Preached Liberty.* Indianapolis, Ind.: Liberty Press, n.d.

Conkin, Paul K. "The Religious Pilgrimage of Thomas Jefferson." In *Jeffersonian Legacies*, edited by Peter S. Onuf. Charlottesville: University Press of Virginia, 1993.

"Constitutional Fiction: An Analysis of the Supreme Court's Interpretation of the Religion Clauses." *Louisiana Law Review* 47 (1986): 169–198.

Cord, Robert L. "Church–State Separation: Restoring the 'No Preference' Doctrine of the First Amendment." *Harvard Journal of Law and Public Policy* 9 (1986): 129–172.

———. "Mr. Jefferson's 'Nonabsolute' Wall of Separation between Church and State." In *Religion and Political Culture in Jefferson's Virginia*, edited by Garrett Ward Sheldon and Daniel L. Dreisbach. Lanham, Md.: Rowman and Littlefield, 2000.

———. "Original Intent Jurisprudence and Madison's 'Detached Memoranda.'" *Benchmark* 3, nos. 1–2 (1987): 79–85.

Cord, Robert L. *Separation of Church and State: Historical Fact and Current Fiction*. New York: Lambeth Press, 1982.

Cornelison, Isaac A. *The Relation of Religion to Civil Government in the United States of America: A State without a Church, but not without a Religion*. New York: G. P. Putnam's Sons, 1895.

Corwin, Edward S. "The 'Higher Law' Background of American Constitutional Law." *Harvard Law Review* 42 (1928–29): 149–185, 365–409.

———. "The Supreme Court as National School Board." *Law and Contemporary Problems* 14 (1949): 3–22.

Costanzo, Joseph F. "Religious Heritage of American Democracy." *Thought* 30 (Winter 1955–56): 485–506.

———. *This Nation under God: Church, State and Schools in America*. New York: Herder and Herder, 1964.

———. "Thomas Jefferson, Religious Education and Public Law." *Journal of Public Law* 8 (1959): 81–108.

Cousins, Norman, ed. *"In God We Trust": The Religious Beliefs and Ideas of the American Founding Fathers*. New York: Harper and Brothers, 1958.

Curry, Thomas J. *The First Freedoms: Church and State in America to the Passage of the First Amendment*. New York: Oxford University Press, 1986.

Dalin, David G. "How High the Wall?: American Jews and the Church–State Debate." In *Liberty under Law: American Constitutionalism, Yesterday, Today and Tomorrow*, 2d ed., edited by Kenneth L. Grasso and Cecilia Rodriguez Castillo. Lanham, Md.: University Press of America, 1997.

Davis, Derek H. *Original Intent: Chief Justice Rehnquist and the Course of American Church/State Relations*. Buffalo, N.Y.: Prometheus Books, 1991.

———. *Religion and the Continental Congress, 1774–1789: Contributions to Original Intent*. New York: Oxford University Press, 2000.

De Jong, Norman. "Separation of Church and State: Historical Reality or Judicial Myth?" *Fides et Historia* 18, no. 1 (January 1986): 25–37.

De Jong, Norman, with Jack Van Der Slik. *Separation of Church and State: The Myth Revisited*. Jordan Station, Ontario, Canada: Paideia Press, 1985.

Dickson, Charles Ellis. "Jeremiads in the New American Republic: The Case of National Fasts in the John Adams Administration." *New England Quarterly* 60 (1987): 187–207.

Drakeman, Donald L. *Church–State Constitutional Issues: Making Sense of the Establishment Clause*. Westport, Conn.: Greenwood Press, 1991.

———. "Religion and the Republic: James Madison and the First Amendment." *Journal of Church and State* 25 (1983): 427–445.

Dreisbach, Daniel L. "Church–State Debate in the Virginia Legislature: From the Declaration of Rights to the Statute for Establishing Religious Freedom." In *Religion and Political Culture in Jefferson's Virginia*, edited by Garrett

Ward Sheldon and Daniel L. Dreisbach. Lanham, Md.: Rowman and Littlefield, 2000.

———. "The Constitution's Forgotten Religion Clause: Reflections on the Article VI Religious Test Ban." *Journal of Church and State* 38 (1996): 261–295.

———. "*Everson* and the Command of History: The Supreme Court, Lessons of History, and Church–State Debate in America." In *Everson Revisited: Religion, Education, and Law at the Crossroads*, edited by Jo Renée Formicola and Hubert Morken. Lanham, Md.: Rowman and Littlefield, 1997.

———. "George Mason's Pursuit of Religious Liberty in Revolutionary Virginia." *Virginia Magazine of History and Biography* 108, no. 1 (2000): 5–44.

———. "In Search of a Christian Commonwealth: An Examination of Selected Nineteenth–Century Commentaries on References to God and the Christian Religion in the United States Constitution." *Baylor Law Review* 48 (1996): 927–1000.

———. "A Lively and Fair Experiment: Religion and the American Constitutional Tradition." *Emory Law Journal* 49, no. 1 (2000): 223–253.

———. "A New Perspective on Jefferson's Views on Church–State Relations: The Virginia Statute for Establishing Religious Freedom in Its Legislative Context." *American Journal of Legal History* 35 (1991): 172–204.

———. *Real Threat and Mere Shadow: Religious Liberty and the First Amendment*. Westchester, Ill.: Crossway Books, 1987.

———. "'Sowing Useful Truths and Principles': The Danbury Baptists, Thomas Jefferson, and the 'Wall of Separation.'" *Journal of Church and State* 39 (1997): 455–501.

———. "Thomas Jefferson and Bills Number 82–86 of the Revision of the Laws of Virginia, 1776–1786: New Light on the Jeffersonian Model of Church–State Relations." *North Carolina Law Review* 69 (1990): 159–211.

———. "Thomas Jefferson and the Danbury Baptists Revisited." *William and Mary Quarterly*, 3d ser., 56 (1999): 805–816.

———. "Thomas Jefferson, a Mammoth Cheese, and the 'Wall of Separation between Church and State.'" In *Religion and the New Republic: Faith in the Founding of America*, edited by James H. Hutson. Lanham, Md.: Rowman and Littlefield, 2000.

———, ed. *Religion and Politics in the Early Republic: Jasper Adams and the Church–State Debate*. Lexington: University Press of Kentucky, 1996.

Dreisbach, Daniel L., and John D. Whaley. "What the Wall Separates: A Debate on Thomas Jefferson's 'Wall of Separation' Metaphor." *Constitutional Commentary* 16, no. 3 (1999): 627–674.

Dunn, Charles W., ed. *American Political Theology: Historical Perspective and Theoretical Analysis*. New York: Praeger, 1984.

Dunn, Charles W., ed. *Religion in American Politics*. Washington, D.C.: Congressional Quarterly Press, 1989.

Eastland, Terry. "In Defense of Religious America." *Commentary* 71, no. 6 (June 1981): 39–45.

———, ed. *Religious Liberty in the Supreme Court: The Cases That Define the Debate over Church and State*. Washington, D.C.: Ethics and Public Policy Center, 1993.

Eckenrode, Hamilton James. *Separation of Church and State in Virginia: A Study in the Development of the Revolution*. Richmond, Va.: Davis Bottom, 1910.

Eidsmoe, John. *Christianity and the Constitution: The Faith of Our Founding Fathers*. Grand Rapids, Mich.: Baker Book House, 1987.

Eisgruber, Christopher L. "Madison's Wager: Religious Liberty in the Constitutional Order." *Northwestern University Law Review* 89 (1995): 347–410.

Elazar, Daniel J., ed. *Covenant in the Nineteenth Century: The Decline of an American Political Tradition*. Lanham, Md.: Rowman and Littlefield, 1994.

———. "The Political Theory of Covenant: Biblical Origins and Modern Developments." *Publius: The Journal of Federalism* 10, no. 4 (Fall 1980): 3–30.

Elliott, Emory. "The Dove and the Serpent: The Clergy in the American Revolution." *American Quarterly* 31 (1979): 187–203.

Emmerich, Charles J. "The Enigma of James Madison on Church and State." In *Religion, Public Life, and the American Polity*, edited by Luis E. Lugo. Knoxville: University of Tennessee Press, 1994.

Esbeck, Carl H. "Five Views of Church–State Relations in Contemporary American Thought." *Brigham Young University Law Review* 1986 (1986): 371–404.

Estep, William R. *Revolution within the Revolution: The First Amendment in Historical Context, 1612–1789*. Grand Rapids, Mich.: William B. Eerdmans, 1990.

Evans, Bette Novit. *Interpreting the Free Exercise of Religion: The Constitution and American Pluralism*. Chapel Hill: University of North Carolina Press, 1997.

Evans, M. Stanton. *The Theme Is Freedom: Religion, Politics, and the American Tradition*. Washington, D.C.: Regnery, 1994.

Fabian, Bernhard, "Jefferson's *Notes on Virginia*: The Genesis of Query xvii, The different religions received into that State?" *William and Mary Quarterly*, 3d ser., 12 (1955): 124–138.

Feldman, Stephen M. *Please Don't Wish Me a Merry Christmas: A Critical History of the Separation of Church and State*. New York: New York University Press, 1997.

———, ed. *Law and Religion: A Critical Anthology*. New York: New York University Press, 2000.

Field, Peter S. *The Crisis of the Standing Order: Clerical Intellectuals and Cultural Authority in Massachusetts, 1780–1833.* Amherst: University of Massachusetts Press, 1998.

"First Amendment Religion Clauses: Historical Metamorphosis." *Northwestern University Law Review* 61 (1966): 760–776.

Fleet, Elizabeth, ed. "Madison's 'Detached Memoranda.'" *William and Mary Quarterly*, 3d ser., 3 (1946): 534–568.

Foote, Henry Wilder. *The Religion of Thomas Jefferson.* Boston: Beacon Press, 1947.

Foster, Charles I. *An Errand of Mercy: The Evangelical United Front, 1790–1837.* Chapel Hill: University of North Carolina Press, 1960.

Gaustad, Edwin Scott. "The Backus–Leland Tradition." *Foundations: A Baptist Journal of History and Theology* 2 (1959): 131–152.

———. "A Disestablished Society: Origins of the First Amendment." *Journal of Church and State* 11 (1969): 409–425.

———. *Faith of Our Fathers: Religion and the New Nation.* San Francisco: Harper and Row, 1987.

———. *Liberty of Conscience: Roger Williams in America.* Grand Rapids, Mich.: William B. Eerdmans, 1991.

———. *A Religious History of America*, rev. ed. San Francisco: Harper and Row, 1990.

———. *Sworn on the Altar of God: A Religious Biography of Thomas Jefferson.* Grand Rapids, Mich.: William B. Eerdmans, 1996.

———. "Thomas Jefferson, Danbury Baptists, and 'Eternal Hostility.'" *William and Mary Quarterly*, 3d ser., 56 (1999): 801–804.

———. "Thomas Jefferson, Religious Freedom, and the Supreme Court." *Church History* 67 (December 1998): 682–694.

Gifford, Frank Dean. "The Influence of the Clergy on American Politics from 1763 to 1776." *Historical Magazine of the Protestant Episcopal Church* 10 (June 1941): 104–123.

Glenn, Gary D. "Forgotten Purposes of the First Amendment Religion Clauses." *Review of Politics* 49 (1987): 340–367.

Goldwin, Robert A., and Art Kaufman, eds. *How Does the Constitution Protect Religious Freedom?* Washington, D.C.: American Enterprise Institute for Public Policy Research, 1987.

Good, Douglas L. "The Christian Nation in the Mind of Timothy Dwight." *Fides et Historia* 7, no. 1 (1974): 1–18.

Gould, William D. "The Religious Opinions of Thomas Jefferson." *Mississippi Valley Historical Review* 20 (1933): 191–208.

Greene, Evarts B. *Religion and the State: The Making and Testing of an American Tradition.* New York: New York University Press, 1941.

Greene, M. Louise. *The Development of Religious Liberty in Connecticut.* Boston: Houghton Mifflin, 1905.

Grenz, Stanley J. "Church and State: The Legacy of Isaac Backus." *Center Journal* 2, no. 2 (Spring 1983): 73–94.

———. "Isaac Backus and Religious Liberty." *Foundations: A Baptist Journal of History, Theology, and Ministry* 22 (1979): 352–360.

Gribbin, William. "The Covenant Transformed: The Jeremiad Tradition and the War of 1812." *Church History* 40 (1971): 297–305.

Griffin, Clifford S. *Their Brothers' Keepers: Moral Stewardship in the United States, 1800–1865.* New Brunswick, N.J.: Rutgers University Press, 1960.

Griffin, Keith L. *Revolution and Religion: American Revolutionary War and the Reformed Clergy.* New York: Paragon House, 1994.

Guliuzza, Frank, III. *Over the Wall: Protecting Religious Expression in the Public Square.* Albany: State University of New York Press, 2000.

———. "The Practical Perils of an Original Intent–Based Judicial Philosophy: Originalism and the Church–State Test Case." *Drake Law Review* 42 (1993): 343–383.

Hall, J. Lesslie. "The Religious Opinions of Thomas Jefferson." *Sewanee Review* 21 (1913): 164–176.

Hall, Thomas Cuming. *The Religious Background of American Culture.* Boston: Little, Brown, 1930.

Hall, Timothy L. "Roger Williams and the Foundations of Religious Liberty." *Boston University Law Review* 71 (1991): 455–524.

———. *Separating Church and State: Roger Williams and Religious Liberty.* Urbana: University of Illinois Press, 1998.

Hamburger, Philip A. "A Constitutional Right of Religious Exemption: An Historical Perspective." *George Washington Law Review* 60 (1992): 915–948.

———. "Equality and Diversity: The Eighteenth–Century Debate about Equal Protection and Equal Civil Rights." In *1992 The Supreme Court Review*, edited by Dennis J. Hutchinson, David A. Strauss, and Geoffrey R. Stone. Chicago: University of Chicago Press, 1993.

———. *Separation of Church and State.* Cambridge, Mass.: Harvard University Press, 2002.

Hammett, Harold D. "The Homogenized Wall." *American Bar Association Journal* 53 (October 1967): 929–936.

———. "Separation of Church and State: By One Wall or Two?" *Journal of Church and State* 7 (1965): 190–206.

Handy, Robert T. "The American Tradition of Religious Freedom: An Historical Analysis." *Journal of Public Law* 13 (1964): 247–266.

———. *A Christian America: Protestant Hopes and Historical Realities.* 2d ed. New York: Oxford University Press, 1984.

————. "The Magna Charta of Religious Freedom in America." *Union Seminary Quarterly Review* 38 (1984): 301–317.

Hanley, Mark Y. *Beyond a Christian Commonwealth: The Protestant Quarrel with the American Republic, 1830–1860.* Chapel Hill: University of North Carolina Press, 1994.

Harriman, John C., ed. "'Most Excellent—far fam'd and far fetch'd Cheese': An Anthology of Jeffersonian Era Poetry." *American Magazine and Historical Chronicle* 2, no. 2 (Autumn/Winter 1986–87): 1–26.

Hart, Benjamin. *Faith and Freedom: The Christian Roots of American Liberty.* Dallas, Tex.: Lewis and Stanley, 1988.

————. "The Wall That Protestantism Built: The Religious Reasons for the Separation of Church and State." *Policy Review* no. 46 (Fall 1988): 44–52.

Hartnett, Robert C. "The Religion of the Founding Fathers." In *Wellsprings of the American Spirit*, edited by F. Ernest Johnson. New York: Cooper Square, 1964.

Hatch, Nathan O. "The Christian Movement and the Demand for a Theology of the People." *Journal of American History* 67 (December 1980): 545–567.

————. *The Democratization of American Christianity.* New Haven, Conn.: Yale University Press, 1989.

————. *The Sacred Cause of Liberty: Republican Thought and the Millennium in Revolutionary New England.* New Haven, Conn.: Yale University Press, 1977.

Headley, J. T. *The Chaplains and Clergy of the Revolution.* New York: Charles Scribner, 1864.

Healey, Robert M. *Jefferson on Religion in Public Education.* New Haven, Conn.: Yale University Press, 1962.

————. "Thomas Jefferson's 'Wall': Absolute or Serpentine?" *Journal of Church and State* 30 (1988): 441–462.

Heimert, Alan. *Religion and the American Mind: From the Great Awakening to the Revolution.* Cambridge, Mass.: Harvard University Press, 1966.

Hirsch, Elisabeth Feist. "John Cotton and Roger Williams: Their Controversy Concerning Religious Liberty." *Church History* 10 (1941): 38–51.

Hood, Fred J. *Reformed America: The Middle and Southern States, 1783–1837.* Tuscaloosa: University of Alabama Press, 1980.

————. "Revolution and Religious Liberty: The Conservation of the Theocratic Concept in Virginia." *Church History* 40 (1971): 170–181.

Howe, Mark DeWolfe. *The Garden and the Wilderness: Religion and Government in American Constitutional History.* Chicago: University of Chicago Press, 1965.

Hudson, Winthrop S. *Religion in America: An Historical Account of the Development of American Religious Life*, 3d ed. New York: Charles Scribner's Sons, 1981.

Humphrey, Edward Frank. *Nationalism and Religion in America, 1774–1789.* Boston: Chipman Law Publishing Co., 1924.

Hunt, Gaillard. "James Madison and Religious Liberty." *Annual Report of the American Historical Association for the Year 1901* 1 (1902): 163–171.

Huntley, William B. "Jefferson's Public and Private Religion." *South Atlantic Quarterly* 79 (1980): 286–301.

Hutson, James H. *Religion and the Founding of the American Republic.* Washington, D.C.: Library of Congress, 1998.

———. "Thomas Jefferson's Letter to the Danbury Baptists: A Controversy Rejoined." *William and Mary Quarterly*, 3d ser., 56 (1999): 775–790.

———. "'A Wall of Separation': FBI Helps Restore Jefferson's Obliterated Draft." *Library of Congress Information Bulletin* 57, no. 6 (June 1998): 136–139, 163.

———, ed. *Religion and the New Republic: Faith in the Founding of America.* Lanham, Md.: Rowman and Littlefield, 2000.

Hyneman, Charles S., and Donald S. Lutz, eds. *American Political Writing during the Founding Era: 1760–1805.* 2 vols. Indianapolis, Ind.: Liberty Press, 1983.

Isaac, Rhys. "'The Rage of Malice of the Old Serpent Devil': The Dissenters and the Making and Remaking of the Virginia Statute for Religious Freedom." In *The Virginia Statute for Religious Freedom: Its Evolution and Consequences in American History*, edited by Merrill D. Peterson and Robert C. Vaughan. New York: Cambridge University Press, 1988.

Ivers, Gregg. *To Build a Wall: American Jews and the Separation of Church and State.* Charlottesville: University Press of Virginia, 1995.

———. *Lowering the Wall: Religion and the Supreme Court in the 1980s.* New York: Anti-Defamation League, 1991.

Ives, J. Moss. *The Ark and the Dove: The Beginning of Civil and Religious Liberties in America.* New York: Cooper Square, 1969.

———. "The Catholic Contribution to Religious Liberty in Colonial America." *Catholic Historical Review* 21 (1935): 283–298.

James, Charles F. *Documentary History of the Struggle for Religious Liberty in Virginia.* Lynchburg, Va.: J. P. Bell, 1900.

Jayne, Allen. *Jefferson's Declaration of Independence: Origins, Philosophy and Theology.* Lexington: University Press of Kentucky, 1998.

"Jefferson and the Church–State Wall: A Historical Examination of the Man and the Metaphor." *Brigham Young University Law Review* 1978 (1978): 645–674.

Johnson, F. Ernest, ed. *Wellsprings of the American Spirit.* New York: Cooper Square, 1964.

Jones, Archie Preston. "Christianity in the Constitution: The Intended Meaning of the Religion Clauses of the First Amendment." Ph.D. diss., University of Dallas, 1991.

Joyce, Lester Douglas. *Church and Clergy in the American Revolution: A Study in Group Behavior.* New York: Exposition Press, 1966.

Kerr, Harry P. "The Election Sermon: Primer for Revolutionaries." *Speech Monographs* 29 (1962): 13–22.

———. "Politics and Religion in Colonial Fast and Thanksgiving Sermons, 1763–1783." *Quarterly Journal of Speech* 46 (December 1960): 372–382.

Kessler, Sanford. "John Locke's Legacy of Religious Freedom." *Polity* 17 (1985): 484–503.

———. "Locke's Influence on Jefferson's 'Bill for Establishing Religious Freedom.'" *Journal of Church and State* 25 (1983): 231–252.

———. *Tocqueville's Civil Religion: American Christianity and the Prospects for Freedom.* Albany: State University of New York Press, 1994.

———. "Tocqueville's Puritans: Christianity and the American Founding." *Journal of Politics* 54 (1992): 776–792.

Ketcham, Ralph L. "James Madison and Religion — A New Hypothesis." *Journal of the Presbyterian Historical Society* 38 (June 1960): 65–90.

Knoles, George Harmon. "The Religious Ideas of Thomas Jefferson." *Mississippi Valley Historical Review* 30 (1943): 187–204.

Koch, G. Adolf. *Republican Religion: The American Revolution and the Cult of Reason.* Gloucester, Mass.: Peter Smith, 1964.

Konvitz, Milton R. "Separation of Church and State: The First Freedom." *Law and Contemporary Problems* 14 (1949): 44–60.

Kramer, Leonard J. "Muskits in the Pulpit: 1776–1783." *Journal of the Presbyterian Historical Society* 31 (December 1953): 229–244, 32 (March 1954): 37–51.

———. "Presbyterians Approach the American Revolution." *Journal of the Presbyterian Historical Society* 31 (June 1953): 71–86, (September 1953): 167–180.

Kramnick, Isaac, and R. Laurence Moore. "The Baptists, the Bureau, and the Case of the Missing Lines." *William and Mary Quarterly*, 3d ser., 56 (1999): 817–822.

———. *The Godless Constitution: The Case Against Religious Correctness.* New York: W. W. Norton, 1996.

Kruse, Clifton B. "The Historical Meaning and Judicial Construction of the Establishment of Religion Clause of the First Amendment." *Washburn Law Journal* 2, no. 1 (1962): 65–141.

Kurland, Philip B. "The Irrelevance of the Constitution: The Religion Clauses of the First Amendment and the Supreme Court." *Villanova Law Review* 24 (1978–79): 3–27.

Kurland, Philip B. "The Origins of the Religion Clauses of the Constitution." *William and Mary Law Review* 27 (1986): 839–861.

Kurland, Philip B., and Ralph Lerner, eds. *The Founders' Constitution*. 5 vols. Chicago: University of Chicago Press, 1987.

Lambert, Frank. "'God—and a Religious President . . . [or] Jefferson and No God': Campaigning for a Voter–Imposed Religious Test in 1800." *Journal of Church and State* 39 (1997): 769–789.

Lash, Kurt T. "The Second Adoption of the Establishment Clause: The Rise of the Nonestablishment Principle." *Arizona State Law Journal* 27 (1995): 1085–1154.

———. "The Second Adoption of the Free Exercise Clause: Religious Exemptions under the Fourteenth Amendment." *Northwestern University Law Review* 88 (1994): 1106–1156.

Laycock, Douglas. "'Noncoercive' Support for Religion: Another False Claim about the Establishment Clause." *Valparaiso University Law Review* 26 (1991): 37–69.

———. "'Nonpreferential' Aid to Religion: A False Claim about Original Intent." *William and Mary Law Review* 27 (1986): 875–923.

Lerche, Charles O., Jr. "Jefferson and the Election of 1800: A Case Study in the Political Smear." *William and Mary Quarterly*, 3d ser., 5 (1948): 467–491.

Levy, Leonard W. *The Establishment Clause: Religion and the First Amendment*, 2d ed. Chapel Hill: University of North Carolina Press, 1994.

———. *Jefferson and Civil Liberties: The Darker Side*. Cambridge, Mass.: Belknap Press, Harvard University Press, 1963.

Lindsay, Thomas. "James Madison on Religion and Politics: Rhetoric and Reality." *American Political Science Review* 85 (1991): 1321–1337.

Littell, Franklin Hamlin. "The Basis of Religious Liberty in American History." *Journal of Church and State* 6 (1964): 314–332.

———. *From State Church to Pluralism: A Protestant Interpretation of Religion in American History*. Garden City, N.Y.: Doubleday, 1962.

Little, David. "Roger Williams and the Separation of Church and State." In *Religion and the State: Essays in Honor of Leo Pfeffer*, edited by James E. Wood, Jr. Waco, Tex.: Baylor University Press, 1985.

———. "Thomas Jefferson's Religious Views and Their Influence on the Supreme Court's Interpretation of the First Amendment." *Catholic University Law Review* 26 (1976): 57–72.

Little, Lewis Peyton. *Imprisoned Preachers and Religious Liberty in Virginia*. Lynchburg, Va.: J. P. Bell, 1938.

Lloyd, Gordon, and Margie Lloyd, eds. *The Essential Bill of Rights: Original Arguments and Fundamental Documents*. Lanham, Md.: University Press of America, 1998.

Loveland, Anne C. *Southern Evangelicals and the Social Order, 1800–1860*. Baton Rouge: Louisiana State University Press, 1980.

Luebke, Fred C. "The Origins of Thomas Jefferson's Anti–Clericalism." *Church History* 32 (1963): 344–356.

Lugo, Luis E., ed. *Religion, Public Life, and the American Polity*. Knoxville: University of Tennessee Press, 1994.

Lutz, Donald S. "From Covenant to Constitution in American Political Thought." *Publius: The Journal of Federalism* 10, no. 4 (Fall 1980): 101–133.

Lynch, Joseph M. "Madison's Religion Proposals Judicially Confounded: A Study in the Constitutional Law of Conscience." *Seton Hall Law Review* 20 (1990): 418–477.

Maas, David E. "The Ideological and Political Roots of the Religious Clause in the Constitution." *Fides et Historia* 19, no. 2 (1987): 32–46.

———. "The Philosophical and Theological Roots of the Religious Clause in the Constitution." In *Liberty and Law: Reflections on the Constitution in American Life and Thought*, edited by Ronald A. Wells and Thomas A. Askew. Grand Rapids, Mich.: William B. Eerdmans, 1987.

———. "The Watchwords of 1774." *Fides et Historia* 18, no. 3 (1986): 15–34.

Maclear, James Fulton. "'The True American Union' of Church and State: The Reconstruction of the Theocratic Tradition." *Church History* 28 (1959): 41–62.

Magnuson, Roger P. "Thomas Jefferson and the Separation of Church and State." *Education Forum* 27 (May 1963): 417–421.

Malbin, Michael J. *Religion and Politics: The Intentions of the Authors of the First Amendment*. Washington, D.C.: American Enterprise Institute for Public Policy Research, 1978.

Malone, Dumas. *Jefferson and His Time*. 6 vols. Boston: Little, Brown, 1948–1981.

Marnell, William H. *The First Amendment: The History of Religious Freedom in America*. Garden City, N.Y.: Doubleday, 1964.

Marsden, George M. "America's 'Christian' Origins: Puritan New England as a Case Study." In *John Calvin: His Influence in the Western World*, edited by W. Stanford Reid. Grand Rapids, Mich.: Zondervan, 1982.

Marshall, William P. "The Case against the Constitutionally Compelled Free Exercise Exemption." *Case Western Reserve Law Review* 40 (1989–1990): 357–412.

Marty, Martin E. *The Infidel: Freethought and American Religion*. Cleveland, Ohio: Meridian Books, 1961.

———. "Living with Establishment and Disestablishment in Nineteenth–Century Anglo–America." *Journal of Church and State* 18 (1976): 61–77.

Mathews, Donald G. "The Second Great Awakening as an Organizing Process, 1780–1830: An Hypothesis." *American Quarterly* 21 (1969): 23–43.

Mayer, David N. *The Constitutional Thought of Thomas Jefferson.* Charlottesville: University Press of Virginia, 1994.

McBrien, Richard P. *Caesar's Coin: Religion and Politics in America.* New York: Macmillan, 1987.

McCarthy, Rockne. "Civil Religion in Early America." *Fides et Historia* 8, no. 1 (1975): 20–40.

McClellan, James. "Hand's Writing on the Wall of Separation: The Significance of *Jaffree* in Future Cases on Religious Establishment." In *How Does the Constitution Protect Religious Freedom?*, edited by Robert A. Goldwin and Art Kaufman. Washington, D.C.: American Enterprise Institute for Public Policy Research, 1987.

———. *Joseph Story and the American Constitution: A Study in Political and Legal Thought.* Norman: University of Oklahoma Press, 1971.

———. "The Making and the Unmaking of the Establishment Clause." In *A Blueprint for Judicial Reform*, edited by Patrick B. McGuigan and Randall R. Rader. Washington, D.C.: Free Congress Research and Education Foundation, 1981.

McConnell, Michael W. "Coercion: The Lost Element of Establishment." *William and Mary Law Review* 27 (1986): 933–941.

———. "The Origins and Historical Understanding of Free Exercise of Religion." *Harvard Law Review* 103 (1990): 1409–1517.

McLoughlin, William G. "Isaac Backus and the Separation of Church and State in America." *American Historical Review* 73 (1968): 1392–1413.

———. *New England Dissent, 1630–1833: The Baptists and the Separation of Church and State.* 2 vols. Cambridge, Mass.: Harvard University Press, 1971.

———. "Religious Freedom and Popular Sovereignty: A Change in the Flow of God's Power, 1730–1830." *Union Seminary Quarterly Review* 38 (1984): 319–336.

———. *Revivals, Awakenings, and Reform: An Essay on Religion and Social Change in America, 1607–1977.* Chicago: University of Chicago Press, 1978.

———. "The Role of Religion in the Revolution: Liberty of Conscience and Cultural Cohesion in the New Nation." In *Essays on the American Revolution*, edited by Stephen G. Kurtz and James H. Hutson. Chapel Hill: University of North Carolina Press, 1973.

———. *Soul Liberty: The Baptists' Struggle in New England, 1630–1833.* Hanover, N.H.: University Press of New England, 1991.

Mead, Sidney E. "American Protestantism during the Revolutionary Epoch." *Church History* 22 (1953): 279–297.

———. *The Lively Experiment: The Shaping of Christianity in America.* New York: Harper and Row, 1963.

———. *The Nation with the Soul of a Church.* New York: Harper and Row, 1975.

———. "Neither Church nor State: Reflections on James Madison's 'Line of Separation.'" *Journal of Church and State* 10 (1968): 349–363.

———. *The Old Religion in the Brave New World: Reflections on the Relation between Christendom and the Republic.* Berkeley: University of California Press, 1977.

Meyer, Jacob C. *Church and State in Massachusetts: From 1740 to 1833.* Cleveland, Ohio: Western Reserve University Press, 1930.

Miller, Glenn T. *Religious Liberty in America: History and Prospects.* Philadelphia: Westminster Press, 1976.

Miller, Howard. "The Grammar of Liberty: Presbyterians and the First American Constitutions." *Journal of Presbyterian History* 54 (1976): 142–164.

Miller, Perry. "The Contribution of the Protestant Churches to Religious Liberty in Colonial America." *Church History* 4 (1935): 57–66.

———. *The Life of the Mind in America: From the Revolution to the Civil War.* New York: Harcourt, Brace and World, 1965.

Miller, William Lee. *The First Liberty: Religion and the American Republic.* New York: Alfred A. Knopf, 1986.

Moehlman, Conrad Henry. *The Wall of Separation between Church and State: An Historical Study of Recent Criticism of the Religious Clause of the First Amendment.* Boston: Beacon Press, 1951.

———. "The Wall of Separation: The Law and the Facts." *American Bar Association Journal* 38 (April 1952): 281–284, 343–348.

Monsma, Stephen V. *Positive Neutrality: Letting Religious Freedom Ring.* Westport, Conn.: Greenwood Press, 1993.

Moore, Frank, ed. *The Patriot Preachers of the American Revolution, 1766–1783.* New York, 1860.

Moore, LeRoy. "Religious Liberty: Roger Williams and the Revolutionary Era." *Church History* 34 (1965): 57–76.

———. "Roger Williams as an Enduring Symbol for Baptists." *Journal of Church and State* 7 (1965): 181–189.

Moore, R. Laurence. "The End of Religious Establishment and the Beginning of Religious Politics: Church and State in the United States." In *Belief in History: Innovative Approaches to European and American Religion,* edited by Thomas Kselman. Notre Dame, Ind.: University of Notre Dame Press, 1991.

Morgan, Edmund S. "The Puritan Ethic and the American Revolution." *William and Mary Quarterly,* 3d ser., 24 (1967): 3–43.

———. *Roger Williams: The Church and the State.* New York: Harcourt, Brace and World, 1967.

Morgan, Richard E. *The Supreme Court and Religion.* New York: Free Press, 1972.

Morris, B. F. *Christian Life and Character of the Civil Institutions of the United States, Developed in the Official and Historical Annals of the Republic.* Philadelphia: George W. Childs, 1864.

Morrison, Jeffry Hays. "John Witherspoon and 'The Public Interest of Religion.'" *Journal of Church and State* 41 (1999): 551–573.

Morton, R. Kemp. *God in the Constitution.* Nashville, Tenn.: Cokesbury Press, 1933.

Mott, Royden J. "Sources of Jefferson's Ecclesiastical Views." *Church History* 3 (1934): 267–284.

Murray, Iain H. *Revival and Revivalism: The Making and Marring of American Evangelicalism, 1750–1858.* Carlisle, Pa.: Banner of Truth Trust, 1994.

Nagel, Paul C. *This Sacred Trust: American Nationality, 1798–1898.* New York: Oxford University Press, 1971.

Neuhaus, Richard John. "Contending for the Future: Overcoming the Pfefferian Inversion." *Journal of Law and Religion* 8 (1990): 115–129.

———. *The Naked Public Square: Religion and Democracy in America.* Grand Rapids, Mich.: William B. Eerdmans, 1984.

Nichols, James Hastings. "John Witherspoon on Church and State." *Journal of Presbyterian History* 42 (1964): 166–174.

Niebuhr, H. Richard. "The Idea of Covenant and American Democracy." *Church History* 23 (1954): 126–135.

———. *The Kingdom of God in America.* New York: Harper and Brothers, 1937.

"Nineteenth Century Judicial Thought Concerning Church–State Relations." *Minnesota Law Review* 40 (1956): 672–680.

Noll, Mark A. *Christians in the American Revolution.* Washington, D.C.: Christian University Press, 1977.

———. *A History of Christianity in the United States and Canada.* Grand Rapids, Mich.: William B. Eerdmans, 1992.

———. "The Image of the United States as a Biblical Nation, 1776–1865." In *The Bible in America: Essays in Cultural History*, edited by Nathan O. Hatch and Mark A. Noll. New York: Oxford University Press, 1982.

———. *One Nation under God?: Christian Faith and Political Action in America.* San Francisco: Harper and Row, 1988.

———, ed. *Religion and American Politics: From the Colonial Period to the 1980s.* New York: Oxford University Press, 1990.

Noll, Mark A., Nathan O. Hatch, and George M. Marsden. *The Search for Christian America.* Westchester, Ill.: Crossway Books, 1983.

Noonan, John T., Jr. *The Believer and the Powers That Are: Cases, History, and Other Data Bearing on the Relation of Religion and Government.* New York: Macmillan, 1987.

———. *The Lustre of Our Country: The American Experience of Religious Freedom.* Berkeley: University of California Press, 1998.

Noonan, John T., Jr., and Edward McGlynn Gaffney, Jr. *Religious Freedom: History, Cases, and Other Materials on the Interaction of Religion and Government.* New York: Foundation Press, 2001.

Novak, Michael. *On Two Wings: Humble Faith and Common Sense at the American Founding.* San Francisco: Encounter Books, 2002.

Oaks, Dallin H., ed. *The Wall between Church and State.* Chicago: University of Chicago Press, 1963.

O'Brien, Charles F. "The Religious Issue in the Presidential Campaign of 1800." *Essex Institute Historical Collections* 107, no. 1 (1971): 82–93.

O'Brien, Francis William. *Justice Reed and the First Amendment: The Religion Clauses.* Washington, D.C.: Georgetown University Press, 1958.

———. "The States and 'No Establishment': Proposed Amendments to the Constitution since 1798." *Washburn Law Journal* 4 (1965): 183–210.

O'Neil, Robert M. "The 'Wall of Separation' and Thomas Jefferson's Views on Religious Liberty." *William and Mary Quarterly*, 3d ser., 56 (1999): 791–794.

O'Neill, James M. "Nonpreferential Aid to Religion Is Not an Establishment of Religion." *Buffalo Law Review* 2 (1953): 242–266, 272–278.

———. *Religion and Education under the Constitution.* New York: Harper and Brothers, 1949.

Parsons, Wilfrid. *The First Freedom: Considerations on Church and State in the United States.* New York: Declan X. McMullen, 1948.

Pasley, Jeffrey L. *"The Tyranny of Printers": Newspaper Politics in the Early American Republic.* Charlottesville: University Press of Virginia, 2001.

Perry, Barbara A. "Justice Hugo Black and the 'Wall of Separation between Church and State.'" *Journal of Church and State* 31 (1989): 55–72.

Peters, Thomas Nathan. "Religion, Establishment, and the Northwest Ordinance: A Closer Look at an Accommodationist Argument." *Kentucky Law Journal* 89 (2000–2001): 743–780.

Peterson, Merrill D. *The Jefferson Image in the American Mind.* New York: Oxford University Press, 1960.

———. *Thomas Jefferson and the New Nation: A Biography.* New York: Oxford University Press, 1970.

Peterson, Merrill D., and Robert C. Vaughan, eds. *The Virginia Statute for Religious Freedom: Its Evolution and Consequences in American History.* New York: Cambridge University Press, 1988.

Pfeffer, Leo. *Church, State, and Freedom.* Boston: Beacon Press, 1953; rev. ed. 1967.

———. "The Deity in American Constitutional History." *Journal of Church and State* 23 (1981): 215–239.

———. "Madison's 'Detached Memoranda': Then and Now." In *The Virginia Statute for Religious Freedom: Its Evolution and Consequences in American History,* edited by Merrill D. Peterson and Robert C. Vaughan. New York: Cambridge University Press, 1988.

———. "No Law Respecting an Establishment of Religion." *Buffalo Law Review* 2 (1953): 225–241, 267–272.

Plöchl, Willibald M. "Thomas Jefferson, Author of the Statute of Virginia for Religious Freedom." *Jurist* 3 (1943): 182–230.

Plumstead, A. W., ed. *The Wall and the Garden: Selected Massachusetts Election Sermons, 1670–1775.* Minneapolis: University of Minnesota Press, 1968.

Ramsay, William M. *The Wall of Separation: A Primer on Church and State.* Louisville: Westminster/John Knox Press, 1989.

Reichley, A. James. *Religion in American Public Life.* Washington, D.C.: Brookings Institution, 1985.

"Rethinking the Incorporation of the Establishment Clause: A Federalist View." *Harvard Law Review* 105 (1992): 1700–1719.

Rice, Charles E. *The Supreme Court and Public Prayer.* New York: Fordham University Press, 1964.

Richards, Peter Judson. "'A Clear and Steady Channel': Isaac Backus and the Limits of Liberty." *Journal of Church and State* 43 (2001): 447–482.

Richey, Russell E., and Donald G. Jones, eds. *American Civil Religion.* New York: Harper and Row, 1974.

Riemer, Neal. "Covenant and the Federal Constitution." *Publius: The Journal of Federalism* 10, no. 4 (Fall 1980): 135–148.

———. "Madison: A Founder's Vision of Religious Liberty and Public Life." In *Religion, Public Life, and the American Polity,* edited by Luis E. Lugo. Knoxville: University of Tennessee Press, 1994.

———. "Religious Liberty and Creative Breakthroughs: The Contributions of Roger Williams and James Madison." In *Religion in American Politics,* edited by Charles W. Dunn. Washington, D.C.: Congressional Quarterly Press, 1989.

Ross, Thomas. "Metaphor and Paradox." *Georgia Law Review* 23 (1989): 1053–1084.

Rutland, Robert Allen. *The Birth of the Bill of Rights, 1776–1791.* Chapel Hill: University of North Carolina Press, 1955.

Safranek, Stephen J. "Can Science Guide Legal Argumentation?: The Role of Metaphor in Constitutional Cases." *Loyola University Chicago Law Journal* 25 (1994): 357–403.

Sandler, S. Gerald. "Lockean Ideas in Thomas Jefferson's *Bill for Establishing Religious Freedom.*" *Journal of the History of Ideas* 21 (1960): 110–116.

Sandoz, Ellis. *A Government of Laws: Political Theory, Religion and the American Founding.* Baton Rouge: Louisiana State University Press, 1990.

———. "Religious Liberty and Religion in the American Founding Revisited." In *Religious Liberty in Western Thought,* edited by Noel B. Reynolds and W. Cole Durham, Jr. Atlanta: Scholars Press, 1996.

———, ed. *Political Sermons of the American Founding Era: 1730–1805.* Indianapolis, Ind.: Liberty Press, 1991.

Sanford, Charles B. "The Religious Beliefs of Thomas Jefferson." In *Religion and Political Culture in Jefferson's Virginia,* edited by Garrett Ward Sheldon and Daniel L. Dreisbach. Lanham, Md.: Rowman and Littlefield, 2000.

———. *The Religious Life of Thomas Jefferson.* Charlottesville: University Press of Virginia, 1984.

Schaff, Philip. *Church and State in the United States; or, The American Idea of Religious Liberty and Its Practical Effects.* New York: G. P. Putnam's Sons; American Historical Society, 1888.

Schultz, Roger. "Covenanting in America: The Political Theology of John Witherspoon." *Journal of Christian Reconstruction* 12, no. 1 (1988): 179–289.

Schulz, Constance B. "'Of Bigotry in Politics and Religion': Jefferson's Religion, the Federalist Press, and the Syllabus." *Virginia Magazine of History and Biography* 91 (1983): 73–91.

Schwartz, Bernard. *The Bill of Rights: A Documentary History.* 2 vols. New York: Chelsea House, 1971.

———. *The Great Rights of Mankind: A History of the American Bill of Rights.* New York: Oxford University Press, 1977.

Segers, Mary C., and Ted G. Jelen. *A Wall of Separation?: Debating the Public Role of Religion.* Lanham, Md.: Rowman and Littlefield, 1998.

Shain, Barry Alan. *The Myth of American Individualism: The Protestant Origins of American Political Thought.* Princeton, N.J.: Princeton University Press, 1994.

Sheldon, Garrett Ward. *The Political Philosophy of James Madison.* Baltimore, Md.: Johns Hopkins University Press, 2001.

———. *The Political Philosophy of Thomas Jefferson.* Baltimore, Md.: Johns Hopkins University Press, 1991.

Sheldon, Garrett Ward, and Daniel L. Dreisbach, eds. *Religion and Political Culture in Jefferson's Virginia.* Lanham, Md.: Rowman and Littlefield, 2000.

Sheridan, Eugene R. "Liberty and Virtue: Religion and Republicanism in Jeffersonian Thought." In *Thomas Jefferson and the Education of a Citizen,* edited by James Gilreath. Washington, D.C.: Library of Congress, 1999.

Singer, C. Gregg. *A Theological Interpretation of American History*, rev. ed. Phillipsburg, N.J.: Presbyterian and Reformed Publishing Co., 1981.

Singleton, Marvin K. "Colonial Virginia as First Amendment Matrix: Henry, Madison, and Assessment Establishment." *Journal of Church and State* 8 (1966): 344–364.

Sky, Theodore. "The Establishment Clause, the Congress and the Schools: An Historical Perspective." *Virginia Law Review* 52 (1966): 1395–1466.

Smith, Craig R. *To Form a More Perfect Union: The Ratification of the Constitution and the Bill of Rights, 1787–1791*. Lanham, Md.: University Press of America, 1993.

Smith, Elwyn A. *Religious Liberty in the United States: The Development of Church–State Thought since the Revolutionary Era*. Philadelphia: Fortress Press, 1972.

———, ed. *The Religion of the Republic*. Philadelphia: Fortress Press, 1971.

Smith, Gary Scott. *The Seeds of Secularization: Calvinism, Culture, and Pluralism in America, 1870–1915*. Grand Rapids, Mich.: Christian University Press, 1985.

Smith, Rodney K. "Getting Off on the Wrong Foot and Back on Again: A Reexamination of the History of the Framing of the Religion Clauses of the First Amendment and a Critique of the *Reynolds* and *Everson* Decisions." *Wake Forest Law Review* 20 (1984): 569–643.

———. "Nonpreferentialism in Establishment Clause Analysis: A Response to Professor Laycock." *St. John's Law Review* 65 (1991): 245–271.

———. *Public Prayer and the Constitution: A Case Study in Constitutional Interpretation*. Wilmington, Del.: Scholarly Resources, 1987.

Smith, Steven D. *Foreordained Failure: The Quest for a Constitutional Principle of Religious Freedom*. New York: Oxford University Press, 1995.

Smith, Timothy L. *Revivalism and Social Reform in Mid–Nineteenth–Century America*. New York: Abingdon Press, 1957.

Smylie, James H. "Madison and Witherspoon: Theological Roots of American Political Thought." *Princeton University Library Journal* 22 (Spring 1961): 118–132.

———. "Protestant Clergy, the First Amendment, and Beginnings of a Constitutional Debate, 1781–1791." In *The Religion of the Republic*, edited by Elwyn A. Smith. Philadelphia: Fortress Press, 1971.

Sorauf, Frank J. *The Wall of Separation: The Constitutional Politics of Church and State*. Princeton, N.J.: Princeton University Press, 1976.

Spiegel, Jayson L. "Christianity as Part of the Common Law." *North Carolina Central Law Journal* 14 (1984): 494–516.

Stokes, Anson Phelps. *Church and State in the United States*. 3 vols. New York: Harper and Brothers, 1950.

Story, Joseph. "Christianity a Part of the Common Law." *American Jurist and Law Magazine* 9 (April 1833): 346–348.

———. *Commentaries on the Constitution of the United States.* 3 vols. Boston: Hilliard, Gray, 1833.

Stout, Harry S. *The New England Soul: Preaching and Religious Culture in Colonial New England.* New York: Oxford University Press, 1986.

———. "Religion, Communications, and the Ideological Origins of the American Revolution." *William and Mary Quarterly,* 3d ser., 34 (1977): 519–541.

———. "Rhetoric and Reality in the Early Republic: The Case of the Federalist Clergy." In *Religion and American Politics: From the Colonial Period to the 1980s,* edited by Mark A. Noll. New York: Oxford University Press, 1990.

Strout, Cushing. *The New Heavens and New Earth: Political Religion in America.* New York: Harper and Row, 1974.

Sutherland, Arthur. "Historians, Lawyers, and Establishment of Religion." In *Religion and the Public Order,* An Annual Review of Church and State, and of Religion, Law, and Society, Number Five, edited by Donald A. Giannella. Ithaca, N.Y.: Cornell University Press, 1969.

Swancara, Frank. *The Separation of Religion and Government: The First Amendment, Madison's Intent, and the McCollum Decision: A Study of Separationism in America.* New York: Truth Seeker, 1950.

Sweet, Douglas H. "Church Vitality and the American Revolution: Historiographical Consensus and Thoughts towards a New Perspective." *Church History* 45 (1976): 341–357.

Sweet, William Warren. *Religion in Colonial America.* New York: Charles Scribner's Sons, 1942.

———. *Religion in the Development of American Culture, 1765–1840.* New York: Charles Scribner's Sons, 1952.

———. *The Story of Religions in America.* New York: Harper and Brothers, 1930.

Swomley, John M. *Religious Liberty and the Secular State: The Constitutional Context.* Buffalo, N.Y.: Prometheus Books, 1987.

Thornton, John Wingate, ed. *The Pulpit of the American Revolution; or, The Political Sermons of the Period of 1776.* Boston: Gould and Lincoln, 1860.

Turner, James. *Without God, Without Creed: The Origins of Unbelief in America.* Baltimore, Md.: Johns Hopkins University Press, 1985.

Tuveson, Ernest Lee. *Redeemer Nation: The Idea of America's Millennial Role.* Chicago: University of Chicago Press, 1968.

Van Der Slik, Jack R. "Respecting an Establishment of Religion in America." *Christian Scholar's Review* 13 (1984): 217–235.

Van Patten, Jonathan K. "In the End Is the Beginning: An Inquiry into the Meaning of the Religion Clauses." *Saint Louis University Law Journal* 27 (1983): 1–93.

———. "Standing in Need of Prayer: The Supreme Court on James Madison and Religious Liberty." *Benchmark* 3, nos. 1–2 (1987): 59–69.

Van Tyne, Claude H. "Influence of the Clergy, and of Religious and Sectarian Forces, on the American Revolution." *American Historical Review* 19 (October 1913): 44–64.

Veit, Helen E., Kenneth R. Bowling, and Charlene Bangs Bickford, eds. *Creating the Bill of Rights: The Documentary Record from the First Federal Congress.* Baltimore, Md.: Johns Hopkins University Press, 1991.

Waite, Edward F. "Jefferson's 'Wall of Separation': What and Where?" *Minnesota Law Review* 33 (1949): 494–516.

Wald, Kenneth D. *Religion and Politics in the United States.* 3d ed. Washington, D.C.: Congressional Quarterly Press, 1997.

Weber, Donald. *Rhetoric and History in Revolutionary New England.* New York: Oxford University Press, 1988.

Weber, Paul J. "James Madison and Religious Equality: The Perfect Separation." *Review of Politics* 44 (1982): 163–186.

———, ed. *Equal Separation: Understanding the Religion Clauses of the First Amendment.* Westport, Conn.: Greenwood, 1990.

Weisberger, Bernard A. *America Afire: Jefferson, Adams, and the Revolutionary Election of 1800.* New York: William Morrow, 2000.

Wells, Ronald A., and Thomas A. Askew, eds. *Liberty and Law: Reflections on the Constitution in American Life and Thought.* Grand Rapids: William B. Eerdmans, 1987.

West, Ellis M. "The Case against a Right to Religion–Based Exemptions." *Notre Dame Journal of Law, Ethics and Public Policy* 4 (1990): 591–638.

———. "The Right to Religion–Based Exemptions in Early America: The Case of Conscientious Objectors to Conscription." *Journal of Law and Religion* 10 (1993–94): 367–401.

West, John G., Jr. *The Politics of Revelation and Reason: Religion and Civic Life in the New Nation.* Lawrence: University Press of Kansas, 1996.

West, Thomas G. "Religious Liberty: The View from the Founding." In *On Faith and Free Government,* edited by Daniel C. Palm. Lanham, Md.: Rowman and Littlefield, 1997.

Whipple, Leon. *Our Ancient Liberties: The Story of the Origin and Meaning of Civil and Religious Liberty in the United States.* New York: H. W. Wilson, 1927.

White, Ronald C., Jr., and Albright G. Zimmerman, eds. *An Unsettled Arena: Religion and the Bill of Rights.* Grand Rapids, Mich.: William B. Eerdmans, 1990.

Wills, Garry. *Under God: Religion and American Politics.* New York: Simon and Schuster, 1990.

Wilson, John F. *Public Religion in American Culture.* Philadelphia: Temple University Press, 1979.

———, ed. *Church and State in America: A Bibliographical Guide; The Colonial and Early National Periods.* Westport, Conn.: Greenwood Press, 1986.

Wilson, John F., and Donald L. Drakeman, eds. *Church and State in American History: The Burden of Religious Pluralism*, 2d ed. Boston: Beacon Press, 1987.

Wilson, John K. "Religion under the State Constitutions, 1776–1800." *Journal of Church and State* 32 (1990): 753–773.

Witte, John, Jr. "The Essential Rights and Liberties of Religion in the American Constitutional Experiment," *Notre Dame Law Review* 71 (1996): 371–445.

———. "How to Govern a City on a Hill: The Early Puritan Contribution to American Constitutionalism." *Emory Law Journal* 39 (1990): 41–64.

———. "'A Most Mild and Equitable Establishment of Religion': John Adams and the Massachusetts Experiment." In *Religion and the New Republic: Faith in the Founding of America*, edited by James H. Hutson. Lanham, Md.: Rowman and Littlefield, 2000.

———. *Religion and the American Constitutional Experiment: Essential Rights and Liberties*. Boulder, Colo.: Westview Press, 2000.

Wood, Gordon S. *The Creation of the American Republic, 1776–1787*. Chapel Hill: University of North Carolina Press, 1969.

Wood, James E., Jr., ed. *Religion and the State: Essays in Honor of Leo Pfeffer*. Waco, Tex.: Baylor University Press, 1985.

Wood, James E., Jr., E. Bruce Thompson, and Robert T. Miller. *Church and State in Scripture, History, and Constitutional Law*. Waco, Tex.: Baylor University Press, 1958.

Wyndham, Mark. "The Historical Background to the Issue of Religious Liberty in the Revolutionary Era." *Journal of Christian Reconstruction* 3, no. 1 (Summer 1976): 152–171.

Yarbrough, Jean M. *American Virtues: Thomas Jefferson on the Character of a Free People*. Lawrence: University Press of Kansas, 1998.

Zuckert, Catherine. "Not by Preaching: Tocqueville on the Role of Religion in American Democracy." *Review of Politics* 43 (1981): 259–280.

# Acknowledgments

For most of my professional life, I have been thinking, reading, and writing about church and state in American history. During these years, I have encountered the "wall of separation" metaphor in scholarly literature and popular discourse more times than I can remember. Indeed, on more than a few occasions I made uncritical references to the metaphor in my own work. Not until a few years ago did it occur to me that, although Jefferson's trope is ubiquitous in church-state literature, almost nothing had been written that examined in detail the origins of this figurative phrase and the historical and political context in which Jefferson used it. That was the genesis of this book. Although I first considered writing this book only in mid-1999, it is the product of two decades of research. Consequently, there is a *very* long list of individuals and institutions that have generously assisted me in researching and writing this volume. Even if I could remember everyone who has contributed to the project, I could not possibly name them all. In the course of writing the book, I benefited in countless ways from numerous individuals whose fellowship, encouragement, and provocative ideas deserve much more than these few lines of acknowledgment. I trust those individuals whose contributions I fail to identify by name will accept my thanks anonymously. There are a few individuals and institutions, however, that must escape anonymity.

The outline for this book first appeared as "'Sowing Useful Truths and Principles': The Danbury Baptists, Thomas Jefferson, and the 'Wall of Separation,'" *Journal of Church and State* 39 (1997): 455–501. Many acquaintances and complete strangers wrote or called to comment on the article or to suggest new avenues of inquiry. The favorable response was so overwhelming that I decided to expand the article into a book. I thank the *Journal of Church and State* for publishing the article and for permission to publish revised excerpts.

A sabbatical leave from American University and a fellowship research grant from the Earhart Foundation afforded me the time and resources to devote to this project. This book would not have been written without the very generous support of these two institutions.

I also wish to acknowledge the assistance of archivists, curators, and reference librarians at American University, the Library of Congress, Georgetown University, the University of Virginia, the Virginia Historical Society, the Virginia State Library, and the Virginia Room at the Fairfax County Public Library. I would be remiss if I did not specifically thank the staff of the Bender Library, at American University, who handle interlibrary loan transactions for their patience in processing my seemingly endless requests for obscure documents.

I am grateful for the following friends and mentors who read and commented on large portions of the penultimate draft: Thomas E. Buckley, S.J., Mark David Hall, James H. Hutson, and Jeffry Hays Morrison. Their substantive and stylistic suggestions made for a much improved final draft. I also want to thank the following colleagues who read and commented on sections of either the book or the original article on which it is based: William F. Cox, Jr., Sherry Ederheimer, Edwin S. Gaustad, Robert M. Healey, David Little, and John Witte, Jr. Philip Hamburger generously allowed me to review the unpublished manuscript of his excellent treatise, *Separation of Church and State* (Harvard University Press, 2002). The debt I owe to his research is reflected in the many references I make to this work. Much credit is due my very able and enthusiastic research assistants, John D. Whaley, Meredith Rucker Hunter, Toni Chayt, and Allison Henry-Plotts. My appreciation also extends to the editorial staff at New York University Press for their help and encouragement in bringing this volume to print.

The views expressed in this book, as well as any errors, are mine alone and should not be attributed to the individuals and institutions whose assistance I have acknowledged.

Finally, this book would not have been written without the endless patience and good humor of my wife, to whom this volume is dedicated, and my daughters. To my great joy, Mollie and Moriah did much to distract me from this project and to remind me that there are things in life more important than book credits and footnotes. When they are old enough to read this book, I hope these pages will help them to understand where I was and what I was doing when I was not with them. My wife and daughters graciously bore the burden of living with a writer preoccupied by a simple, yet enigmatic, metaphor. Words are inadequate to express my gratitude to, and my affection for, them.

# Index

# About the Author

Daniel L. Dreisbach is a professor of justice, law, and society at American University in Washington, D.C. He received a D.Phil. degree from Oxford University, where he studied as a Rhodes Scholar, and a J.D. degree from the University of Virginia. He has authored or edited several books, as well as numerous chapters and articles in scholarly publications, on religion, politics, and law in American history. He lives in Virginia with his wife and two daughters.